SAINT JOHN CHRYSOSTOM
HIS LIFE AND TIMES

A Sketch of the Church and the Empire in the Fourth Century

COLLECTOR'S EDITION
Includes Index, Footnotes and Quick Dictionary

WILLIAM STEPHENS

MAGDALENE
PRESS

Saint John Chrysostom,
His Life and Times
A Sketch of the Church and the Empire in the Fourth Century
Collector's Edition
Includes Index, Footnotes and Quick Dictionary

By William Stephens

Cover design, layout, index, quick qictionary
by Magdalene Pagratis

Image of Saint John Chrysostom:

"Copied from a frontispiece to the edition by Fronto DUC/EUS, A.D. 1636, of St. Chrysostom's Works (In The Cathedral Library, Chichester). The original is stated to have been engraved from an eikon of great antiquity, at Constantinople, and agrees with the notices of Chrysostom's appearance by Greek writers, who describe him as short, with a large head, ample, wrinkled forehead, eyes deep-set but pleasing, hollow cheeks, and a scanty grey beard."

ISBN 9781773351421

Creative Content Copyright © Magdalene Press, 2022

First Edition Published in 1872
Second Edition Published in 1880
by Edinburgh University Press:
Thomas and Archibald Constable,
Printers to her Majesty

This Collector's Edition is published by
Magdalene Press, 2022

CONTENTS

PREFACE TO THE SECOND EDITION 10
PREFACE TO THE FIRST EDITION 11

CHAPTER 1
INTRODUCTORY 16

CHAPTER 2
FROM HIS BIRTH TO HIS APPOINTMENT TO THE OFFICE OF READER, A.D. 345 OR A.D. 347 TO A.D. 370. 23

CHAPTER 3
COMMENCEMENT OF ASCETIC LIFE—STUDY UNDER DIODORUS—FORMATION OF AN ASCETIC BROTHERHOOD—THE LETTERS TO THEODORE. A.D. 370 36

CHAPTER 4
CHRYSOSTOM EVADES FORCIBLE ORDINATION TO A BISHOPRIC—THE TREATISE "ON THE PRIESTHOOD." A.D. 370, 371 50

CHAPTER 5
NARROW ESCAPE FROM PERSECUTION—HIS ENTRANCE INTO A MONASTERY—THE MONASTICISM OF THE EAST, A.D. 372. 64

CHAPTER 6
WORKS PRODUCED DURING HIS MONASTIC LIFE—THE LETTERS TO DEMETRIUS AND STELECHIUS—TREATISES ADDRESSED TO THE OPPONENTS OF MONASTICISM—LETTER TO STAGIRIUS. 74

CHAPTER 7
ORDINATION AS DEACON—DESCRIPTION OF ANTIOCH—WORKS COMPOSED DURING HIS DIACONATE. A.D. 381-386. 88

CHAPTER 8
ORDINATION TO THE PRIESTHOOD BY FLAVIAN—INAUGURAL DISCOURSE IN THE CATHEDRAL—HOMILIES AGAINST THE ARIANS—ANIMADVERSIONS ON THE CHARIOT RACES. A.D. 386..102

CHAPTER 9
HOMILIES AGAINST PAGANS AND JEWS—CONDITION OF THE JEWS IN ANTIOCH—JUDAISING CHRISTIANS—HOMILIES ON CHRISTMAS DAY AND NEW YEAR'S DAY—CENSURE OF PAGAN SUPERSTITIONS. A.D. 386, 387. 117

CHAPTER 10
SURVEY OF THE FIRST DECADE OF THE REIGN OF THEODOSIUS—HIS CHARACTER—HIS EFFORTS FOR THE EXTIRPATION OF PAGANISM AND HERESY—THE APOLOGIES OF SYMMACHUS AND LIBANIUS. A.D. 379-389.. 131

CHAPTER 1
THE SEDITION AT ANTIOCH—THE HOMILIES ON THE STATUES—THE RESULTS OF THE SEDITION. A.D. 387. 140

CHAPTER 12
ILLNESS OF CHRYSOSTOM—HOMILIES ON FESTIVALS OF SAINTS AND MARTYRS—CHARACTER OF THESE FESTIVALS—PILGRIMAGES—RELIQUES—CHARACTER OF PEASANT CLERGY IN NEIGHBOURHOOD OF ANTIOCH. A.D. 387.. 162

CHAPTER 13
SURVEY OF EVENTS BETWEEN A.D. 387 AND A.D. 397—AMBROSE AND THEODOSIUS—REVOLT OF ARBOGASTES—DEATH OF

THEODOSIUS—THE MINISTERS OF ARCADIUS—RUFINUS AND EUTROPIUS. 169

CHAPTER 14
DEATH OF NECTARIUS, ARCHBISHOP OF CONSTANTINOPLE— EAGER COMPETITION FOR THE SEE—ELECTION OF CHRYSOSTOM—HIS COMPULSORY REMOVAL FROM ANTIOCH— CONSECRATION—REFORMS—HOMILIES ON VARIOUS SUBJECTS— MISSIONARY PROJECTS..191

CHAPTER 15
THE FALL OF EUTROPIUS— HIS RETREAT TO THE SANCTUARY OF THE CHURCH— RIGHT OF SANCTUARY MAINTAINED BY CHRYSOSTOM— DEATH OF EUTROPIUS— REVOLT OF GOTHIC COMMANDERS TRIBIGILD AND GAÏNAS— DEMAND OF GAÏNAS FOR AN ARIAN CHURCH REFUSED BY CHRYSOSTOM— DEFEAT AND DEATH OF GAÏNAS. A.D. 399-401. 199

CHAPTER 16
CHRYSOSTOM'S VISIT TO ASIA— DEPOSITION OF SIX SIMONIACAL BISHOPS— LEGITIMATE EXTENT OF HIS JURISDICTION— RETURN TO CONSTANTINOPLE— RUPTURE AND RECONCILIATION WITH SEVERIAN, BISHOP OF GABALA— CHRYSOSTOM'S INCREASING UNPOPULARITY WITH THE CLERGY AND WEALTHY LAITY— HIS FRIENDS— OLYMPIAS THE DEACONESS— FORMATION OF HOSTILE FACTIONS, WHICH INVITE THE AID OF THEOPHILUS, PATRIARCH OF ALEXANDRIA. A.D. 400, 401..219

CHAPTER 17
CIRCUMSTANCES WHICH LED TO THE INTERFERENCE OF THEOPHILUS WITH THE AFFAIRS OF CHRYSOSTOM— CONTROVERSY ABOUT THE WRITINGS OF ORIGEN— PERSECUTION BY THEOPHILUS OF THE MONKS CALLED "THE TALL BRETHREN"— THEIR FLIGHT TO PALESTINE— TO

CONSTANTINOPLE— THEIR RECEPTION BY CHRYSOSTOM— THEOPHILUS SUMMONED TO CONSTANTINOPLE. A.D. 395-403. ...237

CHAPTER 18
THEOPHILUS ARRIVES IN CONSTANTINOPLE— ORGANISES A CABAL AGAINST CHRYSOSTOM— THE SYNOD OF THE OAK— CHRYSOSTOM PRONOUNCED CONTUMACIOUS FOR NON-APPEARANCE AND EXPELLED FROM THE CITY— EARTHQUAKE— RECALL OF CHRYSOSTOM— OVATIONS ON HIS RETURN— FLIGHT OF THEOPHILUS. A.D. 403. 254

CHAPTER 19
AN IMAGE OF EUDOXIA PLACED IN FRONT OF THE CATHEDRAL— CHRYSOSTOM DENOUNCES IT— ANGER OF THE EMPRESS— THE ENEMY RETURNS TO THE CHARGE— ANOTHER COUNCIL FORMED— CHRYSOSTOM CONFINED TO HIS PALACE— VIOLENT SCENE IN THE CATHEDRAL AND OTHER PLACES— CHRYSOSTOM AGAIN EXPELLED. A.D. 403, 404..................271

CHAPTER 20
FURY OF THE PEOPLE AT THE REMOVAL OF CHRYSOSTOM— DESTRUCTION OF THE CATHEDRAL CHURCH AND SENATE-HOUSE BY FIRE— PERSECUTION OF CHRYSOSTOM'S FOLLOWERS— FUGITIVES TO ROME— LETTERS OF INNOCENT TO THEOPHILUS— TO THE CLERGY OF CONSTANTINOPLE— TO CHRYSOSTOM— DEPUTATION OF WESTERN BISHOPS TO CONSTANTINOPLE REPULSED— SUFFERINGS OF THE EASTERN CHURCH— TRIUMPH OF THE CABAL. A.D. 404, 405. 284

CHAPTER 21
CHRYSOSTOM ORDERED TO BE REMOVED TO CUCUSUS— PERILS ENCOUNTERED AT CÆSAREA— HARDSHIPS OF THE JOURNEY— REACHES CUCUSUS— LETTERS WRITTEN THERE TO OLYMPIAS AND OTHER FRIENDS. A.D. 404. 300

CHAPTER 22
CHRYSOSTOM'S SUFFERINGS FROM THE WINTER COLD— DEPREDATIONS OF THE ISAURIANS— THE MISSION IN PHŒNICIA— LETTERS TO INNOCENT AND THE ITALIAN BISHOPS— CHRYSOSTOM'S ENEMIES OBTAIN AN ORDER FOR HIS REMOVAL TO PITYUS— HE DIES AT COMANA, A.D. 407— RECEPTION OF HIS RELIQUES AT CONSTANTINOPLE, A.D. 438. ...316

CHAPTER 23
SURVEY OF CHRYSOSTOM'S THEOLOGICAL TEACHING— PRACTICAL TONE OF HIS WORKS— REASON OF THIS— DOCTRINE OF MAN'S NATURE— ORIGINAL SIN— GRACE— FREE-WILL— HOW FAR CHRYSOSTOM PELAGIAN— LANGUAGE ON THE TRINITY— ATONEMENT— JUSTIFICATION— THE TWO SACRAMENTS— NO TRACE OF CONFESSION, PURGATORY, OR MARIOLATRY— RELATIONS TOWARDS THE POPE— LITURGY OF CHRYSOSTOM— HIS CHARACTER AS A COMMENTATOR— VIEWS ON INSPIRATION— HIS PREACHING— PERSONAL APPEARANCE— REFERENCES TO GREEK CLASSICAL AUTHORS— COMPARISON WITH ST. AUGUSTINE. 325

APPENDIX 359
FOOTNOTES..361
INDEX..401
QUICK DICTIONARY 412

SAINT JOHN CHRYSOSTOM

HIS LIFE AND TIMES

PREFACE TO THE SECOND EDITION

THE PRESENT EDITION OF this Essay is substantially a reproduction of the first. It is possible, indeed, and I hope probable, that the fruits of nine years' more experience and study would have manifested themselves in some marked improvements upon the former work had I rewritten or recast the whole of it. But after mature consideration it did not seem to me that the defects of my original attempt were sufficient to warrant such an expenditure of time and toil.

I have therefore contented myself with carefully revising the text and references, and making here and there a few slight alterations in the way either of addition or omission.

WOOLBEDING RECTORY,
Feby. 20, 1880.

PREFACE TO THE FIRST EDITION

THE CONSIDERATIONS WHICH INDUCED me to undertake this monograph are mentioned in the introductory chapter. How far the design there indicated has been satisfactorily fulfilled, it is for others to decide. I am of course conscious of defects, for every workman's ideal aim should be higher than what he can actually accomplish. The work has incurred a certain risk from having been once or twice suspended for a considerable period; but I have always returned to it with increased interest and pleasure, nor can I charge myself with having wittingly bestowed less pains on one part than another. I have endeavoured to make it a trustworthy narrative by drawing from the most original sources to which I could gain access; and where, as in those portions which touch on secular history, the lead of general historians, such as Gibbon or De Broglie has been followed, I have, as far as possible, consulted the authorities to which they refer. To modern authors from whom I have derived valuable assistance for special parts of the work, such as M. Amédée Thierry and Dr. Foerster, my obligations are acknowledged in their proper place.

Neander's Life of St. Chrysostom has, of course, throughout been frequently consulted. It is marked by the customary merits and defects of that historian. It is full of research, information, thought, and refined religious sentiment; but he fails to bring out strongly the personality of his subject. We have abundance of Chrysostom's sayings and opinions, but somehow too little of Chrysostom himself. The fact is that Neander seems always to be thinking more of those views and theories about the growth of Christian doctrine and the Church, which he wishes to impress upon men's minds, than of the person about whom he is writing. Thus, the subject of his biography becomes too much a mere vehicle for conveying Neander's own opinions, and the personality of the character fades away in proportion. Some passages in the life of his subject are related at inordinate length; others, because less illustrative of Neander's views, are imperfectly sketched, if not omitted.

In extracts from the works of Chrysostom, the somewhat difficult question of the comparative advantages of translation and paraphrase has been decided, on the whole, in favour of the latter. The condensation of matter gained by a paraphrase is an important, indeed necessary, object, if many specimens are to be given from such a very voluminous author as Chrysostom. A careful endeavour, at the same time, has been made to render faithfully the general sense of the original; and wherever the peculiar beauty of the language or the importance of the subject seemed to demand it, a translation has been given.

From an early date in the sixteenth century down to the present time the works of Chrysostom have occupied the attention of learned editors. The first attempts, after the invention of printing, were mainly confined to Latin translations of different portions. Afterwards appeared—

(1.) In 1529 the Greek text of the Homilies on St. Paul, published at Vienna, "typis Stephani et fratrum," with a preface by Maximus Donatus. This was followed by the Commentaries on the New Testament, published by Commelin, a printer at Heidelberg, four vols. folio, A.D. 1591-1602.

(2.) In 1612 appeared a magnificent edition of the whole works, in eight thick folio volumes, printed at Eton, and prepared by Sir Henry Savile. Savile, born in 1549, was equally distinguished for his knowledge of mathematics and Greek, in which he acted for a time as tutor to Queen Elizabeth. He became Warden of Merton in 1585, and Provost of Eton in 1596. Promotion in Church and State was offered to him by James I., but declined, though he accepted a knighthood in 1604. His only son died about that time, and he devoted his fortune henceforth entirely to the promotion of learning. The Savilian Professorships of Geometry and Astronomy in Oxford were founded by him, and a library furnished with mathematical books for the use of his Professors. He spared no labour or expense to make his edition of St. Chrysostom handsome and complete. He personally examined most of the great libraries in Europe for mss., and, through the kindness of English ambassadors and eminent men of learning abroad, his copyists were admitted to the libraries of Paris, Basle, Augsburg, Munich, Vienna, and other cities. He used the Commelinian edition as his printer's copy, carefully compared with five mss., the various readings of which are marked (by a not very distinct plan) in the margin. The chief value of the work consists in the prefaces and notes, contributed some of them by Casaubon and other learned men, though by far the best are Savile's own. The whole cost of bringing out this grand edition is said to have been £8000. Savile's wife was so jealous of her husband's attachment to the work that she threatened to burn it.

(3.) Meanwhile, Fronton le Duc, a French Jesuit, had been labouring independently, but in most amicable intercourse with Savile, not only to edit the works of Chrysostom complete, but accompanied by a Latin translation, which he supplied himself for those pieces of which he failed to find any good one already existing. His death arrested the work, which was taken up, after a time, by the two brothers, Frederick and Claude Morel, and completed by the latter in 1633. It was published in Paris in 1636, in twelve large folio volumes. The Commelinian was again used as the printer's copy, with fewer alterations than in the edition of Savile.

(4.) We now come to the great Benedictine edition, prepared under the care of Bernard de Montfaucon, who deserted the profession of arms at the age of twenty to become, as a member of the brotherhood of St. Maur, one of the most marvellously industrious workers in literature that the world has ever seen. In 1698, when the Benedictines had completed their editions of SS. Augustine and Athanasius, they began to prepare for an edition of Chrysostom, which they had intended to do for more than thirty years. Montfaucon was sent to Italy, where he spent three years in examining libraries; and, on his return, obtained leave from the presidents of the congregation to employ four or five of the brethren in collating mss. in the Royal Library at Paris, and in those of Colbert and Coislin. Their labours extended over thirteen years; more than 300xi mss., containing different portions of Chrysostom's works, having been discovered in those libraries. Montfaucon, meanwhile, corresponded with learned men in all parts of Europe, in order to procure materials and further collations. His correspondents in England were Potter, Bishop of Oxford, Bentley, and Needham; and in Ireland, Godwin, Bishop of Kilmore. The result was that, after more than twenty years of incessant toil, Montfaucon produced an edition, in which several pieces saw the light for the first time, and others, imperfect in previous editions, were presented entire. The text after all is the least satisfactory part of the work. Mr. Field has discovered that the eight principal mss. employed were not very carefully collated, and that, though Savile's text is extremely praised, that of Morel, by a curious inconsistency, is most closely followed, which is little more than a reproduction of the original Commelinian. The main value of the edition consists in the prefaces, written by Montfaucon to every set of homilies and every treatise, in which the chronology, contents, and character of the composition are most fully and ably discussed. The chronological arrangement also of the pieces is a great improvement on the editions of Savile and Fronton le Duc, who had made no attempt of that kind. The last volume, the thirteenth, contains a life of St. Chrysostom, a most copious index, and dissertations on the doctrine, discipline, and heresies prevalent in his age, illustrated by notices collected from his works. On the whole, the edition must be pronounced a marvellous monument of ability and industry, especially when it is considered that at the date of its completion, 1738, Montfaucon was eighty-three years of age, and had been engaged for upwards of fifty years in literary work of a most laborious description. He died in 1741.

(5.) The last edition, which leaves little or nothing to be desired, is that which I have used in preparing this volume—the Abbé Migne's, in 13 vols., Paris, 1863. It is substantially a reproduction of the Benedictine, in a rather less cumbrous size, and embodies some of the best corrections, notes, and prefaces of modern commentators, especially those of Mr. Field to the Homilies of St. Matthew, and some by the learned editor himself.

A brief sketch of the principal forms in which Chrysostom's works have appeared seemed an appropriate introduction to the history of the man himself. If the perusal of that history shall afford to readers half as much interest, pleasure, and instruction as I have myself derived from the composition of it, I shall feel amply rewarded for my labour; and I gladly take this opportunity of expressing my gratitude to my father-in-law for originally suggesting a work of this kind, and to many friends, and especially my wife, for constant encouragement, without which a mixture of indolence and diffidence might have prevented the completion of my design.

DENSWORTH COTTAGE, CHICHESTER,
All Saints Day 1871.

CHAPTER 1

INTRODUCTORY

I. THERE ARE MANY GREAT names in history which have been familiar to us from almost our earliest years, but of the personal character, the actual life of those who bore them, we are comparatively ignorant. We know that they were men of genius; industrious, energetic workers, who, as statesmen, reformers, warriors, writers, speakers, exercised a vital influence for good or ill upon their fellow-men. They have achieved a reputation which will never die; but from various causes their personality does not stand out before us in clear and bold relief. We know something about some of the most important passages in their life, a few of their sayings, a little of their writings; but the men themselves we do not know.

Frequently the reason of this is, that though they occupy a place, perhaps an important place, in the great drama of history, yet they have not played one of the *foremost* parts; and general history cannot spare much time or space beyond what is necessary to describe the main progress of events, and the actions and characters of those who were most prominently concerned in them. Other men may have been greater in themselves; they may have been first-rate in their own sphere, but that sphere was too much secluded or circumscribed to admit of the extensive and conspicuous public influence of which alone history takes much cognisance. They are to history what those side or background figures in the pictures of great medieval painters are to the grand central subject of the piece: they do but help to fill up the canvas, yet the picture would not be complete without them. They are notable personages, well worthy of being separately depicted, though in the large historical representation they play a subordinate part.

To take out one of these side figures of history, and to make it the centre of a separate picture, grouping round it all the great events and characters among which it moved, is the work of a biographer. And by many it will be felt that nothing invests the general history of any period with such a living interest as viewing it through the light of some one human life. How was this individual soul affected by the movement of the great forces with which it was surrounded? How did it affect them, in its turn, wherever in its progress it came into contact with them? This one consideration will confer on many details of history an importance and freshness of which they seemed too trivial or too dull to be susceptible.

II. Among these side characters in history, characters of men in themselves belonging to the first rank, men whose names will be renowned and honoured to the end of time, but precluded, by disposition or circumstances, from taking the foremost place in the larger canvas of general history, must be reckoned many of the great ecclesiastics of the first four or five centuries of Christianity. Every one recognises as great such names as Origen, Tertullian, Cyprian, Basil, the two Gregories, and many more. Every one would admit that the Church owes them a debt, but it may be safely affirmed that here the acquaintance of many with these eminent men begins and ends. A few scraps from their writings quoted in commentaries, one or two remarkable acts or sayings which have been thought worthy to be handed down, a few passages in which their lives flit across the stage of general history, complete the knowledge of many more. Such men, indeed, as Athanasius and Ambrose are to some extent exceptions. The magnitude of the principles for which they contended, the energy and ability which they displayed in the contest, were too conspicuous to be passed over by the general historian, civil or ecclesiastical. The proverbial expression "Athanasius contra mundum" attests of itself the pre-eminent greatness of the man. But with other luminaries of the Church, whose powers were perhaps equally great, but not exercised on so public a field or on behalf of such apparently vital questions, history has not dealt, perhaps cannot consistently with its scope deal, in any degree commensurate with their merits. Nor does this remark apply entirely to civil history. Ecclesiastical history also is so much occupied with the consideration of subjects on a large scale and covering a large space of time,—the course of controversies, the growth of doctrines, the relations between Church and State, changes in discipline, in liturgies, in ritual,—that the history of those who lived among these events, and who by their ability made or moulded them, is comparatively lost sight of. The outward operations are seen, but the springs which set them going are concealed. How can general history, for instance, adequately set forth the character and the work of such men as Savonarola or Erasmus, both in their widely different ways men of such incomparable genius and incessant activity? It does not; it only supplies a glimpse, a sketch, which make us long for a fuller vision, a more finished picture.[1]

III. It is designed to attempt, in the following pages, such a supplementary chapter in ecclesiastical history. An endeavour will be made not merely to chronicle the life and estimate the character of the great preacher of Antioch and Constantinople, but to place him in the centre of all the great movements, civil as well as religious, of his time, and see what light he and they throw upon one another.

The age in which he lived was a troublous one. The spectacle of a tempestuous sea may in itself excite our interest and inspire us with awe, but place in the midst of it a vessel containing human life, and how deeply is our interest intensified!

What was the general character and position of the clergy in the fourth century? What was the attitude of the Church towards the sensuality, selfishness, luxury, of an effete and debased civilisation on the one hand, and the rude ferocity of young and strong barbarian races on the other? To what extent had Christianity leavened, or had it appreciably leavened at all, popular forms of thought and popular habits of life? What was the existing phase of monasticism? what the ordinary form of worship in the Catholic Church? what the established belief respecting the sacraments and the great verities of the Christian faith? In answer to such inquiries, and to many more, much useful information may be extracted from the works of so prolific a writer and preacher as Chrysostom. Being concerned also, as a preacher, with moral practice more than with abstract theology, his homilies reflect, like the writings of satirists, the manners of the age. The habits of private life, the fashionable amusements, the absurdities of dress, all the petty foibles, as well as the more serious vices of the society by which he was surrounded, are dragged out without remorse, and made the subjects of solemn admonition, or fierce invective, or withering sarcasm, or ironical jest.

IV. Nor does secular history, from which not a single chapter in ecclesiastical history can without injury be dissociated, want for copious illustration. Not only from the memorable story of the sedition at Antioch, and from the public events at Constantinople, in which Chrysostom played a conspicuous part, but from many an allusion or incidental expression scattered up and down his works, we may collect rays of light on the social and political condition of the Empire. We get glimpses in his pages of a large mass of the population hovering midway between Paganism and Christianity; we detect an oppressive system of taxation, a widely-spread venality in the administration of public business, a general insecurity of life arising from the almost total absence of what we understand by police regulations, a depressed agriculture, a great slave population, a vast turbulent army as dangerous to the peace of society as the enemies from whom it was supposed to defend it, the presence of barbarians in the country as servants, soldiers, or colonists, the constantly-impending danger from other hordes ever hovering on the frontier, and, like famished wolves, gazing with hungry eyes on the plentiful prey which lay beyond it. But in the midst of the national corruption we see great characters stand out; and it is remarkable that they belong, without exception, to the two elements which alone were strong and progressive in the midst of the general debility and decadence. All the men of commanding genius in this era were either Christian or barbarian. A young and growing faith, a vigorous and manly race: these were the two forces destined to work hand in hand for the destruction of an old and the establishment of a new order of things. The chief doctors of Christianity in the fourth century—Augustine, Chrysostom, Ambrose—are incomparably greater than their contemporary advocates of the old religion and philosophy, Symmachus or Libanius; even as the Gothic Alaric and Fravitta, and the Vandal Stilicho, were the only generals who did not disgrace the Roman arms.

V. Some remarks on the theology of Chrysostom will be found in the concluding chapter. The appellation of preacher,[2] by which he is most generally known, is a true indicator of the sphere in which his powers were greatest. It was in upholding a pure and lofty standard of Christian morality, and in denouncing unchristian wickedness, that his life was mainly spent, rather than, like Augustine's, in constructing and teaching a logical system of doctrine. The rage of his enemies, to which he ultimately fell a victim, was not bred of the bitterness of theological controversy, but of the natural antagonism between the evil and the good. And it is partly on this account that neither the remoteness of time, nor difference of circumstances, which separate us from him, can dim the interest with which we read his story. He fought not so much for any abstract question of theology or point of ecclesiastical discipline, which may have lost its meaning and importance for us, but for those grand principles of truth and justice, Christian charity, and Christian holiness, which ought to be dear to men equally in all ages.

VI. But there is also in the struggle of Chrysostom with the secular power an ecclesiastical and historical interest, as well as a moral one. We see prefigured in his deposition the fate of the Eastern Church in the Eastern capital of the Empire. As the papacy grew securely by the retreat from the old Rome of any secular rival, so the patriarchate of the new Rome was constantly, increasingly depressed by the presence of such a rival. Of all the great churchmen who flourished in the fourth century, Athanasius, Basil, the Gregories, Ambrose, Jerome, Augustine, and Chrysostom, the last three alone survived into the fifth century. But the glory of the Western Church was then only in its infancy; the glory of the Eastern culminated in Chrysostom. From his time the patriarchs of Constantinople fell more and more into the servile position of court functionaries. The working out of that grand idea, a visible organised Catholic Church, uniform in doctrine and discipline, an idea which grew more and more as the political disintegration of the Empire increased, was to be accomplished by the more commanding, law-giving spirit of the West. Intrepid in spirit, inflexible of purpose, though Chrysostom was, he could not subdue, he could only provoke to more violent opposition, the powers with which he was brought into collision. Ineffectual was his contest with ecclesiastical corruption and secular tyranny, as compared with a similar contest waged by his Western contemporary, Ambrose; ineffectual also were the efforts, after his time, of the Church which he represented to assert the full dignity of its position.

VII. Chrysostom, and the contemporary fathers of the Eastern Church, naturally seem very remote from us; but, in fact, they are nearer to us in their modes of thought than many who in point of time are less distant. They were brought up in the study of that Greek literature with which we are familiar. Philosophy had not stiffened into scholasticism. The ethics of Chrysostom are substantially the same with the ethics of Butler. So, again, Eastern fathers of the fourth century are far more nearly allied to us in theology than writers of a few centuries later. If we are to look to "the rock" whence our Anglican liturgy "was hewn," and "to the hole of the pit" whence Anglican reformed theology "was digged," we must turn our eyes, above all other directions, to the Eastern Church and the Eastern fathers. It was observed by Mr. Alexander Knox,[3] that the earlier days of the Greek Church seem resplendent with a glow of simple, fervent piety, such as in a Church, as a whole, has never since been seen; and that this character is strikingly in harmony with our own liturgy, so overflowing with sublime aspirations, so Catholic, not bearing the impress of any one system of theology, but containing what is best in all. We may detect in Chrysostom the germ of medieval corruptions, such as the invocation of saints, the adoration of relics, and a sensuous conception of the change effected in the holy elements in the Eucharist; but these are the raw material of error, not yet wrought into definite shape. The Bishop of Rome is recognised, as will be seen from Chrysostom's correspondence with Innocent, as a great potentate, whose intercessions are to be solicited in time of trouble and difficulty, and to whose judgment much deference is to be paid, but by no means as a supreme ruler in Christendom.

Thus, the tone of Chrysostom's language is far more akin to that of our own Church than of the medieval or present Church of Rome. In his habit of referring to Holy Scripture as the ultimate source and basis of all true doctrine, "so that whatsoever is not read therein, nor may be proved thereby, is not to be required of any man as an article of faith;" in his careful endeavour to ascertain the real meaning of Scripture, not seeking for fanciful or mystical interpretations, or supporting preconceived theories, but patiently labouring, with a mixture of candour, reverence, and common sense, to ascertain the exact literal sense of each passage;—in these points, no less than in his theology, he bears an affinity to the best minds of our own reformed Church, and fairly represents that faith of the Catholic Church before the disruption of East and West in which Bishop Ken desired to die; while his fervent piety, and his apostolic zeal as a preacher of righteousness, must command the admiration of all earnest Christians, to whatever country, age, or Church, they may belong.

CHAPTER 2

FROM HIS BIRTH TO HIS APPOINTMENT TO THE OFFICE OF READER, A.D. 345 OR A.D. 347 TO A.D. 370.

IT HAS BEEN WELL remarked by Sir Henry Savile, in the preface to his noble edition of Chrysostom's works, published in 1612, that, as with great rivers, so often with great men, the middle and the close of their career are dignified and distinguished, but the primary source and early progress of the stream are difficult to ascertain and trace. No one, he says, has been able to fix the exact date, the year, and the consulship of Chrysostom's birth. This is true; but at the same time his birth, parentage, and education are not involved in such obscurity as surrounds the earliest years of some other great luminaries of the Eastern Church; his own friend, for instance, Theodore, Bishop of Mopsuestia, and yet more notably, the great Athanasius.

There is little doubt that his birth occurred not later than the year A.D. 347, and not earlier than the year A.D. 345; and there is no doubt that Antioch in Syria was the place of his birth, that his mother's name was Anthusa, his father's Secundus, and that both were well born. His mother was, if not actually baptized, very favourably inclined to Christianity,[4] and, indeed, a woman of no ordinary piety. The father had attained the rank of "magister militum" in the Imperial army of Syria, and therefore enjoyed the title of "illustris." He died when his son John was an infant, leaving a young widow, about twenty years of age, in comfortable circumstances, but harassed by the difficulties and anxieties of her unprotected condition as mistress of a household in days when servants were slaves, and life in large cities altogether unguarded by such securities as are familiar to us. Greatly did she dread the responsibility of bringing up a son in one of the most turbulent and dissolute capitals of the Empire. Nothing, she afterwards[5] declared to him, could have enabled her to pass through such a furnace of trial but a consoling sense of divine support, and the delight of contemplating the image of her husband as reproduced in his son. How long a sister older than himself may have lived we do not know; but the conversation between him and his mother, when he was meditating a retreat into a monastery, seems to imply that he was the only surviving child. All her love, all her care, all her means and energies, were concentrated on the boy destined to become so great a man, and exhibiting even in childhood no common ability and aptitude for learning. But her chief anxiety was to train him in pious habits, and to preserve him uncontaminated from the pollutions of the vicious city in which they resided. She was to him what Monica was to Augustine, and Nonna to Gregory Nazianzen.

The great influence, indeed, of women upon the Christianity of domestic life in that age is not a little remarkable. The Christians were not such a pure and single-minded community as they had been. The refining fires of persecution which burnt up the chaff of hypocrisy or indifference were now extinguished; Christianity had a recognised position; her bishops were in kings' courts. The natural consequences inevitably followed this attainment of security; there were more Christians, but not more who were zealous; there were many who hung very loosely to the Church—many who fluctuated between the Church and Paganism. In the great Eastern cities of the Empire, especially Alexandria, Antioch, Constantinople, the mass of the so-called Christian population was largely infected by the dominant vices— inordinate luxury, sensuality, selfish avarice, and display. Christianity was in part paganised long before it had made any appreciable progress towards the destruction of Paganism. But the sincere and ardent piety of many amongst the women kept alive in many a home the flame of Christian faith which would otherwise have been smothered. The Emperor Julian imagined that his efforts to resuscitate Paganism would have been successful in Antioch but for the strenuous opposition of the Christian women. He complains "that they were permitted by their husbands to take anything out of the house to bestow it upon the Galilæans, or to give away to the poor, while they would not expend the smallest trifle upon the worship of the gods."[6] The efforts also of the Governor Alexander, who was left in Antioch by the Emperor to carry forward his designs of Pagan reformation, were principally baffled through this female influence. He found that the men would often consent to attend the temples and sacrifices, but afterwards generally repented and retracted their adherence. This relapse Libanius the sophist, in a letter[7] to the Governor, ascribes to the home influence of the women. "When the men are out of doors," he says, "they obey you who give them the best advice, and they approach the altars; but when they get home, their minds undergo a change; they are wrought upon by the tears and entreaties of their wives, and they again withdraw from the altars of the gods."

Anthusa did not marry again; very possibly she was deterred from contracting a second marriage by religious scruples which Chrysostom himself would certainly have approved.[8] The Pagans themselves admired those women who dedicated themselves to a single life, or abstained from marrying again. Chrysostom himself informs us that when he began to attend the lectures of Libanius, his master inquired who and what his parents were; and on being told that he was the son of a widow who at the age of forty had lost her husband twenty years, he exclaimed in a tone of mingled jealousy and admiration: "Heavens! what women these Christians have!"[9]

What instruction he received in early boyhood, beside his mother's careful moral and religious training; whether he was sent, a common custom among Christian parents in that age,[10] to be taught by the monks in one of the neighbouring monasteries, where he may have imbibed an early taste for monastic retirement, we know not. He was designed, however, not for the clerical but for the legal profession, and at the age of twenty he began to attend the lectures of one of the first sophists of the day, capable of giving him that secular training and learning which would best enable him to cope with men of the world.

Libanius had achieved a reputation as a teacher of general literature, rhetoric, and philosophy, and as an able and eloquent defender of Paganism, not only in his native city Antioch, but in the Empire at large. He was the friend and correspondent of Julian, and on amicable terms with the Emperors Valens and Theodosius. He had now returned to Antioch after lengthened residence in Athens (where the chair of rhetoric had been offered to him, but declined), in Nicomedia, and in Constantinople.[11] In attending daily lectures at his school, the young Chrysostom became conversant with the best classical Greek authors, both poets and philosophers. Of their teaching he in later life retained little admiration,[12] and to the perusal of their writings he probably seldom or never recurred for profit or recreation, but his retentive memory enabled him to the last to point and adorn his arguments with quotations from Homer, Plato, and the Tragedians. In the school of Libanius also he began to practise those nascent powers of eloquence which were destined to win for him so mighty a fame, as well as the appellation of Chrysostomos, or the Golden Mouth, by which, rather than by his proper name of John, he will be known to the end of time.[13] Libanius, in a letter to Chrysostom, praises highly a speech composed by him in honour of the Emperors, and says they were happy in having so excellent a panegyrist.[14] The Pagan sophist helped to forge the weapons which were afterwards to be skilfully employed against the cause to which he was devoted. When he was on his deathbed, he was asked by his friends who was in his opinion capable of succeeding him. "It would have been John," he replied, "had not the Christians stolen him from us."[15] But it did not immediately appear that the learned advocate of Paganism was nourishing a traitor; for Chrysostom had not yet been baptized, and began to seek an opening for his powers in secular fields of activity.[16] He commenced practice as a lawyer; some of his speeches gained great admiration, and were highly commended by his old master Libanius. A brilliant career of worldly ambition was open to him. The profession of the law was at that time the great avenue to civil distinction. The amount of litigation was enormous. One hundred and fifty advocates were required for the court of the Prætorian Prefect of the East alone. The display of talent in the law-courts frequently obtained for a man the government of a province, whence the road was open to those higher dignities of vice-prefect, prefect, patrician, consul, which were honoured by the title of "illustrious."[17]

But the pure and upright disposition of the youthful advocate recoiled from the licentiousness which corrupted society; from the avarice, fraud, and artifice which marked the transactions of men of business; from the chicanery and rapacity that sullied the profession which he had entered.[18] He was accustomed to say later in life that "the Bible was the fountain for watering the soul." If he had drunk of the classical fountains in the school of Libanius, he had imbibed draughts yet deeper of the spiritual well-spring in quiet study of Holy Scripture at home. And like many another in that degraded age, his whole soul revolted from the glaring contrast presented by the ordinary life of the world around him to that standard of holiness which was held up in the Gospels.

He had formed also an intimate friendship with a young man, his equal in station and age, by whose influence he was diverted more and more from secular life, and eventually induced altogether to abandon it. This was Basil, who will come before us in the celebrated work on the priesthood. He must not be confounded with the great Basil,[19] Bishop of Cæsarea, in Cappadocia, who was some fifteen years older than Chrysostom, having been born in A.D. 329, nor with Basil, Bishop of Seleucia, who was present at the Council of Chalcedon in A.D. 451, and must therefore have been considerably younger. Perhaps he may be identified with a Basil, Bishop of Raphanea in Syria, not far from Antioch, who attended the Council of Constantinople in A.D. 381.

Chrysostom has described his friendship with Basil in affecting language:[20] "I had many genuine and true friends, men who understood and strictly observed the laws of friendship; but one there was out of the many who exceeded them all in attachment to me, and strove to leave them all behind in the race, even as much as they themselves surpassed ordinary acquaintances. He was one of those who accompanied me at all times; we engaged in the same studies, and were instructed by the same teachers; in our zeal and interest for the subjects on which we worked, we were one. As we went to our lectures or returned from them, we were accustomed to take counsel together on the line of life it would be best to adopt; and here, too, we appeared to be unanimous."

Basil early determined this question for himself in favour of monasticism; he decided, as Chrysostom expresses it, to follow the "true philosophy." This occasioned the first interruption to their intercourse. Chrysostom, soon after the age of twenty, had embarked on a secular career, and could not immediately make up his mind to tread in the footsteps of his friend. "The balance," he says, "was no longer even;" the scale of Basil mounted, while that of Chrysostom was depressed by the weight of earthly interests and desires.[21] But the decisive act of Basil made a deep impression on his mind; separation from his friend only increased his attachment to him, and his aversion from life in the world. He began to withdraw more from ordinary occupations and pleasures, and to spend more of his time in the study of Holy Scripture. He formed acquaintance with Meletius, the deeply respected Catholic Bishop of Antioch, and after three years, the usual period of probation for catechumens, was baptized by him.

A natural question arises: Why was he not baptized before, since his mother was a Christian, and there is abundant evidence that infant baptism was and had been the ordinary practice of the Church?[22] In attempting a solution of the difficulty, it will be proper to mention first certain reasons for delaying baptism which were prevalent in that age, and which may partially have influenced the mind of Chrysostom's mother or himself. It may sound paradoxical to say that an exaggerated estimation of the import and effect of baptism contributed in two ways to its delay. But such appears to have been the case. It was regarded by many as the most complete and final purgation of past sin, and the most solemn pledge of a new and purified life for the future. To sin, therefore, before baptism was comparatively harmless, if in the waters of baptism the guilty stains could be washed away; but sin after the reception of that holy sacrament was almost, if not altogether, unpardonable—at least fraught with the most tremendous peril. Hence some would delay baptism, as many now delay repentance, from a secret or conscious reluctance to take a decisive step, and renounce the pleasures of sin; and under the comfortable persuasion that some day, by submitting to baptism, they would free themselves from the responsibilities of their past life. Others, again, were deterred from binding themselves under so solemn a covenant by a distrust of their ability to fulfil their vows, and a timorous dread of the eternal consequences if they failed. Against these misconceptions of the true nature and proper use of the sacrament, the great Basil, the two Gregories, and Chrysostom himself contend[23] with a vehemence and indignation which proves them to have been common. Many parents thought they would allow the fitful and unstable season of youth to pass before they irrevocably bound their children under the most solemn engagements of their Christian calling. The children, when they grew up, inherited their scruples, and so the sacrament was indefinitely deferred.

It is not impossible that such feelings may have influenced Chrysostom's mother and himself; but considering the natural and healthy character of his piety, which seems to have grown by a gentle and unintermitting progress from his childhood, they do not seem very probable in his case. A more cogent cause for the delay may perhaps be found in the distracted state of the Church in Antioch, which lasted, with increasing complications, from A.D. 330, or fifteen years prior to Chrysostom's birth, up to the time of his baptism by Meletius, when a brighter day was beginning to dawn.

The vicissitudes of the Church in Antioch during that period form a curious, though far from pleasing, picture of the inextricable difficulties, the deplorable schisms, into which the Church at large was plunged by the Arian controversy. Two years after the Council of Nice, A.D. 327, the Arians, through the assistance of Constantia, the Emperor's sister, won the favour of Constantine. He lost no time during this season of prosperity in procuring the deposition of Catholic bishops. Eminent among these was Eustathius, Bishop of Antioch. He was ejected by a synod held in his own city on false charges of Sabellianism and adultery.[24] An Arian Bishop, Euphronius, was appointed, but the Catholic congregation indignantly withdrew to hold their services in another quarter of the town, on the opposite side of the Orontes.[25] The see remained for some time entirely in the hands of the Arians. When the Council of Sardica met in A.D. 342, and the Arian faction seceded from it to hold a Council of their own in Philippopolis, Stephen, Bishop of Antioch, was their president. He was deposed in A.D. 349 by the Emperor Constantius, having been detected as an accomplice in an infamous plot against some envoys from the Western Church.[26] But "uno avulso non deficit alter;" he was succeeded by another Arian, the eunuch Leontius.[27] He tried to conciliate the Catholics by an artful and equivocating policy, of which his manner of chanting the doxology was an instance. The Arian form of it was "Glory be to the Father BY the Son *in* the Holy Ghost;" this the bishop was accustomed to slur in such an indistinct voice that the prepositions could not be clearly if at all heard, while he joined loudly in the second part of the hymn where all were agreed.[28] He died towards the close of A.D. 357, when the see was fraudulently seized by Eudoxius, Bishop of Germanicia. He favoured the extreme Arians so openly that the Semi-Arians appealed to the Emperor Constantius to summon a General Council. Their request was granted; but the Arians, fearing that the Catholics and Semi-Arians would coalesce to overwhelm them, artfully suggested that Rimini, the place proposed for the Council, was too distant for the Eastern prelates, and that the Assembly should be divided, part meeting at Rimini, and part at Nice.[29] Their suggestion was accepted, and the result is well known. Partly by arguments, partly by artifices and delays which wore out the strength and patience of the members, the Arians completely carried the day; the creed of Rimini was ordered by the Emperor to be everywhere signed, and in the words of Jerome, "the world groaned and found itself Arian."[30] An Arian synod sat at Constantinople. Macedonius, the archbishop, being considered too moderate, was deposed, and Eudoxius, the usurper of Antioch, was elevated to the see in his stead;[31] and Meletius, Bishop of Sebaste, in Armenia, was translated to the vacant see of Antioch, A.D. 361. But in him the Arians had mistaken their man. He was one of those who attended more to the practical moral teaching than to the abstract theology of Christianity; and, being not perhaps very precise in his language on doctrinal points, he had been reckoned an Arian.[32] After his elevation to the See of Antioch, he confined himself in his discourses to those practical topics on which all could agree. But this was not allowed to last long. The Emperor Constantius paid a visit to Antioch soon after the appointment of Meletius, and he was instigated by the Arians to put the bishop to a crucial test. He was commanded to preach on Proverbs viii. 22: "The Lord *possessed* me" (Septuagint ἔκτισε, that was the fatal word) "in the beginning," etc. The interpretation put on the word "formed" ἔκτισε would reveal the man. Two other bishops discoursed first upon the same text: George of Laodicea, Acacius of Cæsarea. The first construed the passage in a purely Arian sense: the Word was a κτίσμα, "a created being," though the first in time and rank; the second preacher took a more moderate line. Then came the turn of Meletius; short-hand writers took down every word as it fell. Meletius was a mild and temperate man, but he had his convictions, and he was no coward. To the horror of the Arians (the secret joy, perhaps, of those who disliked him) he entirely dissented from the Arian interpretation. The people loudly applauded his sermon, and called aloud for some brief and compendious statement of his doctrine. Meletius replied by a symbolical action: he held up three fingers, and then closing two of them, he said: "Our minds conceive of three, but we speak as to one."[33] This was conclusive; the objectionable prelate was banished to Melitene, his native place in Armenia, thirty days after he had entered Antioch. Euzoius, who had been an intimate friend and constant associate of Arius himself, was put into the see. The Church of Antioch now split into three parties: the old and rigid orthodox set, who, ever since the deposition of Eustathius in A.D. 327, had adhered to his doctrine, and were called after his name; the moderate Catholics, who regarded Meletius as their bishop; and the Arians under Euzoius. The synod which had deposed him published a thoroughly Arian creed, which declared the Son to have been created out of nothing, and to be unlike the Father both in substance and will.[34]

This first banishment of Meletius, which occurred in A.D. 361, did not last long. Julian, who became Emperor the same year, recalled all the prelates who had been exiled in the two preceding reigns; partly, perhaps, from a really liberal feeling, partly from a willingness to foment the internal dissensions of the Church by placing the rival bishops in close antagonism. Athanasius returned to Alexandria amidst great ovations.[35] One of the questions which occupied the attention of a synod convened by him was the schism of Antioch. Eusebius, Bishop of Vercelli, a staunch Italian friend of Athanasius, was despatched to Antioch in order to heal the division; but he had been unhappily anticipated by another Western prelate, Lucifer of Cagliari, in Sardinia, a brave defender of orthodoxy, for which with Eusebius he had suffered exile, but a most unskilful peacemaker. He only complicated the existing confusion by consecrating as bishop a priest of the old Eustathian party, named Paulinus, instead of strengthening the hands of Meletius.[36] The unhappy Church at Antioch, where the whole Christian community amounted to not more than 100,000 souls,[37] was thus torn to tatters. There were now three bishops: the Arian Euzoius, Meletius, generally acknowledged by the Eastern Church, and Paulinus by the Western. And, as if three rival heads were not sufficient, the Apollinarians soon afterwards added a fourth. But the mild, prudent, and charitable disposition of Meletius procured for him the affection and esteem of the largest and most respectable part of the population, as well as of the common people. Even when he was banished for the first time after he had been only a month in Antioch, the populace endeavoured to stone the prefect as he was conducting the bishop out of the city. He was saved by Meletius himself, who threw a part of his own mantle round him, to protect him from their fury. And after he returned from exile the popularity of Meletius increased. In paintings on the walls of houses and engravings on signet rings, his face was often represented, and parents gave his name to their children both to perpetuate his memory and to remind them of an example which was worthy of their imitation.[38] Once more in A.D. 367, and yet again in A.D. 370 or A.D. 371, when the Arians recovered the favour of the Court under the Emperor Valens, he was sent into exile, but he returned after the death of Valens in A.D. 378; and it was as Bishop of Antioch that he presided over the Council of Constantinople in A.D. 381, and died during its session.[39] His funeral oration, pronounced by Gregory Nyssen, is extant. The final reparation of that schism which he nobly and constantly endeavoured to heal was not effected for nearly twenty years, when Chrysostom, then Archbishop of Constantinople, accomplished that good service for his native city.

It is interesting to dwell at some length upon the history of the Church in Antioch at this period, because it represents the painful feuds in which the Church at large became entangled through the baneful influence of the Arian controversy, that first great blow to the unity of Christendom; when bishop was set up against bishop, and rival councils manufactured rival creeds, when violence, and intrigue, and diplomatic arts were employed too often by both sides to gain their ends. But the distracted state of the Church at Antioch also supplies a possible answer to the question why the baptism of Chrysostom was delayed so long. One of the reasons frequently alleged for deferring the reception of that sacrament was the desire of the candidate to receive it at the hands of some particular bishop.[40] Now who were the bishops of Antioch during the infancy and boyhood of Chrysostom? The Arians were in possession of the see at the time of his birth, and retained it till A.D. 361, when Meletius was appointed, but banished almost immediately. The pious sensible mother and the well-disposed youth would not unnaturally hold aloof from a Church over which presided such prelates as Stephen, Leontius, Eudoxius, Euzoius. Their minds may well have been so sorely perplexed and suspended between the claims of opposing factions as to delay the reception of baptism from the hands of any.

But the prudent, conciliatory policy, the mild and amiable disposition of Meletius, would engage the sympathy and respect of an affectionate, pious, and sensible youth, such as Chrysostom was. He was about twenty when Meletius was banished in 367 by the Emperor Valens; but the bishop returned in a short time, when Chrysostom's friend Basil had withdrawn into religious seclusion, and he himself was feeling an increasing repugnance to the world. He presented himself as a candidate for baptism to the bishop, and after the usual three years of preparation as a catechumen, was admitted into the Christian Church.

There can be no doubt that baptism, from whatever cause delayed, must on that very account have come home to the recipient with a peculiar solemnity of meaning. It was an important epoch, often a decisive turning-point in the life, a deliberate renunciation of the world, and dedication of the whole man to God. So Chrysostom evidently felt it; from this point we enter on a new phase in his life. He becomes for a time an enthusiastic ascetic, and then settles down into that more tranquil and steady, but intense glow of piety and love to God which burned with undiminished force till the close of his career.

The wise Bishop Meletius, however, desired to employ his powers in some sphere of active labour in the Church. As a preliminary step to this end, he ordained him soon after his baptism to the office of reader. This order appears not to have been instituted in the Church before the third century; at least there is no allusion to it in writers of the first two centuries, and frequent references in writers of the third and fourth.[41] The duty of readers was to read those portions of Scripture which were introduced into the first service or "Missa Catechumenorum," which preceded the Communion, or "Missa Fidelium," so called because only the baptized were admitted to it. They read from the Pulpitum or Tribunal Ecclesiæ, or Ambo, the reading-desk of the Church, which must not be confounded with the Bema, or Tribunal of the Sanctuary. This last was identical with the altar, or rather the steps of the altar, and no rank lower than that of deacon was permitted to read from this position. By the Novells of Justinian,[42] eighteen was fixed as the youngest age at which any one could be ordained to this office. But previous to this limitation, it was not uncommon to appoint mere children. Cæsarius of Arles is said to have been made a reader at the tender age of seven, and Victor Uticensis, describing the cruelties of the Vandalic persecution in Africa, affirms that among 500 clergy or more who perished by sword or famine, were many "infant readers."[43]

The ceremony of ordination appears to have been very simple. The Fourth Council of Carthage ordains that the bishop should testify before the congregation to the purity, the faith, and conversation of the candidate. Then in their presence he is to place a Bible in his hands with these words: "Take thou this book, and be thou a reader of the word of God, which office if thou discharge faithfully and profitably thou shalt have part with those who have ministered the word of God."[44]

CHAPTER 3

COMMENCEMENT OF ASCETIC LIFE—STUDY UNDER DIODORUS—FORMATION OF AN ASCETIC BROTHERHOOD—THE LETTERS TO THEODORE. A.D. 370.

THE ENTHUSIASM OF MINDS newly awakened to a full perception of Christian holiness, and a deep sense of Christian obligations, was in early times seldom contented with anything short of complete separation from the world. The Oriental temperament especially has been at all times inclined to passionate extremes. It oscillates between the most abandoned licentiousness and intense asceticism. The second is the corrective of the first; where the disease is desperate, the remedies must be violent. Chrysostom, as will be perceived throughout his life, was never carried to fanatical extremes; a certain sober-mindedness and calm practical good sense eminently distinguished him, though mingled with burning zeal. But in his youth especially he was not exempt from the spirit of the age and country in which he lived. He irresistibly gravitated towards that kind of life which his friend Basil had already adopted—a life of retirement, contemplation, and pious study—"the philosophy" of Christianity, as it was called at that time.[45]

It does not appear that Basil had actually joined any monastic community, but merely that he was leading a life of seclusion, and practising some of the usual monastic austerities. Chrysostom, indeed, distinctly asserts that, previous to his own baptism, their intercourse had not been entirely broken off; only that it was impossible for him, who had his business in the law-courts and found his recreation in the theatre, to be so acceptable as formerly to one who now never entered public places, and who was wholly devoted to meditation, study, and prayer.[46] Their intercourse was necessarily more rare, though their friendship was substantially unshaken. "When, however, I had myself also lifted my head a little above this worldly flood, he received me with open arms" (probably referring here to his baptism or preparation for it); "but even then I was not able to maintain my former equality, for he had the advantage of me in point of time, and having manifested the greatest diligence, he had attained a very lofty standard, and was ever soaring beyond me."[47]

This disparity, however, could not diminish their natural affection for one another; and Basil at length obtained Chrysostom's consent to a plan which he had frequently urged—that they should abandon their present homes and live together in some quiet abode, there to strengthen each other in undisturbed study, meditation, and prayer. But this project of the young enthusiasts was for a time frustrated by the irresistible entreaties of Chrysostom's mother, that he would not deprive her of his protection, companionship, and help. The scene is described by Chrysostom himself,[48] with a dramatic power worthy of Greek tragedy. It reminds the reader of some of those long and stately, yet elegant and affecting, narratives of the messenger who, at the close of the play, *describes* the final scene which is not represented. Certainly it bespeaks the scholar of a man who had made his pupils familiar with the best classical writers in Greek. "When she knew that we were meditating this course, my mother took me by the right hand and led me into her own chamber, and there, seating herself near the bed on which she had given birth to me, wept fountains of tears; to which she added words of lamentation more pitiable even than the tears themselves. 'I was not long permitted to enjoy the virtue of thy father, my child: so it seemed good to God. My travail-pangs at your birth were quickly succeeded by his death; bringing orphanhood upon thee, and upon me an untimely widowhood, with all those miseries of widowhood which those only who have experienced them can fairly understand. For no description can approach the reality of that storm and tempest which is undergone by her who having but lately issued from her father's home, and being unskilled in the ways of the world, is suddenly plunged into grief insupportable, and compelled to endure anxieties too great for her sex and age. For she has to correct the negligence, to watch against the ill-doings, of her slaves, to baffle the insidious schemes of kinsfolk, to meet with a brave front the impudent threats and harshness of tax-collectors.'"[49]

She then describes minutely the expense, and labour, and constant anxiety which attended the education of a son; how she had refrained from all thoughts of second marriage, that she might bestow her undivided energies, time, and means upon him; how amply it had all been rewarded by the delight of his presence, recalling the image of her husband;—and now that he had grown up, would he leave her absolutely forlorn? "In return for all these my services to you," she cried, "I implore you this one favour only—not to make me a second time a widow, or to revive the grief which time has lulled. Wait for my death—perhaps I shall soon be gone; when you have committed my body to the ground, and mingled my bones with your father's bones, then you will be free to embark on any sea you please." Such an appeal to his sense of filial gratitude and duty could not be disregarded. Chrysostom yielded to his mother's entreaties, although Basil did not desist from urging his favourite scheme.[50]

At the same time he assimilated his life at home as much as possible to the condition of a monk. He entirely withdrew from all worldly occupations and amusements. He seldom went out of the house; he strengthened his mind by study, his spirit by prayer, and subdued his body by vigils and fasting, and sleeping upon the bare ground. He maintained an almost constant silence, that his thoughts might be kept abstracted from mundane things, and that no irritable or slanderous speech might escape his lips. Some of his companions naturally lamented what they regarded as a morose and melancholy change.[51]

But the intercourse between him and Basil was more frequent than before; and two other young men, who had been their fellow-students at the school of Libanius, were persuaded to adopt the same kind of secluded life. These two were Maximus, afterwards Bishop of

Seleucia, in Isauria; and Theodore, who became Bishop of Mopsuestia, in Cilicia.[52] This little fraternity formed, with some others not named, a voluntary association of youthful ascetics. They did not dwell in a separate building, nor were they in any way established as a monastic community, but (like Wesley and his young friends at Oxford) they lived by rule, and practised monastic austerities. The superintendence of their studies and general conduct they submitted to Diodorus and Carterius, who were presidents of monasteries in the vicinity of Antioch.[53] In addition to his own intrinsic merits and eminence, Diodorus claims our attention, because there can be no doubt that he exercised a great influence upon the minds of his two most distinguished scholars, Chrysostom and Theodore. Indeed, judging from the fragments of his works, and the notices of him by historians, it is not too much to say that he was the founder of a method of Biblical interpretation of which Chrysostom and Theodore became the most able representatives.

He was of noble family, and the friend of Meletius, who confided to him and the priest Evagrius the chief care of his diocese during his second exile under Valens about A.D. 370. And one of the first acts of Meletius, on his return in A.D. 378, was to make Diodorus Bishop of Tarsus. His writings in defence of Christianity were sufficiently powerful and notorious to provoke the notice of Julian, who, in a letter to Photinus, attacks him with no small asperity.[54] The Emperor finds occasion for ridicule in the pale and wrinkled face and the attenuated frame of Diodorus, wasted by his severe labours and ascetic practices; and represents these disfigurements as punishments from the offended gods against whom he had directed his pen. Being well known as a warm friend of Meletius, Diodorus was exposed to some risk from the Arian party during the exile of the bishop from A.D. 370-378. But he was not deterred from frequenting the old town on the south side of the Orontes, where the congregation of Meletius held their assemblies, and diligently ministering to their spiritual needs. He accepted no fixed stipend, but his necessities were supplied by the hospitality of those among whom he laboured.[55] Of his voluminous writings, a commentary on the Old and New Testament is that most frequently quoted by ecclesiastical writers. They expressly and repeatedly affirm that he adhered very closely to the literal and historical meaning of the text, and that he was opposed to those mystical and allegorical interpretations of Origen and the Alexandrian school, which often disguised rather than elucidated the true significance of the passage.[56] One evil of the allegorical method was, that it destroyed a clear and critical perception of the differences between the Older Revelation and the New. The Old Testament was regarded as a kind of vast enigma, containing *implicitly* the facts and doctrines of the New. To detect subtle allusions to the coming of our Saviour, to the events of his life, to his death and resurrection, in the acts, speeches, and gestures of persons mentioned in the Old Testament, was regarded as a kind of interpretation no less satisfactory than it was ingenious. To believe indeed that the grand intention running through Scripture from the beginning to the end is to bring men to Jesus Christ; that the history of the fall of man is given to enable us to appreciate the need of a Restorer, and to estimate his work at its proper value; that the history of a dispensation based on law enables us to accept with more thankfulness a dispensation of spirit; that the history of the Jewish system of sacrifices is intended to conduct us to the one great Sacrifice as the substance of previous shadows, the fulfilment of previous types; that, alike in the law and the prophets, intimations and hints and significant parallels of the subsequent history to which they lead on are to be discerned;—this may be reasonable, profitable, and true: but it can be neither profitable nor true to see allusions, prophecies, and parallels in every minute and trivial detail of that earlier history.

From this vital error Diodorus appears to have emancipated himself and his disciples. He perceived, as we shall see Chrysostom perceived, a gradual development in Revelation: that the knowledge, and morality, and faith of men under the Old Dispensation were less advanced than those of men who lived under the New. One instance must suffice. He remarks that the Mosaic precept, directing the brother of a man who had died childless to raise up posterity to his brother by marrying his wife, was given for the consolation of men who had as yet received no clear promise respecting a resurrection from the dead.[57] There is an approach to what some might deem rationalistic criticism, when he affirms that the speech of God to men in the Old Testament was not an external voice, but an inward spiritual intimation. When, for instance, it is said that God gave a command to Adam, it is evident, he says, that it was not made by a sound audible to the bodily ear, but that God impressed the knowledge of the command upon him according to his own proper energy, and that when Adam had received it his *condition* was the same *as* if it had come to him through the actual hearing of the ear. And this, he observes, is what God effected also in the case of the prophets.[58] A similar rationalistic tendency is observable in his explanation of the relation between the Divine and human elements in the person of our blessed Lord. His language, in fact, on this subject is Nestorian: a distinction was to be made between Him who, according to his essence, *was* Son of God—the Logos—and Him who through Divine decree and adoption *became* Son of God. He who was born as Man from Mary was Son according to grace, but God the Logos was Son according to nature. The Son of Mary became Son of God because He was selected to be the receptacle or temple of God the Word. It was only in an improper sense that God the Word was called Son of David; the appellation was given to Him merely because the human temple in which He dwelt belonged to the lineage of David.[59] It is clear that Diodorus would have objected equally with Nestorius to apply the title of "God-bearer" (Θεοτόκος) to the blessed Virgin. Sixty years later, in A.D. 429, the streets of Constantinople and Alexandria resounded with tumults excited by controversy about the subject of which this was the watchword. But Diodorus happily lived too early for these dreadful conflicts, and his scholar Theodore was not personally disturbed; though long after his death, in A.D. 553, his writings were condemned by the Fifth Œcumenical Council, because the Nestorians appealed to them in confirmation of their tenets, and revered his memory. The practical element in Diodorus, his method of literal and common-sense interpretation of Holy Scripture, was inherited chiefly by Chrysostom; the intellectual vein, his conceptions of the relation between the Godhead and Manhood in Christ, his opinions respecting the final restoration of mankind, which were almost equivalent to a denial of eternal punishment, were reproduced mainly by Theodore.

It was inevitable that those who, in an access of religious fervour, had renounced the world and subjected themselves to the sternest asceticism, should sometimes find that they had miscalculated their powers. The passionate enthusiasm which for a time carried them along the thorny path would begin to subside; a hankering after a more natural, if not more worldly, life ensued; and occasionally the reaction was so violent, the passions kept down in unnatural constraint reasserted themselves with such force, that the ascetic flew back to the pleasures and sometimes to the sins of the world, with an appetite which was in painful contrast to his previous abstinence. The youthful Theodore was for a time an instance, though far from an extreme instance, of such reaction: the strain was too great for him; he relapsed for a season into his former habits of life; he retired from the little ascetic brotherhood to which Chrysostom and Basil belonged. There is no evidence that he fell into any kind of sin; he simply returned to the occupations and amusements of ordinary life. He was in love with and desirous of marrying a young lady named Hermione. But Chrysostom was at this period such an ardent ascetic; he was so deeply impressed with the evil of the world; and regarded an austere and absolute separation from it as so indispensable to the highest standard of Christian life, that to him any divergence from that path, when once adopted, seemed a positive sin. The relapse of Theodore called forth two letters of lamentation, remonstrance, and exhortation from his friend. They are the earliest of his extant works, and exhibit a command of language which does credit to the training of Libanius as well as to his own ability, and an intimate acquaintance with Holy Scripture, which proves how much time he had already spent in diligent and patient study. Since these epistles have been justly considered among the finest of his productions, and represent his opinions at an early stage of his life respecting repentance, a future life, the advantages of asceticism and celibacy, some paraphrases from them will be presented to the reader.

He begins his first letter by quoting the words of Jeremiah: "Oh that my head were waters, and mine eyes a fountain of tears!"

"If the prophet uttered that lamentation over a ruined city, surely I may express a like passionate sorrow over the fallen soul of a brother. That soul which was once the temple of the Holy Spirit now lies open and defenceless to become the prey of any hostile invader. The spirit of avarice, of arrogance, of lust, may now find a free passage into a heart which was once as pure and inaccessible to evil as heaven itself. Wherefore I mourn and weep, nor will I cease from my mourning until I see thee again in thy former brilliancy. For though this may seem impossible to men, yet with God it is possible, for He it is who lifteth the beggar from the earth and taketh the poor out of the dunghill, that He may set him with the princes, even with the princes of his people." An eminent characteristic of Chrysostom is that he is always hopeful of human nature; he never doubts the capacity of man to rise, or the willingness of God to raise him. Theodore himself appears to have been stricken with remorse, and to have drooped into despondency, to rouse him from which and lead him to repose more trustfully on the goodness of God, was one main purpose of Chrysostom's letters. "Despair was the devil's work;" "it is he who tries to cut off that hope whereby men are saved, which is the support and anchor of the soul, which, like a long chain, let down from heaven, little by little draws those who hold tightly to it up to heavenly heights, and lifts them above the storm and tempest of these worldly ills. The devil tries to extinguish that trust which is the source and strength of prayer, which enables men to cry, 'as the eyes of a maiden look unto the hand of her mistress, even so our eyes wait upon the Lord our God until He have mercy upon us.' Yet if man will only believe it, there is never a time at which any one, even the most abandoned sinner, may not turn and repent and be accepted by God. For God being impassible, his wrath is not a passion or an emotion; He punishes not in anger, since He is unsusceptible by nature of injury from any insult or wrong done by us, but in mercy, that He may bring men back to Himself.[60] The many instances of God's mercy; his relenting towards the Jews, and even to Ahab, when he humbled himself; the repentance of Manasseh—of the Ninevites—of the penitent thief—all accepted, although preceded by a long course of sin, prove that the words 'today if ye will hear his voice' are applicable to any time:—it is always 'to-day' as long as a man lives; repentance is estimated not by length of time, but by the disposition of the heart." He acutely observes that "despondency often conceals moral weakness; a secret though perhaps unconscious sympathy with the sin which the man professes to deplore and hate." "To fall is natural, but to remain fallen argues a kind of acquiescence in evil, a feebleness of moral purpose which is more displeasing to God than the fall itself."[61]

But although he speaks in the most hopeful, encouraging language of the efficacy of repentance, however late, if sincere, in *this life*, no one can assert more strongly the impossibility of restoration when the limits of this present existence have once been passed. In this respect he differs alike from Origen, Diodorus, and his fellow-student Theodore, and from believers in the later developed doctrine of purgatory. "As long as we are here, it is possible, even if we sin ten thousand times, to wash all away by repentance; but when once we have been taken to that other world, even if we manifest the greatest penitence, it will avail us naught, but however much we may gnash with our teeth, and beat our breasts, and pour forth entreaties, no one will be able even with the tip of his finger to cool us in the flame; we shall only hear the same words as the rich man: 'between us and you there is a great gulf fixed.'"[62] Nothing is more remarkably characteristic of Chrysostom's productions, especially the earlier, than a frequent recurrence to this truth: the existence of a great impassable chasm between the two abodes of misery and bliss. Heaven and hell were no distant dreamlands to him, but realities so nearly and vividly present to his mind that they acted as powerful motives, encouraging to holiness, deterring from vice. He paints the two pictures in glowing colours, and submits them to the contemplation of his friend. "When you hear of fire, think not that the fire in that other world is like it; for this earthly fire burns up and consumes whatever it lays hold of, but that burns continually those who are seized by it and never ceases, wherefore it is called unquenchable. For sinners must be clothed with immortality, not for honour, but merely to supply a constant material for this punishment to feed upon; and how terrible this is, a description would indeed never be able to present, but from our experience of small sufferings it is possible to form some little conception of those greater miseries. If you should ever be in a bath which has been overheated, then I pray you consider the fire of hell; or if ever you have been parched by a severe fever, transfer your thoughts to that flame, and you will be able clearly to distinguish the difference. For if a bath or a fever so distress and agitate us, what will be our condition when we fall into that river of fire which flows past the terrible Judge's throne."[63] "Heaven is, indeed, a subject which transcends the powers of human language, yet we can form a dim image of what it is like. It is the place 'whence sorrow and sighing shall flee away' (Is. xxxv. 10); where poverty and sickness are not to be dreaded; where no one injures or is injured, no one provokes or is provoked; no one is harassed by anxiety about the necessary wants, or frets over the loftier ambitions, of life; it is the place where the tempest of human passions is lulled; where there is neither night nor cold nor heat, nor changes of season, nor old age; but everything belonging to decay is taken away, and incorruptible glory reigns alone. But far above all these things, it is the place where men will continually enjoy the society of Jesus Christ, together with angels and archangels and all the powers above."[64] "Open your eyes," he cries in a transport of feeling, "and contemplate in imagination that heavenly theatre crowded not with men such as we see, but with those who are nobler than gold or precious stones or sunbeams, or any brilliant thing that can be seen; and not with men only, but angels, thrones, dominions, powers ranged about the King whom we dare not describe for his transcendent beauty, majesty, and splendour. If we had to suffer ten thousand deaths every day; nay, if we had to undergo hell itself, for the sake of beholding Christ coming in his glory, and being numbered among the band of saints, would it not be well to submit to all these things? 'Master, it is a good thing for us to be here:' if such an exclamation burst from St. Peter on witnessing a partial and veiled manifestation of Christ's glory, what are we to say when the reality shall be displayed, when the royal palace shall be thrown open and we shall see the King Himself; no longer by means of a mirror, or as it were in a riddle, but face to face; no longer through faith, but actual sight."[65] He passes on to some remarks upon the soul, which are Platonic in character: "Man cannot alter the shape of his body, but God has conceded to him a power, with the assistance of Divine grace, of increasing the beauty of the soul. Even that soul which has become deformed by the ugliness of sin may be restored to its pristine beauty. No lover was ever so much captivated by the beauty of the body as God loves and longs for the beauty of the human soul.[66] You who are now transported with admiration of Hermione's beauty" (the girl whom Theodore wished to marry) "may, if you will, cultivate a beauty in your own soul as far exceeding hers as heaven surpasses earth. Beauty of the soul is the only true and permanent kind, and if you could see it with the eye, you would admire it far more than the loveliness of the rainbow and of roses, and other flowers which are evanescent and feeble representations of the soul's beauty."[67] He tells some curious stories of men who had relapsed from monastic life and subsequently been reclaimed to it. One, a young man of noble family and heir to great wealth, had thrown up all the splendour which he might have commanded, and exchanged his riches and his gay clothing for the poverty and mean garb of a recluse upon the mountains, and had attained an astonishing degree of holiness. But some of his relations seduced him from his retreat, and once more he might be seen riding on horseback through the forum followed by a crowd of attendants. But the holy brethren whom he had deserted ceased not to endeavour to recover him; at first he treated them with haughty indifference, when they met and saluted him, as he proudly rode through the streets. But at last, as they desisted not day by day, he would leap from his horse when they appeared, and listen with downcast eyes to their warnings; till, as time went on, he was rescued from his worldly entanglements, and restored to his desert and the study of the true philosophy, and now, when Chrysostom wrote, he bestowed his wealth upon the poor, and had attained the very pinnacle of virtue.[68] Earnestly, therefore, does he implore Theodore to recover his trust in God, to repent and return to the brotherhood which was buried in grief at his defection. "Now the unbelieving and the worldly rejoice; but return to us, and our sorrow and shame will be transferred to the adversary's side." "It was the beginning of penitence which was arduous; the devil met the penitent at the door of the city of refuge, but, if defeated there, the fury of his assaults would diminish." He warned him against an idle confession of sinfulness not accompanied by any honest effort to amend. "Such was no true confession, because not joined with the tears of contrition or followed by alteration of life."[69] But of Theodore he hoped better things; as there were different degrees of glory reserved for men, implied in our Lord's mention of "many mansions," and his declaring that every one should be rewarded according to his works, he trusted that Theodore might still obtain a high place; that he might be a vessel of silver, if not of gold or precious stone, in the heavenly house.[70]

In the second epistle Chrysostom expresses more distinctly his view respecting the solemn obligations of those who joined a religious fraternity. "If tears and groanings could be transmitted through a letter, this of mine would be filled with them; I weep that you have blotted yourself out of the catalogue of the brethren, and trampled on your covenant with Christ." "The devil assaulted him with peculiar fury, because he was anxious to conquer so worthy an antagonist; one who had despised delicate fare and costly dress, who had spent whole days in the study of Holy Scripture, and whole nights in prayer, who had regarded the society of the brethren as a greater honour than any worldly dignity. What, I pray you, is there that appears blessed and enviable in the world? The prince is exposed to the wrath of the people and the irrational outbursts of popular feeling—to the fear of princes greater than himself—to anxieties about his subjects; and the ruler of to-day is to-morrow a private man: for this present life no way differs from a stage; as on that, one man plays the part of a king, another of a general, a third of a common soldier; but when evening has come the king is no king, the ruler no ruler, the general no general; so will it be in *that* day; each will receive his due reward, not according to the character which he has enacted, but according to the works which he has done."[71] Theodore had clearly expressed his intention of honourably marrying Hermione; but though Chrysostom allows that marriage is an honourable estate, yet he boldly declares that for one who like Theodore had made such a solemn renunciation of the world, it was equally criminal with fornication. He had wholly dedicated himself to the service of God, and he had no right to bind himself by any other tie: to marry would be as culpable as desertion in a soldier. He points out the miseries, the anxieties, the toils, often fruitless, which accompanied secular life, especially in the married state. From all such ills the life of the brotherhood was exempt: he alone was truly free who lived for Christ; he was like one who, securely planted on an eminence, beholds other men below him buffeting with the waves of a tumultuous sea. For such a high vantage-ground Chrysostom implores Theodore to make. He begs him to pardon the length of his letter: "nothing but his ardent love for his friend could have constrained him to write this second epistle. Many indeed had discouraged what they regarded as a vain task and sowing upon a rock; but he was not so to be diverted from his efforts: he trusted that by the grace of God his letters would accomplish something; and if not, he should at least have delivered himself from the reproach of silence."[72]

These letters are the productions of a youthful enthusiast, and as such, allowances must be made for them. They abound not only in eloquent passages, but in very fine and true observations upon human nature—on penitence—on God's mercy and pardon. It is only the application of them to the case of Theodore which seems harsh and overstrained. At a later period Chrysostom's views on ascetic and monastic life were modified; but in early life, though never fanatical, they were what we should call extreme. His earnest efforts for the restoration of his friend were crowned with success. Theodore abandoned the world once more and his matrimonial intentions, and retired into the seclusion of the brotherhood. Some twenty years later, in A.D. 394, he was made Bishop of Mopsuestia, which is pretty nearly all we know about him, but the extant fragments of his voluminous writings prove him to have been a man of no ordinary ability, and a powerful commentator of the same sensible and rational school as Chrysostom himself. We may be disposed to say, What of Hermione? Had she no claims to be considered? But the ascetic line of life was regarded by the earnest-minded as so indisputably the noblest which a Christian could adopt, that her disappointment would not have been allowed to weigh in the balance for a moment against what was considered the higher call.[73]

CHAPTER 4

CHRYSOSTOM EVADES FORCIBLE ORDINATION TO A BISHOPRIC—THE TREATISE "ON THE PRIESTHOOD." A.D. 370, 371.

WE NOW COME TO a curious passage in Chrysostom's life; one in which his conduct, from our moral standpoint, seems hardly justifiable. Yet for one reason it is not to be regretted, since it was the originating cause of his treatise "De Sacerdotio;" one of the ablest, most instructive, and most eloquent works which he ever produced.

Bishop Meletius had been banished in A.D. 370 or 371. The Arian Emperor Valens, who had expelled him, was about to take up his residence in Antioch. It was desirable therefore, without loss of time, to fill up some vacant sees in Syria. The attention of the bishops, clergy, and people was turned to Chrysostom and Basil, as men well qualified for the episcopal office.

According to a custom prevalent at that time, they might any day be seized and compelled, however reluctant, to accept the dignity. So St. Augustine was dragged, weeping, by the people before the bishop, and his immediate ordination demanded by them, regardless of his tears.[74] So St. Martin, Bishop of Tours, was torn from his cell, and conveyed under a guard to his ordination.[75] The two friends were filled with apprehension and alarm. Basil implored Chrysostom that they might act in concert at the present crisis, and together accept or together evade or resist the expected but unwelcome honour.

Chrysostom affected to consent to this proposal, but in reality determined to act otherwise. He regarded himself as totally unworthy and incompetent to fill so sacred and responsible an office; but considering Basil to be far more advanced in learning and piety, he resolved that the Church should not, through his own weakness, lose the services of his friend. Accordingly, when popular report proved correct, and some emissaries from the electing body were sent to carry off the young men (much, it would seem from Chrysostom's account, as policemen might arrest a prisoner), Chrysostom contrived to hide himself. Basil, less wary, was captured, and imagined that Chrysostom had already submitted; for the emissaries acted with subtlety when he tried to resist them. They affected surprise that he should make so violent a resistance, when his companion, who had the reputation of a hotter temper, had yielded so mildly to the decision of the Fathers.[76] Thus Basil was led to suppose that Chrysostom had already submitted; and when he discovered too late the artifice of his friend and his captors, he bitterly remonstrated with Chrysostom upon his treacherous conduct. "The character of them both," he complained, "was compromised by this division in their counsels." "You should have told us where your friend was hidden," said some, "and then we should have contrived some means of capturing him;" to which poor Basil was ashamed to reply that he had been ignorant of his friend's concealment, lest such a confession should cast a suspicion of unreality over the whole of their supposed intimacy. "Chrysostom, on his side, was accused of haughtiness and vanity for declining so great a dignity; though others said that the electors deserved a still greater dishonour and defeat for appointing over the heads of wiser, holier, and older men, mere lads,[77] who had been but yesterday immersed in secular pursuits; that they might now for a little while knit their brows, and go arrayed in sombre robes and affect a grave countenance."[78] Basil begged Chrysostom for an explanation of his motives in this proceeding. "After all their mutual protestations of indivisible friendship, he had been suddenly cast off and turned adrift, like a vessel without ballast, to encounter alone the angry tempests of the world. To whom should he now turn for sympathy and aid in the trials to which he would surely be exposed from slander, ribaldry, and insolence? The one who might have helped him stood coldly aloof, and would be unable even to hear his cries for assistance."[79]

We may be strongly disposed to sympathise with the disconsolate Basil. But the conscience of Chrysostom appears to have been quite at ease from first to last in this transaction. He regarded it as a "pious fraud." "When he beheld the mingled distress and displeasure of his friend, he could not refrain from laughing for joy, and thanking God for the successful issue of his plan."[80] In the ensuing discussion he boldly asserted the principle that deceit claims our admiration when practised in a good cause and from a good motive. The greatest successes in war, he argues, have been achieved through stratagem, as well as by fair fighting in the open field; and, of the two, the first are most to be admired, because they are gained without bloodshed, and are triumphs of mental rather than bodily force.[81] But, retorts poor Basil, I was not an enemy, and ought not to have been dealt with as such. "True, my excellent friend," replies Chrysostom, "but this kind of fraud may sometimes be exercised towards our dearest acquaintance." "Physicians were often obliged to employ some artifice to make refractory patients submit to their remedies. Once a man in a raging fever resisted all the febrifugal draughts administered to him, and loudly called for wine. The physician darkened the room, steeped a warm oyster shell in wine, then filled it with water, and put it to the patient's lips, who eagerly swallowed the draught, believing it, from the smell, to be wine."[82] In the same category of justifiable stratagem he places, not very discriminatingly, the circumcision of Timothy by St. Paul, in order to conciliate the Jews, and St. Paul's observance of the ceremonial law at Jerusalem (Acts xxi. 26), for the same purpose. Such contrivances he calls instances, not of treachery, but of "good management" (οἰκονομία). There is something highly Oriental, and alien to our Western moral sense, in the sophistical tone of this whole discussion. If Basil really submitted to such arguments, he was easily vanquished. He says, however, no more about the injustice of his treatment, but, apparently accepting Chrysostom's position that for a useful purpose deceit is justifiable, he begs to be informed "what advantage Chrysostom thought he had procured for himself or his friend by this piece of management, or good policy, or whatever he pleased to call it."

The remaining books on the Priesthood are occupied with the answer to this inquiry. The line which Chrysostom takes is to point out the pre-eminent dignity, difficulty, and danger of the priestly office, and then to enlarge upon the peculiar fitness of his friend to discharge its duties.[83] "What advantage could be greater than to be engaged in that work which Christ had declared with his own lips to be the special sign of love to Himself? For when He put the question three times to the leader of the apostles (κορυφαῖος), 'Lovest thou me?' and had been answered by a fervent asseveration of attachment, he added each time, 'Feed my sheep,' or 'Feed my lambs.' 'Lovest thou me *more* than these?' had been the question, and the charge which followed it had been always, 'Feed my sheep;' not, If thou lovest Me, practise fasting, or incessant vigils, and sleep on the bare ground, or protect the injured and be to the orphans as a father, and to their mother as a husband; no, he passes by all these things, and says, 'Feed my sheep.' Could his friend, therefore, complain that he had done ill in compassing, even by fraud, his dedication to so glorious an office?[84] As for himself, it was obvious that he could not have refused so great an honour out of haughty contempt or disrespect to the electors. On the contrary, it was when he considered the exceeding sanctity and magnitude of the position, and its awful responsibilities—the heavenly purity, the burning love towards God and man, the sound wisdom and judgment, and moderation of temper required in those who were dedicated to it—that his heart failed him. He felt himself utterly incompetent and unworthy for so arduous a task. If some unskilled person were suddenly to be called upon to take charge of a ship laden with a costly freight, he would immediately refuse; and in like manner he himself dared not risk by his present inexperience the safety of that vessel which was laden with the precious merchandise of souls.[85] Vain-glory, indeed, and pride would have induced him not to reject, but to covet, so transcendent a dignity. The office of priest was discharged indeed on earth, yet it held a place among heavenly ranks. And rightly; for neither man, nor angel, nor archangel, nor created power of any kind, but the Paraclete Himself, ordained this ministry. Therefore, it became one who entered the priesthood to be as pure as if he had already taken his stand in heaven itself among the powers above. 'When thou seest the Lord lying slain, and the priest standing and praying over the sacrifice, when thou seest all sprinkled with that precious blood, dost thou deem thyself still among men, still standing upon this earth? art thou not rather transported immediately to heaven, and, every carnal imagination being cast out, dost thou not, with soul unveiled and pure mind, behold the things which are in heaven? O miracle! O the goodness of God! He who is sitting with the Father is yet at that hour held in the hands of all, and gives Himself to be embraced and grasped by those who desire it. And this all do through the eye of faith. Do these things seem to you to merit contempt? does it seem possible to you that any one should be so elated as to slight them?"[86]

"Human nature possessed in the priesthood a power which had not been committed by God to angels or archangels; for to none of *them* had it been said, 'Whatsoever ye shall bind on earth or loose on earth shall be bound or loosed in heaven.' Was it possible to conceive that any one should think lightly of such a gift? Away with such madness!—for stark madness it would be to despise so great an authority, without which it was not possible for man to obtain salvation, or the good things promised to him. For if it were impossible for any one to enter into the kingdom of heaven, except he were born again of water and the Spirit; and if he who did not eat the flesh of the Lord and drink his blood was ejected from life eternal, and if these things were administered by none but the consecrated hands of the priest, how would any one, apart from them, be able to escape the fire of hell, or obtain the crown laid up for him?"[87]

There are, perhaps, no passages elsewhere in Chrysostom expressed in such a lofty sacerdotal tone; but it must be remembered that on any supposition as to the date of this treatise, he was young when it was composed, holding therefore, as on the subject of monasticism, more enthusiastic, highly-wrought opinions than he afterwards entertained; and moreover, that the whole treatise is written in a somewhat vehement and excited style, as by one who was maintaining a position against an antagonist.

Having proved that his evasion of the episcopal office could have arisen from no spirit of pride, but from a consciousness of his infirmity and incapacity, he proceeds to point out the manifold and peculiar dangers which encompassed it. "Vain-glory was a rock more fatal than the Sirens. Many a priest was shipwrecked there, and torn to pieces by the fierce monsters which dwelt upon it—wrath, despondency, envy, strife, slander, falsehood, hypocrisy, love of praise, and a multitude more. Often he became the slave and flatterer of great people, even of women who had most improperly mixed themselves up with ecclesiastical affairs, and especially exercised great influence in the elections."[88]

The scenes, indeed, which often took place about this period at the elections to bishoprics occasioned much scandal to the Church. In earlier times, when the Christians were less numerous, more simple in their habits, more unanimous,—when liability to persecution deterred the indifferent, or pretenders, from their ranks,—the episcopal office could be no object of worldly ambition. The clergy and the people elected their bishop; and the fairness and simplicity with which the election was usually conducted won the admiration of the Emperor Alexander Severus.[89] But when Christianity was recognised by the State, a bishopric in towns of importance became a position of high dignity; and warm debates, often fierce tumults, attended the election of candidates. Up to the time of Justinian at least, the whole Christian population of the city or region over which the bishop was to preside possessed a right to elect. Their choice was subject to the approval of the bishops, and the confirmation of the metropolitan of the province; but, on the other hand, neither the bishops nor the metropolitan could legally obtrude a candidate of their own upon the people. A charge brought against Hilary of Arles was, that he ordained several bishops against the will and consent of the people. A just and legitimate ordination, according to Cyprian, was one which had been examined by the suffrage and judgment of all, both clergy and people. Such, he observes, was the election of Cornelius to the See of Rome in A.D. 251.[90] If the people were unanimous, there were loud cries of ἄξιος, *dignus*, ἀνάξιος, *indignus*, as the case might be; but if they were divided, it was usual for the metropolitan to give the preference to the choice of the majority; or, if they appeared equally divided, the metropolitan and his synod selected a man indifferent, if possible, to both parties. Occasionally also, as in the case of Nectarius, the predecessor of Chrysostom in the See of Constantinople, the Emperor interposed, and appointed one chosen by himself. Sanguinary often were the tumults which attended contested elections. The greater the city, the greater the strife. In the celebrated contest for the See of Rome in A.D. 366, between Damasus and Ursicinus, there was much hard fighting and copious bloodshed. Damasus, with a furious and motley mob, broke into the Julian Basilica, where Ursicinus was being consecrated by Paul, Bishop of Tibur, and violently stopped the proceedings. Frays of this kind lasted for some time. On one occasion, one hundred and thirty dead bodies strewed the pavement of the Basilica of Licinius till Damasus at last won the day. It is especially mentioned that the ladies of Rome favoured his side.[91] It seems scarcely possible to doubt that as these events must have been fresh in Chrysostom's recollection, he must be specially referring to them when, insisting on freedom from ambition as one grand qualification for the priesthood, he says "that he will pass by, lest they should seem incredible, the tales of murders perpetrated in churches, and havoc wrought in cities by contentions for bishoprics;" and when also he alludes indignantly to the interference of women in the elections. "The elections," he says, "were generally made on public festivals, and were disgraceful scenes of party feeling and intrigue. The clergy and the people were never unanimous. The really important qualifications for the office were seldom considered. Ambitious men spared no arts of bribery or flattery by which to obtain places for themselves in the Church, and to keep them when obtained. One candidate for a bishopric was recommended to the electors because he belonged to a distinguished family; another because he was wealthy, and would not burden the funds of the Church."[92] The provocations to ambition and worldly glory were so great, both in the acquisition and in the exercise of the episcopal office, that Chrysostom says he had "determined partly for these reasons to avoid the snare."[93] He shrank also from many other trials incident to the office. There were always persons ready to detect and magnify the slightest mistake or transgression in a priest. One little error could not be retrieved by a multitude of successes, but darkened the man's whole life; for a kind of immaculate purity was exacted by popular opinion of a priest, as if he were not a being of flesh and blood, or subject to human passions. Often his brethren, the clergy, were the most active in spreading mischievous reports about him, hoping to rise themselves upon his ruin; like avaricious sons waiting for their father's death. Too often St. Paul's description of the sympathy between the several parts of the Christian body was inverted. 'If one member suffered, all the others rejoiced; if one member rejoiced, the others suffered pain.' A bishop had need be as impervious to slander and envy as the three children in the burning fiery furnace.[94] What a rare and difficult combination of qualities was required for the efficient discharge of his duties in the face of such difficulties! 'He must be dignified, yet not haughty; formidable, yet affable; commanding, yet sociable; strictly impartial, yet courteous; lowly, but not subservient; strong, yet gentle; promoting the worthy in spite of all opposition, and with equal authority rejecting the unworthy, though pushed forward by the favour of all; looking always to one thing only— the welfare of the Church; doing nothing out of animosity or partiality.'[95] The behaviour also of a priest in ordinary society was jealously criticised. The flock were not satisfied unless he was constantly paying calls. Not the sick only, but the sound desired to be 'looked after' (ἐπισκοπεῖσθαι),—not so much from any religious feeling, as because the reception of such visits gratified their sense of their own importance. Yet if a bishop often visited the house of a wealthy or distinguished man to interest him in some design for the advantage of the Church, he would soon be stigmatised as a parasitical flatterer. Even the manner of his greetings to acquaintance in the streets was criticised: 'He smiled cordially on Mr. Such-an-one, and talked much with him; but to me he only threw a commonplace remark.'"[96]

It is amusing and instructive to read these observations. They prove what important personages bishops had become. The interests of the people were violently excited over their elections. They were subjected to the mingled reverence, deference, and court, criticism, scandal, and gossip, which are the inevitable lot of all persons who occupy an exalted position in the world.

In the fourth book Chrysostom speaks of some of the more mental qualifications indispensable for a priest. Foremost among these was a power of speaking: "That was the one grand instrument which enabled him to heal the diseases of the body intrusted to his care. And, in addition to this, he must be armed with a prompt and versatile wit, to encounter the various assaults of heretics. Jews, Greeks, Manichæans, Sabellians, Arians, all were narrowly watching for the smallest loophole by which to force a breach in the walls of the Church. And, unless the defender was very vigilant and skilful, while he was keeping out the one he would let in the other. While he opposed the blind deference of the Jews to their Mosaic Law, he must take care not to encourage the Manichæans, who would eliminate the Law from the Scriptures. While he asserted the Unity of the Godhead against the Arians, there was danger of slipping into the Sabellian error of confounding the Persons; and, while he divided the Persons against the Sabellians, he must be careful to avoid the Arian error of dividing the substance also. The line of orthodoxy was a narrow path hemmed in by steep rocks on either side. Therefore it was of the deepest importance that the priest should be a learned and effective speaker, that he might not fall into error himself or lead others astray. For, if he was seen to be worsted in a controversy with heretics, many became alienated from the truth, mistaking the weakness of the defender for a weakness in the cause itself."[97]

"But there was yet another task fraught with peril—the delivery of sermons. The performances of a preacher were discussed by a curious and critical public like those of actors. Congregations attached themselves to their favourite preachers. Woe to the man who was detected in plagiarisms! He was instantly reprobated like a common thief.

"To become an effective preacher two things were necessary: first, indifference to praise; secondly, power of speech; two qualities, the one moral, the other intellectual, which were rarely found coexisting. If a man possessed the first only, he became distasteful and despicable to his congregation; for if he stood up and at first boldly uttered powerful words which stung the consciences of his hearers, but, as he proceeded, began to blush and hesitate and stumble, all the advantage of his previous remarks would be wasted. The persons, who had secretly felt annoyed by his telling reproofs would revenge themselves by laughing at his embarrassment in speaking. If, on the other hand, he was a weighty speaker, but not indifferent to applause, he would probably trim his sails to catch the popular breeze, and study to be pleasant rather than profitable, to the great detriment of himself and of his flock."[98]

He makes some remarks eminently wise and true on the necessity of study for the preparation of sermons. "It might seem strange, but in truth study was even more indispensable for an eloquent than for an ordinary preacher. Speaking was an acquired art, and when a man had attained a high standard of excellence he was sure to decline unless he kept himself up by constant study. The man of reputation was always expected to say something new, and even in excess of the fame which he had already acquired. Men sat in judgment on him without mercy, as if he were not a human being subject to occasional despondency, or anxiety, or irritation of temper; but as if he were an angel or some infallible being, who ought always to remain at the same high level of excellence. The mediocre man, on the other hand, from whom much was not expected, would obtain a disproportionate amount of praise if he said a good thing now and then.[99] The number of persons, however, in any congregation, who were capable of appreciating a really learned and powerful preacher, was very small; therefore a man ought not to be much disheartened or annoyed by unfavourable criticisms. He should be his own critic, aiming in all his work to win the favour of God. Then, if the admiration of men followed, he would quietly accept it; or, if withheld, he would not be distressed, but seek his consolation in honest work and in a conscience void of offence.[100] But if a priest was not superior to the love of admiration, all his labour and eloquence would be wasted; either he would sacrifice truth to popularity, or, failing to obtain so much applause as he desired, he would relax his efforts. This last was a common defect in men whose powers of preaching were only second-rate. Perceiving that even the highly gifted could not sustain their reputation without incessant study and practice, while they themselves, by the most strenuous efforts, could gain but a very slender meed of praise, if any, they abandoned themselves to indolence. The trial was especially great when a man was surpassed in preaching by one who occupied an inferior rank in the hierarchy, and who perhaps took every opportunity of parading his superior powers. A kind of passion for listening to preaching possessed, he says, both Pagans and Christians at this time; hence it was very mortifying for a man to see a congregation looking forward to the termination of his discourse, while to his rival they listened with the utmost patience and attention, and were vexed only when his sermon had come to an end."[101]

In the sixth book, Chrysostom enlarges on the dangers and trials which beset the priest as compared with the tranquillity and security of the monk—that life to which he still felt himself powerfully attracted. "'Who watch for your souls as they that must give an account.' The dread of the responsibility implied in that saying constantly agitated his mind. For if it were better to be drowned in the sea than to offend one of the little ones of Christ's flock, what punishment must they undergo who destroyed not one or two but a whole multitude?"[102] "Much worldly wisdom was required in the priest; he must be conversant with secular affairs, and adapt himself with versatility to all kinds of circumstances and men; and yet he ought to keep his spirit as free, as unfettered by worldly interests and ambitions as the hermit dwelling on the mountains."[103]

The trials, indeed, which beset the priest so far exceeded those of the monk, that Chrysostom considered the monastery, on the whole, a bad school for active clerical life. "The monk lived in a calm; there was little to oppose or thwart him. The skill of the pilot could not be known till he had taken the helm in the open sea amidst rough weather. Too many of those who had passed from the seclusion of the cloister to the active sphere of the priest or bishop proved utterly incapable of coping with the difficulties of their new situation. They lost their head (ἰλιγγιῶσιν), and, often, instead of adding to their virtue, were deprived of the good qualities which they already possessed. Monasticism often served as a screen to failings which the circumstances of active life drew out, just as the qualities of metal were tested by the action of fire."[104]

Chrysostom concludes by saying that he was conscious of his own infirmities; the irritability of his temper, his liability to violent emotions, his susceptibility to praise and blame. All such evil passions could, with the help of God's grace, be tamed by the severe treatment of the monastic life; like savage beasts who must be kept on low fare. But in the public life of a priest they would rage with incontrollable fury, because all would be pampered to the full—vain-glory by honour and praise, pride by authority, envy by the reputation of other men, bad temper by perpetual provocations, covetousness by the liberality of donors to the Church, intemperance by luxurious living.[105] He bids Basil picture the most implacable and deadly contest between earthly forces which his imagination could draw, and declares that this would but faintly express the conflict between the soul and evil in the spiritual warfare of the world. "Many accidents might put an end to earthly combat, at least for a time—the approach of night, the fatigue of the combatants, the necessity of taking food and sleep. But in the spiritual conflict there were no breathing spaces. A man must always have his harness on his back, or he would be surprised by the enemy."[106]

It is not surprising that Basil, after the fearful responsibilities and perils of his new dignity had been thus powerfully set before him, should declare that his trouble now was not so much how to answer the accusers of Chrysostom as to defend himself before God. He besought his friend to promise that he would continue to support and advise him in all emergencies. Chrysostom replied that as far as it was possible he would do so; but that he doubted not Christ, who had called Basil to this good work, would enable him to discharge it with boldness. They wept, embraced, and parted. And so Basil went forth to the unwelcome honours and trials of his bishopric, while Chrysostom continued to lead that monastic kind of life which was only a preparatory step to the monastery itself. His friendship with Basil is curious and romantic. Their intercourse was brought to a singular conclusion by the stratagem of Chrysostom. Basil may have, according to his own earnest request, continued to consult his friend in any difficulty or distress; but he is never mentioned again. Although so intimately bound up with this passage in Chrysostom's life, there is something indistinct and shadowy about his whole existence. He flits across the scene for a few moments, and then disappears totally and for ever.

The books on the Priesthood may be regarded as containing partly a real account of an actual conversation between the two friends. But, as in the dialogues of Plato, far more was probably added by the writer, so that in parts the dialogue is only a form into which the opinions of the author at the time of composition were cast. It is impossible to decide with certainty the exact time at which the treatise may have been written. It is not likely to have been later than his diaconate in 381,[107] but more probably[108] the work may be assigned to the six years of leisure spent in the seclusion of the monastery and mountains—that is, to the period between Basil's election to the bishopric, and his own ordination as deacon. The treatise reads like the production of one who had acquired considerable experience of monastic life; who had deliberately calculated its advantages on the one hand, and, on the other, had keenly observed and seriously weighed the temptations and difficulties which attended the more secular career of priest or bishop. It is a more mature work than the Epistles to Theodore, and is free from such rapturous and excessive praise of the ascetic life as they contain.

NOTE TO FOREGOING CHAPTER

It may excite surprise that men so young as Chrysostom and Basil, the former at least being not more than twenty-five or twenty-six, and not as yet ordained deacon, should have been designated to the highest office in the Church. The Council of Neocæsarea (about A.D. 320—*vide* Hefele, vol. i., Clark's transl. p. 222) fixed thirty as the age at which men became eligible for the priesthood. The same age, then, at least, must have been required for a bishop.

The Constitutions called Apostolical fix the age at fifty, but add a clause which really lets in all the exceptions, "unless he be a man of singular merit and worth, which may compensate for the want of years." And, in fact, there are numerous instances of men, both before and after the time of Chrysostom, who were consecrated as bishops under the age of thirty. The Council of Nice was held not more than twenty years after the persecution of Maximian, which Athanasius (Epist. ad Solitar., p. 382, Paris edition) says he had only heard of from his father, yet in five months after that Council he was ordained Archbishop of Alexandria. Remigius of Rheims was only twenty-two when he was made bishop, in A.D. 471. In like manner, though it was enacted by the Council of Sardica, A.D. 343-344, that none should rise to the Episcopal throne *per saltum*, yet there are not a few examples of this rule being transgressed.

Augustine, when he created a see at Fassula, presented Antonius, a reader (the very position Chrysostom now filled) to the Primate, who ordained him without scruple on Augustine's recommendation (Aug. Ep. 261, ad Cælest.). Cyprian, Ambrose, and Nestorius are celebrated instances of the consecration of laymen to bishoprics.

CHAPTER 5

NARROW ESCAPE FROM PERSECUTION—HIS ENTRANCE INTO A MONASTERY—THE MONASTICISM OF THE EAST, A.D. 372.

ABOUT THIS TIME, 372-373, while Chrysostom was still residing in Antioch, he narrowly escaped suffering the penalties of an imperial decree issued by Valentinian and Valens against the practisers of magical arts, or possessors even of magical books. A severe search was instituted after suspected persons; soldiers were everywhere on the watch to detect offenders. The persecution was carried on with peculiar cruelty at Antioch, where it had been provoked by the detection of a treasonable act of divination. The twenty-four letters of the alphabet were arranged at intervals round the rim of a kind of charger, which was placed on a tripod, consecrated with incantations and elaborate ceremonies. The diviner, habited as a heathen priest, in linen robes, sandals, and with a fillet wreathed about his head, chanted a hymn to Apollo, the god of prophecy, while a ring in the centre of the charger was slipped rapidly round a slender thread. The letters in front of which the ring successively stopped indicated the character of the oracle. The ring on this occasion was supposed to have pointed to the first four letters in the name of the future Emperor, Θ Ε Ο Δ. Theodorus, and probably many others who had the misfortune to own the fatal syllables, were executed. There were, of course, multitudes of eager informers, and zealous judges, who strove to allay the suspicious fears of the Emperors, and to procure favour for themselves by vigorous and wholesale prosecutions. Neither age, nor sex, nor rank was spared; women and children, senators and philosophers, were dragged to the tribunals, and committed to the prisons of Rome and Antioch from the most distant parts of Italy and Asia. Many destroyed their libraries in alarm—so many innocent books were liable to be represented as mischievous or criminal; and thus much valuable literature perished.[109] It was during this dreadful time, when suspicion was instantly followed by arrest, and arrest by imprisonment, torture, and probably death, that Chrysostom chanced to be walking with a friend to the Church of the Martyr Babylas, outside the city. As they passed through the gardens by the banks of the Orontes, they observed fragments of a book floating down the stream. Curiosity led them to fish it out; but, to their dismay, on examining it, they found that it was inscribed with magical formulæ, and, to increase their alarm, a soldier was approaching at no great distance. At first they knew not how to act; they feared the book had been cast into the river by the artifice of an informer to entrap some unwary victim. They determined, however, to throw their dangerous discovery back into the river, and happily the attention or suspicions of the soldier were not roused. Chrysostom always gratefully looked back to this escape as a signal instance of God's mercy and protection.[110]

It must have been soon after this incident and previous to the edict of persecution against the monks issued by Valens in 373, that Chrysostom exchanged what might be called the amateur kind of monastic life passed in his own home for the monastery itself. Whether his mother was now dead or had become reconciled to the separation, or whether her son's passionate enthusiasm for monastic retirement became irresistible, it is impossible to determine. His mother is not mentioned by him in his writings after this point, except in allusion to the past, which is a strong presumption that she was no longer living. Bishop Meletius would probably have endeavoured to detain him for some active work in the Church, but he was now in exile; and to Flavian, the successor of Meletius, Chrysostom was possibly not so intimately known.

During the first four centuries of the Christian era, the enthusiasm for monastic life prevailed with ever increasing force. We are, perhaps, naturally inclined to associate monasticism chiefly with the Western Christianity of the Middle Ages. But the original and by far the most prolific parent of monasticism was the East. There were always ascetics in the Christian Church; yet asceticism is the product not so much of Christianity as of the East; of the oriental temperament, which admires and cultivates it; of the oriental climate, which makes it tolerable even when pushed to the most rigorous extremes. Asceticism is the natural practical expression of that deeply-grounded conviction of an essential antagonism between the flesh and spirit which pervades all oriental creeds. Even the monastic form of it was known in the East before Christianity. The Essenes in Judæa, the Therapeutæ in Egypt, were prototypes of the active and contemplative communities of monks.

The primitive ascetics of the Christian Church were not monks. They were persons who raised themselves above the common level of religious life by exercises in fasting, prayer, study, alms-giving, celibacy, bodily privations of all kinds. These habits obtained for them great admiration and reverence. Such persons are frequently designated by writers of the first three centuries as "an ascetic," "a follower of the religious ascetics."[111] But they did not form a class distinctly marked off by dress and habitation from the rest of the world, like the monks or even the anchorites of later time. They lived in the cities or wherever their home might be, and were not subject to any rules beyond those of their own private making. Eusebius calls them σπουδαῖοι, "earnest persons;" and Clemens Alexandrinus ἐκλεκτῶνἐκλεκτότεροι, "more elect than the elect."[112] Midway between the primitive ascetic and the fully-developed monk must be placed the anchorite or hermit, who made a step in the direction of monasticism by withdrawing altogether from the city or populous places into the solitudes of mountain or desert. Persecution assisted the impulse of religious fervour. Paul retired to the Egyptian Thebaid during the persecution of Decius in A.D. 251, and Antony during that of Maximin in A.D. 312. They are justly named the fathers or founders of the anchorites, because, though not actually the first, they were the most distinguished; and the fame of their sanctity, their austerities, their miracles, produced a tribe of followers. The further Antony retired into the depths of the wilderness the more numerous became his disciples. They grouped their cells around the habitation of the saintly father, and out of the clusters grew in process of time the monastery. A number of cells ranged in lines like an encampment, not incorporated in one building, was called a "Laura" or street.[113] This was the earliest and simplest kind of monastic establishment. It was a community, though without much system or cohesion.

The real founder of the Cœnobia or monasteries in the East was the Egyptian Pachomius; he was the Benedict of the East. His rule was that most generally adopted, not only in Egypt but throughout the oriental portions of the Empire. He and Antony had now been dead about twenty years, and Hilarius, the pupil and imitator of Antony, had lately introduced monasticism on the Pachomian model into Syria. In about fifty years more, the nomadic Saracens will gaze with veneration and awe at the spectacle of Simeon on his pillar, forty miles from Antioch. Thousands will come to receive baptism at his hands; his image will have been placed over the entrance of the shops in Rome.[114] The spirit had been already caught in the West. The feelings of abhorrence with which the Italians first beheld the wild-looking Egyptian monks who accompanied Athanasius to Rome had soon been exchanged for veneration. The example of Marcellina, and the exhortations of her brother Ambrose of Milan, had induced multitudes of women to take vows of celibacy.[115] Most of the little islands on the coasts of the Adriatic could boast of their monasteries or cells.[116] St. Martin built his religious houses near Poitiers and Tours, and was followed to his grave by two thousand brethren.[117] But St. Jerome, perhaps, more than any one else, promoted the advance of monasticism in the West. Born on the borders of East and West,[118] he mingled with the Eastern Church at Antioch and Constantinople, and in the desert of Chalcis had inured himself to the most severe forms of oriental asceticism, and returned to Rome eager to impart to others a kindred spirit of enthusiasm for the ascetic life. A little later, early in the fifth century, John Cassianus, president of a religious establishment in Marseilles, propagated monastic institutions of an oriental type in the south of France, and made men conversant with the system by his work on the rules of the cloister. These were the scattered forces which in the West awaited the master mind and strong hand of Benedict to mould and discipline them into a mighty system. The nearest approach in the West to the Egyptian system of Pachomius was among the Benedictines of Camaldoli.

There is every reason to suppose on general grounds, and the supposition is corroborated by notices in the writings of Chrysostom, that the monasteries near Antioch, like the rest of the Syrian monasteries, were based on the Pachomian model. Pachomius was a native of the Thebaid, born in A.D. 292. He began to practise asceticism as a hermit, but, according to the legend, was visited by an angel who commanded him to promote the salvation of other men's souls besides his own, and presented him with a brazen tablet, on which were inscribed the rules of the Order which he was to found. He established his first community on Tabennæ, an island in the Nile, which became the parent of a numerous offspring. Pachomius had the satisfaction in his lifetime of seeing eight monasteries, containing in all 3000 monks, acknowledging his rule; and after his death, in the first half of the fifth century, their numbers had swelled to 50,000.[119] Chrysostom exulted with Christian joy and pride over the spectacle of "Egypt, that land which had been the mother of pagan literature and art, which had invented and propagated every species of witchcraft, now despising all her ancient customs, and holding up the Cross, in the desert no less if not more than in the cities: ... for the sky was not more beautiful, spangled with its hosts of stars, than the desert of Egypt studded in all directions with the habitations of monks."[120]

By the Pachomian rule no one was admitted as a full monk till after three years of probation, during which period he was tested by the most severe exercises. If willing, after that period, to continue the same exercises, he was admitted without further ceremony beyond making a solemn declaration that he would adhere to the rules of the monastery. That no irrevocable vow was taken by the members of the monastery near Antioch which Chrysostom joined seems proved by his return to the city after a residence in the monastery of several years' duration. According to Sozomen, the several parts of the dress worn by Pachomian monks had a symbolical meaning. The tunic (a linen garment reaching as far as the knees) had short sleeves, to remind the wearers that they should be prompt to do such honest work only as needed no concealment. The hood was typical of the innocence and purity of infants, who wore the same kind of covering; the girdle and scarf, folded about the back, shoulders, and arms, were to admonish them that they should be perpetually ready to do active service for God. Each cell was inhabited by three monks. They took their chief meal in a refectory, and ate in silence,[121] with a veil so arranged over the face that they could see only what was on the table. No strangers were admitted, except travellers, to whom they were bound, by the rule of their Order, to show hospitality. The common meal or supper took place at three o'clock,[122] up to which time they usually fasted. When it was concluded, a hymn was sung, of which Chrysostom gives us a specimen, though not in metrical form:[123] "Blessed be God, who nourisheth me from my youth up, who giveth food to all flesh: fill our hearts with joy and gladness, that we, having all sufficiency at all times, may abound unto every good work, through Jesus Christ our Lord, with Whom be glory, and honour, and power to Thee, together with the Holy Ghost, for ever and ever, Amen. Glory to Thee, O Lord! Glory to Thee, Holy One! Glory to Thee, King, who hast given us food to make us glad! Fill us with the Holy Spirit, that we may be found well pleasing in thy sight, and not ashamed when Thou rewardest every man according to his works."

The whole community in a Pachomian monastery was divided into twenty-four classes, distinguished by the letters of the Greek alphabet; the most ignorant, for instance, under class Iota, the more learned under Xi or Zeta, such letters being in shape respectively the simplest and the most complicated in the alphabet. Those hours which were not devoted to services or study were occupied by manual labour, partly to supply themselves with the necessaries of life, partly to guard against the incursion of evil thoughts. There was a proverbial saying attributed to some of the old Egyptian fathers, that "a labouring monk was assaulted by one devil only, but an idle one by an innumerable legion." They wove baskets and mats, agriculture was not neglected, nor even, among the Egyptian monks, ship-building. Palladius, who visited the Egyptian monasteries about the close of the fourth century, found, in the monastery of Panopolis, which contained 300 members, 15 tailors, 7 smiths, 4 carpenters, 12 camel-drivers, 15 tanners. Each monastery in Egypt had its steward, and a chief steward stationed at the principal settlement had the supervision of all the rest. All the products of monkish labour were shipped under his inspection on the Nile for Alexandria. With the proceeds of their sale, stores were purchased for the monasteries, and the surplus was distributed amongst the sick and poor.[124]

A monastery founded on this model might be fairly described as a kind of village containing an industrial and religious population; and had the Eastern monks adhered to this simple and innocent way of life, such communities might have become more and more schools of learning, centres of civilisation, and homes of piety. But they were increasingly forgetful of the wholesome saying of Antony, that a monk in the city was like "a fish out of water." Instead of attending exclusively to their pious and industrial exercises, they mixed themselves up with the theological and political contests which too often convulsed the cities of the Eastern Empire. Their influence or interference was frequently the reverse of peace-making, judicious, or Christian. They would rush with fanatical fury into the city, to rescue the orthodox, or to attack those whom they considered heretical. The evil had grown to such a height by the reign of Arcadius, that a law was passed by which monks were strictly forbidden to commit such outrages on civil order, and bishops were commanded to prosecute the authors of such attempts.[125] Eastern monasticism, in fact, partook of the character which distinguished the Eastern Church as a whole, and which we may regard as one principal cause of its corruption and decay. A certain stability, sobriety, self-control, a law-making and law-respecting spirit, as it is the peculiar merit of the Western, so the want of it is the peculiar defect of the Oriental temperament. Hence a curious co-existence of extremes; the passions, unnaturally repressed at one outlet by intense asceticism, burst forth with increased fury at another. He who had subdued his body in the wilderness or on the mountains by fastings and macerations entertained the most implacable animosity towards pagans and heretics, and fought them like a ruffian (the word is not too strong for truth), when some tumult in an adjacent city afforded him an opportunity for this robust mode of displaying and defending his orthodoxy. Western monasticism, on the other hand, is distinguished by more gravity, more of the old Roman quality, a love of stern discipline. It did not run to such lengths of fanatical asceticism, and consequently was exempt from such disastrous reactions. It never produced such a caricature of the anchorite as Simeon Stylites, or such savage zealots as the monkish bands who dealt their sturdy blows in the religious riots of Constantinople and Alexandria. From the notices scattered up and down Chrysostom's writings of the monasteries in the neighbourhood of Antioch, it appears that they conformed in all essential respects to the Pachomian model. We might anticipate, indeed, that, where such a man as Diodorus was president or visitor, they would be conducted on a simple and rational system.

South of Antioch were the mountainous heights of Silpius and Casius, whence rose the springs which in a variety of channels found their way into the city, provided it with a constant and abundant supply of the purest water, and irrigated the gardens for which it was celebrated.[126] In this mountain region dwelt the communities of monks, in separate huts or cells (κάλυβαι[127]), but subject to an abbot, and a common rule. Chrysostom has in more passages than one furnished us with a description of their ordinary costume, fare, and way of life. He is fond of depicting their simple, frugal, and pious habits, in contrast to the artificial and luxurious manners of the gay and worldly people of the city. They were clad in coarse garments of goat's hair or camel's hair, sometimes of skins, over their linen tunics, which were worn both by night and day.¹²⁸ Before the first rays of sunlight, the abbot went round, and struck those monks who were still sleeping with his foot, to wake them. When all had risen,—fresh, healthy, fasting, they sang together, under the precentorship of their abbot, a hymn of praise to God. The hymn being ended, a common prayer was offered up (again under the leadership of their abbot), and then each at sunrise went to his allotted task, some to read, others to write, others to manual labour, by which they made a good deal to supply the necessities of the poor. Four hours in the day, the third, the sixth, the ninth, and some time in the evening, were appointed for prayers and psalms. When the daily work was concluded, they sat down, or rather reclined, on strewn grass, to their common meal, which was sometimes eaten out of doors by moonlight, and consisted of bread and water only, with occasionally, for invalids, a little vegetable food and oil. This frugal repast was followed by hymns, after which they betook themselves to their straw couches, and slept, as Chrysostom observes, free from those anxieties and apprehensions which beset the worldly man. There was no need of bolts and bars, for there was no fear of robbers. The monk had no possession but his body and soul, and if his life was taken he would regard it as an advantage, for he could say that to live was Christ, and to die was gain.¹²⁹ Those words "mine and thine," those fertile causes of innumerable strifes, were unknown.¹³⁰ No lamentations were to be heard when any of the brethren died. They did not say, "such a one is dead," but, "he has been perfected" (τετελείωται), and he was carried forth to burial amidst hymns of praise, thanksgiving for his release, and the prayers of his companions that they too might soon see the end of their labours and struggles, and be permitted to behold Jesus Christ.¹³¹ Such was the simple and industrial kind of monastic body to which Chrysostom for a time attached himself; and to the end of his life he regarded such communities with the greatest admiration and sympathy. But he never failed to maintain also the duty of work against those who represented the perfection of the Christian life as consisting in mere contemplation and prayer. Such a doctrine of otiose Christianity he proved to be based on a too exclusive attention to certain passages in the New Testament. If, for instance, our blessed Lord said to Martha, "Thou art careful and troubled about many things, but one thing is needful;" or again, "Take no thought for the morrow;" or, "Labour not for the meat that perisheth"—all such passages were to be balanced and harmonised by others, as, for example, St. Paul's exhortation to the Thessalonians to be "quiet and to do their own business," and "let him that stole steal no more, but rather let him labour, working with his hands that which is good, that he may have to give to him that needeth." He points out that the words of our Lord do not inculcate total abstinence from work, but only censure an undue anxiety about earthly things, to the exclusion or neglect of spiritual concerns. The contemplative form of monasticism, based on misconception of Holy Scripture, had, he observes, seriously injured the cause of Christianity, for it occasioned practical men of the world to deride it as a source of indolence.[132]

CHAPTER 6

WORKS PRODUCED DURING HIS MONASTIC LIFE—THE LETTERS TO DEMETRIUS AND STELECHIUS—TREATISES ADDRESSED TO THE OPPONENTS OF MONASTICISM—LETTER TO STAGIRIUS.

SEVERAL TREATISES WERE COMPOSED by Chrysostom during his monastic life. Among the first must be placed two books addressed to Demetrius and Stelechius. Of these the former was evidently written soon after the commencement of his retreat, for he speaks of having recently determined to take the step, and of the petty anxieties about food and other personal comforts which had at first unsettled his purpose a little. But he had soon conquered these hankerings after the more luxurious life which he had abandoned. It seemed to him a disgrace that one to whom heaven and celestial joys were offered, such as eye had not seen nor ear heard, should be so hesitating and timorous, when those who undertook the management of public affairs did not shrink from dangers and toil, and long journeys, and separation from wife and children, and perhaps unfavourable criticism, but only inquired whether the office were honourable and lucrative.[133]

The aim of the books is to animate torpid characters to a warmer piety, first by drawing a lively picture of the depravity of the times, secondly by a glowing description of the fervent energy of apostles and apostolic saints, and insisting that those lofty heights of Christian holiness were not unattainable by the Christian of his own day, if he bent the whole energy of his will, aided by Divine grace, to the attempt.

"So great," he observes, "was the depravity of the times that if a stranger were to compare the precepts of the Gospel with the actual practice of society, he would infer that men were not the disciples, but the enemies of Christ. And the most fatal symptom was their total unconsciousness of this deep corruption. Society was like a body which was outwardly vigorous, but concealed a wasting fever within; or like an insane person who says and does all manner of shocking things, but, instead of being ashamed, glories in the fancied possession of superior wisdom."[134] Chrysostom applies the test of the principal precepts of morality in the Sermon on the Mount to the existing state of Christian morals. Every one of them was shamelessly violated. A kind of regard, superstitious or hypocritical, was paid to the command in the letter, which was broken in the spirit. Persons, for instance, who scrupled to use the actual expressions "fool" or "Raca," heaped all kinds of opprobrious epithets on their neighbours.[135] So the command to be reconciled with a brother before approaching the altar was really broken though formally kept. Men gave the kiss of peace at the celebration of Holy Communion when admonished by the deacon so to do, but continued to nourish resentful feelings in the heart all the same.[136] Vainglory and ostentation robbed prayer, fasting and almsgiving of their merit; and as for the precept "Judge not," a most uncharitable spirit of censoriousness pervaded every class of society, including monks and ecclesiastics.[137] Contrast with this false and hollow religion of the world the condition of one in whom a deep compunction for sin, and a genuine love of Jesus Christ, was awakened. The whole multitude of vain frivolous passions was dispersed like dust before the wind. So it was with St. Paul. Having once turned the eye of his soul towards heaven, and being entranced by the beauty of that other world, he could not stoop to earth again. As a beggar, in some gloomy hovel, if he saw a monarch glittering with gold and radiant with jewels, might altogether for a time forget the squalor of his dwelling-place in his eagerness to get inside the palace of the king, so St. Paul forgot and despised the poverty and hardship of this present world because the whole energy of his being was directed to the attainment of that heavenly city.[138] But men objected to the citation of apostolic examples. Paul and Peter, they said, were superhuman characters; models beyond our limited powers. "Nay,"

Chrysostom replies, "these are feeble excuses. The Apostles were in all essential points like ourselves. Did they not breathe the same kind of air? eat the same kind of food? were not some of them married men? did they not follow mechanical trades? nay more, had not some of them deeply sinned? Men at the present day did not indeed receive grace at baptism to work miracles, but they received enough to enable them to lead a good and holy Christian life.[139] And the highest blessing of Christ—his invitation to those who were called 'blessed children' to inherit the kingdom prepared for them—was addressed, not to those who had wrought miracles, but to those who had ministered to himself through feeding the hungry, entertaining the stranger, visiting the sick and the prisoners, who were his brethren. But grace, though undoubtedly given by God, required man's own co-operation to become effectual. Otherwise, since God is no respecter of persons, it would have resided in equal measure in all men; whereas we see that with one man it remains, from another it departs; a third is never affected by it at all."[140] The second book on the same subject, addressed to another friend, named Stelechius, is an expression of more rapturous and highly-wrought feeling, and is more rhetorical in style. His description in the beginning of the blessed freedom of the monk's life from secular vanities and cares, his remarks on David and St. Paul,[141] two of his most favourite characters, and still more his masterly enumeration of the manifold ways in which God manifests his providential care for man,[142] well deserve to be read. They are too long to be translated here in full, and a paraphrase would very inadequately represent such passages, of which the peculiar beauty consists in the language more even than in the ideas. One special interest of these books, written immediately after his retirement from the world, is that they put clearly before us what it was which drove him and many another to the monastic life. It was a sense of the glaring and hideous contrast between the Christianity of the Gospel and the Christianity of ordinary society. A kind of implacable warfare,[143] as he expresses it, seemed to be waged in the world against the commands of Christ; and he had therefore determined, by seclusion from the world, to seek that kind of life which he saw exhibited in the Gospels, but nowhere else.[144]

But the largest and most powerful work which Chrysostom produced during this period was occasioned by the decree of the Emperor Valens in A.D. 373—a decree which struck at the roots of monasticism. It directed that monks should be dragged from their retreats, and compelled to discharge their obligations as citizens, either by serving in the army, or performing the functions of any civil office to which they might be appointed.[145] The edict is said to have been enforced with considerable rigour, and in Egypt this seems to have been the case. But it was evidently far from complete or universal in its operation. None of Chrysostom's brethren appear to have been compelled to return to the city; certainly he himself was not. But they were liable, of course, to the persecution which, under the shelter of the decree, all the enemies of their order directed against them. These enemies of monasticism were of several kinds. There were the zealous adherents of the old paganism; men like Libanius, who were opposed to Christianity on principle, and especially to the monastic form of it, as encouraging idleness, and the dereliction of the duties of good citizens. There were also the more worldly-minded Christians who had adopted Christianity more from impulse or conformity than from conviction, and who disliked the standing protest of monastic life against their own frivolity. They were irritated also by the influence which the monks often acquired over their wives and children, sometimes alluring the latter from that lucrative line of worldly life which their fathers had marked out for them. And lastly, there were those who regretted that some men should have taken up a position of direct antagonism to the world, instead of mingling with it, and infusing good leaven into the mass of evil. The treatise of Chrysostom addressed "to the assailants of monastic life" was intended to meet most of these objections.

A friend had brought the terrible tidings to his retreat of the authorised persecution which had just broken out. He heard it with indescribable horror. It was a sacrilege far worse than the destruction of the Jewish Temple. That an Emperor (an Arian, indeed, yet professing himself Christian) should organise the persecution, and that some actually baptized persons should take, as his friend informed him, a part in it, was an intolerable aggravation of the infliction. He would rather die than witness such a calamity, and was ready to exclaim with Elijah, "Now, O Lord, take away my life!" His friend roused him from this state of despondency by suggesting that, instead of giving way to useless lamentations, he should write an admonitory treatise to the originators and abettors of this horrible persecution. At first Chrysostom refused, partly from a feeling of incompetency, partly from a dread of exposing to the pagans by his writings some of the internal corruptions, dissensions, and weaknesses of the Church. His friend replies that these were already but too notorious; and as for the sufferings of the monks, they formed the topic of public conversation, too often of public jest. In the market-place and in the doctors' shops the subject was freely canvassed, and many boasted of the part which they had taken against the victims. "I was the first to lay hands on such a monk," one would cry, "and to give him a blow;" or, "I was the first to discover his cell;" or, "I stimulated the judge against him more than any one." Such was the spirit of cruelty and profanity by which even Christians were animated; and, as for the pagans, they derided both parties. Roused by these dreadful communications, the indignation of Chrysostom no longer hesitated to set about the task.[146]

His pity, he says, was excited chiefly for the persecutors; they were purchasing eternal misery for themselves, while the future reward of their victims would be in proportion to the magnitude of their present sufferings, since "Blessed were those whom men should hate, persecute, and revile for Christ's sake, and great was to be their reward in heaven."[147]

To persecute monks was to hinder that purity of life to which Christ attached so deep an importance. It might be objected, Cannot men lead lives uncontaminated at home? to which Chrysostom replies that he heartily wishes they could, and that such good order and morality might be established in cities as to make monasteries unnecessary. But at present such gross iniquity prevailed in large towns, that men of pious aspirations were compelled to fly to the mountain or the desert. The blame should fall, not on those who escaped from the city, but on those who made life there intolerable to virtuous men. He trusted the time might come when these refugees would be able to return with safety to the world.[148]

If it was objected that on this principle of reasoning the mass of mankind was condemned, he could only reply, in the words of Christ himself, "Narrow is the way which leadeth unto life, and few there be that find it." We must not honour a multitude before truth. If all flesh was once destroyed except eight persons, we cannot be surprised if the number of men eventually saved shall be few. "I see," he says, "a constant perpetration of crimes which are all condemned by Christ as meriting the punishment of hell—adultery, fornication, envy, anger, evil speaking, and many more. The multitude which is engaged in this wickedness is unmolested, but the monks who fly from it themselves, and persuade others to take flight also, are persecuted without mercy." So much for the Christianity of the world.[149]

In Book II he expresses his astonishment that fathers should so little understand what was best for their sons as to deter them from studying "the true philosophy." But in combating this error he will put forward all that can be urged on their side. He imagines the case of a pagan father, possessed of great worldly distinction and wealth. He has an only son, in whom all his pride and hopes are centred; one whom he expects to surpass himself in riches and honour. Suddenly this son becomes converted to monasticism; this rich heir flies to the mountains, puts on a dress coarser than that of the meanest servant, toils at the menial occupations of gardening and drawing water, becomes lean and pale. All the schemes of his father for the future are frustrated, all past efforts for his education seem to have been squandered. The little vessel which was his pride and pleasure is wrecked at the very mouth of the harbour from which it was setting out on the voyage of life. The parent has no longer any pleasure in life; he mourns for his son as for one already dead.[150]

Having thus stated the case on his adversary's side as strongly as possible, Chrysostom begins his own defence by asking which would be best: that a man should be subject to thirst all his life, or wholly exempt from it? Surely to be exempt from it. Apply this to the moral appetites—love, avarice, and the rest. The monk is exempt from them; the man of the world is distracted by them, if not overwhelmed. Again, if the monk has no wealth of his own, he exercises a powerful influence in directing the wealth of others. Religious men will part with much of their riches according to his suggestions; if one refuses, another will give. The resources, in fact, of the monk are quite inexhaustible; many will subscribe to supply his wants or to execute his wishes, as Crito said that he and his friends would subscribe for Socrates. It is impossible to deprive the monk of his wealth or of his home; if you strip him of everything he has, he rejoices, and thanks you for helping him to live the life which he desires; and as for his home, the world is his home; one place is the same as another to him; he needs nothing but the pure air of heaven, wholesome streams, and herbs. As for high place and rank, history suffices to teach us that the desert does not destroy, and the palace does not give, true nobility. Plato—planting, watering, and eating olives—was a far nobler personage than Dionysius the Tyrant of Sicily, amidst all the wealth and splendour of a monarch. Socrates—clad in a single garment, with his bare feet and his meagre fare of bread, and dependent upon others for the mere necessaries of life—was a far more illustrious character than Archelaus, who often invited him, but in vain, to court. Real splendour and distinction consisted not in fine raiment, or in positions of dignity and power, but only in excellence of the soul and in philosophy.[151]

He then proceeds to maintain that the influence of the monk was more powerful than that of the man of the world, however distinguished he might be. If he descended from his mountain solitude, and entered the city, the people flocked round him, and pointed him out with reverence and admiration, as if he were a messenger from heaven. His mean dress commanded more respect than the purple robe and diadem of the monarch. If he was required to interfere in matters of public interest, his influence was greater than that of the powerful or wealthy; for he could speak before an emperor with boldness and freedom, and without incurring the suspicion of self-interested or ambitious motives. He was a more effectual comforter of the mourners than any one in a prosperous worldly condition was likely to be. If a father had lost his only son, the sight of other men's domestic happiness only revived his grief; but the society of the monk, who disdained the ties of home and family, and who talked to him of death as only a sleep, soothed his grief. Thus the man who wished his son to possess real honour and power would permit him to become a monk; for monks who were once mere peasants had been visited in their cells and consulted by kings and ministers of state.

Chrysostom concludes this book by relating the history of one of his own brethren in the monastery, who, when first he desired to become a monk, had been disowned by his father, a wealthy and distinguished pagan, who threatened him with imprisonment, turned him out of doors, and allowed him almost to perish with hunger. But, finding him inflexible in his purpose, the father at last relented, and, at the time when Chrysostom wrote, honoured, he might say venerated, that son, considering the others, who occupied distinguished positions in the world, scarcely worthy to be his servant.[152]

As the second book was intended to meet the objections of a pagan father, so the third contains admonitions to one who was professedly Christian, but worldly-minded, on the duty of parents in regard to the moral and religious education of their children.

It appeared to him that the fathers of that day gave their sons none but worldly counsel, inculcated none but worldly industry and prudence, and encouraged to the emulation of none but worldly examples.[153] The force of habit was intensely strong, especially when pleasure co-operated with it, and parents, instead of counteracting habits of worldliness, promoted them by their own example. God led the Israelites through the wilderness as a kind of monastic training, to wean them from the luxurious and sensual habits of an Egyptian life; yet even then they hankered after the land of their bondage. How, then, could the children of parents who left them in the midst of the Egypt of vice, escape damnation? If they achieved anything good of themselves, it was speedily crushed by the flood of worldly conversation which issued from the parent. All those things which were condemned by Christ—as wealth, popularity, strife, an evil eye, divorce—were approved by parents of that day, and they threw a veil over the ugliness of these vices, by giving them specious names. Devotion to the hippodrome and theatre was called fashionable refinement; wealth was called freedom; love of glory, high spirit; folly, boldness; prodigality, benevolence; injustice, manliness. Virtues, on the contrary, were depreciated by opprobrious names: temperance was called rusticity; equity, cowardice; justice, unmanliness; modesty, meanness; endurance of injury, feebleness. He truly remarks, that nothing contributes so much to deter men from vice as calling vices plainly by their proper names.[154]

"How can children escape moral ruin, when all the labour of their fathers is bestowed on the provision of superfluous things—fine houses, dress, horses, beautiful statues, gilded ceilings—while they take no pains about the soul, which is far more precious than any ornament of gold?"[155] And there were worse evils behind: vice too monstrous and unnatural to be named, but to which he was constrained to allude, because he felt that it was poisoning with deadly venom the very vitals of the social body. "Well," but worldly men reply, "Would you have us all turn philosophers, and let our worldly affairs go to ruin? Nay," says Chrysostom, "it is the want of the philosophic spirit and rule which ruins everything now; it is your rich men—with troops of slaves and swarms of parasites, eager for wealth and ambitious of distinction, building fine houses, adding field to field, lending money at a usurious rate of interest—who propagate the strife and litigation, and envy, and murder, and general confusion, by which life is distracted. These are they who bring down the vengeance of Heaven, in the shape of droughts, and famines, and inundations, and earthquakes, and submersion of cities, and pestilences. It is not the simple monk, or the philosophic Christian, who is contented with a humble dwelling, a mean dress, a little plot of ground. These last, shining like bright beacons in a dark place, hold up the lamp of philosophy on high, and endeavour to guide those who are tossing on the open sea in a dark night into the haven of safety and repose."[156]

"In spite of law, disorder prevailed to such an extent, that the very idea of God's providence was lost. Men assigned the course of events to fate, or to the stars, or to chance, or to spontaneous force. God did, indeed, still rule; but He was like a pilot in a storm, whose skill in managing and conducting the vessel in safety was not perceived or appreciated by the passengers, owing to the confusion and fright caused by the raging of the elements. In the monastery, on the other hand, all was tranquillity and peace as in a community of angels. He strenuously combated the error of supposing that sin was more pardonable in a man of the world than in a monk. Anger, uncleanness, swearing, and the like, were equally sinful in all. Christ made no distinctions, but propounded one standard of morality for all alike. Nothing had inflicted more injury on the moral tone of society than the supposition that strictness of life was demanded of the monk only."[157] He strongly urges the advantage of sending youths for education to monasteries, even for so long a period as ten or twenty years. Men consented, he says, to part with their children, for the purpose of learning some art or trade, or even so low an accomplishment as rope-dancing; but when the object was to train their souls for heaven, all kinds of impediments were raised. To object that few attained through residence in a monastery that perfection of spiritual life which some expected of them, was a mere excuse. In the case of worldly things, on which men's hearts were set, they thought of getting as much as they could, not of reaching absolute perfection. A man did not prevent his son from entering military service because the chances of his becoming a prefect were small; why, then, hesitate to send your son to a monastery because all monks do not become angels?[158]

These treatises are remarkable productions, and deserve to be read, not only because they exhibit Chrysostom's best powers of argument and style, but also because they throw light upon the character of the man and the times in which he lived. He pleads his cause with the ingenuity, as well as eloquence, of a man who had been trained for the law courts. We find, indeed, that his opinions on the advantages of the monastic life were modified as he grew older; but his bold condemnation of worldliness, his denunciation of a cold secularised Christianity, as contrasted with the purity of the Gospel standard, the deep aspirations after personal holiness, the desire to be filled with a fervent and overflowing love of Christ, the firm hold on the idea of a superintending Providence, amidst social confusion and corruption; these we find, as here, so always, conspicuous characteristics of the man, and principal sources of his influence.

From the frightful picture here drawn of social depravity, we perceive the value—we might say, the necessity—of monasteries, as havens of refuge for those who recoiled in horror from the surrounding pollution. It is clear also that the influence of the monks was considerable. Monasteries were recognised places of education, where pious parents could depend on their children being virtuously brought up. The Christian wife of a pagan or worldly husband could here find a safe home for her boy, where he could escape the contamination of his father's influence or example. Chrysostom relates, in chapter 12, how a Christian lady in Antioch, being afraid of the wrath of a harsh and worldly-minded husband if she sent away her son to school at the monastery, induced one of the monks, a friend of Chrysostom's, to reside for a time in the city, in the character of pedagogue. The boy, thus subjected to his training, afterwards joined the society of the monks; but Chrysostom, fearing the consequences both to the youth and to the monastic body, should his father detect his secession, persuaded him to return to the city, where he led an ascetic life, though not habited in monkish dress. Out of these monastic schools, after years of discipline and prayer, and study of the Word, there issued many a pastor and preacher, well-armed champions of the truth, strong in the Lord, and in the power of His might; like Chrysostom himself, instant in season and out of season; stern denouncers of evil, even in kings' courts; holding out the light of the Gospel in the midst of a dark and crooked generation.

The foregoing extracts and paraphrases from these treatises prove also that as philosophy was considered the highest flight in the intellectual culture of the pagan, so was asceticism regarded as the highest standard of Christian life; it was to the education of the soul what philosophy was to the education of the mind, and hence it was called by the same name. Possessed by this idea, Chrysostom threw himself at this period of his life into the system with all the ardour of his nature. If asceticism was good, it was right to carry it as far as nature could bear it. He adopted the habits of an old member of the brotherhood named Syrus, notorious for the severity of his self-inflicted discipline. The day and greater part of the night were spent in study, fastings and vigils. Bread and water were his only habitual food. At the end of four years he proceeded a step further. He withdrew from the community to one of those solitary caves with which the mountains overhanging Antioch on its southern side abounded. In fact, he exchanged the life of a monk for that of an anchorite. His frame endured this additional strain for nearly two years, and then gave way. His health was so much shattered that he was obliged to abandon monastic life, and to return to the greater comfort of his home in Antioch.[159]

Meanwhile a friend of his, Stagirius by name—a person of noble birth, who, in spite of his father's opposition, had embraced monasticism—was reduced to a more deplorable condition. While Chrysostom was confined to his house by illness, a friend common to him and Stagirius brought him the sad intelligence that Stagirius was affected with all the symptoms of demoniacal possession—wringing of the hands, squinting of the eyes, foaming at the mouth, strange inarticulate cries, shiverings, and frightful visions at night.[160] We shall perhaps find little difficulty in accounting for these distressing affections, as the consequence of excessive austerities. The young man, who formerly lived a gay life in the world, and in the midst of affluence, had in the monastery fared on bread and water only, often kept vigil all night long, spent his days in prayer and tears of penitence, preserved an absolute silence, and read so many hours continuously, that his friends and brother monks feared that his brain would become disordered.[161] Very probably it was, and hence his visions and convulsions; but those were not days in which men readily attributed any strange phenomena, mental or bodily, to physical causes. We may believe in the action of a spirit-world on the inhabitants of this earth; but we require good evidence that any violent or strange affection of mind or body is due to a directly spiritual agency, rather than to the operation of God according to natural law. The cases of demoniacs in the Gospel stand apart. Our Lord uses language which amounts to a distinct affirmation that those men were actually possessed by evil spirits. To use such expressions as "come out of him," "enter no more into him," and the like, if there was no spirit concerned in the case at all, would have been, to say the least, a mere unmeaning piece of acting, of which it would be shocking to suppose our Lord capable. But to admit the direct agency of spirit, when confirmed by such authoritative testimony, is widely different from the hasty ascription to spiritual agency, by an uncritical and unscientific age, of everything which cannot be accounted for by the most superficial knowledge and observation. Chrysostom, of course, not being beyond his age in such matters, did not for a moment dispute the supposition that Stagirius was actually possessed by a demon, but he displays a great deal of good sense in dealing with the case. As the state of his own health did not permit him to pay Stagirius a visit in person, he wrote his advice instead. He perceived the fatal temptation to despair in a man who imagined that the devil had got a firm hold upon him, and that every evil inclination proceeded directly from this demoniacal invader. He will not allow that the suggestion to suicide, of which Stagirius complained, came direct from the demon, but rather from his own despondency,[162] with which the devil had endeavoured to oppress him, that he might, under cover of that, work his own purposes more effectually, just as robbers attack houses in the dark. But this was to be shaken off by trust in God; for the devil did not exercise a compulsory power over the hearts of men; there must be a co-operation of the man's own will. Eve fell partly through her own inclination to sin: "When she saw that the tree was good for food, and pleasant to the eyes, she took of the fruit thereof and did eat;" and if Adam was so easily persuaded to participate in her sin, he would have fallen even had no devil existed.

Chrysostom endeavours also to console his friend by going through the histories of saints in all times who have been afflicted. His sufferings were not to be compared to those of Abraham, Isaac, Jacob, Moses, David, and St. Paul. "These afflictions were sent for remedial, purgatorial purposes—that the soul might be saved in the day of the Lord. It was not easy to say why such a person was tried by this or that form of suffering, but if we knew exactly God's motives, there would be no test of faith. The indispensable thing was to be firmly convinced that whatever God sent was right. Some men were disturbed because the good were often troubled, and the wicked prosperous; but such inequality in the distribution of reward and punishment in this life suggested a future state where they would be finally adjusted. The wicked who had here received his good things would there receive his evil.[163] Stagirius had not been attacked by any demon when he was living in carelessness and worldly pleasure, but when he had buckled on his armour and appeared as an antagonist, then the devil descended to the assault. Hence he had no need to be ashamed of his affliction; the only thing to be ashamed of was sin, and it was owing to his renunciation of sin that the devil assailed him. The real demoniacs were those who were carried away by the impulses of unregulated passions." His summaries of the lives of the Old Testament saints, which fill the rest of the second book and most of the third, are very masterly, and display most intimate acquaintance with Holy Scripture in all its parts. A powerful mind and retentive memory had profited by six years of retirement largely devoted to study.

CHAPTER 7

ORDINATION AS DEACON—DESCRIPTION OF ANTIOCH—
WORKS COMPOSED DURING HIS DIACONATE. A.D. 381-386.

PROBABLY ONE OF THE last acts of Bishop Meletius before he left Antioch to attend the Council of Constantinople in 381, was to ordain Chrysostom a deacon. The bishop never returned. He died during the session of the council of which he was president, leaving both that and the See of Antioch distracted by the most deplorable factions. It will be remembered[164] that the Catholics of Antioch had, ever since the ill-judged mission of Lucifer of Cagliari, been divided between allegiance to Paulinus, a priest of the old Eustathian party, who had been consecrated bishop by Lucifer, and Meletius, bishop of the more moderate party. With the laudable purpose of healing this schism, it is said that several of the clergy at Antioch, who were considered most likely to succeed to a vacancy, bound themselves under an oath, that in the event of either bishop dying, they would decline the offer of the see, if made, and acknowledge the survivor. But on the death of Meletius, their plan was frustrated. Either the Asiatics, who generally favoured Meletius, refused to submit to the authority of Paulinus, because he had been ordained by a Western prelate, or the Eustathians who acknowledged Paulinus were unwilling on their side to admit Meletians into their fold. In any case, the earnest endeavours of Gregory of Nazianzum, now President of the Council, to unite the two factions under one prelate were unsuccessful.[165] The Meletians elected Flavian to be their bishop, one of the very priests who had, under oath, renounced their pretensions to the see. This appointment of course exposed Flavian to the imputation of perjury, but we may hope that, like Gregory, he yielded to a pressing necessity only, and to a conviction that the dissension would have been aggravated and protracted if he had obdurately refused.[166] At any rate, as will hereafter appear, his conduct, wherever it comes before us, is worthy of all admiration, and Chrysostom must have filled the office of deacon with happiness under his administration. A greater contrast than the initiation of Chrysostom into clerical life, and that of a young deacon in modern times, can scarcely be imagined. He was in his thirty-seventh year, and had supplemented the good liberal education of his youth by several years of devotion to close study of Scripture, to rigorous mortification of the body, to prayer and meditation, and to every means of promoting the culture of the soul. After this long and careful training, he enters the subordinate ranks of the clergy, not to discharge, like a modern deacon, duties as laborious, and often as responsible, as those which pertained to the priest, but such light and irresponsible tasks as were suitable to men who might be young, and were necessarily inexperienced in pastoral work. The deacons were sometimes called the Levites of the Christian Church.[167] It was their office to take care of the holy table and its furniture, to administer the cup to the laity, but not to a priest or a bishop, and occasionally to read the Gospel.[168] They were in most churches permitted to baptize.[169] But their peculiar duty in the services of the Church was to call the attention of the people to every fresh movement, to use a musical expression, in the progress of the service. Thus at the close of the sermon, the deacon's voice was heard crying: "Let the hearers [*i.e.* the second order of catechumens who were permitted to hear the sermon, but not the conclusion of the Eucharistic service] and the unbelievers depart!"[170] Then he bid the remaining orders of the catechumens, *i.e.* the energumens, the competentes, and the penitents to pray for one another, and the people also to pray for them; ἐκτενῶςδεηθῶμεν, "let us ardently pray for them"—such was the form. Again when they were dismissed by the command ἀπολύεσθε, "disperse," the faithful were invited by the deacon to pray for the whole state of Christ's Church.[171] Thus the deacons were the sacred criers or heralds of the Church; they "proclaimed or bid prayer," they announced each part as it was unfolded in the sacred drama of the Liturgy. The frequent recurrence in our own Liturgy, without much apparent significance, of the form "Let us pray," is a remnant of these old diaconal invitations. The deacons were not permitted to preach except by a special direction of the bishop. Their duty in part corresponded to that of our churchwardens; they were to reprove any improper behaviour during divine service,[172] to bring cases of poverty and sickness before the notice of the bishop, to distribute the alms under his direction, and also to report to him grave moral offences.[173] They were essentially, as the name implies, ministers to the bishops and priests, and were often styled, in symbolical language, "the bishop's eyes," or "ears," or "right hand." The attitude of respect, which they were bound to maintain in church towards bishops and priests was in keeping with the servitorial character of their office as a whole. While the priests had their chairs ranged on either side of the central chair of the bishop in the choir, the deacons stood humbly by, as if ready to receive and execute the directions of their superiors.[174] Even the Roman deacons, who rose rather above the natural lowliness of their office, did not presume to sit in the church.[175]

The duties of the diaconate must have brought Chrysostom into constant intercourse with the Christian population of Antioch, and especially with the poorer portion of it. The whole population of the city amounted, according to Chrysostom's statement, to 200,000,[176] and the Christians to 100,000,[177] of whom 3000 were indigent, and mainly supported by the bounty of the Church.[178] The deacon's function of searching out and relieving the necessitous by distribution of alms must have been peculiarly congenial to him. There is no Christian duty on which he more constantly and earnestly insists than that of almsgiving, not only in order to alleviate the sufferings of poverty, but as a means of counteracting the inordinate avarice and selfish luxury which were the prevailing vices in the higher ranks of society, both in Antioch and Constantinople. His hold upon the affections of the common people, partly no doubt through his sympathy with their needs, partly by his bold denunciation of the vices of the wealthy, partly by his affectionate and earnest plain-speaking of Christian truth, was remarkably strong throughout his life. As during the secluded leisure of his monastic life he had acquired a profound intimacy with Holy Scripture, so in the more active labours of his diaconate he enlarged his knowledge of human nature, and stored up observations on the character and manners of the people among whom he moved; qualifications no less important for the formation of a great and effective preacher.

It may not be uninteresting to take a brief glance at the character of the city and its inhabitants among whom he was destined to labour for the next seventeen years of his life.

Both nature and art combined to make Antioch one of the most delectable and luxurious residences in the world. The advantages of its situation, in some most important respects, could scarcely be exceeded. The river Orontes, connecting it with the sea about three miles distant, was the throat through which the city was fed with merchandise from all parts of the world. The wooded shores of the large lake of Antioch some miles above the city, supplied the inhabitants with fuel, and its waters yielded fish in great abundance. The hills which impended over the town on the southern side sent down numerous and copious streams, whose water, unsurpassed in purity, bubbled up through the fountains which stood in the court of every house. Northwards extended a fertile plain between the Orontes and Mount Coryphæus. The northern winds were occasionally keen and searching, but the prevailing western breezes coming up from the sea were so delicately soft, yet refreshing, that the citizens delighted in summer to sleep upon the flat roofs of their dwellings. These advantages, however, were in some degree balanced by a liability to inundations and earthquakes. Those hill-streams, the blessing and delight of the inhabitants in summer, were sometimes swollen in winter by excessive rains into torrents of incontrollable fury, and caused much damage to the buildings which were situated near their course. But far more destructive were the earthquakes. More than once, indeed, especially in the reigns of Caligula, Claudius, and Trajan, the whole city was almost shattered to pieces; but on each occasion, through public and private exertions, it arose from its ruins in new and, if possible, increased magnificence. The peculiar glories of Antioch were its gardens, and baths, and colonnaded streets. As in its population, and religion, and customs, so also in its architecture, it presented, as time went on, a remarkable mixture of Asiatic, Greek, and Roman elements. The aim of each Greek king and Roman emperor was to leave it more beautiful than he had received it from the hands of his predecessor. Each marked his reign by the erection of a temple or basilica, or bath, or aqueduct, or theatre, or column. The church in which Chrysostom officiated, usually called "the great Church," to distinguish it from the smaller and older church, called the Church of the Apostles, was begun by Constantine and finished by Constantius. In the main principles of structure, we may find some parallel to it in St. Vitale at Ravenna. It stood in the centre of a large court, and was octangular in shape; chambers, some of them subterranean, were clustered round it; the domed roof, of an amazing height, was gilded on the inside; the floor was paved with polished marbles; the walls and columns were adorned with images, and glistened with precious stones; every part, indeed, was richly embellished with bronze and golden ornament.[179] Among the principal wonders of Antioch was the great street constructed by Antiochus Epiphanes, nearly four miles in length, which traversed the city from east to west; the natural inequalities of the ground were filled up, so that the thoroughfare was a perfect level from end to end; the spacious colonnades on either side were paved with red granite. From the centre of this magnificent street, where stood a statue of Apollo, another street, similar in character, but much shorter, was drawn at right angles, leading northwards in the direction of the Orontes. Many of the other streets were also colonnaded, so that the inhabitants, as they pursued their errands of business or pleasure, were sheltered alike from the scorching sun of summer and the rains of winter. Innumerable lanterns at night illuminated the main thoroughfares with a brilliancy which almost rivalled the light of day, and much of the business, as well as the festivity, of the inhabitants was carried on by night.[180]

The character of the inhabitants partook of the various elements—Asiatic, Syrian, Greek, Jewish, Roman—which composed the whole population. But the impulsive oriental temperament, subject at times to fits of gloomy despondency, and to outbursts of wild ferocity, was undoubtedly the most dominant. When not driven under the pressure of excitement to either of these extremes, they abandoned themselves very freely to those voluptuous recreations for which the character of their city and climate afforded every facility and inducement. The bath, the circus, the theatre, were the daily amusements of the citizen; the Olympic games (instituted in the time of Commodus), which were celebrated in the grove of Daphne, and the festivities held at particular seasons in honour of different deities, were the greater occasions to which he looked forward with all the eagerness of a pleasure-loving nature.

These main characteristics of the people are abundantly illustrated in detail, as will be seen hereafter, in the homilies of Chrysostom. He is ever, in them, labouring with indefatigable industry and earnestness to lift the Christians above the frivolity and vices of the rest of the population. His opportunities for investigating the condition of the Christian community were great during his diaconate. He did not as yet preach; but by observations on life and manners, he laid up copious materials for preaching. And he was not idle in the use of his pen, for to this period may be assigned the treatise on Virginity; a letter addressed to a young widow; a book on the martyr Babylas; and, perhaps, though this cannot certainly be determined, the six books on the Priesthood.[181]

The letter to a young widow must have been written soon after the destruction of the Emperor Valens and his army by the Goths in A.D. 378, since it contains a reference to that event as a recent occurrence,[182] yet it must have been antecedent to the crushing defeats inflicted on them by Theodosius in A.D. 382, because the writer implies that at the time of composition the Goths were overrunning large tracts of the empire with impunity, and mocking the helplessness and timidity of the imperial troops.[183] The whole book is penetrated with that profound sense of the misery and instability of things human, which the corruption of society and recent calamities of the empire impressed with peculiar force on the minds of reflecting persons; which produced among pagans either melancholy or careless indifference, but made Christians cling with a more earnest and tenacious trust to the hopes and consolations of the Gospel.

Therasius, the husband of the young widow, had died after five years of married life. He is described by Chrysostom as having been distinguished in rank, in ability, and, above all, in virtue; as having held a high position in the army, with a reasonable expectation of soon becoming a prefect. But these very excellencies and brilliant prospects, which seemed to aggravate the sense of his loss, "ought," Chrysostom observes, "to be regarded as sources of consolation. If death were a final and total destruction, then indeed it would have been reasonable to lament the extinction of one so benevolent, so gentle, so humble, prudent, and devout, as her late husband. But if death was only the landing of the soul in a tranquil haven, only a transition from the worse to better, from earth to heaven, from men to angels and archangels, and to Him who is the Lord of angels, then there was no place left for tears. It was better that he should depart and be with Christ, his true King, serving Whom in that other world, he would not be exposed to the dangers and animosities which attended the service of an earthly monarch. They were, indeed, separated in body, but neither length of time nor remoteness of place could sunder the friendship of the soul. Endure patiently for a little time, and you will behold again the face of your desire; perhaps even now, in visions, his form will be permitted to visit you."[184] If it was the loss of the prefecture that she specially deplored, let her think from what dangerous ambitions her husband had been preserved; think of the fate of Theodorus, who was tempted by his high station to lay a plot against the Emperor, and suffered capital punishment for his treason.[185] The loftier a man's ambitions in life, the more probable a disastrous fall. Look at the tragical fate of the Emperors in the course of the past fifty years. Two only, out of nine, had died natural deaths; of the other seven, one had been killed by a usurper,[186] one in battle,[187] one by a sedition of his domestic guards,[188] one by the man who had invested him with the purple.[189] Julian had fallen in battle in the Persian expedition. Valentinian I. died in a fit of rage, and Valens had been burnt, together with his retinue, in a house to which the Goths set fire. And of the widows of these Emperors, some had perished by poison, others had died of despair and broken hearts. Of those who yet survived, one was trembling for the safety of an orphan son,[190] another had with difficulty obtained permission to return from exile.[191] Of the wives of the present Emperors, one was racked by constant anxiety on account of the youth and inexperience of her husband,[192] the other was subject to no less anxiety for her husband's safety, who ever since his elevation to the throne had been engaged in incessant warfare with the Goths.[193] Human ambition was a hard taskmistress, who employed arrogance and avarice as her agents; "do not then, mourn that your husband has been emancipated from her tyranny." Most of the wisest and noblest characters even of the pagan world had resisted the allurements of ambition—Socrates, Epaminondas, Aristides, Diogenes, Crates. Shall the Christian then complain, if God takes one away from these temptations? He who cared least about glory, who was natural and modest, and unambitious, often acquired most glory, whereas he who was most eager and anxious to secure it, often obtained nothing but derision and reproach. She believed that her husband might have obtained the prefecture; it was a reasonable hope, but there was many a slip betwixt the cup and the lip, and he who was king to-day was dead to-morrow. "Strive, then, to equal and even surpass your husband in piety and goodness, that you may be admitted into the same home, and reunited to him in a bond far more lovely and enduring than that of earthly wedlock."

In the long treatise "De Virginitate," Chrysostom boldly declares his preference for celibacy, but at the same time he exposes and denounces the mischievous error of Marcionites and Manichæans, who condemned marriage altogether as positive sin. "They were mistaken in supposing that abstinence from marriage would procure them a high place in heaven, because, even if it were granted that marriage was a positive sin, it must be remembered that not those who abstained from sin, but those who did positive good, would receive the highest rewards; not one who abstained from calling his brother 'Raca,' but he who loved his enemies. The celibacy of heretics, such as the Manichæans, was based on the false conception that all created matter was evil, and that the Creator Himself was an inferior being to the Supreme Deity. Hence their celibacy was the work of the devil; they belonged to those mentioned only to be condemned in 1 Tim. iv. 1-3 'as forbidding to marry.'[194] Chastity of body was worthless, if the soul within was depraved; but celibacy rightly cultivated, to preserve the purity of the soul towards God, was better than marriage, better as heaven was better than earth, and angels better than men." He confronts the common objection: if all men embraced celibacy, how would the race be propagated? "Myriads of angels inhabit heaven, yet we believe they are not propagated by matrimony, and it was only by the special provision and will of God, that matrimony itself produced offspring. Sarah was barren till God vouchsafed her Isaac. Marriage was the inferior state to conduct us to the higher; it was to celibacy as the Law to the Gospel, it was a crutch to support those who would otherwise fall into sin, but to be dispensed with when possible. Let those, then, who reproached and derided celibacy, put a restraint upon their lips, lest like Miriam, or the children who mocked Elisha, they should be severely punished for pouring contempt on so holy a state."[195]

We are enabled to understand from this work why the best Christianity in the East was so disparaging of the married state. The woman had not attained her proper place in society. She seems to have been ill-educated, to have been kept, especially before marriage, in a state of unnatural seclusion, which she broke when she could, and was too often treated by the husband like a slave, with severity and distrust. This degrading position was partly a remnant of a pagan state of society, partly the offspring of oriental character and habits of life. Christianity perceived the evil, but had not effected much towards a remedy. Instead of endeavouring to elevate, to soften, and refine the relation of one sex to the other, it encouraged rather a total separation. The treatise now under notice presents curious pictures of domestic life, if such it can be called, in that age. Matrimonial matches were arranged entirely by the parents, the attentions of the suitors were paid to the parents, not to the maiden herself. She suffered an agony of suspense, while the favourite of yesterday was supplanted by the superior charms of some rival of to-day, who in his turn was superseded by a third. Sometimes, on the very eve of marriage, the suitor whom she herself preferred was dismissed, and she was finally handed over to another whom she disliked. The suitors also, on their side, were racked by anxiety; for it was difficult to ascertain what the real character, personal appearance, and manners were of the maiden, who was always kept in the strictest seclusion. Then there was often great difficulty in getting the dowry paid by the father-in-law, which was an annoyance to each of the newly-married pair.[196]

He draws a highly-wrought picture, with some caustic humour, of the miseries of jealous wives and husbands. When a man constantly suspects "his dearest love,"[197] for whom he would willingly sacrifice life itself, what can console him? By day and night he has no peace, and is irritable to all. Some men have even slain their wives, without succeeding in cooling their own jealous rage. The trials of the wife were more severe; her words, her very looks and sighs, were watched by slaves, and reported to her husband, who was too jealous to distinguish false tales from the true. The poor woman was reduced to the wretched alternative of keeping her own apartment, or, if she went out, of rendering an exact account of her proceedings. Untold wealth, sumptuous fare, troops of servants, distinguished birth, amounted to nothing when placed in the balance against such miseries as these. If it was the woman who was jealous, she suffered more than the man, for she could not keep him at home, or set the servants to watch him. If she remonstrated with him, she would be told that she had better hold her tongue, and keep her suspicions to herself. If the husband instituted a suit against the wife, the laws were favourable to him, and he could procure her condemnation, and even death; but if she were the petitioner, he would escape.[198]

It was very natural that the woman, who, before marriage, was cooped up like a child in the parental home, should break out afterwards into extravagance, dissipation, and frivolity, if not worse. An inordinate amount of time and money was bestowed upon dress, though perhaps not more than by the fashionable ladies of modern times. Women loaded themselves with ornaments, under the delusion that these added to their charms, whereas, Chrysostom observes, if the woman was naturally beautiful, the ornaments only concealed and detracted from her charms. If she was ugly, they only set off her ugliness by the glaring contrast, and the effect on the spectator was ludicrous or painful. But the adornment of the virgin who had dedicated herself to God was altogether spiritual. She arrayed herself in gentleness, modesty, poverty, humility, fasting, vigils. Incorporeal graces and incorporeal beauty were the objects of her love and contemplation. She treated enemies with such perfect courtesy and forbearance, that even the depraved were put to shame in her presence. The goodness of the soul within overflowed into all her outer actions.[199] From this rapturous description of a highly spiritual kind of life, Chrysostom passes, with versatile quickness, to a somewhat ludicrous picture of the petty cares of life in the world. "The worldly lady thinks it a fine thing to drive round the Forum; how much better to be independent, and use her feet for the purpose for which God gave them! There was always some difficulty about the mules: she and her husband wanted them at the same time; one or both were lame or turned out to grass. A quiet and modestly-dressed woman needed no carriage and attendants to protect her in her passage through the streets, but might walk through the Forum, free from any annoyance. Some might say it was pleasant to be waited on by a troop of handmaids; but, on the contrary, such a charge was attended with much anxiety. Not only had the sick to be taken care of, but the indolent to be chastised, mischief, quarrels, and all kinds of evil doings to be corrected; and if there happened to be one distinguished by personal beauty, jealousy was added to all these other cares, lest the husband should be so captivated by her charms as to pay more attention to her than to her mistress.[200] If it was replied to all these objections against married life, that Abraham and other saints in the Old Testament were all married men, it must be remembered that a much higher standard was required under the New Dispensation. There were degrees of perfection. When Noah was said to be 'perfect in his generation,' it meant relatively to that age in which he lived, for what is perfect in relation to one era becomes imperfect for another. Murder was forbidden by the Old Law, but hatred and wrath under the New. A larger effusion of the Holy Spirit rendered Christian men fully grown as compared with the children of the Old Dispensation. Degrees of virtue, impossible then, were attainable now; and as the moral standard under the Old Dispensation was lower, so the rewards of obedience were less exalted. The Jews were encouraged to obedience by the promise of an earthly country, Christians by the prospect of heaven. The Jews were deterred from sin by menaces of temporal calamity; the Christian, of eternal punishment. Let us, therefore, not spend our care upon money-getting and wives and luxurious living, else how shall we ever become men rather than children, and live in the spirit? for when we have taken our journey to that other world, the time for contest will have passed; then those who have not oil in their lamps will be unable to borrow it from their neighbours, or he who has a soiled garment to exchange it for another robe. When the Judge's throne has been placed, and He is seated upon it, and the fiery stream is 'coming forth from before Him' (Dan. vii. 10), and the scrutiny of past life has begun: though Noah, Daniel, and Job were to implore an alteration of the sentence passed upon their own sons and daughters, their intercession would not avail."[201]

The long treatise "De S. Babyla contra Julianum et Gentiles" presents several interesting subjects for consideration. In the history of the grove of Daphne we have a singular instance of the way in which Grecian legend was transplanted into foreign soil. Daphne, the daughter of the Grecian river-god Ladon, was, according to the Syrian version of the myth, overtaken by Apollo near Antioch. Here it was, on the banks, not of the Peneus, but of the Orontes, that the maiden prayed to her mother earth to open her arms and shelter her from the pursuit of the amorous god, and that the laurel plant sprang out of the spot where she disappeared from the eyes of her disappointed lover. The horse of Seleucus Nicator, founder of the Syrian monarchy, was said to have struck his hoof upon one of the arrows which Apollo had dropped in the hurry of his chase; in consequence of which the king dedicated the place to the god. A temple was erected in his honour, ample in proportions, and sumptuous in its adornments; the interior walls were resplendent with polished marbles, the lofty ceiling was of cypress wood. The colossal image of the god, enriched with gold and gems, nearly reached the top of the roof; the draped portions were of wood, the nude portions of marble. The fingers of the deity lightly touched the lyre which hung from his shoulders, and in the other hand he held a golden dish, as if about to pour a libation on the earth, "and supplicate the venerable mother to give to his arms the cold and beauteous Daphne."[202] The whole grove became consecrated to pleasure, under the guise of festivity in honour of the god. A more beautiful combination of delights cannot well be conceived. The grove was situated five miles to the south-west of Antioch, among the outskirts of the hills, where many of the limpid streams, rushing down towards the valley of the Orontes, mingled their waters. The road which connected the city with this spot was lined on the left hand with large gardens and groves, baths, fountains, and resting-places; on the right were villas with vineyards and rose-gardens irrigated by rivulets. Daphne itself was, according to Strabo,[203] eighty stadia, or about ten miles, in circumference. It contained everything which could gratify and charm the senses; the deep impenetrable shade of cypress trees, the delicious sound and coolness of falling waters, the fragrance of aromatic shrubs. Such a combination of all that was voluptuous told with fatal and enervating effect upon the morals of a people who were at all times disposed to an immoderate indulgence in luxurious pleasures. Roman troops, and even Roman emperors, fell victims to the allurements of the spot.[204] The annual celebration of the Olympian games instituted here by Commodus was especially the occasion of shocking excesses of every kind. But by the order of Gallus Cæsar an attempt was made to introduce a pure association into the spot hitherto abandoned to the licentiousness of pagan rites. The remains of Babylas, the Bishop of Antioch, who had suffered martyrdom in the reign of Decius, were transferred from their resting-place in the city to the grove of Daphne. The chapel or martyry erected over the bones of the Christian saint stood hard by the temple of the pagan deity. Here it confronted the Christian visitor, as a warning to him not to take part in pagan and licentious rites, abhorrent to the faith for which the Bishop had died. But the remains of the martyr were not permitted to rest in peace. When Julian visited Antioch, he consulted the oracle of Apollo at Daphne respecting the issue of the expedition which he was about to make into Persia. But the oracle was dumb. At length the god yielded to the importunity of repeated prayers and sacrifices so far as to explain the cause of his silence. He was disturbed by the proximity of a dead body: "Break open the sepulchres, take up the bones, and remove them hence." The demand was interpreted as referring to the remains of Babylas, and the wishes of the crestfallen oracle were complied with.[205] But the insult done to the Christian martyr was speedily avenged. Soon after the accomplishment of the impious act, a violent thunderstorm broke over the temple, and the lightning consumed both the roof of the building and the statue of the deity. At the time when Chrysostom wrote, some twenty years after the occurrence, the mournful wreck was yet standing; but the chapel again contained the relics of the saint and martyr, and conferred blessings on the pilgrims who resorted thither in crowds. The ruined and deserted temple, side by side with the carefully-preserved church of the martyr, thronged by devotees, presented a striking emblem of the fate of paganism, crumbling and vanishing away before the presence of the new faith, blasted by the lightning flash of a mightier force. A great portion of the treatise of Chrysostom is occupied by an analysis of his old master Libanius's elegy over the fate of the stricken shrine of pagan worship. The affected and inflated tone of the sophist's composition deserves the sarcasm and scorn which his pupil unsparingly pours upon it.

CHAPTER 8

ORDINATION TO THE PRIESTHOOD BY FLAVIAN—INAUGURAL DISCOURSE IN THE CATHEDRAL—HOMILIES AGAINST THE ARIANS—ANIMADVERSIONS ON THE CHARIOT RACES. A.D. 386.

CHRYSOSTOM HAD USED THE office of a deacon well. The lofty tone of Christian piety, the boldness, the ability, the command of language manifested in his writings, marked him out as eminently qualified for a preacher. His treatises, indeed, are distinguished by a vehemence and energy which belong more to the fervour of the orator than to the calmness of the writer. No doubt also men had not forgotten the talent for speaking which he had displayed when he began to practise, nearly twenty years before, as a lawyer. The Bishop Flavian ordained him a priest in 386, and immediately appointed him to be one of the most frequent preachers in the church. The bishop of a see like Antioch at that time rather resembled the rector of a large town parish than the bishop of modern times. He resided in Antioch, and discharged the duties of a chief pastor, assisted by his staff of priests and deacons. Where the whole Christian population amounted to not more than 100,000 souls, as in Antioch,[206] that division into distinct districts, such as were formed in Alexandria,[207] Rome, and Constantinople, with separate churches, served by members of the central staff in rotation, or by pastors especially appropriated to them, does not seem to have been made. Chrysostom officiated and preached in the great church, where the bishop also officiated. The less learned and less able priests were appointed to the less responsible duties of visiting the sick and the poor, and administering the sacraments. The vocation of Chrysostom, however, was especially that of a teacher. It will be readily acknowledged how difficult, how delicate an office preaching was, in an age when Christianity and Paganism were still existing side by side, and when the opinions of many men were floating in suspense between the old faith and the new, and were liable to be distracted from a firm hold upon the truth by Judaism and heresies of every shade.

Either on the occasion of his ordination, or very soon after it, Chrysostom preached an inaugural discourse, in the presence of the bishop. It is distinguished by that flowery and exaggerated kind of rhetoric which he occasionally displays in all its native oriental luxuriance, and which is due to the school in which he was brought up, rather than to the man. On such a public and formal occasion he appears less as the Christian teacher than as the scholar of Libanius the Rhetorician. His self-disparagement at the opening of his discourse, and his flattering encomiums on Flavian and Meletius at the close, would to modern, certainly at least to English, ears sound intolerably affected. No doubt, however, they were acceptable to the taste of his audience at Antioch; and, indeed, the whole discourse contains nothing more overstrained or ornate than is to be found in some of the most celebrated performances of the great French preachers in the seventeenth and eighteenth centuries.

A few paraphrases will suffice to illustrate the character of his discourse.

"He could scarcely believe what had befallen him, that he, an insignificant and abject youth,[208] should find himself elevated to such a height of dignity. The spectacle of so vast a multitude hanging in expectation on his lips quite unnerved him, and would have dried up fountains of eloquence, had he possessed such. How, then, could he hope that his little trickling stream of words would not fail, and that the feeble thoughts which he had put together with so much labour would not vanish from his mind?

"Wherefore he besought them to pray earnestly that he might be inspired with courage to open his mouth boldly in this hitherto unattempted work."[209] He wished to offer the first-fruits of his speech in praise to God. As the tiller of the ground gave of his wheat, grapes, or olives, so he would fain make an offering in kind; he would 'praise the name of God with a song, and magnify it with thanksgiving.' But the consciousness of sin made him shrink from the task, for as in a wreath not only must the flowers be clean, but also the hands which wove it, so in sacred hymns not only must the words be holy, but also the soul of him who composed them. The words of the wise man who said, 'praise is not becoming in the mouth of a sinner,'[210] sealed up his lips, and when David invited all creation, animate and inanimate, visible and invisible, to 'praise the Lord of Heaven, to praise him in the height,' he did not include the sinner in the invitation. He would rather therefore dilate on the merits of some of his fellow-men who were worthier than himself. The mention of their Christian virtues would be an indirect way, legitimate for a sinner, of paying glory and honour to God himself. And to whom should he address his praises first but to their bishop, whom he might call the teacher of their country, and through their country of the world at large? To enter fully, however, into his manifold virtues was to dive into so deep a sea that he feared he should lose himself in its profundities. To do justice to the task would require an inspired and apostolic tongue. He must confine himself to a few points. Although reared in the midst of affluence, Flavian had surmounted the difficulties which impeded the entrance of a rich man into the kingdom of heaven. He had been distinguished from youth by perfect temperance and control over the bodily appetites, by contempt of luxury and a costly table. Though untimely deprived of parental care, and exposed to the temptations incident to wealth, youth, and good birth, yet had he triumphed over them all. He had assiduously cultivated his mind, and had put the bridle of fasting on his body sufficient to curb excess, without impairing its strength and usefulness; and though he had now glided into the haven of a calm old age, yet he did not relax the severity of this personal discipline. The death of their beloved father Meletius had caused great distress and perplexity to the Church, but the appearance of his successor had dispersed it, as clouds vanished before the sun. When Flavian mounted the episcopal throne, Meletius himself seemed to have risen from his tomb."

All that can be collected from history respecting Flavian's character confirms and justifies these eulogiums, though English taste would prefer them to have been uttered after his death rather than in his actual presence. Chrysostom concludes by saying that he had prolonged his address beyond the bounds which became his position, but the flowery field of praise had tempted him to linger. "He would conclude his task by asking their prayers: prayers that their common mother the Church might remain undisturbed and steadfast, and that the life of their father, teacher, spiritual shepherd, and pilot, might be prolonged; prayers finally that he, the preacher, might be strengthened to bear the yoke which was laid upon him, might in the great day restore safely the deposit which his Master had committed to his trust, and obtain mercy for his sins through the grace and goodness of the Lord Jesus Christ, to whom be glory, and power, and worship for ever and ever."

We now enter on a period of ten years, during which Chrysostom constantly resided in Antioch, and was occupied in the almost incessant labour of preaching. The main bulk of those voluminous works which have been preserved to our times belongs to this period; yet there can be no doubt that, numerous as are the extant works, they represent but a fraction of the discourses which he actually delivered. For we know, on his own authority, that he frequently preached twice, occasionally oftener, in the course of a week.[211]

It does not fall within the scope of this essay to determine how many of the homilies which we possess were delivered in each year, or to enter into a critical examination of every set. But an attempt will be made to extract from them whatever seems to throw light upon the life and times of their author, upon events in which he played a conspicuous part, or which were of great public importance; whatever also illustrates the special condition of the Church,—her general practice, her merits and defects, the dangers and difficulties with which, from dissension within or heresy without, she had at this era to contend.

The field of subjects on which the preacher was called to exercise his powers was varied and extensive. Christianity was imperilled by corruption of morals and corruption of faith. Not the laity only, but the clergy also, at least in the great towns, had become deeply infected by the prevalent follies and vices of the age. Again, between the orthodox Christian and the Pagan every variety of heresy intervened. The Arian, the Manichæan, the Marcionite, the Sabellian, the Jew,—all were, so to say, touching and fraying the edge of pure Christianity; the danger was, lest they should gradually so wear it away as to injure the very vitals of the faith. Such were the evils which Chrysostom bent his energies to redress, such the enemies whom he manfully endeavoured to repel. He is alternately the champion of a pure morality and of a sound faith.

Among the discourses which belong to the first year of his priesthood falls one delivered in commemoration of Bishop Meletius, the predecessor of Flavian.[212] He had died at Constantinople about the end of May A.D. 381, and Chrysostom in the commencement of his homily remarks, that five years had now elapsed since the bishop had taken his journey to the "Saviour of his longings." The tone of the discourse illustrates a characteristic of the times; a passionate devotion to the memory of departed saints which was rapidly passing into actual adoration; a subject on which more will be said hereafter. The shrine which contained the reliques of Meletius was placed in the sight of the preacher and the congregation, who swarmed round it like bees.[213] When Chrysostom looked at the great multitude assembled he congratulated the holy Meletius on enjoying such honour after his death, and he congratulated the people also on the endurance of their affection to their late spiritual father. Meletius was like the sound root which though invisible proved its strength by the vigour of its fruit. When he had returned from his first banishment the whole Christian population had streamed forth to meet him. Happy those who succeeded in clasping his feet, kissing his hand, hearing his voice. Others who beheld him only at a distance felt that they too had obtained a blessing from the mere sight. A kind of spiritual glory emanated from his holy person, even as the shadows of St. Peter and St. John had healed the sick on whom they fell.

"Let us all, rulers and ruled, men and women, old and young, free men and slaves, offer prayer, taking the blessed Meletius into partnership with this our prayer (since he has more confidence now in offering prayer, and entertains a warmer affection towards us), that our love may be increased and that as now we stand beside his shrine, so one day we may all be permitted to approach his resting-place in the other world."

The discourses of Chrysostom against Arians and Jews fall within the first year of his priesthood.[214] They are among the finest of his productions, and deserve perusal on account of their intrinsic merit no less than of the important points of doctrine with which they are concerned. Antioch, indeed, may in some sort be regarded as the cradle of Arianism. Paul of Samosata, who was deposed from the See of Antioch in A.D. 272, advocated doctrines of a Sabellian character, but that sophistical dialectical school of thought of which the Arians were the most conspicuous representatives may be traced to him. His original calling had been that of a sophist, and he was therefore by training more fitted to attack established doctrines than to build up a definite system of his own. Hence it is not surprising that, though his own tendency was to Sabellian opinions, Lucian, his intimate friend and fellow-countryman, held doctrines diametrically opposite, or what were afterwards called Arian.[215] Lucian, when presbyter at Antioch, was the teacher of Eusebius, Bishop of Nicomedia, of Leontius, the Arian Bishop of Antioch, and perhaps also of Arius himself.[216] Aëtius, and his pupil Eunomius, originators of the most extreme and undisguised form of Arianism, resided in the beginning of their career at Antioch. Eunomius, in fact, was the founder of a sect which was called Eunomian after him; or sometimes Anomœan, because it denied not only equality but even similarity (ὁμοιότης) between the Father and the Son in the Holy Trinity. It was the most materialistic phase which Arianism developed. Mystery was to be eliminated from revelation as much as possible, sacramental grace was little recognised, asceticism disparaged. Adherents of this school seem to have existed still in some force at Antioch. A system marked by so much of cold intellectual pride was especially repugnant to the fervid and humble faith of Chrysostom. Yet in his assaults upon it he was neither precipitate nor harsh. In his first homily "On the incomprehensible Nature of God," he says that, having observed several persons who were infected by this heresy listening to his discourses, he had abstained from attacking their errors, wishing to gain a firmer hold upon their interest before engaging with them in controversy. But having been invited by them to undertake the contest, he could not decline it, but would endeavour to conduct it in a spirit of gentleness and love, since "the servant of the Lord must not strive, but be gentle towards" all, as well as "apt to teach." He urges all disputants to remember our Lord's answer when He was buffeted, "If I have spoken evil, bear witness of the evil; but if well, why smitest thou me?"[217]

He dilates on the arrogance of the Anomœans in pretending to understand and to define the exact nature of God. "Professing themselves wise they only discovered their folly. Imperfect knowledge on so profound a subject was an inevitable part of the imperfection of our human state. The condition of our present knowledge was this: we know many things *about* God, but we do not know *how* they are or take place. For example, we may know that He is everywhere and without beginning or end, but *how* He is thus, we know not. We know that He begat the Son, and that the Holy Spirit proceeded from Him, but *how* these things can be we are unable to tell. This is analogous to our knowledge of many things which are called natural. We eat various kinds of food, but *how* they nourish us and are transmuted into the several humours of the body we do not understand."[218]

"Again, if the wisest and holiest men have confessed themselves incompetent to fathom the *purposes* and *dispensations* of God, how far more inscrutable must His *essence* be! If David exclaims 'Such knowledge is too wonderful and excellent for me, I cannot attain unto it;' and St. Paul, 'Oh the depth of the riches and wisdom of God! how unsearchable are His judgments, how untraceable His ways!' if the very angels do not presume to discuss the nature of God, but humbly adore Him with veiled faces, crying 'Holy, Holy, Holy,' how monstrous is the conceit and irreverence of those who curiously investigate and pretend to define the exact nature of the Godhead!"[219]

He proceeds to dwell upon the littleness and feebleness of man, as contrasted with the amazing and boundless power of God. The Eunomians maintained that man could know the nature of God as much as God Himself knew it. "What mad presumption was this! The Prophets exhaust all available metaphors to express the insignificance of man as compared with God. Men are 'dust and ashes,' 'grass,' and the 'flower of grass,' 'a vapour,' 'a shadow.' Inanimate creation acknowledges the irresistible supremacy of His power; 'if He do but touch the hills they shall smoke,' 'He shaketh the earth out of her place, and the pillars thereof tremble' (Job ix. 6)." "Seest thou not yon sky, how beautiful it is, how vast, spangled with what a choir of stars? Five thousand years and more has it stood, yet length of time has left no mark of old age upon it: like a youthful vigorous body it retains the beauty with which it was endowed at the beginning. This beautiful, this vast, this starry, this ancient firmament, was made by that God into whose nature you curiously pry, was made with as much ease as a man might for pastime construct a hovel: 'He established the sky like a roof, and stretched it out like a tent over the earth' (Isa. xl. 22). The solid, durable earth He made, and all the nations of the world, even as far as the British Isles, are but as a drop in a bucket; and shall man, who is but an infinitesimal part of this drop, presume to inquire into the nature of Him who made all these forces and whom they obey?"[220] "God dwells in the light which no man can approach unto. If the light which surrounds Him be inaccessible, how much more God Himself who is within it? St. Paul rebukes those who presume to question the dispensation of God. 'Nay but, O man, who art thou that repliest against God? Shall the thing formed say unto him that formed it, Why hast thou made me thus?' How much more, then, would he have reproved dogmatic assumptions respecting the nature of the great Dispenser?[221] The declaration of St. John, that no man had seen God at any time, might appear at variance with the descriptions in the prophets of visions of the Deity. As: 'I saw the Lord sitting on His throne, high and lifted up' (Isa. vi. 1). 'I saw the Lord standing above the altar' (Amos ix. 1). 'I beheld till the thrones were cast down, and the Ancient of days did sit, whose garment was white as snow,' etc. (Dan. vii. 9). But the very variety of forms under which God is said to have appeared proves that these manifestations were merely condescensions to the weakness of human nature, which requires something that the eye can see and the ear can hear. They were only manifestations of the Deity adapted to man's capacity; not the Divine Nature itself, which is simple, incomposite, devoid of shape. So also, when it is said of God the Son that He is 'in the bosom of the Father,' when He is described as standing, or sitting, on the right hand of God, these expressions must not be interpreted in too material a sense; they are expressions accommodated to our understandings, to convey an idea of such an intimate union and equality between the two Persons as is in itself incomprehensible."[222]

And this leads him on to consider the second error of the Arians—their denial of absolute equality between the three Persons in the Godhead. His arguments are based, as usual, entirely on an appeal to Holy Scripture. He makes a skilful selection and combination of texts to prove his point: that the titles "God" and "Lord" are common to the first two Persons in the Trinity—the names Father and Son being added merely to distinguish the Personality. Had the Father alone been God, then it would have been superfluous to add the name Father at all: "there is one God" would have been sufficient. But, as it was, the titles "God" and "Lord" were applied to both Persons to prove their equality in respect of Godhead. That the appellation of Lord no way indicated inferiority was plain, because it was frequently applied to the Father. "The Lord our God is one Lord," Exod. xx. 2. "Great is our Lord, and great is his power," Ps. cxlvii. 5. On the other hand, Christ is frequently entitled *God*, e.g. "Immanuel—*God* with us." "Christ according to the flesh, who is over all, *God* blessed for ever." In some instances the Father and the Son are both called Lord, or both God, in the *same* passage; as, for example, "The Lord said unto my Lord, ... Thy throne, O God (the Son), is for ever and ever; ... wherefore God (the Father), even thy God, hath anointed thee with the oil of gladness," etc.[223]

The reason why Christ sometimes acted and spoke in a manner which implied human infirmity and inferiority to the Father was twofold: First, that men might be convinced that He did really, substantially, exist in the truth of our human nature; that He was not a mere phantom—the error of Marcion, Manes, and Valentinus—an error which would have been still more prevalent had He not so clearly manifested the reality of his humanity. On the other hand, He was reserved and cautious in declaring the highest mystery—his divine union and equality with the Father—out of condescension to the weakness of man's intellect, which recoiled from the more recondite mysteries. When He told them that "Abraham rejoiced to see his day," that "before Abraham was He was," "that the bread from heaven was his flesh, which He would give for the life of the world," that "hereafter they should see the Son of Man coming in the clouds," they were invariably offended. But, on the contrary, He was chiefly accepted when He spoke words implying more humiliation—for example, "I can of my own self do nothing, but as my Father taught me, even so I speak." "As He spake these words," we are told, "many believed on Him."[224]

Two other reasons might be assigned for this language of self-abasement. One was, that He came to teach us humility,—"Learn of me, for I am meek and lowly of heart." He "came not to be ministered unto but to minister." He who bids others be lowly must first and pre-eminently be lowly himself. Therefore He performed such acts as washing his disciples' feet; and the Incarnation itself was no sign, as the Arian maintained, of inferiority, but only the highest expression of that great principle of self-sacrificing love which He came to teach. Lastly, by such language He directs our minds to the apprehension of a clear distinction between the Persons in the Godhead. If his sayings about Himself had all been of the same type as "I and my Father are one," the Sabellian error of confounding the Persons would have become yet more prevalent than it was. Thus, we find throughout our Lord's life, in his acts and language, a careful mixture and variation of character in order to present the two elements—the human and divine—in equal proportions. He predicts his own sufferings and death, yet quickly afterwards He prays the Father that He might be, if possible, spared undergoing them. In the first act is pure divinity; in the second, humanity shrinking from that pain which is abhorrent to human nature.[225]

This very fact, however, of our Lord's praying, was laid hold of by the Arians to prove the inferiority of his nature. This argument Chrysostom meets in Homilies IX. and X. The raising of Lazarus had been read in the Gospel for the day. "I perceive," he says, "that many of the Jews and heretics will find an excuse, in the prayer offered by Christ before performing this miracle, to impugn his power, and say He could not have done it without the Father's assistance." But this fell to the ground, because on most other occasions our Lord wrought his miracles without any prayer at all. To the dead maiden he simply said, "Talitha cumi," and she arose; the woman with an issue of blood was healed without any word or touch from Him. In the case of Lazarus He prayed, as He Himself declared, for the sake of the people, that they might perceive that God heard his prayers—that there was a perfect unanimity between the Father and the Son. Martha, in fact, had asked for a prayer—"I know whatsoever thou shalt ask of God, God will give it thee;" therefore He prayed; just as, when the centurion said, "Speak the word only," He spake the word and the servant was healed. If He had needed help He would have invoked it before all his miracles. In fact there was no kind of sovereign power which He hesitated to exercise. "Son, be of good cheer, thy sins be forgiven thee" ... "the Son of man hath power on earth to forgive sins;"—to an evil spirit, "*I* charge thee, come out of him, and enter no more into him;" ... "to them of old it was said, Thou shalt not kill; but *I* say, whosoever is angry with his brother without a cause," etc. He represents Himself as saying on the final day, "Come, ye blessed;" or "Depart, ye cursed." Thus He claims authority to absolve, to judge, to legislate.

Homilies XI. and XII., against the Anomœans, were delivered some ten years later at Constantinople, but as they contain no special references to the events of that time, the continuity of this subject may be maintained by extracting from them the argument there employed to prove the equality of the Son with the Father. It is based on the passage, "My Father worketh hitherto, and I work" (St. John v. 17); by which our

Saviour justified Himself from the accusation of breaking the Sabbath when He healed the paralytic. The words "My Father worketh," Chrysostom observes, refer to the daily operations of God's providence, by which he sustains in being those things which he commanded into existence.

This upholding energy, our Lord declares, is active at all times and on all days alike; and if it were not, the fabric of the universe would fall to pieces. He claims a similar right to providential rule, which implies equality with the Father. "My Father worketh, *and I* work." If the Son had been inferior, such a method of justifying Himself would only have added force to the charges of his enemies. If a subject of the Emperor were to put on the imperial diadem and purple, it would be no excuse to say that he wore them *because* the Emperor wore them—"the Emperor wears them, *and I* wear them;"—on the contrary, it would augment the offensiveness of his presumption and arrogance. If Christ were not equal with the Father, it was the height of presumption to use those words, "My Father worketh hitherto, and I work."

In dealing with such lengthy homilies, it has been impossible to do more than give specimens in a very condensed form of the main lines of argument which Chrysostom adopts. They vary greatly in value; but two points cannot fail to arrest the notice of any one who reads these homilies through:—First, the profound acquaintance of their author with Holy Scripture; extending apparently with equal force to every part of the sacred volume. Old and New Testament and Apocrypha are almost equally employed for argument, illustration, adornment; he is at home everywhere. Secondly, upon Scripture all his arguments are based: in none of his controversial homilies does Chrysostom take his stand upon the platform of existing tradition, or rely on the authority of the Church alone; "to the law and to the testimony" is always the way with him. And this was a test at that time universally accepted. The dispute with the most rationalistic and critical Arians seems never to have turned on the *authority*, but only on the *interpretation* of Scripture. Scripture is appealed to as the supreme court for trying all their differences; the only question was, as to the exact meaning of its decisions.

Again, we cannot fail to be struck by the ease and rapidity with which he glances off from the most controversial and theological parts of his discourse to practical reproof and exhortation. Nothing provoked him more than to see the bulk of that large concourse of people, who had been listening with profound attention to his address, leave the church just as the celebration of the Eucharist was about to commence. "Deeply do I groan to perceive that when your fellow-servant is speaking, great is your earnestness, strained your attention, you crowd one upon another, and stay till the very end; but that, when Christ is about to appear in the holy mysteries, the church is empty and deserted.... If my words had been laid up in your hearts they would have kept you here, and brought you to the celebration of these most solemn mysteries with greater piety; but as it is, my speech seems as fruitless as the performance of a lute-player, for as soon as I have finished you depart. Away with the frigid excuse of many: I can say prayers at home, but I cannot at home hear homilies and doctrine. Thou deceivest thyself, O man; you may indeed pray at home, but it is impossible to pray *in the same manner* as at church, where there is so large an assembly of your spiritual fathers, and the cry of the worshippers is sent up with one accord; where there is unanimity and concert in prayer; and where the priests preside, that the weaker supplications of the multitude being supported by theirs, which are more powerful, may ascend together with these to heaven. First prayer, then discourse; so say the Apostles—"But we will give ourselves to *prayer and* to the ministry of the word."[226]

Again, as frequently in other discourses, he reproves the congregation for testifying their admiration of his words by applause. "You praise what I have said, you receive my exhortation with tumults of applause; but show your approbation by obedience; that is the praise which I seek, the applause which comes through deeds."[227]

His hearers, in fact, were so closely packed, and so much absorbed in listening to his discourse, that pickpockets often practised on them with some success. Chrysostom advises them, therefore, to bring no money or ornaments about their persons to church. It was a device of the devil, who hoped by means of this annoyance to chill their zeal in attending the services, just as he stripped Job of everything, not merely to make him poor but to rob him if possible of his piety.[228]

But the most inveterate enemy with which Chrysostom had to contend was the circus. Against this he declaims with all the vehemence of Evangelical invectives against horse-racing in modern times. The indomitable passion for the chariot-races, and the silly eagerness displayed about them by the inhabitants of Rome, Constantinople, and Antioch, are among the most remarkable symptoms of the depraved state of society under the later Empire. The whole populace was divided into factions distinguished by the different colours adopted by the charioteers, of which green and blue were the two chief favourites. The animosity, the sanguinary tumults, the superstitions,[229] folly, violence of every kind, which were mixed up with these popular amusements, well deserved the unsparing severity with which they were lashed by the great preacher.

A few specimens shall be collected here from other homilies, as well as from those immediately under consideration.

"Again we have the horse-races; again our assembly is thinned. There were many indeed whose absence he little regretted: they were to the faithful amongst the congregation only as leaves to fruit.[230] Sometimes, however, the church was deserted by those of whom he had expected more fidelity. He felt disheartened, like a sower who had scattered good seed plentifully, but with no adequate result. Gladly and eagerly would he continue his exertions could he see any fruit of his labours; but when, forgetful of all his exhortations and warnings, and solemn reminders of the terrible doom, the unquenchable fire, the undying worm, they again abandoned themselves to the diabolical exhibitions of the race-course, with what heart could he return to the unthankful task? They manifested, indeed, by applause, the pleasure with which they heard his words, and then they hurried off to the circus, and, sitting side by side with Jew or Pagan, they applauded with a kind of frenzied eagerness the efforts of the several charioteers; they rushed tumultuously along, jostling one another, and shouting, 'that horse didn't run fairly,' 'that was tripped up and fell,' and the like.[231] Various excuses were pleaded for absence from church—the exigencies of business, poverty, ill health, lameness; but these impediments never prevented attendance at the Hippodrome. In the church the chief places even were not always all occupied, but *there* old and young, rich and poor, crowded every available space for standing or sitting; pushing, and squeezing, and trampling on one another's feet, while the sun poured down on their heads: yet they appeared thoroughly to enjoy themselves, in spite of all these discomforts; while in the church the length of the sermon, or the heat, or the crowd, were perpetual subjects of complaint."[232]

Such are a few illustrations of one, but perhaps the most notable, form among many in which the impulsiveness and frivolity of the people of Antioch were displayed. "The building which the preacher had so laboriously and industriously reared in the hearts of his disciples was thus cruelly dashed down and levelled to the very ground by a few hours of dissolving pleasure and iniquitous frivolity."[233]

Truly indeed might the lamentation of the prophet over the evanescent piety of Ephraim and Judah have been applied to these people: "Your goodness is as a morning cloud, and as the early dew it goeth away" (Hos. vi. 4).

CHAPTER 9

HOMILIES AGAINST PAGANS AND JEWS—CONDITION OF
THE JEWS IN ANTIOCH—JUDAISING CHRISTIANS—
HOMILIES ON CHRISTMAS DAY AND NEW YEAR'S DAY—
CENSURE OF PAGAN SUPERSTITIONS. A.D. 386, 387.

IN DEALING WITH THE Arians, the contest mainly turned, as has been pointed out in the previous chapter, on the interpretation of Scripture; but in doing battle with Pagans and Jews, with the former especially, Chrysostom had of course to take up a different attitude. The method which he adopts towards the Jew is to demonstrate the fulfilment of Old Testament prophecy in the person and work of Jesus Christ, and to insist on the consequent abrogation of the Jewish dispensation. The ground on which he mainly relies against the Pagan is the miraculous establishment and progress of Christianity in the face of unprecedented opposition, as an evidence of its divine origin.

The treatise addressed to Jews and Gentiles combined exhibits a powerful application of both these methods.[234] "He would first of all enter the lists against the Pagan. And here caution was requisite. He would not say, when the Pagan asked how the divinity of Christ was to be proved, that Christ created the world, raised the dead, healed the sick, expelled demons, promised a resurrection and a heavenly kingdom, because these were the very questions upon which they joined issue. But he would start from a ground which even the Pagan would accept: no one would venture to deny that the Christian religion was founded by Jesus Christ, and from this simple fact he would undertake to prove that Christ could be no less than God. No mere man could, in so short a time, with such feeble instruments, and in the face of such opposition arising from inveterate custom and forms of faith, have subdued so many and such various races of mankind.[235] How contrary to the common course of events, that He who was despised, weak, and put to an ignominious death, should now be honoured and adored in all regions of the earth! Emperors who have made laws, and altered the constitution of states, who have ruled nations by their nod, in whose hands was the power of life and death, pass away; their images are in time destroyed, their actions forgotten, their adherents despised, their very names buried in oblivion:—present grandeur is succeeded by nothingness. In the case of Jesus Christ all is reversed. During his lifetime, all seemed failure and degradation, but a career of glory and triumph succeeded his death.[236] Before his death Judas betrayed him, St. Peter denied him; after his death, St. Peter and the rest of the Apostles traversed the world to bear witness to his truth, and thousands of people have died rather than utter what the chief of the Apostles once uttered from fear of a maid-servant's taunts. 'His rest shall be glorious:'—this was true, not only of the Master, but also of his disciples. In that most royal city of Rome, monarchs, prefects, generals, flocked to the sepulchres of the fisherman and the tent-maker; and in Constantinople they who wore the diadem were content to lay their bones in the porch of the Apostles' Church, and to become as it were the door-keepers of humble fishermen.[237] Christ had made the most ignominious death, and the instrument of it, glorious. It was written, 'Cursed is he that hangeth on a tree,' yet the cross had become the object of desire and love; it was more honourable than the whole world, for the imperial crown itself was not such an ornament to the head: princes and subjects, men and women, bond and free, all delighted to wear it imprinted on the brow. It was conspicuous on the Holy Table, and in the ceremony of ordaining priests; in houses, in market-places, by the wayside, and on mountain sides, on couches and on garments, on ships, on drinking vessels, in mural decorations, the cross was depicted. Whence all this extraordinary honour to a piece of wood, unless the power of him who died upon it was divine?'"[238]

Christ had declared that the gates of hell should not prevail against his Rock-founded Church. How far had this prediction been verified? In a short space of time Christianity had abolished ancestral customs, plucked up deeply-rooted habits, overturned altars and temples, caused unclean rites and ceremonials to vanish away. Christian altars had been erected in Italy, in Persia, in Scythia, in Africa. "What say I? even the British Isles, which lie outside the boundaries of our world and our sea, in the midst of the ocean itself, have experienced the power of the Word, for even there churches and altars have been set up." Thus the world had been, so to say, cleared of thorns, and purified to receive the seed of godliness. What a proof of superhuman power! The progress of the Church had been encountered by customs which were not only venerated but pleasant; yet these traditions, handed down through long lines of ancestors, were abandoned for a religion far more severe and laborious, a religion which substituted fasting for enjoyment, poverty for money-getting, temperance for lasciviousness, meekness for wrath, benevolence for ill-will. Men who had long been enervated by luxury, and accustomed to the broad way, had been converted into the narrow, rugged path, not by tens or twenties, but by multitudes under the whole heaven. By whose agency had these mighty results been wrought? By a few unlearned obscure men, without illustrious ancestors, without money, without eloquence."[239] And all this in the teeth of opposition of the most varied kind. For where the new doctrine penetrated, it excited divisions and strife; children were set at variance with parents, brother with brother, husband with wife, master with servant. Yet, in spite of persecution and disruption of social ties, the new faith grew and flourished. How could such unprecedented marvels have come to pass but through the divine power, and in obedience to that Word of God which is creative of actual results? Just as, when He said "Let the earth bring forth grass," the wilderness became a garden, so when the expression of His purpose had gone forth, "I will build my Church," straightway the process began, and though tyrants and people, sophists and orators, custom and religion, had been arrayed against it, yet the

Word, going forth like fire, consumed the thorns, and scattered the good seed over the purified soil.[240]

In attempting to convince the Jews of the divinity of Jesus Christ by proving the exact fulfilment of Old Testament prophecy in his person and work, Chrysostom displays that intimate familiarity with every part of Scripture which is his eminent characteristic.

The passages are, on the whole, most judiciously selected; some corresponding passage from the New Testament being placed, if possible, against each, with a careful attention even to verbal parallelism. For instance, against the passage in Isaiah, "The Spirit of the Lord shall *rest* upon him," he places the verse from St. John i. 32, "I beheld the Spirit descending like a dove, and it *abode* upon him."[241] He refers each event in Christ's life, his Incarnation, his rejection by the Jews, his betrayal, crucifixion, burial, resurrection, the descent of the Holy Ghost, and the beginning of the Apostolic labours to some corresponding prediction.[242] He sometimes, however, falls into the error, less common in him than in other patristic interpreters, of seeing direct references to the Messiah and the Messianic kingdom, to the almost total exclusion of any other meaning. For instance, such passages as "Their sound is gone out into all lands," "That thou mayest make princes in all lands," are cited as if exclusively predictive of the propagation of Christianity. In such words as "The virgins that be her fellows shall bear her company," he sees a distinct foreshadowing of the honour to be paid to virginity under Christianity.[243] In other passages, again, he is misled by ignorance of the Hebrew, and a too literal adherence to the Septuagint translation. In the passage, "I will make thy officers peace," thine "exactors" being rendered in the Septuagint bishops or overseers, he extracts from this word a direct reference to the Christian priesthood.[244] "He shall descend like rain into a fleece of wool" is interpreted as significant of the extreme secrecy of Christ's birth, and the noiseless gentleness with which his kingdom was founded.[245] Whereas, the strict translation being "like rain upon new-mown grass," it is rather illustrative of the fruitful results of Christ's advent.[246]

Such occasional defects, however, will not prevent us from according the praise due to the great skill with which, on the whole, he has worked out this method of argument, and the noble vindication of Christianity in this treatise has seldom if ever been surpassed by Chrysostom elsewhere. The several parts of his argument are unfolded in orderly procession, and expressed with an eloquence at once luminous and earnest, and which, though at times copious and ornate, does not degenerate into the mere redundancy, still less into the affectations and flowery artifices, of rhetoric; he is always real and earnest, he is sometimes sublime.

Closely connected with this treatise in subject, and not far distant in time of composition, are the Homilies directed against Jews and Judaising Christians. The Jews, ever since the time of Antiochus the Great, were a considerable body in Antioch, and over the Christian population exerted a seriously pernicious influence. Their position, indeed, in the Empire at large had been increasingly favourable from the reign of Hadrian to Constantine. Though they were not permitted to approach Jerusalem, yet the worship in their synagogues was freely tolerated; they were permitted to circumcise their own children though not the children of proselytes; and their religious organisation in the Empire was held together under the sway of the Patriarch of Tiberias.[247] After the recognition of Christianity by the Empire, the Jews, as a natural consequence, were less favourably treated. The statutes of Constantine and Constantius were severe. Those Jews who attempted the life of a Christian were to be burned. No Christians were to become Jews, under pain of punishment. Jews were forbidden to marry Christian women or to possess Christian slaves. The national character of the Jew seems to have deteriorated, as the race became more widely dispersed, and as their wealth and importance increased. They were no longer indeed so morosely and sullenly proud as when they gloried in the possession of a holy city and distinct religious ordinances, and a geographical position which isolated them from the rest of mankind, but neither were their faith or morals so pure. Self-indulgence, sensualism, and low cunning corrupted their life; a superstitious and material cast of thought depraved their faith. Their habits harmonised too well with that propensity to luxury and licentiousness which was the besetting vice of the people of Antioch; their materialism worked hand in hand with the prevailing Arianism, if, indeed, Arianism may not be regarded as in some sort its product. Certainly, whenever popular insurrections caused by religious dissensions occurred either in Antioch or in Alexandria, the Jews ranged themselves on the Arian side, as if the spirit and character of the Arian sect were the most congenial to their own.[248]

Allowing for some exaggerations in the preacher, carried away by the impulse of the moment, the invectives of Chrysostom must be permitted to prove that the Jewish residents in Antioch were of a low and vicious order. They seem to have been regarded by the common people with a mixture of dislike and awe; the age was superstitious, and the Jews availed themselves of superstitious terrors to make a livelihood, especially through a kind of quackery in medicine. Their quarters are denounced by Chrysostom as dens of robbers and habitations of demons.[249] A whole day would not suffice to tell the tale of their extortions, their thefts, their deceptions, their base methods of traffic, such as the sale of amulets and charms.[250] Their priests were no better than counterfeits, because they had not gone through all the elaborate rites of consecration. They had no sacred ephod, no Urim and Thummim, no altar, no sacrifice, no prophecy.

The Festival of Trumpets was a scene of great debauchery, more iniquitous than the proceedings in the theatre. Any catechumen who was detected attending that festival was to be excluded from the porch of the church; any communicant so detected was to be denied access to the Holy Table. The booths erected at the Feast of Tabernacles were like taverns, crowded with flute-players and ill-conditioned women. The synagogues were frequented by the most abandoned characters of both sexes, and dancers, actors, and charioteers were largely drawn from the Jewish population. In spite of this, many Christians were seduced to attend the Jewish festivals and fasts, and even to swear Jewish oaths in the synagogues, under the superstitious impression that such were more solemn and binding than any Christian forms. He had himself, only three days ago, rescued a woman being dragged off, against her will, to take an oath of this kind, by a man who professed himself a Christian. On stopping to rebuke him in the sternest language, Chrysostom was shocked to learn that the practice was extremely common among Christians. He passionately exhorts the faithful to reclaim their deluded brethren from these pernicious ways:—If twelve Apostles had converted the larger part of the world, it would be a shame that the Christians, who were the majority in the population of Antioch, should fail to allay the plague of Judaism. What treason! what inconsistency, that they, who worshipped the Crucified One, should associate with the race which crucified Him.[251] The synagogue ought not to be an object of reverence because it contained the Books of the Law and the Prophets, but rather of abhorrence, because those who possessed the Prophets refused to recognise Him of whom their writings spoke. Was the temple of Serapis holy because it contained the Septuagint, deposited there by Ptolemy Philadelphus?[252]

Christians seem to have attended Jewish services much in that spirit of curiosity with which Protestants sometimes go to Roman Catholic churches, to be entertained by music, incense, and a grand ritual. They maintained that the effect was solemnising; but, observes Chrysostom, the value of the offering to God depends not on the nature of the offering, but on the heart of the offerers. The worshippers sanctify the temple, not the temple the worshippers. You would not touch or address the murderer of your own son, and will you court the society of those who slew the Son of God?[253] Let them consider that cry uttered by the deacon from time to time in the celebration of the holy mysteries: "Discern one another."[254] So let them do. "If you discern any one Judaising, hold him fast and expose him, that you may not yourself participate in the danger."

"In military camps, if any soldier be detected sympathising with the barbarian or the Persian, not only does he himself run a risk of his life, but also any of his comrades who were conscious of his defection, but did not represent it to the general. Since, then, you are the army of Christ, search diligently whether any stranger has intruded into your camp, and expose him, not that we may put him to death, but that we may punish him, deliver him from his error and impiety, and render him wholly our own; but if you willingly conceal him, be well assured that you will sustain the same punishment with him." This homily is concluded by a solemn adjuration: "In the words of Moses, I call heaven and earth to record against you this day, that if any of you now present or absent attend the Feast of Trumpets, or enter a synagogue, or observe a fast, or a sabbath, or any Jewish rite whatever, I am guiltless of your blood. These discourses will rise up for both of us in the great day of our Lord: if you shall have obeyed them, they will give you confidence; but if otherwise, they will stand as severe accusers against you." Therefore he implored them to institute the most rigorous search after the Judaising brethren. When their mother the Church had lost a child, it was criminal to conceal either the captor or the captured; let the men seek out the men, the women the women, the slave his fellow-servant, and present the culprit to him before the next assembly.

Another Judaising practice, which he condemns in the severest language, was the custom of keeping Easter on the 14th day of the month, according to Jewish calculation, irrespective of the week-day on which it might fall; thus sometimes feasting when the rest of the Church was fasting, or fasting when the rest was feasting. The existence of such a practice at this time was a remarkable instance of the increasing influence of the Jews in Antioch and the neighbouring regions. For up to the year A.D. 276, the Antiochene patriarchate had observed Easter in conformity with the Catholic usage; the adoption of the Jewish calculation was made after that date, when most of the rest of Christendom had dropped it, and was therefore the subject of special condemnation at the Council of Nice.[255] Such a discrepancy in practice was regarded as a most serious rent in the unity of the Church. Chrysostom denounces it especially as a contumacious disregard of the Council of Nice, which had distinctly ordained by the mouths of three hundred bishops that Easter should be kept at one and the same time throughout Christendom. He implores the Judaisers to desist from the idle inquiry into the exact dates of seasons; to follow the Church, and to place harmony and charitable peace before all things. It was impossible, in fact, to fix the actual day on which Christ rose; therefore let them observe that day which the Church through her bishops had prescribed. It was a less offence to fast on the wrong day than to rend the unity of the Church. "How long halt ye between two opinions?" if Judaism be true, embrace it altogether, and "cease to annoy the Church; if Christianity be true, abide in it, and follow it."[256]

The Jews themselves could not, in Chrysostom's opinion, legally perform sacrifices, or observe festivals of any kind. Jerusalem was the only place in which such observances were commanded; and Jerusalem being destroyed they became void.[257] They had been suspended during the Captivity, to be resumed when the people returned to the holy soil. If the Jews of the present day also expected restoration, let them likewise suspend their rites; but, in fact, this never would occur. The Temple never would be rebuilt, and restoration was a vain hope. Jerusalem was to be trodden down of Gentiles till the times of the Gentiles were fulfilled; and by the fulfilment of those times Chrysostom understood the end of the world.[258] All four Captivities of the Jews—their subjection to the Egyptians, Babylonians, Antiochus, and the Romans—had been distinctly foretold. To each of the *first three* prophecy had assigned a limit; but to the last *none*—it reached into all time; there was no sign or intimation of any probable cessation.[259] The revolt of the Jews under Hadrian, and under Constantine,[260] had ignominiously failed; the attempt of Julian to rebuild the Temple had been frustrated by portents: fire issuing from the foundations had consumed some of the workmen, and scared the spectators; the naked substructions, left just as they were when the work was abandoned, presented a visible monument of the divinely-arrested work.[261]

The eager exhortation reiterated in his last homily, that the faithful should seek out their brethren who had been caught in the Jewish snare, is a powerful rush of indignant eloquence, and a wholesome admonition on the responsibility of all for the spiritual welfare of their fellow-men. "Say not within thyself, I am a man of the world; I have a wife and children; these matters belong to the priests and the monks. The

Samaritan in the parable did not say, Where are the priests? where are the Pharisees? where are the Jewish authorities? but seized the opportunity of doing a good deed, as if it was a great advantage. In like manner, when you see any one requiring bodily or spiritual care, say not within thyself, Why did not this or that man attend to him?—but deliver him from his infirmity. If you find a piece of gold in your path, you do not say, Why did not some other person pick it up? but you eagerly anticipate others by seizing it yourself. Even so, in the case of your fallen brethren, consider that you have found a treasure in them and give the attention necessary for their wants." He besought them not to proclaim the calamity of the Church by idly gossiping about the numbers of those who had observed some Jewish custom, but to search them out; and, if necessary, to enter their houses, tax them with their guilt, and solemnly warn them against the iniquity of consorting with the enemies of Jesus Christ. "Listen not to any excuses which they may plead on the ground of cures effected by the Jews; expose their impostures, their incantations, their amulets, their charms, their drugs." Even if they really effected cures, it would be better to die and save the soul, than resort to the enemies of Christ to heal the body. Let them rather appeal to the assistance of the martyrs and saints who were His friends, and had great confidence in addressing Him. "Why did the Son of Man Himself enter the world? Was it not to seek and to save wandering sheep? This do thou, according to thy ability. I will not cease to speak, whether you hear or whether you forbear. If you heed not, I shall do it, but with grief; if you listen and obey, I shall do it, but with joy."[262]

It is difficult for us, in our altered position towards Jews and heretics of all kinds, to sympathise with the vehemence of Chrysostom's feelings and language. Yet there can be no doubt that such dabbling, if the word may be used, in the customs, the observances, the ritual of an obsolete dispensation, and a debased people, did seriously imperil purity of faith and morals, and unity of discipline, in the Christian Church.

Towards dissentient Christians, not infected by Judaism, Chrysostom adopts a milder tone, and indeed restrains the immoderation of party feeling in others with wholesome censure. He laments[263] the distracted state of the Church in Antioch, which was now divided into the three sections of Meletians, Eustathians, and Arians; but he denounces the practice of anathematising. It was uncharitable and presumptuous. St. Paul anathematised once only; the casting off of a heretic ought to be as painful as plucking out an eye or cutting off a limb. A holy man before their times, one of the successors of the Apostles, and judged worthy of the honour of martyrdom, used to say, that to assume the right to anathematise was as great a usurpation of Christ's authority as for a subject to put on the Imperial purple. In dealing with erring brethren, the Christian should "in meekness instruct those that oppose themselves, if God, peradventure, will give them repentance to the acknowledging of the truth." "If a man accepts your counsel and confesses his error, you have saved him, and delivered your own soul also; but if he will not, do you nevertheless continue to testify with long-suffering and kindness, that the Judge may not require his soul at thy hand. Hate him not; turn not from him; persecute him not, but catch him in the net of sincere and genuine charity. The person whom you anathematise is either living or dead; if living, you do wrong to cut off one who may still be converted; if dead, much more you do wrong; 'to his own master he standeth or falleth;' and 'who hath known the mind of the Lord, or who hath been his counsellor?' You may anathematise heretical dogmas, but towards the persons who hold them show the greatest possible forbearance, and pray for their salvation."

In the winter of 386, Chrysostom preached a sermon on Christmas Day, which, though not distinguished by any unusual merit, possesses an interest of its own. We learn from it, that this festival was not originally celebrated in the Eastern Church; it had been adopted from the West, and, in Antioch at least, less than ten years before the year of Chrysostom's discourse. It had gradually increased in popularity, and this year Chrysostom rejoiced to observe that the church was crowded to overflowing. Rome had fixed the observance of the 25th of December, and this was the day kept throughout Christendom from Thrace to Gades; but the propriety of the date was much debated in the Eastern Churches, and the observance of the festival at all was considered by some as a questionable innovation. Chrysostom energetically vindicates the dignity of the festival and the correctness of the date.[264] It was the metropolis, so to say, of all other festivals, and as such it was the most solemn and awful. For the incarnation of Christ was the necessary condition of all the succeeding events of His career on earth, and in the profundity of its mystery it exceeded them all. That Christ should die was a natural consequence of human nature once assumed; but that He, being God, should have stooped so low as to assume that nature, was a mystery unfathomable to the mind of man! "Wherefore I specially welcome and belove this day, and desire to make you partakers in my affection. I pray and implore you all to come with zeal and alacrity, every man first purging his own house, to behold our Lord wrapped in swaddling clothes and lying in a manger; for if we come with faith, we shall indeed behold Him lying in the manger; for this Table supplies the place of the manger, and here also the body of the Lord will lie, not wrapped in swaddling clothes, but invested on all sides by the Holy Spirit. The initiated (or the baptized) understand what I mean."[265] But he warns his hearers against crowding in a tumultuous and disorderly manner to partake of the holy feast. "Approach with fear and trembling, with fasting and prayer, not making an uproar, hustling and jostling one another: consider, O man, what kind of sacrifice thou art about to handle; consider that thou, who art dust and ashes, dost receive the body and blood of Christ."[266] This irreverent conduct at the reception of the Eucharist frequently provoked the indignation and censure of Chrysostom. It occurred especially at the greater festivals, because on those days multitudes received the Eucharist who did not enter the church at other times. "How," he cries in the homily on the Epiphany, "shall we teach you what is necessary concerning your soul, immortality, the kingdom of heaven, the long-suffering and mercy of God, and a future judgment, when you come to us only once or twice in the year?" Many of those who pushed and kicked one another in the eagerness of each to get foremost to the holy Table, withdrew from the church before the final thanksgiving. "What," Chrysostom cries, "when Christ is present, and the angels are standing by, and this awe-inspiring Table is spread before you, and your brethren are still partaking of the mysteries, will you hurry away?" Too often they who thronged the church on these great occasions led worldly and even vicious lives; they hurried away before the sacred feast was ended, like Judas, to do the devil's work.[267] Such is one among many examples which may be elicited from Chrysostom's works of that Pagan grossness and superstition which was mingled with the faith and the most solemn observances of Christianity. The vitality of superstitious customs, the subtlety with which they have grafted themselves upon Christianity, the tenacity with which they have clung to men in spite of it late into modern times, is indeed extraordinary; but for centuries their existence and influence were not appreciably if at all affected by Christianity. A half Oriental, half Greek, partly Jewish population, like that of Antioch, whose purer feelings and nobler reason were seriously impaired by habits of licentiousness and luxury, was naturally liable to superstitious terrors, and addicted to superstitious practices of all kinds. Chrysostom is frequently reproving his people for being anxious and afraid where there was no cause, while they abandoned themselves to vice, the only worthy cause for fear, without scruple or alarm. If Christmas Day was observed as a Christian festival, though without becoming reverence, New Year's Day was given up to riotous festivity, thoroughly Pagan in character. The houses were festooned with flowers, the inns were scenes of the most disgraceful intemperance; men and women drinking undiluted wine there from an early hour in the morning; auguries and omens were consulted by which the horoscope of the year was cast. Good luck in the coming year was supposed to depend (how is not clearly stated) on the manner in which the first day was spent. This is the theme of the preacher's righteous indignation. The real happiness of the year was determined, not by the observation of particular feasts, but by the amount of goodness which we put into it. Sin was the only real evil, virtue the only real good; therefore, if a man practised justice, almsgiving, and prayer, his year could not fail to be propitious; for he who had a clean conscience carried about with him a perpetual holy day, and without this, the most brilliant and joyous festival was obscured by darkness. "When thou seest the year completed, thank God that He has brought thee safely to the conclusion of the cycle: prick thine heart, reckon up the time of thy life, and say to thyself, The days are hurrying along, the years are being fulfilled, I have advanced far on the road, the judgment is at the doors, my life is pressing on towards old age: well! what good have I done? shall I depart hence destitute and empty of all righteousness?"[268]

There is a fuller notice, in some of his homilies on the Epistle to the Ephesians, of the many gross and senseless forms of superstition which prevailed even among the communicants in the Christian Church. He laments the decay of discipline, by which a more rigorous scrutiny was once instituted into the characters of those who came to the holy feast. If any one were to examine the lives of all those who partake of the mysteries on Easter Day, he would find amongst them persons who consulted auguries, who used drugs, and omens, and incantations; even the adulterer, curser, and drunkard, dared to partake. Iniquitous men had crept into the Church, the highest places of command were bought and sold, till the pure livers had betaken themselves to the mountains to escape from the contamination.[269] Some of the vulgar superstitions of the day were ludicrously puerile. "This or that man was the first to meet me as I walked out; consequently innumerable ills will certainly befall me: that confounded servant of mine, in giving me my shoes, handed me the left shoe first; this indicates dire calamities and insults: as I stepped out, I started with the left foot foremost; this too is a sign of misfortune: my right eye twitched upwards as I went out; this portends tears."[270] To strike the woof with the comb in a particular way, the braying of a donkey, the crowing of a cock, a sudden sneeze,—all these were indications of something or other. "They suspect everything, and are more in bondage than if they were slaves many times over. But let not us, brethren, fear such things, but laughing them to scorn as men who live in the light, and whose citizenship is in heaven, and who have nothing in common with this earth, let us regard one thing only as terrible,—and that is, sin."[271]

CHAPTER 10

SURVEY OF THE FIRST DECADE OF THE REIGN OF THEODOSIUS—HIS CHARACTER—HIS EFFORTS FOR THE EXTIRPATION OF PAGANISM AND HERESY—THE APOLOGIES OF SYMMACHUS AND LIBANIUS. A.D. 379-389.

BEFORE CHRYSOSTOM HAD LABOURED two full years in "confirming the souls of the disciples" at Antioch, that city became the scene of events memorable in history; and events in which the great preacher played an honourable and distinguished part.

The foremost man of the age, not only by position but also to a great extent in character, was Theodosius the Emperor; Theodosius the Great, deservedly so called in spite of one prominent defect in character, and a few glaring misdeeds which tarnish his reputation. The military exploits of his father, Theodosius the elder, had provoked the jealousy of the court[272] and cost him his life, and the son, who had manifested ability almost equal, in serving under him both by land and sea against Scots and Saxons, Moors and Goths, was glad to escape a similar ungrateful return for his services, by retiring to the obscurity of his native village in Spain. He was disgraced when the Empire had been liberated from danger by the exertions of his father and himself; but in the hour of its utmost jeopardy, and direst distress, he was recalled to more than his former position. The total defeat and death of Valens, and the almost extermination of his army before Hadrianople in A.D. 378, placed the Empire at the mercy of victorious barbarians within the frontier, and on the edge of the horizon more storm-clouds of Gothic or Hunnish invasion were lowering. There was but one person to whom the mind of Gratian, the young Emperor of the West, and his advisers, overwhelmed by the prospect of impending calamity, instinctively turned as capable of saving the State in this crisis. For three years Theodosius had been quietly cultivating his farm between Valladolid and Segovia, when he was summoned to accept the title of Augustus, together with all the responsibilities and perils which attended the possessor, at such a time, of that venerable name. He was equal to the situation; handsome with a manly beauty, courageous and determined of purpose, just and politic in intention if not always in act, he was endowed with some of the noblest qualities of a soldier and a statesman, by which to rescue and reorganise a panic-stricken and crumbling State. This is not the place to narrate the military achievements of Theodosius. The original materials for information respecting them are scanty; but they have been collected and arranged by that historian whose indefatigable industry brings order out of confusion, and whose luminous style lights up with interest even the darkest and most meagre annals.[273] It is sufficient to remind the reader of Gibbon, that Theodosius subdued the Goths, not in any one or two great battles, but by frequent and skilfully contrived engagements on a smaller scale. He thus gradually revived the drooping courage and discipline of the imperial troops, and wore out the enemy. The several tribes, on their submission, were settled in the waste tracts of country, which they were to occupy free of taxation, on the wise condition that they kept the land in a state of cultivation. So a numerous colony of Visigoths was established in Thrace, and of Ostrogoths in Phrygia and Lydia. The ability of Theodosius is proved more by the results of his energy than by anything that we know of the manner in which he accomplished them. He not only vanquished the Goths, but arrested the progress of the usurper Maximus in the West, who was leading his victorious legions to Italy, flushed with success after the ignominious flight and assassination of Gratian. Theodosius was not in a position, surrounded as he was by half-vanquished barbarians, to dispute the passage of the conqueror; but by assuming a firm tone in negotiations, he secured for Valentinian,

Gratian's brother and successor, the sovereignty of Italy, Africa, and Western Illyricum, surrendering for the present to the usurper the regions north of the Alps.

Theodosius was a Christian; as a Spaniard he was a Trinitarian, and as a soldier he was anxious to establish one uniform type of religious faith and ecclesiastical discipline throughout the Empire. But such a task proved more impracticable than the reduction of military foes. Neither Paganism nor Arianism could be extinguished in a few years by suppressive edicts. Theodosius himself had been baptized in the first year of his reign, A.D. 380, when his life was threatened by a severe illness, and he had then announced his will and pleasure that his own solemn declaration of faith should be accepted by his subjects also. That faith which was "professed by the Pontiff Damasus, and Peter, Bishop of Alexandria" was to be the faith of the Empire. "Let us believe the sole deity of the Father, the Son, and the Holy Ghost, under an equal majesty and a pious Trinity. We authorise the followers of this doctrine to assume the title of Catholic Christians, and as we judge that all others are extravagant madmen, we brand them with the infamous name of heretics."[274] Their places of assembly were not to enjoy the title of churches, and they themselves were to expect severe civil penalties as well as the Divine condemnation. Damophilus, the Arian Bishop of Constantinople, preferred exile to signing the creed of Nice; and Gregory of Nazianzus was conducted by the Emperor in person through the streets of Constantinople (though not without a strong guard) to occupy the episcopal throne. A project for another general council (after the Council of Constantinople, A.D. 381) was entertained but abandoned, for the factious demeanour of the several prelates and their partisans on their arrival did not augur a very successful settlement of differences by that method. The Emperor fell back, for the accomplishment of his object, on his own authority. On July 25, A.D. 383, an edict was posted in Constantinople, prohibiting all the heretics therein named, Arians, Eunomians, Macedonians, and Manichæans, from holding any kind of assembly, public or private, either in the cities or in the country. Any ground or building used for such illegal purpose was to be confiscated to the State; and the penalty of banishment was pronounced against those who allowed themselves to be ordained priests or bishops of the heretical sects. Historians concur in the opinion that few of these penalties were actually enforced. The heretical sects were not animated by a spirit of martyrdom; the intimidation was generally sufficient.[275] The hypocrite or the indifferent conformed, the more conscientious retired into obscurity. There seem to have been few if any Arian prelates of great and commanding ability. All the leading ecclesiastics of the day—Chrysostom, Jerome, Basil, the two Gregories, and Ambrose—were by conviction on the side of the Emperor, and added all the weight of their influence to his decrees.

When measures had been taken for the suppression of heresy, it was the Pagan's turn to suffer. The spectacle of temples standing open for worship side by side with Christian churches was a painful incongruity in the eyes of Theodosius, with his soldier-like ideas of uniformity and discipline. The first blow was directed against those disloyal sons of the Church who had seceded to Paganism. They were deprived of the power to make wills or to receive bequests.[276] The second step was absolutely to prohibit all sacrifices in those temples which were still open. Nearly twenty years before, the sacrifice of animals had been forbidden by Valentinian and Valens, owing to their connection with arts of divination, which were used for political purposes. As long as such sacrifices were permitted, the priests could not refrain from consulting the entrails of the victims, and pretending to read therein future events: the death of this Emperor, the elevation of that, the success or failure of expeditions, and the like, were intimated to the people, always eager to know what is beyond the limits of human knowledge. Such divinations encouraged a restless spirit in the subjects, and often disaffected them towards the ruling power. That these laws of Valentinian were renewed by Theodosius in 381, and again in A.D. 385, proves that they had been imperfectly obeyed.[277]

They were followed up by a yet more decisive step in A.D. 392. Cynegius, the Prætorian Prefect of the East, the Counts Jovinus and Gaudentius in the West, were commissioned to shut up the temples, to destroy their contents, images, and vessels, and to confiscate their property. In many instances the executors of the edict, aided by the fanatical fury of monks, seem to have exceeded their instructions. The great temple of Jupiter, at Apamea, in Syria, of which the roof was supported on sixty massive columns, fell, but not unavenged; for the Bishop Marcellus, who headed the assailants, fell a victim to the rage of the exasperated rustics who defended it.[278] The safety of the universe was represented by Pagans to depend on the preservation of the colossal gold and silver image of Serapis at Alexandria. Even Christians beheld with some trepidation an audacious soldier deal a blow with a battle-axe on the cheek of this awful deity; but as the only result of the gash was the issue of a swarm of rats who had harboured in the sacred head, instead of the avenging thunders which had been expected, a revulsion of feeling was experienced. The huge idol was hewn to pieces, the limbs were dragged through the streets, and the remains of the carcase burned in the amphitheatre, amidst the derision of the populace.

These were shattering blows to Paganism. But the religion of sentiment and custom long survives the extinction of more solid if not reasonable convictions. Chrysostom's homily on New Year's Day is only one among many illustrations of the way in which Pagan rites and superstitions lingered, especially in connection with public festivals. All the Pagan concomitants of these festivals in the country districts—hymns, libations, garlands, incense, lights—were strictly prohibited, under heavy penalties, by Theodosius in A.D. 392, but, in the West especially, the extirpation was very incomplete. The Bishops of Verona and of Brescia protested, but in vain, against the proprietors of land indulging their tenantry in these practices. Sicily, Corsica, and Sardinia, were strongholds of Paganism as late as A.D. 600. Sacrifices were offered to Apollo on Monte Casino till the establishment of St. Benedict's monastery in A.D. 529.

The riotous populace of towns, and the simple country folk attached to old customs, thus evinced some spirit in their resistance to repressive enactments. But the hold which Paganism retained upon intellectual people was feeble indeed. Two apologists only, with any pretensions to ability, stepped forward to plead for the sinking cause: Symmachus[279] in the West, and Libanius in the East; and their intercessions are addressed to sentiments of affection for antiquity, and compassion for oppressed weakness, rather than to the reason. Symmachus, as is well known, pleaded twice for the retention of the altar and statue of Victory in the senate-house at Rome. Eloquent and touching, his appeal is directed to patriotic feeling and a sense of political expediency, not to religious conviction. He does not profess to *believe* in the Pagan deities, but regards with a philosophic eye the various kinds of faith in the world as so many forms of homage to the great unknown Being who presides over the universe. "It is right to recognise that what all adore can be at bottom but one Being only. We contemplate the same stars; the same sky covers us; the same universe encloses us. What matters it by what reasonings each seeks the truth? a single path cannot conduct us to the grand secret of nature. As an individual, a man may be a worshipper of Mithras, or of Christ, but as a citizen it is his duty to conform to that worship which is bound up with the history and glory of his country; to part from it is heartless and disloyal."[280]

The memorial of Symmachus got into the hands of Ambrose, and was rather rudely treated by him. He subjects it to a stern test of facts. Had the national gods indeed protected the Romans from disaster? It was maintained that by their aid the conquest of Italy by Hannibal had been averted. Why then did they permit the invader to inflict such ravages as he had done? Would not the Gauls also have captured the Capitol, but for the timely cry of the goose? Where was Jupiter *then?* but perhaps he was speaking through the goose. The Carthaginians worshipped some of the same deities as the Romans. If then the gods conquered with the Romans they yielded with the Carthaginians. Paganism declined, notwithstanding support; the Church flourished, in spite of opposition. As to the abandonment of ancient customs, was not progress the law of improvement? The glimmering dawn gradually brightened into the full and perfect day; the riches of harvest and vintage came in the maturity of the year; even so the faith of Christ had gradually planted itself on the ruins of a worn-out creed, and was now reaping an abundant harvest among all nations of the earth.[281] The whole reply of Ambrose is pitched in the positive, confident, authoritative tone of one who speaks from a conviction that he stands on the platform of absolute truth, and that his cause is therefore inevitably destined to win.

If the appeal of Symmachus was addressed to the sentiment of reverence for *national* antiquity, that of Libanius was directed to a sentiment of attachment to *classical* antiquity. The citizen mourns over the suppression of a worship which was bound up with the history and the glory of his country; the scholar sighs over the degradation of that which was connected with all that was most beautiful in the literature and life of the olden time—with the poetry of Homer and the tragedians—with the festive song and dance—with the hills, and fountains, and groves of Greece. He clings to the past with the love of the antiquarian. Though his actual belief in the myths of the classical era may not have been very deep or earnest, there is no doubt that he entertained a genuine animosity towards the new faith which was usurping their place. A flowery description of the origin and antiquity of the honour paid to the gods is followed by a vehement invective against the monks, "those black-robed creatures, more voracious than elephants, who rush upon the temples, armed with stones, wood, and fire; who break up the roofs, destroy the walls, throw down the statues, raze the altars." They glaringly exceeded the edicts of the Emperor, which had forbidden the offering of sacrifice in the temples, but had not commanded the actual destruction of the buildings.[282] There is real feeling also in his description of the distress caused in country districts by the demolition of the temples. "They were the centres round which human habitations and civilisation grew; in them the labourer placed all his hopes; to them he commended his wife, his children, his plantation, his crops. Deprived of the gods, from whom he expected the rewards of toil, he felt as if henceforth his labours would be vain. Sometimes the very land was wrested from them on the pretext that it had been consecrated to gods; if the poor despoiled owners sought redress from the pastor (*i.e.* the bishop) of the neighbouring town (falsely called pastor, since there was no gentleness in his nature), he praised the robber and dismissed the complainers." No doubt to a great extent this was a true picture, and such harshness and injustice must have retarded (as always happens when an attempt is made to coerce opinion) the cause of Christianity, which the law was intended to promote.

Theodosius, however, was in principle far too upright to treat the Church with a blind partiality. Cynegius, the Prefect, was ordered to enforce the law at Alexandria with full rigour against those despicable beings who sought to make traffic by informing against Pagans. Constantine had exempted the clergy from serving in curial offices; Theodosius compelled them to pay for substitutes, and renounce their claims to patrimony. They were to enjoy immunity from torture when brought to trial, but if detected in falsehood were to be visited with penalties of peculiar severity, because they had abused the shelter of the law which favoured them.[283]

Such was Theodosius—a prudent and skilful general, a firm and upright ruler; a sincere and simple-minded believer in Christianity, who did his best, as head at once of the army, the civil government, and the Church, to consolidate the fabric of the Empire. The barbarians were repelled, or held down; taxes were collected with honesty and firmness,—some of the most burdensome were taken off; Paganism and heresy languished, however far from being extinguished, and the Emperor fondly hoped that uniformity in faith and discipline would soon be established throughout Christendom.

The good genius of his life was the Empress Flacilla; she was a Christian of a pure and noble type; imperial state had not corrupted the simplicity or hardened the tenderness of her disposition. She was accustomed to visit the hospitals in Constantinople, not attended by a single slave or waiting-woman; administered food and medicine to the patients, and dressed their wounds with her own hands. She was wont to remind her husband of the great change in their worldly position, as a motive to humility and gratitude to God. "It behoves thee to consider what thou wert and what thou hast become; by constantly reflecting on this thou wilt not be ungrateful to thy benefactor, but wilt guide the kingdom which thou hast received with a due regard to law, and by so doing wilt pay homage to Him who gave it thee."

She, we may well believe, restrained the impulses of that choleric temper which was the principal defect in the Emperor's character, and which occasionally after her death burst forth into acts of deplorable violence. This wise and pious monitress was taken from him in A.D. 385. She died at a watering-place in Thrace, whither she had gone to recover her health after the shock caused by the death of the infant Princess Pulcheria. Her body was brought back to Constantinople on a melancholy day in autumn, when the skies poured down a gentle rain, as if mingling their tears with those of the disconsolate people.[284]

This condensed survey of the character and work of Theodosius, during the first ten years of his reign, will assist us in forming a proper estimate of his conduct in that memorable occurrence which brings his life into contact with the life of Chrysostom.

CHAPTER 11

THE SEDITION AT ANTIOCH—THE HOMILIES ON THE STATUES—THE RESULTS OF THE SEDITION. A.D. 387.

THE WISE COUNSEL AND softening influence of the Empress were removed from her husband at an inopportune season. Political storms were approaching, and the passionate temper of Theodosius was soon to be subjected to a most severe trial.

The year 388 would have completed the first decade of his reign. The year 387 was the fifth of the reign of his son Arcadius, whom he had nominally associated with himself in the government. The celebration of these two events Theodosius, from motives of prudent economy and convenience, resolved to combine. The army on such occasions claimed a liberal donative, five gold pieces to each man. It was obviously desirable, therefore, to avoid, if possible, the repetition of such a donative within a short space of time. It was always a strain on the royal treasury, and at the present juncture the strain was increased, for the Goths were assuming a menacing attitude on the Danubian frontier. It was necessary to mass troops in that direction, and, with a view to provide for these expenses, it was proposed to raise a special subsidy from the opulent cities of the Eastern empire. But the inhabitants of Alexandria and Antioch were loath to part with any of the wealth which they had accumulated during nearly ten years of peace and exemption from onerous taxation. Large meetings were held by the citizens of Alexandria in the theatres and other public places; inflammatory and seditious speeches were made. "If we are to be treated thus," they cried, "a simple remedy is open: we will appeal to Maximus in the West; he knows how to shake off a troublesome tyrant."

Fortunately the Prefect Cynegius was a man of firmness and promptitude; he made some arrests of the most conspicuous leaders of the mutinous faction, and enforced an immediate payment of the tribute, and by these decisive measures public order was restored. Either the people of Antioch were more deeply disaffected, or no such energetic officer was in that city to nip the spirit of rebellion in the bud. It is said that the inhabitants entertained a grudge against the Emperor, because he had never visited their city, which had been frequently graced by the royal presence of his predecessors.[285]

The edict which enjoined the levying of the tribute was proclaimed by a herald on February 26. Large numbers of the people assembled on the spot, collected chiefly into groups, amongst which were some persons of distinction, senators and other civic functionaries, noble ladies, and retired soldiers. An ominous silence succeeded the announcement of the edict. The crowd then dispersed, but reassembled about the prætorium, where the governor resided.[286] There they stood in gloomy silence, save that the women, from time to time, raised a wailing lamentation, crying that the ruin of the city was determined, and that since the Emperor had abandoned them, God alone from henceforth could come to their succour. At last a little band detached itself from the mass, shouting that they must go and seek the Bishop Flavian, and constrain him to intercede with the Emperor on their behalf. Flavian, by accident or design, was absent from the episcopal residence, and the mob returned to the prætorium, crying that the governor must do them justice. The people appear to have been excited to violence chiefly by those turbulent foreign adventurers who abounded in Antioch, sordid venal creatures, often hired by actors to get up applause in the theatres, or by great men not over popular to raise cheers when they appeared in public places. But however stimulated, the passions of the mob were thoroughly roused, and their fury vented itself in a tumultuous rush into one of the great public baths, where they soon tore everything to pieces. Having completed this work of destruction, they hurried back once more to the hall of the unfortunate governor. Here they were kept at bay by a guard for a sufficient time to enable the governor to escape by a back-door, and when they at last succeeded in bursting in, the vacancy of the place aggravated their rage. The governor was not seated in the judicial chair, but they found themselves face to face with the statues of the imperial family, which as emblems of authority were ranged above it. They paused for a few moments; highly excited as they were, imperial majesty, even so represented, had some deterrent influence upon their fury.

But, unfortunately, there were boys in the crowd; the love of stone-throwing without respect of persons was as ardent in boy nature fifteen hundred years ago as it is now. A stone was cast by one of these juvenile hands, which hit one of the sacred statues. The momentary feelings of reverence which had arrested the people were dissipated. The images were mutilated, almost battered to pieces, and the fragments dragged through the streets. Other images of the imperial family with which the city was adorned were treated in the same manner; the equestrian statue of Count Theodosius, father of the Emperor, was dislodged from its pedestal and hacked about, amidst derisive shouts of "Defend thyself, grand cavalier!"[287]

The unrestrained fury of the people was inflamed by success; they began to bring up torches and actually set fire to one of the principal buildings of the city, when the governor, who had escaped their hands, returned at the head of a company of archers. As usual with disorderly mobs, however furious, they were unable to face the discipline of military force; the soldiers were no sooner drawn up and preparing to fix their weapons than rage turned to panic, and the mob, lately so formidable, melted away.

The whole tumult had not lasted more than three hours; before noon, every one had returned to his home, the streets and squares were empty, and a death-like stillness pervaded the city. Remorse was mingled with great terror respecting the consequences of the outrage which had been perpetrated. The Emperor, indeed, was humane and forgiving of wrongs which concerned himself alone, but how would he brook the insults done to the memory of his father and his tenderly beloved Empress? One hope remained: Flavian, the bishop, was a favourite at court; his intercessions might avail; the people besought him with tears to stand their friend in this distress. From Antioch to Constantinople was a long and perilous journey of 800 miles, and the winter was not yet ended. Flavian was old, his only sister was seriously ill, and the approaching season of Lent required his presence at Antioch, but a sense of the emergency prevailed over all these obstacles. Animated by the spirit of the Good Shepherd the intrepid old man was ready to lay down his life for his flock, and set out upon his errand of mercy with all possible speed, in the hope of overtaking the messengers who had started before him, but had been detained at the foot of Mount Taurus by a fall of snow.[288]

During the absence of Flavian all the powers of Chrysostom as an orator, a pastor, and a citizen, were called forth in attempting to calm the fears and revive the deeply-dejected spirits of the people. Perseveringly did he discharge this anxious and laborious task; almost every day, for twenty-two days, that small figure was to be seen either sitting in the Ambo, from which he sometimes preached on account of his diminutive stature, or standing on the steps of the altar, the preacher's usual place;[289] and day after day, the crowds increased which came to listen to the stream of golden eloquence which he poured forth. With all the versatility of a consummate artist, he moved from point to point. Sometimes a picture of the city's agony melted his hearers to tears, and then again he struck the note of encouragement and revived their spirits by bidding them take comfort from the well-known clemency of the Emperor, the probable success of the mission of Flavian, and, above all, from trust in God.

"The gay and noisy city, where once the busy people hummed like bees around their hive, was petrified by fear into the most dismal silence and desolation; the wealthier inhabitants had fled into the country, those who remained shut themselves up in their houses, as if the town had been in a state of siege. If any one ventured into the market-place, where once the multitude poured along like the stream of a mighty river, the pitiable sight of two or three cowering dejected creatures in the midst of solitude soon drove him home again. The sun itself seemed to veil its rays as if in mourning. The words of the prophet were fulfilled, 'Their sun shall go down at noon, and their earth shall be darkened in a clear day' (Amos viii. 9). Now they might cry, 'Send to the mourning women, and let them come, and send for cunning women that they may come' (Jer. ix. 17). Ye hills and mountains, take up a wailing, let us invite all creation to commiserate our woes, for this great city, this capital of Eastern cities, is in danger of being destroyed out of the midst of the earth, and there is no man to help her, for the Emperor, who has no equal among men, has been insulted; therefore let us take refuge with the King who is above, and summon Him to our aid."[290]

The chief reason of the people's extreme dejection was, that the governor and magistrates, probably to disarm any suspicion at court of their own complicity in the sedition, were daily seizing real or supposed culprits, and punishing them with the utmost rigour. Even those who might have been pardoned on account of their tender age were mercilessly handed over to the executioner. Chrysostom speaks of some even having been burnt, and others thrown to wild beasts. The weeping parents followed their unhappy offspring at a distance, powerless to help but fearing to plead, like men on shore beholding with grief shipwrecked sailors struggling in the water, but unable to rescue them.[291]

But the object of Chrysostom was, not to utter ineffectual lamentations. He aimed at rousing the people from their profound dejection, and printing, if possible, on their hearts, humbled and softened by distress, deep and lasting impressions of good. He told them that there was everything to be hoped for from the embassy of Flavian. "The Emperor was pious, the bishop courageous, yet prudent and adroit; God would not suffer his errand to be fruitless. The very sight of that venerable man would dispose the royal mind to clemency. Flavian would not fail to urge how especially suitable an act of forgiveness was to that holy season, in which was commemorated the Death of Christ for the sins of the whole world. He would remind the Emperor of the parable of the two debtors, and warn him not to incur the risk of being one day addressed by the words, 'Thou wicked servant, I forgave thee all that debt; shouldest not thou also have had compassion on thy fellow-servants?' He would represent that the outrages had not been committed by the whole community, but chiefly by some lawless strangers. He would plead that the inhabitants, even had they all offended, had already undergone sufficient punishment in the anxiety and alarm which they endured. It would be unreasonable to visit the crime of a few by the extirpation of a whole city, a city which was the most populous capital of the East, and dear to Christians as the place where they had first received that sweet and lovely name."[292]

Meanwhile he earnestly calls upon the people to improve this season of humiliation by a thorough repentance and reformation in respect of the prevailing vices and follies. The words of St. Paul in writing to the Philippians, "To write the same things to you, to me indeed is not grievous, and for you it is safe," might be aptly applied to Chrysostom. He is never tired of denouncing special sins and exhorting to the renunciation of them in every variety of language. Ostentatious luxury, sordid avarice, religious formalism, a profane custom of taking rash oaths, were the fashionable sins against which he waged an incessant and implacable warfare.

His exhortations are generally based on some passage read in the lesson of the day. "What have we heard today? 'Charge them that are rich in this world, that they be not high-minded.' He who says 'the rich in this world' proves thereby that there are others rich in regard to a future world, like Lazarus in the parable." Wealth of this world was a thankless runaway slave, which, if bound with thousands of fetters, made off, fetters and all. Not that he would quarrel with wealth; it was good in itself, but became evil when inordinately desired and paraded, just as the evil of intoxication lay not in wine itself, but in the abuse of it. The Apostle did not charge those who were rich to become poor, but only not to be high-minded. "Let us adorn our own souls before we embellish our houses. Is it not disgraceful to overlay our walls with marbles and to neglect Christ, who is going about unclothed? What profit is there, O man, in thy house? Wilt thou carry it away with thee? Nay, thou must leave thy *house*; but thy *soul* thou wilt certainly take with thee. Lo! how great the danger which has now overtaken us: let our houses, then, be our defenders; let them rescue us from the impending peril;—but they will not be able. Be those witnesses to my words who have now deserted their houses, and hurried away to the wilderness as if afraid of nets and snares. Do you wish to build large and splendid houses? I forbid you not, only build them not upon the earth; build yourselves tabernacles in heaven—tabernacles which never decay. Nothing is more slippery than wealth, which to-day is with thee and to-morrow is against thee; which sharpens the eyes of the envious on all sides; which is a foe in your own camp, an enemy in your own household. Wealth makes the present danger more intolerable; you see the poor man unencumbered and prepared for whatever may happen, but the rich in a state of great embarrassment, and going about seeking some place in which to bury his gold, or some person with whom to deposit it. Why seek thy fellow-servants, O man? Christ stands ready to receive and guard thy deposits—yea, not only to guard, but also to multiply and to return with rich interest. No man plucks out of His hand; men, when they receive a deposit from another, deem that they have conferred a favour upon him; but Christ, on the contrary, declares that He receives a favour, and, instead of demanding a reward, bestows one upon you."[293]

He entreated them to make the present Lent a season of spiritual renovation. Lent fell in the spring, when the stream of industry which the winter had frozen began to flow again. The sailor launched his vessel, the soldier furbished his sword, the farmer whetted his scythe, the traveller set out confidently on his long journey, the athlete stripped for the contest. "Even so let this fast be to us a spiritual spring-tide; let us polish our spiritual armour, let us breast the waves of evil passions, set out like travellers on our journey heavenwards, and prepare like athletes for the combat. For the Christian is both husbandman, and pilot, and soldier, and athlete, and traveller. Hast thou seen the athlete? hast thou seen the soldier? if thou art an athlete thou must strip to enter the lists; if thou art a soldier thou must put on armour before taking thy place in the ranks. How then to the same man can both these things be possible? How, dost thou ask? I will tell thee. Strip thyself of thy worldly business, and thou hast become an athlete; clothe thyself with spiritual armour, and thou hast become a soldier. Strip thyself, for it is a season of wrestling; clothe thyself, for we are engaged in a fierce warfare with devils. Till thy soul, and cut away the thorns; sow the seed of piety, plant the good plants of philosophy, and tend them with much care, and thou hast become a husbandman, and St. Paul will say to thee, 'The husbandman which laboureth must first be a partaker of the fruits.' Whet thy sickle which thou hast blunted by surfeiting; sharpen it, I say, by fasting. Enter on the road which leads to heaven, the rugged and narrow road, and travel along it. And how shalt thou be able to set out and travel? By buffeting thy body and bringing it into subjection; for where the road is narrow, obesity, which comes from surfeiting, is a great impediment. Repress the waves of foolish passions, repulse the storm of wicked imaginations, preserve the vessel, display all thy skill, and thou hast become a pilot."[294] The originator and instructor of all these arts was abstinence; not the vulgar kind of abstinence, not abstinence from food only, but also from sins. "If thou fastest, show me the results by thy deeds. What deeds, do you ask? If you see a poor man, have pity on him; if an enemy, be reconciled; if a friend in good reputation, regard him without envy. Fast not only by thy mouth, but with thine eyes, thine ears, thy hands, thy feet; avert thine eyes from unlawful sights, restrain thy hands from deeds of violence, keep thy feet from entering places of pernicious amusement, bridle thy mouth from uttering, and stop thine ears from listening to tales of slander." This kind of fast would be acceptable to God, only it should be co-extensive with life. To spend a few days in penance and then to relapse into the former course of life was only an idle mockery.[295] He disparaged that rigorous kind of fasting which some had carried to the extent of taking no food but bread and water. Many boasted of the number of weeks they had fasted; this excessive abstinence was likely to be followed by a reaction. Let them seek rather to subdue evil passions and habits; let one week be devoted to the suppression of swearing, another of anger, a third of slander, and so gradually advancing they might at last attain the consummation of virtue, and propitiate the displeasure of God.[296] "Let us not do now what we have so often done, for frequently when earthquakes, or famine, or drought have overtaken us, we have become temperate for three or four days, and then have returned to our former ways of life. But, if never before, now at least let us remain steadfast in the same state of piety, that we may not again require to be chastised by another scourge."[297]

Almost all the homilies are concluded by an admonition against the sin of swearing, and the greater portion of some is devoted to this topic. The passionate impetuous people of Antioch seem to have been constantly betrayed into the folly of binding themselves by rash oaths. The master, for instance, would take an oath to deprive his slave of food, or the tutor his scholar, till a certain task was accomplished, a threat which it was of course often impossible to enforce. Hence perjury on the part of a superior, and loss of respect on the side of the subordinate. Chrysostom himself had often dined at a house where the mistress swore that she would beat a slave who had made some mistake, while the husband would with another oath forbid the punishment. Thus one of the two would be inevitably involved in perjury.[298] He frequently exhorted his hearers to form a kind of Christian club amongst themselves for the suppression of this vice. In one place he suggests a stern remedy: "When you detect your wife or any of your household yielding to this evil habit, order them supperless to bed, and if you are guilty impose the same penalty on yourself."[299] Near the close of Lent he declares that he will repel from the holy Table at Easter those whom he detects still addicted to this vice.[300]

On the whole, the eager and earnest pastor may be said to have rejoiced at the grand opportunity afforded by the humiliation of the city, to effect a reformation in the moral life of the people. He observed with great satisfaction, that if the forum was deserted the church was thronged, just as in stormy weather the harbour is crowded with vessels.[301] Many an intemperate man had been sobered, the headstrong softened, or the indolent quickened into zeal. Many who once assiduously frequented the theatre now spent their day in the church. Meanwhile they must abide God's pleasure for the removal of their affliction. He had sent it for the purpose of purifying and chastening them; He was waiting till He saw a genuine, an unshakeable repentance, like a refiner watching a piece of precious metal in a crucible, and waiting the proper moment for taking it out.[302] As for those who said what they feared was not so much death, as *ignominious* death by the hand of the executioner, he protested that the only death really miserable was a death in sin. Abel was murdered and was happy, Cain lived and was miserable. John the Baptist was beheaded, St. Stephen was stoned, yet their deaths were happy. To the Christian there was nothing formidable in death itself. To dread death but not to be afraid of sin was to act like children who are frightened by masks whilst they were not afraid of fire. "What, I pray you, is death? It is like the putting off of a garment, for the soul is invested with a body[303] as it were with a garment, and this we shall put off for a little while by death, only to receive it again in a more brilliant form. What, I pray you, is death? It is but to go a journey for a season, or to take a longer sleep than usual." Death was but a release from toil, a tranquil haven. "Mourn not over him who dies, but over him who, living in sin, is dead while he liveth."[304]

Chrysostom's own calmness, and his skill in diverting the thoughts of his flock from present alarm, are manifested by the power and ease with which he dilates on such grand topics as the creation, Divine Providence, the nature of man, and his place in the scale of created beings. His best thoughts, expressed in his best style on these subjects, are to be found in the homilies now under consideration.

The size and beauty of the universe, but still more the perfect regularity with which the system worked, proclaimed a designing power. The succession of day and night, the series of the seasons, like a band of maidens dancing in a circle, the four elements of which the world was composed, mingling in such exquisite proportions that they exactly balanced one another, the sun tempering the action of water, the water that of the sun, the sea unable to break its bounds or reduce the earth to a mass of clay; who could contemplate all these forces at work and suppose that they moved spontaneously, instead of adoring Him who had arranged them all with a wisdom commensurate with the results? As the health of the body depended on the due balance of those humours of which it was composed, if the bile increased fever was produced, or if the phlegmatic element prevailed many diseases were engendered, so was it in the case of the universe: each element observed its proper limits, restrained, as it were, with a bridle by the will of the Maker; and the struggle between these elements was the source of peace for the whole system. As the body failed, languished, died, in proportion as the soul was withdrawn from it, so if the regulating and life-giving power of God's providence were removed from the earth, all would go to rack and ruin, like a vessel deserted by her pilot.[305]

In treating this subject, he manifests a keen appreciation of natural beauties. The infinite varieties of flowers and herbs, trees, animals, insects, and birds—the flowery fields below, the starry fields above—the never-failing fountains—the sea receiving countless streams into its bosom, yet never overflowing,—all proclaimed a Creator and an Upholder, and drew from man the exclamation, "How manifold are Thy works; in wisdom hast Thou made them all!" Yet, lest they should be worshipped instead of the Maker, conditions of change, as decay or death, were imposed upon all.[306] His observation of nature appears in some of his similes. The poor female relatives hovering about the courts of justice, when the culprits of the outrage on the statues were being tried, he compares to parent birds, which wildly flutter round the hunter who has stolen the young from their nest, in an agony of grief, but impotent from weakness and fear.[307] He perceives in some of the lower animals characteristics to be imitated or avoided, and describes them with a kind of humour. The bee especially was a pattern for imitation, not merely because it was industrious, but because it toiled with an unconscious kind of self-sacrifice for the benefit of others as well as itself. It was the most honourable of insects; the spider, on the contrary, was the most ignoble, because it spread its fine web for its own selfish gratification only. The innocence of the dove, the docility of the ox, the light-heartedness of birds, were all examples for imitation. The ferocity, or the cunning of other animals or insects, were examples for avoidance. The good which brutes had by nature man might acquire by force of moral purpose; and the sovereign of the lower animals ought to comprise in his nature all the best qualities of his subjects.[308] The plumage of the peacock, excelling in variety and beauty all possible art of the dyer, evinced the superhuman power of the Maker of all things.[309]

His ethical doctrine bears singular resemblance to that of Butler. God has bestowed on man a faculty of discerning right from wrong; He has impressed upon him a natural law, the law of conscience. Hence some commands are delivered without explanation: for instance, the prohibition to kill, or to commit adultery, because these merely enjoin what is already evident by the light of the natural law. On the other hand, for the command to observe the Sabbath a reason is assigned, because this was a special and temporary enactment. The obligation of the law of conscience was universal and eternal. As soon as Adam had sinned, he hid himself, a clear evidence of his consciousness of guilt, although no written law existed at that time.

The Greeks might attempt to deny the universality of this inherent law, but to what other origin could they ascribe the laws which had been made by their own ancestors concerning respect for life, the marriage bond, covenants, trusts, and the like? They had indeed been handed down from generation to generation; but whence did the first promulgators derive the idea of them, if not from this moral sense? To the law of conscience was added the energy of a moral purpose, προαίρεσις, which enabled man to practise what conscience prescribed: conscience informs man that temperance is right; moral purpose enables him to become temperate. God had also endowed man with some natural virtues: indignation at injustice, compassion for the injured, sympathy with the joys and sorrows of our fellow-men.[310] At the same time Chrysostom fully allows the value of training and teaching as supplementary to and co-operating with all these natural gifts.[311] If conscience grew languid, the admonition of parent and friend, and, in the case of public offences, the law, stepped in, to effect what conscience failed to do; and frequently God sent afflictions for the same remedial purpose.[312]

Thus day after day the indefatigable preacher sounded the note of encouragement, or warning, or instruction. He not only held the Christian flock together, but largely increased its numbers. His eloquence frequently excited rapturous applause, which was invariably repressed with sternness. On one occasion the congregation yielded to a panic; a false rumours was circulated that a body of troops was entering the city, to take vengeance on the inhabitants. The Prefect entered the church to allay the fears of the affrighted people who had fled thither, but Chrysostom was overwhelmed with shame, and sharply upbraided them that a Christian congregation should owe the restoration of calmness to a Pagan, whom they ought to have impressed, like Paul before Agrippa, by a display of Christian firmness and fortitude.[313]

About the middle of Lent, two commissioners, Hellebicus and Cæsarius, arrived at Antioch, invested with full powers to inquire into the late outrage. Their authority was backed by a considerable military force. They were men not only of intelligence and humanity, but Christians in faith; and they had many friends in Antioch. They entered the city, surrounded by a large multitude, who turned weeping faces and held out supplicating hands towards them. The commissioners were moved, and in deep silence entered the lodging provided for them; but it was necessary for them to perform their duty, which was in the first place to announce that Antioch was degraded from the rank of capital of Syria, and its metropolitan honours were transferred to the neighbouring city of Laodicea. Secondly, all the public baths, circuses, theatres, and other places of recreation, were to be closed for an indefinite time. Thirdly, the commissioners were to revise the trials already held by the local governor, and to inflict rigorous sentences upon all the guilty, especially any persons of distinction. These judicial proceedings were to begin on the following day.

The scene at the entrance of the court was a melancholy spectacle; the wives and daughters of the accused hung around it in mean garments sprinkled with ashes, and in attitudes of supplication or despair.

There were no lawyers to plead for the prisoners; they had run away or concealed themselves, to evade the perilous duty. Libanius alone, towards evening, crept timidly into the court. Cæsarius, to whom he was known, observed him, beckoned him to approach, and placed him by his side. In a low voice he bade him take courage; he and his colleague would endeavour as much as possible to spare life. Libanius earnestly thanked him, and promised if he kept his word to immortalise him by an oration in his honour.[314]

An appeal, however, more effectual, was made to the mercy of the commissioners, by persons widely different from Libanius. As they were riding in state to the hall of justice on the second day, they saw amongst the people a group of strange half-wild-looking beings, in rough coarse garments, with long unkempt hair. These were hermits, who had descended from their solitudes in the neighbouring mountains—some who for years had not been seen in the streets of the city, but now appeared to plead on behalf of the offending people. An old man, diminutive in stature, whose clothing was in tatters, started forward from the group as the commissioners passed by, seized the bridle of one, and commanded them in a tone of authority to dismount. "Who is this mad fellow?" inquired the commissioners. They were informed that he was the revered hermit Macedonius, surnamed Crithophagus, or the barley-eater, because barley was his only sustenance. Hellebicus and Cæsarius immediately alighted, and, falling on their knees before him, craved his pardon for having received him so rudely. "My friends," replied the solitary, "go to the Emperor and say, 'You are an emperor, but also a man, and you rule over beings who are of like nature with yourself. Man was created after a Divine image and likeness; do not, then, mercilessly command the image of God to be destroyed, for you will provoke the Maker if you punish his image. For, consider that you are doing this from displeasure at the injury inflicted on a statue of bronze; and how far does a living rational creature exceed the value of such an inanimate object! Let him consider that it is easy to manufacture many statues in the place of those destroyed, but it is wholly impossible for him to make a single hair again of those men who have been put to death.'"[315] The other hermits declared that they were all prepared to shed their blood and lay down their lives for the culprits; that they would not withdraw from the city until they were sent as ambassadors to the Emperor, or until the city itself had been acquitted. The joy of Chrysostom at the courage displayed by these hermits was extreme; their noble conduct compensated for the sad pusillanimity lately exhibited by the congregation in the church. He triumphantly contrasts them with the so-called philosophers of Antioch, who appear to have displayed anything but philosophic calmness in the hour of danger. "Where now are those long-bearded, cloak-wearing, staff-bearing fellows—cynic refuse, more degraded than dogs licking up the crumbs under the table, doing everything for their belly? Why, they have all hurried out of the city and hidden themselves in caves and dens, whilst those who inhabited the caves have entered the city, and boldly walk about the forum as if no calamity had happened. Their conduct illustrates what I have never ceased to maintain, that even the furnace cannot injure one who lives in virtue. Such is the power of philosophy introduced to man by Christ."[316] The result of this singular intercession was, that the commissioners consented to suspend the execution of their sentence on those pronounced guilty, until an appeal had been made to the Emperor. Meanwhile the prisoners were to remain in confinement, and their property to be held by the State.

The hermits were anxious to repair to the court of Theodosius, but the commissioners wisely refused, making the length of the journey an objection, but perhaps really because they feared such excitable zealots might frustrate the object of their embassy by imprudent behaviour. It was finally decided that Hellebicus should remain to preserve order in Antioch, while his colleague went to Constantinople, carrying with him an intercessory letter signed by the hermits, and declaring that they were ready to give their own lives in ransom for the city.

Cæsarius departed amidst the blessings and acclamations of the people.[317]

What had the energetic preacher, who had sustained the spirits of the people so long, been doing, since the arrival of the Emperor's legates? It had been, indeed, a relief to find that the city was not to be surrendered to the sword; but to a proud and luxurious people the loss of metropolitan rank, and the closing of the public baths, theatres, and public places of amusement, were severe blows. Loud and general was the lamentation over their fallen grandeur and their lost enjoyments. Chrysostom expostulated with them on their discontent. The real dignity of a city did not consist in pre-eminence of rank or vastness of population, but in the virtue of its citizens. What constituted the noblest distinction of Antioch?—the fact that the disciples there were the first to be called Christians—that they had sent relief to the distressed brethren in Judæa in the time of the famine (Acts xi. 28, 29)—that they had sent Paul and Barnabas to that Council at Jerusalem which had emancipated the Gentile Christians from Judaic bondage. These were honourable distinctions, which no other city, not even Rome itself, could rival. They enabled Antioch to look the whole Christian world in the face, for they proved how great had been her Christian courage and her Christian love. These were her true metropolitan honours; and, if these were in aught diminished, not by the size or beauty of her buildings, not by her airy colonnades or her spacious porticos and promenades,[318] not by the sacred Grove of Daphne, not by the number and loftiness of her cypresses, not by her fountains or her multitudinous population, or her genial climate,—not by these could she recover her tarnished reputation, but by equity, almsgiving, vigils, prayers, temperance. External size and beauty did not constitute real greatness. David was little of stature, yet he prostrated by a single blow a very tower of flesh. Away with these womanish complaints! "I have heard many in the forum saying, 'Woe to thee, Antioch! what has become of thee? how art thou dishonoured!' and when I heard I laughed at the childish understanding of those who say such things. It behoves you not to speak thus now; but, when you see dancing, and drunkenness, and singing, and blaspheming, and swearing, then utter the cry, 'Woe to thee, O city! what has become of thee?' but when you see only a few equitable, temperate, and moderate men in the forum, then call the city happy."[319]

He remonstrates indignantly with them for their querulous complaints of the prohibition to use the public baths. Bathing, indeed, was a luxury so indispensable to the bodily health and comfort of the people, that they now resorted to the river in large numbers, with very little regard to decency. He reminds those who murmured over this deprivation of their favourite indulgence, that a short time ago, when they were daily expecting an incursion of soldiers, and were flying to the desert and mountains, they would have been too thankful to escape with so cheap a penalty. He urges the duty of reconciliation with enemies as specially incumbent on them when such great efforts were being made to obtain mercy for themselves. They should have one enemy alone, the devil, with whom they should wage an implacable warfare.[320]

Thus the prophet, ever vigilant for the true welfare and honour of his people, ceased not to lift up his voice.

Cæsarius travelled day and night, and in the course of a week accomplished the eight hundred miles which separated Antioch from Constantinople. But his arrival and his errand had been anticipated. Flavian had reached the court a week before, and the pardon of Antioch was already secured. The aged bishop returned to Antioch just in time to celebrate Easter, and to augment the natural joyfulness of the festival by the tidings which he brought. He had, however, been preceded a few days by an express courier, who delivered the imperial rescript to Hellebicus. When the contents were publicly proclaimed, the pent-up feelings of the people burst forth into demonstrations of almost frantic joy. Hellebicus was received with ovation wherever he went. Libanius walked by his side, reciting passages from his orations, in honour of Theodosius and praise of the two commissioners.[321] On Holy Saturday, Flavian himself entered the city, partly attended, partly borne along, by vast crowds of grateful people. On that night the forum was decorated with garlands and illuminated by lanterns. On the next morning, Easter Day, a vast concourse thronged the church, and once more the well-known voice, which had exhorted and encouraged and warned, during the days of their gloom, now poured forth in the sunshine of their joy a pæan of thanksgiving and praise.

"Blessed be God, who hath vouchsafed us to celebrate this holy feast with great joy and gladness, who has restored the Head to the body, the Shepherd to the sheep, the Master to his disciples, the Pontiff to the priests. Blessed be God, who hath done exceeding abundantly above all that we ask or think, for it seemed to us sufficient to be for a time released from the impending calamities; but the merciful God, ever exceeding in His gifts our petitions, has restored to us our father sooner than all our expectation. And not only has our beloved prelate escaped all the perils incident to so long a journey in the winter season, but has found his sister, whom he left on the point of death, still living to welcome his return."[322]

He then proceeds to describe the interview of Flavian with Theodosius, as it had been related to him by an eye-witness. The bishop, when introduced into the royal presence, stood at a distance, silently weeping, bending low, and covering his face, as if he himself had been the author of all the late offences. By this attitude he hoped to expel emotions of anger, and introduce the emotion of pity into the Emperor's breast, before he undertook the actual defence of the city.

Theodosius was moved; he advanced to the bishop, and used no harsh or indignant language, but only mildly reproached with ingratitude a city which he had always treated with lenity, and had long desired and intended to visit. Even had the people been able to accuse him of any injury done to them, they might at least have respected the dead, who could do them no harm (alluding to the destruction of his wife's and father's images).

The aged prelate no longer remained silent. With a fresh flood of tears, he poured forth his pathetic appeal to the Christian clemency and forbearance of the Emperor. "He would not attempt to extenuate the offence, the sense of their ingratitude caused them the deepest distress, and they frankly confessed that it deserved the severest chastisement which could be inflicted. Yet the noblest kind of revenge which he could take was freely to forgive the insult; thereby he would defeat the malice of those demons who had tried to work the ruin of the people by seducing them from their allegiance. In like manner, the devil had tried to compass the death of the human race, but his malevolence had been frustrated by God, who offered even heaven to those who had been excluded from paradise. A free pardon would secure for him a station in the hearts of all his subjects, far more enduring than those statues which had been broken down. He reminded him, how once his great predecessor, Constantine, when urged to revenge some insult done to one of his statues, passed his hand over his face, and observed, with a quiet smile, that he did not feel the blow;—a saying which had endeared him to his people more than his military exploits. But why need he refer to Constantine? Theodosius himself, on a previous Easter, had commanded a general release of prisoners, and had nobly exclaimed, 'Would that it were possible also for me to recall the dead to life!'[323] Now he might in some sort realise that wish, by restoring to life a whole city, which lay, as it were, dead under remorse and fear. Such an act of clemency would both strengthen his own throne and the cause of Christianity. Greeks, Jews, and barbarians were waiting to hear his decision. If it was on the side of mercy, all would applaud it, saying, 'Heavens! how mighty is the power of Christianity, which has restrained the wrath of a monarch who has not his peer in the world.' How noble a tale for posterity to hear, that what the governor and magistrates of a great city dared not ask, had been granted to the prayer of an old man, because he was the priest of God, and from reverence to the Divine laws. He would solemnly remind him of the words, 'If ye forgive not men their trespasses, neither will your Father which is in heaven forgive you your trespasses.' He begged him to remember that there was a day coming in which all men would render an account of their actions, and to imitate the example of God, who, though daily sustaining insults from man, did not cease to bestow blessings upon him. He concluded by declaring that he would never return to Antioch unless he could take back the imperial pardon, but would enrol himself in another city."[324]

If Flavian's intercession was thrown into the form of an oration at all, it is clear that Chrysostom's version of it, which has been here greatly condensed from the original, must be his own, rather than the speech actually delivered. If it had been only half as long, it could not have been accurately related to him from memory, or faithfully rehearsed by him afterwards. The excitement of addressing so large an audience, on so great an occasion, would naturally stimulate him to amplify and embellish.

There is, however, no reason to doubt that Chrysostom has furnished us with an accurate description of Flavian's conduct in the interview, and given us the main substance of his arguments. The whole narrative of the occurrence illustrates the difference between the Eastern and Western character. Compare the demeanour of Ambrose and of Flavian. The first speaks in a tone of majestic authority, which brooks no disputing; the other, though far from deficient in courage, approaches the Emperor with that deferential and submissive manner which the Oriental is accustomed to adopt in the presence of a potentate. His tone is that of an appeal, though based upon the highest grounds; not of a command. There is something of the courtier in Flavian; in Ambrose there is more of the pope.

To conclude Chrysostom's account: the Emperor was deeply affected, though, like Joseph, he refrained himself in the presence of spectators. He declared his intention of granting a free pardon, in language eminently Christian. "If the Lord of the earth, who became a servant for our sakes, and was crucified by those whom He came to benefit, prayed for the pardon of his crucifiers, what wonder was it that a man should forgive his fellow-servants?" He begged Flavian to return with all expedition, that he might release the people from the agony of their suspense. The bishop entreated that the young prince Arcadius might accompany him as a pledge of imperial favour to the city. But Theodosius said that he designed to confer on Antioch a greater honour. He requested the bishop to offer up prayers for the termination of the present war, that he might ratify his pardon by a visit to the city in person. The express courier was then despatched, while Flavian followed at a pace more suitable to his dignity and advanced age.

Chrysostom concludes his discourse by a moral exhortation suggested by those festive demonstrations of joy already described. "Let the lanterns and the chaplets be to them emblems of spiritual things. Let them not cease to be crowned with virtue or to light up a lamp in their soul by the diligent practice of good works; let them rejoice with holy joy, and thank God not only for rescuing them from destruction, but for sending them so wholesome a chastisement, the salutary effects of which would, he trusted, extend to many generations."[325]

Thus terminated the celebrated sedition of Antioch. It is a singular and instructive picture of the times: the impulsive character of the people in the great Eastern cities of the Empire, alternating between frantic rage and abject despondency; the expectation of violent imperial vengeance, nothing less than the extermination of the city; the remarkable veneration paid to monks,—these are points which stand out in vivid colours. But still more remarkably does this event supply an example of the softening, humanising influence of Christianity, in a fierce and heartless age. The issue reflects the greatest honour on those who brought it to pass; and they were *all Christians*: the intrepid old bishop, sacrificing comfort and risking life to intercede, the generous Emperor who yielded to the persuasion of his Christian arguments; the humane commissioners; and last, but not least, the pastor and preacher, who with unwearied patience, invincible courage, unfailing eloquence, sustained the fainting spirits of his flock, and endeavoured to convert their calamity into an occasion of lasting good.

One great and happy result of the recent trouble was a large accession of Pagans to the ranks of the Church. When the city lay under ban, the baths, theatres, and circus were closed, and the panic-stricken people had no heart to pursue their ordinary business. But one place had been constantly open. All knew that in the church prayer was being offered up day by day; and to the first portion of the service, up to the end of the sermon, there was free admission for all without respect of creed. Curiosity alone, if not any deeper feeling, would lead many Pagans to turn into the church, to hear what consolations, what encouragements, the Christian preacher had to offer in this season of general distress and painful suspense. And what had they heard? They had heard an unsparing exposure and denunciation of the follies and vices which prevailed in that great and dissolute city, a trumpet-call to repentance and reformation; they had heard the fleeting nature of earthly honour and earthly riches, their impotence to satisfy the heart or to save the life in the time of danger and distress vividly contrasted with the Christian's aim of laying up incorruptible treasure in an imperishable world; they had heard of the Christian's faith that righteousness was the only permanent good, as sin was the only real evil, that to a good man death was only the transition to a more blessed life, and that affliction was useful in purifying and elevating the soul. They had heard the proofs of a Creator, and of His providential care for the things which he had made as evinced by the majesty, beauty, and organisation of the universe, by the conscience and moral faculties of man, as well as by the more direct testimony of the written word.[326] There is no evidence as to the number of converts reclaimed from Paganism. Chrysostom only informs us[327] that he was occupied for some time after the return of Flavian with confirming in the faith those who "in consequence of the calamity had come to better mind and deserted from the side of Gentile error."

The sermons themselves are lost.

CHAPTER 12

ILLNESS OF CHRYSOSTOM—HOMILIES ON FESTIVALS OF SAINTS AND MARTYRS—CHARACTER OF THESE FESTIVALS—PILGRIMAGES—RELIQUES—CHARACTER OF PEASANT CLERGY IN NEIGHBOURHOOD OF ANTIOCH. A.D. 387.

VERY PROBABLY THE PHYSICAL labour and mental strain which Chrysostom had undergone during the events recorded in the previous chapter may have brought on the illness to which he alludes in the homily preached on the Sunday before Ascension Day.[328] He was prevented by this attack from taking part in the services which were held some time after Easter under the conduct of Bishop Flavian at the chapels built over the remains of martyrs and saints.[329] A variety of homilies delivered by Chrysostom at such "martyries" on other occasions are extant, and it may be as well to introduce here such indications as can be collected from them of the general feeling of the Church, as well as of himself, with regard to saints, and such kindred subjects as pilgrimages and reliques.

Churches had in most instances been erected to commemorate the death of a martyr, or to mark the spot where he died. Tertullian's saying that "the blood of martyrs was the seed of the Church" thus became verified in a literal, material sense. Socrates (iv. 23) even speaks of the churches of St. Paul and St. Peter at Rome as their "martyries," as Eusebius[330] also calls the church which Constantine built on Golgotha the "martyry" of our Saviour. By the age of Chrysostom the festivals of martyrs and saints had grown so numerous that frequently more than one occurred in the same week.[331] Good Friday and Ascension Day, and the Sunday after Whitsun Day (not observed as Trinity Sunday till much later), were especially dedicated to the commemoration of saints.[332] The congregation kept a vigil the night before, or very early before dawn on the Saints' day itself. The vigil consisted of psalms, hymns, and prayers, and was followed early in the day by a full service, when, in addition to the ordinary lessons of the day, the acts or passions of the saint or martyr were read. St. Augustine permitted his people to sit during the reading of them because they were often of great length. Pope Gelasius forbade them to be read because they were so seldom authentic.[333] The martyries were generally outside the city walls, not always built over the grave of the saint, but close to it; in which case the congregation assembled at the grave first, and walked in procession from it to the church, singing hymns as they went. There can be no doubt that Chrysostom believed in the intercessory power of departed saints, and encouraged the invocation of their intercession. They were nearer to the Divine ear, and by virtue of their glorious deaths had justly obtained more confidence in making their requests to God than had the inhabitants of earth. He implores Christians not to resort for medical assistance to Jews, who were the enemies of Christ, but to seek aid from His friends the saints and martyrs, who had much confidence in addressing God.[334] At the close of his homily on the festival of two soldiers who had been beheaded by Julian for obstinate adherence to Christianity, he says: "Let us constantly visit them, touch their shrine, and with faith embrace their reliques, that we may derive some blessing therefrom; for like soldiers who converse freely with their sovereign when they display their wounds, so these, bearing their heads in their hands, are easily able to effect what they desire at the court of the King of Heaven."[335] So, again, in the homily on Bernice and Prosdoke: "Let us fall down before their reliques ... let us embrace their shrines: not only on their festival, but at other times, let us resort to them and invoke them to become our protectors; for they can use much boldness of speech when dead, more, indeed, than when they were alive, for now they bear in their bodies the marks of Jesus Christ ... let us therefore procure for ourselves, through them, favour from God."[336] Thus the saint is to be appealed to as a kind of friend at court, who will present petitions, and use his influence to obtain a favourable answer from the Monarch; but the further step of invoking saints as the *direct* dispensers of spiritual and other benefits had not yet been taken. The feeling of the Church of Smyrna towards their beloved martyr and bishop Polycarp, as expressed in A.D. 160 to the Church of Philomelium, still represented the general state of feeling in the Church.[337] The Jews and other malignants had suggested, when the remains of Polycarp had been earnestly asked for, that the Christians intended to worship him; and "this they said, being ignorant that we should never be able to desert Christ, or worship any other Being. For Him, being the Son of God, we adore, but the martyrs, as the disciples and imitators of the Lord, we love with a deserved affection; desiring to become partners and fellow-disciples with them." The language of St. Augustine and St. Chrysostom thoroughly corresponds to that in the passage just cited. "Our religion," says Augustine, "consists not in the worship of dead men; because if they lived piously they are not considered likely to desire that kind of honour; but would wish Him to be worshipped by us through whose illumination they rejoice to have us partners with them in their merit. They are therefore to be honoured for the sake of imitation, not to be worshipped as a religious act."[338] And in another place: "Christian people celebrate the memory of martyrs with religious solemnity, to stimulate imitation, to become partners in their merits, and to be assisted by their prayers; but in doing this we never offer sacrifice to a martyr, but only to Him who is the God of martyrs."[339] A multitude of passages might be cited from Chrysostom's homilies on Saints' Festivals, in which he passionately exhorts to the imitation and emulation of their noble lives and glorious deaths, and dwells on the great advantages to the Church arising from these solemn commemorations. The very memory of the martyrs wrought upon the minds of men in confirming them against the assaults of wicked spirits, and delivering them from impure and unseemly thoughts; ... the death of the martyrs was the exhortation of the faithful, the confidence of Churches, the confirmation of Christianity, ... the reproach of devils, the condemnation of Satan, a consolation in affliction, a motive to patience, encouragement to fortitude, the root, fountain, mother of all which is good.[340]

But if no inculcations to direct worship of saints are to be found in Chrysostom, it is evident that no small virtue was ascribed by popular faith (and, in his opinion, justly) to their remains.[341] Miracles of healing were wrought, or supposed to be wrought, at their tombs; demons were expelled by the application of their ashes to the persons possessed. It is obvious that, where such a belief has taken possession of the popular mind, prayer will very soon be addressed to the saint for the direct bestowal of those advantages which are supposed to be derivable from his reliques. Pilgrimages were fashionable in all parts of Christendom. Prefects and generals, when they visited Rome, hastened to pay their devotion at the tombs of the tentmaker and fisherman; journeys were made into Arabia to visit the supposed site of Job's dunghill.[342]

Two different causes seem to have led on the mind of the Church to an increasing veneration of martyrs. First, the Church owed to them a real debt; the heroic steadfastness of their deaths contributed much to promote and establish Christianity. Chrysostom observes how the sight of the aged Ignatius going to die at Rome for his faith—going not only with calmness, but even with alacrity—mightily confirmed the souls of the disciples in the several cities through which he passed.[343] "As irrigation made gardens fruitful, so the blood of martyrs gave drink to the Churches."[344] Honour, affection, veneration, easily pass into actual adoration.

Secondly, there is a natural desire to bridge over the chasm which divides the human nature from the Divine, and earth from heaven, by enlisting the agency of some intermediate being. In its earliest conflicts with heresy, theology was chiefly engaged in zealously defending the pure divinity of Christ—his co-equal, co-eternal power and majesty with the Father. The more He was withdrawn into a less accessible region of exalted deity, the more this need of the half-deified human interpositor was felt, and worked itself out at last into a distinct article of faith.

Some of those abuses of saints' days, which we are apt to associate more especially with medieval times, were far from uncommon in the days of Chrysostom. The day which had begun in fasting, and was preceded by a vigil, too often terminated in a very carnal kind of revelry. "Ye have turned night into day by your holy vigils: do not turn day into night by drunkenness, surfeiting, and lascivious songs; let not any one see you misbehaving in an inn on your return home."[345] A custom prevailed of holding a "love-feast," at or near the tomb of the saint, which was furnished by the oblations of the wealthier devotees. Chrysostom on one occasion urges his congregation to attend such a sacred banquet when they dispersed after service, instead of hurrying off to the diabolical entertainments at Daphne. The sight of the martyrs, standing as it were near their table, would prevent their pleasure from running to excess.[346] But there is abundant evidence in other contemporary writers that these meetings too often did degenerate into scenes of mere conviviality and intemperance. St. Augustine speaks of those who "made themselves drunk at the commemoration of martyrs."[347] St. Ambrose prohibited all such feasts in the churches of Milan; and St. Augustine cited his example to obtain a similar prohibition from Aurelius, the Primate of Carthage.[348] St. Basil reprobates a growing custom of trading near the martyries on festival days, under pretence of making a better provision for the feasts, to which we may fairly, perhaps, attribute the universal custom in Christendom of holding fairs on saints' days.[349] As they were in medieval times, so in Roman Catholic countries at the present day, the booths of the fair are in close contiguity with the walls of the church, and they who attend mass in the morning, as well as those who do not attend it at all, may disgrace themselves by drunkenness and all kinds of folly in the evening. Such abuses are an inevitable consequence of keeping up the observance of days after the real enthusiasm for the person or cause which they commemorate has begun to grow, or has altogether grown, cold. Little may ever have been really known about the saint whose memory is celebrated, and that little ceases to speak with any meaning to the minds of later generations. The service, which was once a living reality, becomes a cold and empty form, or the place of religious enthusiasm is supplied by some form of sensual excitement. Crowds of peasants will not fail to be attracted to a church which blazes with thousands of candles arranged in fantastic patterns, and which rings with noisy sensational music: they probably place a superstitious faith in the tutelary power of their patron: but how different is all this from the hearty, genuine, reasonable devotion of more enlightened worshippers to the Lord Himself, and the less strong but more real respect and honour paid by such to His day! It is surely one among many proofs of the deep and lasting hold of Christ's character upon the mind of men, of the applicability of its influence to all times and places, and of its Divine superiority to that of all His followers, however exalted, that abuses which have accompanied the commemorations of saints have never extended in the same degree to His day.[350]

As already remarked, Chrysostom was prevented this year by illness from attending the festivals of saints and martyrs, which fell very thickly between Easter and Whitsun Day. He commences his homily preached on the Sunday before Ascension Day with an allusion to his recent sickness, and tells his congregation that, though absent in body from their sacred festivities, he had been present and rejoiced with them in spirit; and now, though he had not fully recovered his health, he could not refrain from meeting his beloved and much-longed-for flock again. He was the more anxious also to occupy his accustomed place on that day, because large numbers of the rustic population from the neighbouring country had flocked into the city and attended the services of the church. They spoke a different dialect, but they were one with the Christian inhabitants of the town in the soundness of their faith; and their habits of simple piety, pure morality, and honourable industry, put to shame the dissolute manners and indolence which prevailed in the city. Their peasant clergy were a noble race of men; they might be seen, one while yoking their oxen to the plough, and marking out furrows in the soil, another while mounting the pulpit and ploughing the hearts of their flock; now cutting away thorns from the ground with a sickle, now cleansing men's minds from sin by their discourse: for they were not ashamed of hard work, like the people of the city, but of idleness, knowing that it was idleness which taught men vice, and had been from the beginning to those who loved it the schoolmaster of all iniquity. Though little skilled, by training, in reasoning or rhetoric, they proved more than a match for those counterfeit philosophers who paraded themselves about the streets with their professional cloak, staff, and beard, but who could not give any satisfactory information on the subjects upon which they expended such a heap of words,—as the immortality of the soul, the creation of the world, Divine Providence, a future world and judgment. The rustic pastor, being simply and firmly persuaded of the truth of these things, could instruct men with clearness and decision about them; he could give solid matter, the others only polished language, like a man who should have a sword with a silver ornamented hilt, but a weak blade. Their wives were not luxurious creatures, covering themselves with unguents, paints, and dyes, but simple, sober, quiet matrons; which increased the influence of the pastor over the people committed to his charge, and caused the precept of St. Paul, "having food and raiment, let us be therewith content," to be strictly observed[351] among them.

CHAPTER 13

SURVEY OF EVENTS BETWEEN A.D. 387 AND A.D. 397—
AMBROSE AND THEODOSIUS—REVOLT OF ARBOGASTES—
DEATH OF THEODOSIUS—THE MINISTERS OF ARCADIUS—
RUFINUS AND EUTROPIUS.

SOME ACCOUNT HAS NOW been given of the most remarkable among the homilies delivered by Chrysostom during the first year of his priesthood; not only because to follow the course of the Christian seasons through the cycle of one year seemed the most convenient method of giving specimens of his ordinary style of preaching, but also because these first efforts were seldom if ever surpassed in power and beauty by his later productions. A more extensive survey of his theology, under its several heads, is reserved for the concluding chapter; and the remainder of the ten years during which he resided at Antioch being uneventful as regards his life, it will be profitable to fill up the gap by taking a glance at the world outside his present sphere. Some knowledge of contemporary events and men is indeed necessary to a just appreciation of his position and conduct, when he is summoned to occupy a more public and exalted station.

It is a melancholy scene which meets the eye. The mighty fabric of the Empire crumbles, perhaps more rapidly in this decade than in any previous period of equal length—like an old man whose constitution is thoroughly broken.

Effeminate luxury in the civilised population is matched by the rude ferocity of the barbarians who hem it in or mingle with it, and the new barbarian patch agrees ill with the old garment, which is not strong enough to bear it. The pages of historians are filled with tales of murder, massacre, treachery, venality, corruption, everywhere and of all kinds. There is no national greatness, but great men move across the stage: Theodosius himself, generous, just though passionate, vigorous when roused to a sense of emergency; the last Emperor who deserved the name of "great;" Ambrose, the intrepid advocate of religious duty to God and man, the champion of the rights of Church and hierarchy; Stilicho, the skilful commander of armies and able guardian of the Empire after the death of Theodosius; Alaric, the very type of Gothic force; Rufinus and Eutropius, the clever, scheming adventurers, destitute of all nobility, who in a degenerate court contrive to raise themselves to the pinnacle of power, and are suddenly toppled headlong from it.

The most commanding public character in the West at this time was, and for some years had been, Ambrose, Archbishop of Milan. Disliked but feared by the Arian court, respected and beloved by the people, he fought in some respects a similar battle to that in which Chrysostom was afterwards engaged in the East, and amidst many differences there are also many parallels in the character and history of the two men: the same fearless courage to speak what they believed to be God's truth, in the face of royalty itself, animated both; in both cases was it rewarded by virulent persecution; both had to contend with an imperious, passionate woman; both were protected from her fury by the populace keeping guard night and day before the walls of the church. In A.D. 384, Ambrose had been summoned before a royal council, and, in the presence of the young Emperor Valentinian II. and the Queen-mother Justina, had been commanded to surrender the Portian Basilica for the use of the Arians. But Ambrose had replied undauntedly, that not one inch of ground which had been consecrated to truth would he concede to error.[352] For more than two years Ambrose maintained his ground against all the stratagems of his adversaries. On one occasion they seized the Portian Basilica, but dared not hold it in the face of the infuriated people. Messengers from court endeavoured to maintain before the archbishop that the Emperor had a right to dispose of the churches as he pleased, but the argument was contemptuously dismissed as a base sophistry. "What!" he cried; "the Emperor has no right to violate the house of a private individual, and think you that he may do violence to the house of God? No! let him take all that is mine—my land, my money, though these belong to the poor; if he seeks my patrimony, let him seize it; if my person, I will present it to him: but the church it is not lawful for me to surrender, or for him to accept."[353] Force was not more successful than argument. Soldiers were sent to dislodge him and his congregation from one of the basilicas, but instead of drawing their swords they fell on their knees, and declared that they came not to attack the archbishop, but to pray with him. The effect of an edict was tried in A.D. 386,[354] which permitted free worship to all who professed the creed of Rimini (an Arian creed), and rendered liable to capital punishment any who should impede the action of the edict, as offenders against the imperial majesty. Under shelter of this edict, the Portian Basilica was again demanded, but Ambrose refused to recognise such an edict, which militated against his sense of duty to a higher power. "God forbid that I should yield the heritage of Jesus Christ. Naboth would not part with the vineyard of his fathers to Ahab, and should I surrender the house of God? the heritage of Dionysius, who died in exile for the faith; of Eustorgius the confessor; of Miroclus, and all the faithful bishops which were before me?"[355] But though Ambrose disobeyed, the penalties of the edict were not enforced upon him. An order of banishment was served upon him, expressed in vague terms: "Depart from the city, and go where you please." But Ambrose did not please to go anywhere, and remained where he was, moving up and down the city, and officiating as usual in the churches, using in his sermons the same Scripture parallels to indicate the Queen-mother, "Herodias" and "Jezebel," which Chrysostom afterwards applied to the Empress Eudoxia. He preaches day after day, guarded by his faithful flock, who during passion-tide suffered him not to quit the cathedral for fear of violence to his person. Amongst that crowd, touched by the spell of the chants and hymns which Ambrose taught the people[356] to beguile the tediousness of their watch, and impressed by his pungent and decisive doctrine, are two remarkable persons, a mother and her son. They are Monica and Augustine. Monica is among the most faithful in watching, the most earnest in praying for the welfare of the bishop and the church. Augustine is about thirty-two years old; he has been in many places and passed through many phases of thought. He has subdued the vices and follies which stained his youth; he has shaken off the errors of Manicheism which for a time enthralled him; he has been a teacher of rhetoric at Tagaste, at Carthage, at Rome; and Symmachus has now obtained for him a professorial chair at Milan. But Pagan literature is losing its hold upon him. Plato no longer fascinates him equally with Holy Scripture. He is gravitating steadily towards Christianity, and in another year, April 387, just about the time that Chrysostom is delivering his homilies on the Statues, he will crown his mother's hopes by making a public confession of his faith, and receiving baptism at the hands of Ambrose.[357]

One more effort was made to win the contest, this time through diplomacy. The court proposed that the question under dispute should be settled by arbitration, the judges to be selected by Ambrose and Auxentius the Arian bishop. But Ambrose would not accept the arbitrators nominated by Auxentius, four of whom were Pagans and one a catechumen. In the name of himself and the clergy of his province he denied the validity of the tribunal. In an address to the people the same lofty tone of independence was maintained. "He would pay deference to the Emperor, but never yield in things unlawful: the Emperor was 'in the Church, not above it.'"[358] So he remained master of the field. The unfinished basilica, which had been the prize contended for, was consecrated by Ambrose with great pomp, and the joy of the people was completed by the discovery of the martyrs' skeletons beneath the pavement, pronounced to be those of Gervasius and Protasius, who had suffered in the persecution of Diocletian. When demoniacs shuddered on being placed in proximity to these reliques, and a blind man was cured by the application to his eyes of a handkerchief which had been placed in contact with these same reliques, the crown was put on the triumph of Ambrose; the people were more firmly convinced than ever that his cause was the cause of God.[359]

He was so indisputably the ablest man of the time in the West, that, when danger impended over the state, the very court which persecuted him turned to him to rescue the country. Threatening messages came from the court of Maximus at Treves. Ambrose was the ambassador selected to go and pacify or intimidate the tyrant. Maximus was a Catholic, and a ruthless persecutor of those whom he deemed heretics, especially Priscillianists; yet Ambrose did not hesitate to denounce his cruelty to brethren who were Christians, however erring, as well as his disloyal attitude towards Valentinian. The embassy was unsuccessful, but the dignity of the ambassador and of the court which he represented was fully maintained. The artifices by which another ambassador, the Syrian Domninus, was blinded to the preparations of Maximus for the invasion of Italy; the passage of the Alps by the usurper; the flight of Justina and her son to Thessalonica; the prompt march of Theodosius to the succour of Italy, and his complete victory over Maximus, near Aquileia,—belong to the secular historian; but the connection between Theodosius and Ambrose will be related here more in detail.

There is no account of the first meeting between the two great characters of the day—the Emperor and the archbishop. That Ambrose immediately exercised influence over the imperial mind may be inferred from the mildness of the measures by which the embers of the late revolution were extinguished. No bloody executions took place; no rigorous search for rebels was made; the mother and daughter of Maximus—who had been himself beheaded—were provided with a maintenance. Ambrose, in one of his letters, thanks the Emperor for granting liberty, at his request, to several exiles and prisoners, and for remitting the sentence of death to others.

Theodosius could be generous to enemies, and was the zealous friend of Catholic Christianity, but he was a strict punisher of any violations of civil order, even when the offenders were Christian. The people of Callinicum in Osrhoene, instigated by the bishop and some fanatical monks, had set fire to a Jewish synagogue, and to a church of the sect of Valentinians. The Emperor directed the Count of the East to punish the offenders, and commanded the bishop to restore the buildings at the expense of the Church. But the extension of such favour to heretics was in the sight of Ambrose intolerable. It might, indeed, have been wrong to disturb civil order, but it was far more wrong to reinstate error: to order Christians to rebuild a place of worship for those who set Christ at naught was, in his eyes, simple profanity. He expressed his opinion to the Emperor in a letter. It is the first great instance of the Church distinctly claiming a pre-eminence of authority superseding that of civil law. "If I am not worthy to be listened to by you, how can I be worthy to transmit, as your priest, your vows and prayers to God?" Basing on this ground his right to speak out his mind, he declares that "if the Bishop of Callinicum obeyed the imperial command, he would be guilty of culpable weakness, and the Emperor would be responsible for it. If he refused to obey, the Emperor could execute his will by force of arms only; the labarum, perhaps the standard of Christ, would be employed to rebuild a temple where Christ would be denied. What a monstrous inconsistency!" The last words which it contained were: "I have endeavoured to make myself heard in the palace; do not place me under the necessity of making myself heard in the church;" but the letter was unanswered, and so Ambrose put his threat into execution. He preached in Milan in the presence of the Emperor; "he compared the Christian priest to the prophets of the Old Testament, whose duty it was to proclaim God's message to the king himself, as Nathan did to David. As the Israelites were warned not to say, when they entered the land of Canaan, 'My virtue has deserved these good things,' but 'the Lord God has given them,' so the Emperor should remember that he was what he was by the mercy of God. Therefore, he ought to love the body of Christ, the Church—to wash, kiss, and anoint her feet, that all the dwelling where Christ reposes might be filled with the odour; that is, he ought to honour his least disciples, and pardon their faults; every one of the members of the Christian body was necessary to it, and ought to receive his protection."

Having uttered such words, he descended from the altar steps. Theodosius perceived that the archbishop had taken up his parable against him, and as Ambrose was going out of the church he stopped him, saying, "Is it I whom you have made the subject of your discourse?" "I have said that which I deemed useful for you," Ambrose replied. "I perceive it is of the synagogue that you would speak," rejoined Theodosius. "I own that my commands have been a little severe, but I have already softened them, and these monks are troublesome men." "I am going to offer the sacrifice," said Ambrose; "enable me to do so without fear for you; deliver me from the load which oppresses my spirit." "It shall be so," responded the Emperor; "my orders shall be mitigated; I give you my promise." But Ambrose was not satisfied with so vague an assurance. "Suppress the whole matter," he said; "swear it to me, and, on your sworn promise, I proceed to offer the sacrifice." The Emperor swore; Ambrose celebrated mass; "and never," said he, in a letter written the day after to his sister, "did I experience such sensible marks of the presence of God in prayer."[360]

In the spring of A.D. 389, Theodosius made his triumphal entry into Rome, accompanied by Valentinian and his own son Honorius, a boy of ten. His arrival was preceded by two popular enactments: one a decree, renouncing for himself and family all bequests made by codicils—striking a blow at a vicious custom, which had long prevailed, of bribing imperial favour for particular families, by bequeathing large legacies to the reigning sovereign. By heathen emperors these bequests had been sought with great cupidity; sick or old men were sometimes threatened with an acceleration of death, unless they satisfied the royal expectations in this way. The other, no less popular, decree was, to abolish the custom by which royal couriers, when conveying news of victory, exacted donations from the villages through which they passed. The victory of Theodosius over Maximus was the first which had been gratuitously proclaimed along the route to Rome; and the people greeted the Emperor as he made his progress to the capital with all the warmer welcome in consequence.[361]

Rome had at this period scarcely recovered from the ferment into which society had been thrown by the three years' residence of Jerome, A.D. 382-385. His denunciations of clerical luxury; his cutting satires on the vices and follies of the laity; his allurement to monastic life of some of the wealthiest and noblest of the Roman ladies, had stirred up a tumult of feeling for the most part adverse to him. But Theodosius prudently abstained from interfering with the religious debates of Rome. In Constantinople he was the absolute sovereign; in Rome he desired to appear simply as the successful general and the foremost citizen. He assumed no imperial or Asiatic splendour; he exhibited no fastidious abhorrence of statues, temples, and other remnants of Paganism. Symmachus, the most eminent Pagan citizen, was cordially received, and gratified by the promise of consulship. The result of this amiable and moderate conduct was that some of the most powerful Roman families embraced the faith of the Emperor.

A.D. 390. But the generosity which Theodosius had manifested towards the people of Antioch, his moderation after the defeat of Maximus, and during his triumphal residence in Rome, was presently stained by one of those paroxysms of anger to which he was occasionally subject. The intercession of Flavian had averted any such outburst in the case of the sedition of Antioch; the authority of Ambrose, too late to prevent the crime, enforced penance for the cruel vengeance executed on the people of Thessalonica.

Botheric, the governor of Thessalonica, had imprisoned a favourite charioteer for attempting to commit a disgusting crime. The people, passionately attached to the races of the circus, demanded his release on a certain day to take part in the contest. The governor refused, and the people then broke out into rebellion; the tumult was with difficulty quelled by the troops, and not before Botheric had been mortally wounded, several other officers torn to pieces, and their mangled remains dragged through the streets. The irritation of the Emperor, on hearing of this barbarous violence, was extreme; and all the more so, because of Thessalonica he could have expected better things. It did not contain, like Antioch, Rome, or Alexandria, a large mixed population, but one almost exclusively Christian, and for the most part even Catholic. The city was the scene of his early triumphs, and frequently honoured by his visits. It is possible that Ambrose may have pushed his exhortations to clemency too far in the first glow of the Emperor's resentment. At any rate, the counsel of those rivals or enemies of Ambrose, who represented that the affair belonged purely to civil government, and should be decided independently of all clerical interference, prevailed. Rufinus, the flattering, heartless courtier, persuaded Theodosius that a public offence of such magnitude deserved the most merciless punishment which could be inflicted. Orders were issued to the officials at Thessalonica to assemble the populace, as if for a fête, in the circus, and then to let in the troops upon them. This barbarous mandate was too faithfully executed. The unsuspecting victims crowded into their favourite place of amusement; at a given signal the soldiers rushed in, and in the course of two or three hours the ground was strewn with some 7000 corpses of men, women, and children.[362] The horror of the people of Milan was only equalled by their astonishment. Was it possible that he who had displayed such magnanimity and Christian moderation could be guilty of an act which savoured of the most heathen treachery and ferocity? When the Emperor returned from Rome, Ambrose withdrew from Milan into the country, and thence wrote to him a letter expressing his horror at the recent massacre; exhorting him to the deepest repentance and humiliation as the only hope of obtaining mercy from God, and declaring that he could not celebrate mass again in his presence. The mode by which the Emperor was to expiate his guilt is not indicated in this epistle, and he presented himself soon afterwards at the doors of the cathedral church with his usual royal retinue. But he was confronted by Ambrose in his pontifical robes, who with flashing eyes expressed his astonishment at such audacity, and barred the entrance with his person. "I see, Emperor, you are ignorant of the flagrancy of the murder which you have perpetrated. Perhaps your unlimited power blinds you to your guilt, and obscures your reason. Yet consider your frail and mortal nature; think of the dust from which you were formed, and to which you will return, and beneath the splendid veil of your purple recognise the infirmity of the flesh which it covers. You rule over men who are your brethren by nature, and by service to a common King, the Creator of all things. How then will you dare to plant your feet in His sanctuary, and elevate your hands towards Him, all dripping as they are with the blood of men unjustly slain? How will you take into your hands the sacred body of the Lord, or dare to put His precious blood to those lips, which by a word of anger have spilt the blood of so many innocent victims? Withdraw, then, and add not a fresh crime to those with which you are already burdened." The Emperor returned, conscience-stricken and weeping, to his palace. For eight months no intercourse took place between him and Ambrose. Christmas approached; exclusion from the church at such a season seemed insupportable to the Emperor. Rufinus found him one day dissolved in tears. "The church of God," he cried, "is open to the slave and the beggar, but to me it is closed, and with it the gates of heaven; for I remember the words of the Lord: 'Whatsoever ye shall bind on earth shall be bound in heaven.'" Rufinus sought to console him: "I will hasten to Ambrose, and force him to release you from this bond." "No," said the Emperor, "you will not persuade Ambrose to violate divine law from any fear of imperial power." Rufinus, however, sought an interview with the archbishop; but Ambrose spurned him indignantly from him, as being the chief counsellor of the late massacre. Rufinus informed him that the Emperor was approaching. "If he comes," said the prelate, "I will repel him from the vestibule of the church." The minister returned to the Emperor discomfited, and advised him to abstain from visiting the church; but Theodosius had subdued all pride, and replied that he would now go and submit to any humiliation which Ambrose might see proper to impose. He advanced to the church. Perceiving the archbishop in the exterior court or atrium, he cried, "I have come; deliver me from my sins." "What madness," replied Ambrose, "has prompted you to violate the sanctuary, and to trample on divine law?" "I ask for my deliverance," said the humbled monarch; "shut not the door which God has opened to all penitents." "And where is your penitence?" said the archbishop; "show me your remedies for healing your wounds." "It is for *you* to show them to *me*," Theodosius replied; "for me to accept them." Once more Ambrose had gained the day. He could prescribe his own terms. First, he required that the recurrence of a similar crime should be guarded against by a decree which should interpose a delay of thirty days between a sentence of confiscation or death and the execution of it. At the expiration of this period the sentence was to be presented to the Emperor for final reconsideration. Theodosius consented, ordered the law to be drawn up, and subscribed it with his own hand. He was then admitted within the walls, but in deeply penitential guise; stripped of imperial ornaments, prostrate on the pavement, beating his breast, tearing his hair, and crying aloud, "My soul cleaveth unto the dust, quicken thou me according to thy word." So he remained during the first portion of the Liturgy. When the offertory began, he rose, advanced within the choir to present his offering, and was about to resume the place which at Constantinople he usually occupied—a seat in the midst of the clergy, in the more elevated portion of the choir. But Ambrose determined, by taking advantage of the Emperor's present humiliation, to put a stop to this custom. An archdeacon stepped up to Theodosius, and informed him that no layman might remain in the choir during the celebration. The submissive Emperor withdrew outside the rails. When he had returned to Constantinople, he was invited by Nectarius, the archbishop, to occupy his accustomed chair in the choir. "No!" replied Theodosius, with a sigh; "I have learned at Milan the insignificance of an Emperor in the Church, and the difference between him and a bishop. But no one here tells me the truth. I know not any bishop save Ambrose who deserves the name."[363] He had hit the truth. The difference between the conduct of Ambrose and of Nectarius symbolised the difference between the character of the Western and Eastern Church generally: the one stern, commanding, jealous of any encroachment of the civil power; the other, subservient, submissive, courtier-like; the one aspiring and advancing, the other receding and decadent. Chrysostom would have told him the truth; but Chrysostom, in his uncompromising and fearless honesty of purpose and speech, is such a grand exception among the patriarchs of Constantinople, that he proves the general rule. Even Flavian had only *supplicated* mercy from the Emperor; Ambrose *commanded* it.

On one subject the deference of Theodosius for the opinion of Ambrose caused him some embarrassment. Ambrose, in common with the other Western prelates, had recognised Paulinus as Bishop of Antioch—the priest of the Eustathian party who had been consecrated by Lucifer of Cagliari; and he now acknowledged Evagrius, his successor. Theodosius was distracted between his friendship for Flavian, the rival of Evagrius, and for Ambrose. Flavian was summoned to court. The Emperor implored him to go to Rome and justify his claims before the Pope; but Flavian refused. At the suggestion of Ambrose, the Western Bishops assembled in council at Capua, and there delegated the decision to Theophilus, Patriarch of Alexandria. Once more Flavian was summoned to court, and advised to submit to the arbitration of Theophilus; but he was still intractable. "Take my bishopric at once, and give it to whom you please; but I will submit neither my honour nor my faith to the judgment of my equals." Nearly eighteen months were consumed in these negotiations. The West grew impatient. The letters of Ambrose took a severer tone: "Flavian has something to fear; that is why he avoids examination. Will he place himself outside the Church, the communion of Rome, and intercourse with his brethren?" The strife was mercifully broken off by the sudden death of Evagrius, before he had time to designate a successor; and the wound was salved, though not healed. That final good work was destined to be accomplished by Chrysostom.[364]

A.D. 392. Only a few years more of life remained for Theodosius, and his reign was occupied at the end as at the beginning by quelling rebellion in the West. When he returned to the East, in A.D. 391, after the defeat of Maximus, he had generously left the youthful Valentinian in full possession of all his hereditary dominions, which he had rescued for him from the usurper. Arbogastes, a Gaul, was appointed general of the forces; Ambrose was a kind of general counsellor. But Arbogastes was bold, ambitious, unscrupulous. He possessed much power; he determined to acquire the whole. He obeyed the commands of his young sovereign or not, as suited his pleasure and purposes, and surrounded him with creatures of his own, who, under the semblance of courtiers, acted as spies and gaolers. Valentinian's residence at Vienne, in Gaul, became his prison rather than his palace. The sequel belongs to secular history, and is well known. An open rupture took place. Arbogastes threw off the mask. Valentinian was found strangled, too late to receive baptism at the hands of Ambrose, whose coming he had awaited with great eagerness as soon as he knew that his life was in danger.[365] Once more Italy became the prey of a usurper; once more the veteran Emperor of the East roused himself from his well-earned repose, collected a huge force, consulted John, the hermit of the Thebaid, on the issue of the war, solicited the favour of Heaven by visiting the principal places of devotion in the city, and kneeling on flint before the tombs of martyrs and apostles, then set out on his march, and by the summer of A.D. 394 again looked down from the Alps on the plains of Venetia, near the scene of his former victory over one usurper, and now covered with the tents belonging to the army of another. He prosecuted the campaign in the same religious spirit in which he had undertaken it. The first assault made on the 5th of September against the enemy was repulsed. Theodosius rallied and harangued the troops lifted up his eyes to heaven, and cried: "O Lord, Thou knowest that I have undertaken this war only for the honour of thy Son, and to prevent crime going unpunished; stretch forth, I pray Thee, thy hand over thy servants, that the heathen say not of us, 'Where is their God?'" The second assault was more successful; the night was spent by the Emperor in prayer, who was rewarded towards dawn by a vision of two horsemen, clothed in white, who bade him be of good cheer, for that they were the apostles St. Philip and St. John, and would not fail to come to his succour on the following day. The issue of that day was decisive; the overthrow of Arbogastes complete; his army routed; himself slain.[366]

The conqueror was received by Ambrose, at Milan, with transports of joy. The victory was nobly signalised by a display of Christian clemency. Free pardon was proclaimed in the church (whither the offenders had fled for refuge) to all those Milanese who had joined the side of the usurper. Among them were the children of Arbogastes, and of the puppet king whom he had set up, Eugenius. They were made to expiate the crimes of their Pagan fathers by submitting to baptism.[367]

But there was an increasing shade of gloom which overcast the general sunshine of joy. The health of Theodosius, long undermined by a disease, was now manifestly fast giving way. He was sensible of his danger, and despatched a message to Constantinople, desiring that his younger son, Honorius, should be sent to join him at Milan. The young prince, accompanied by his cousin Serena (the wife of Stilicho) and his little sister Placidia, set off without delay. They reached Milan early in the year A.D. 395. Some shocks of earthquake, and terrific storms, which coincided with their arrival, were regarded as portents of future evil. The malady of Theodosius, a dropsical disorder, was rapidly gaining ground. He revived a little at the sight of his son, and received the Eucharist from the hands of Ambrose, which he had hitherto refused, as having too recently been engaged in the sanguinary scenes of war. He gave audience to a deputation of Western bishops, who came to pay him homage, and besought them to heal the schism of Antioch by acknowledging Flavian. He besought the Pagan members of the senate of Rome to embrace the Christian faith, adding the somewhat potent argument, that Pagan worship must no longer expect any pecuniary aid from the State. He appeared for a few times at the circus, where races were held in honour of his victory and the arrival of the young prince; but one day, while dining, he was taken suddenly worse, and expired early the next morning, Jan. 17th, A.D. 395, in the fiftieth year of his age, and the sixteenth of his reign. Those who watched by his bedside thought they detected the name of Ambrose faintly murmured by his dying lips.[368]

So passed away the last great Emperor of the Roman world.[369] He had persistently kept in view a single and noble aim—the consolidation of the Empire. He had repelled invasion, crushed rebellion, laboured to extirpate heathenism, to suppress heresy, to reconcile opposing factions in the Church; and the work seemed advancing when he was called away, and years ensued of misrule and disorder, Gothic devastation, and internal corruption and decadence.

The history of the Empire under Arcadius and Honorius presents a pitiable picture of imbecility on the part of the sovereigns; of infidelity and unscrupulous ambition on the part of their ministers. Theodosius himself, as he lay on his death-bed, was perhaps conscious of impending troubles. The words supposed by Claudian to be spoken by the shade of Theodosius to his son Arcadius: "Res incompositas fateor tumidasque reliqui,"[370] express at any rate the true condition of affairs. To Stilicho he commended his younger son, Honorius, and the interests of the Western Empire, but added a request that he would not neglect Arcadius and the Eastern portion of the Empire also. The legal guardian, however, of Arcadius was not a man who would tamely submit to any supervision, or to any encroachment, fancied or real, upon the rights of his office. He was as jealous of Stilicho as Constantinople was of Rome. Discernment of character cannot be reckoned among the great qualities of Theodosius; otherwise he would not have intrusted his two sons to the guardianship of two men dissimilar in all respects but one—an insatiable love of power. He had placed the two weak princes in the hands of deadly rivals.

Rufinus, the guardian of Arcadius and regent of the East, was an Aquitanian Gaul, born at Elusa, the modern Eauze, at the foot of the Pyrenees.[371] He was the very model of an accomplished adventurer. Sprung from poverty and obscurity, he was gifted by nature with a handsome figure, a noble demeanour, a ready tongue, an inventive, versatile wit.[372] He made his way, after residing in Milan and Rome, to the court of Constantinople; and found in Theodosius a patron who could appreciate his talents without detecting his vices. He rapidly rose till he had attained the high distinction of "Master of the Offices," in A.D. 390; of consul, in connection with Arcadius, in A.D. 392; and, in A.D. 394, prætorian prefect *in presenti*, a position second only to that of the Emperor himself.[373] He affected the warmest zeal for the Catholic faith, and threw himself heartily into the schemes of Theodosius for the suppression of heresy, no less than into those for the consolidation of the social and political fabric.

But underneath this appearance of patriotic enthusiasm he indulged what Claudian terms an "accursed thirst" for gain.[374] By unjust law-suits he wrested patrimonies from the poor, and manœuvred to marry the daughters and widows of the wealthy to his own favourites, in order that he might reap their legacies and gifts. If any exposure of these iniquities was threatened, he stopped the mouths of accusers by large bribes, and compensated his extortions from towns by making presents to their churches or enlarging their public buildings.

When Theodosius departed for the Italian war, Rufinus, being left as guardian of Arcadius, began to conceive the project of elevating himself to the imperial throne. He made a magnificent display of his piety. Hard by his villa, or rather palace, in the suburb of Chalcedon, called the Oak, a spot which afterwards acquired a melancholy notoriety in the history of Chrysostom, he had built a church and a monastery attached to it. This church he now determined to dedicate with great pomp, and at the same time to be baptized himself. For this purpose he assembled nineteen Eastern bishops, chiefly metropolitans, and a number of Egyptian hermits; strange-looking figures, who, with their raiment of skins, their flowing beards and long hair, excited much superstitious reverence. In the midst of this august assembly, the depredator of the East descended into the baptismal waters, arrayed in the white robes typical of innocence. The celebrated Egyptian solitary, Ammonius (who will come before us again), administered the sacrament, and Gregory of Nyssa delivered a discourse.[375] Rufinus now surrounded himself with a powerful party of followers; Arcadius was too stupid to see, or too timid to oppose, the dangerous ambition of his so-called protector.

But the death of Theodosius and the elevation of Stilicho to the guardianship of the West brought the intriguer face to face with an able and determined soldier, who united some of the ferocity of the barbarian with the steadfast patriotism of an old Roman. This last, indeed, was the character which Stilicho, a Vandal by birth, but educated at Rome, more especially emulated. It was his ambition to be compared to Fabricius, Curtius, Camillus.[376] Great was his delight when Claudius, himself called a second Virgil, likened him in his verses to Scipio.[377] The poet declared that Theodosius had never fought without Stilicho, though Stilicho had fought without Theodosius. He was made not only the guardian but father-in-law of Honorius, who was betrothed to his eldest daughter beside the death-bed of Theodosius; the father dying in the happy assurance that, by creating this parental tie, he had secured the fidelity of his minister. The boy and girl were brought into the sick-room, exchanged rings, and repeated the words which were dictated to them.[378]

The regent of the East naturally became profoundly jealous of the regent of the West, and in point of royal connection determined to be even with him. He humoured Arcadius into a consent to marry his own daughter; and his scheme seemed on the point of completion when an inopportune matter of business took him away to Antioch, and his enemy, the chamberlain Eutropius, took advantage of his absence to frustrate the plan. A Frankish general, called Bautho, who had been elevated to the consulship, but had prematurely died, left a daughter of rare beauty named Eudoxia. The orphan girl was brought up by a friend of Bautho, the son of Promotus, a magister militum, whom Rufinus, in revenge for an insult, had caused to be assassinated. Eutropius introduced a portrait of the young beauty to the notice of Arcadius. Curiosity, and soon a tenderer sentiment, were excited in the young Emperor's breast; the cunning chamberlain fanned the flame, till he was able to persuade the royal youth that Eudoxia was a more eligible bride than the daughter of the low-born Gaul.[379] The intrigue was conducted with such secrecy that Rufinus, on his return from Antioch, remained unsuspicious, and his boastful remarks on the approaching nuptials excited the indignation of the public. The wedding-day was fixed for April 25, A.D. 395. Eutropius selected from the imperial wardrobe some of the costliest female robes and jewels which it contained. They were placed on litters, which, escorted by a large train of splendidly apparelled serving-men, paraded the streets, on the way, as was supposed, to the house of Rufinus. What was the astonishment of the populace when the procession suddenly turned in another direction, and presently stopped in front of the house of Promotus! A loud shout of joy burst from the lips of the multitude, and proclaimed to Rufinus the unpopularity of his project, and the general satisfaction at its defeat. The bride thus cunningly substituted was destined to play a conspicuous part in the later scenes of Chrysostom's career. She inherited the fair beauty, the energetic spirit, the impulsive, sometimes fierce, temper of the race from which she sprang. Her father had remained firmly attached to the Pagan religion of his ancestors, but, in deference to Theodosius, his patron, he had allowed his daughter to be baptized and educated in the Christian faith.[380] Impatient of control, she resolved to possess herself of her husband's confidence in order to govern through him, and gradually to disengage herself from the management alike of Rufinus and Eutropius.

Rufinus had been thoroughly outwitted in his matrimonial scheme, but his resources were far from being exhausted. The sequel of his life belongs too exclusively to secular history to be more than glanced at here. He played a subtle and desperate game, seldom if ever surpassed in villainy. Some Hunnish tribes, encouraged by him, made incursions into Armenia, Pontus, Cappadocia, and even as far as the vicinity of Antioch.[381] The court was in the extremity of alarm, for the main forces of the army and treasury had been drained to the West when Theodosius marched against Arbogastes, and remained in the hands of Stilicho. Worse still, the formidable chieftain Alaric, of the royal race of the Visigoths, who had lately distinguished himself in the Italian wars under Theodosius, began to complain of unrequited services, and with a motley force of Huns, Alani, Sarmatians, and Goths, descended into Thrace, and ravaged the country up to the walls of Constantinople. The inhabitants were convulsed with panic; all except the artful intriguer, who had already struck his bargain with the invaders. He rode out of Constantinople accoutred as a Gothic warrior, went through the farce of an interview with Alaric, and returned with the joyful intelligence that his intercessions had saved the city, and that the Gothic prince had consented to withdraw his troops. And so he did; not, however, to retire to the Gothic settlements in the north, but to pour southwards in a devastating flood over Greece. This was the plot of Rufinus. The possession of the Illyrian provinces was disputed between the courts of East and West. Alaric occupied these. Stilicho, with extraordinary energy, collected a large army, advanced against the devastator, who was supposed to be the common enemy of the whole Empire; but when on the point of attacking him, he was arrested by a message from Constantinople, which commanded him to abstain from any hostilities against the ravager of Greece. "He was the good friend of Arcadius: he occupied the province of Illyria as his ally, which Stilicho was to evacuate immediately, and to restore the troops and treasure which belonged to the East." The troops were sent back by Stilicho under the command of Gaïnas, but with the secret understanding that he should compass the death of Rufinus. The result is well known. Rufinus fell just as he was placing his foot on the topmost round of his ladder of ambition. He was standing on the tribune, where Arcadius was to proclaim him Cæsar, in the presence of a vast multitude; he was making a flowery harangue to the troops, complimenting them on their exploits, congratulating them on their restoration to their homes, when those very troops closed in upon him, plunged their swords into his body, and presently hacked it to pieces. A soldier who got hold of his right arm, and having crooked the fingers of the hand, went about the town, holding it in front of him, and crying, "An obol, an obol for him who never had enough," collected a large sum by his grim and savage jest.[382]

Arcadius was quite incapable of handling the reins of government himself, and the downfall of one all-powerful minister would in any case have been quickly followed by the rise of another; but, as it happened, there was one ready to step immediately into the vacant place. The fortunes of this person, the eunuch Eutropius, ran a strange career. Born a slave, somewhere in the region of the Euphrates, and condemned in infancy to the most degraded condition possible even to slavery, he passed in boyhood and youth through the hands of many owners. He performed the most menial offices as a household slave, cutting wood, drawing water, or whisking the flies from his mistress's face with a large fan. Arinthus, an old magister militum, who had become possessed of him, presented him to his daughter on her marriage; and, in the words of

Claudian, "the future consul of the East was made over as part of a marriage dowry."[383] But the young lady grew tired of the slave, who was getting elderly and wrinkled, and without attempting to sell him, simply turned him out of doors.[384] He lived for a time, picking up a precarious livelihood, and often in great want, till an officer about court at Constantinople took pity on him, and with some difficulty obtained for him a situation in the lowest ranks of the imperial chamberlains.[385] This was the beginning of his rise. By the diligence and precision with which he discharged his ordinary duties, by occasional witty sayings, and the semblance of a fervent piety, he attracted the notice of the Emperor Theodosius, and gradually acquired his confidence so as to be employed on difficult and delicate missions. He it was whom the Emperor sent to consult the hermit John in Egypt before undertaking the Italian campaign in A.D. 394.[386]

On the death of Theodosius he became, in the capacity of grand chamberlain, the intimate adviser and constant attendant of Arcadius; and, when Rufinus was removed, the government was practically in his hands, though he was careful to avoid the error of his late rival, and was content with the reality without the display of power. He continued to execute all the household duties which fell to his lot as chamberlain with humble assiduity, and sought no other title than what he possessed.[387] But it was soon apparent, to the amusement of the East and the indignation of the West, that the eunuch slave was really master of the Emperor of half the Roman world. He gradually removed by his arts the friends of Theodosius from the principal posts of trust, and replaced them by creatures of his own. By surrounding his royal charge with a crowd of frivolous companions; by dissipating his thoughts amidst a perpetual round of amusement, public spectacles, chariot races, and the like; by taking him every spring to Ancyra in Phrygia, where he was subjected to the soft enchantments of a delicious climate and luxurious manner of life, he made the naturally feeble mind of Arcadius more feeble still, and withdrew it from the influence of every superior intellect but his own.[388]

Whilst the effeminate monarch languished in inglorious ease in Phrygia, the fairest and most renowned portions of his Empire were overrun by the barbarian forces of Alaric. The sacred pass of Thermopylæ was violated by the Gothic prince, and the ravager spread his devastations over Peloponnesus. Once more Stilicho hastened to the rescue; once more his hand was stayed by the astonishing announcement that Alaric was rewarded for his career of spoliation by being made commander-in-chief of the forces of the East. Thus the invader was turned into the position of friend, and the defender into the position of rebel, who had to withdraw with feelings of shame, disappointment, and rage. To such base arts did the court of Arcadius, under the direction of Eutropius, stoop to protect itself in its pitiful jealousy of its rival in the West.[389]

Eutropius mounted to the summit of power by the simple process of putting all dangerous competitors out of the way, under various pretexts, as treasonable or otherwise public offenders.[390] He deprived them of their last hope of escape, by abolishing the right of the Church to afford asylum to fugitives.[391] He sold the chief functions of the State, and the command of the provinces, to the highest bidders. He was ambitious even of military glory; and, to the amusement of the enemy, as well as of the imperial army, appeared in military costume at the head of the troops, to repel an incursion of Huns. He succeeded, however, more in his negotiations by which he bought off the enemy, than in his martial exploits, and returned mortified by the ridicule which had attended his attempts in war.[392]

From the pettiest detail of domestic life to the most serious affairs of state, the minister was supreme. Arcadius was little more than a magnificently dressed puppet. The descriptions of his palace read like accounts in fairy tales: it swarmed with slaves of every conceivable variety of race, profession, and costume; the floors of the imperial apartments were sprinkled with gold dust, in the carriage of which from Asia a special service of vessels and wagons was constantly engaged.[393] The great annual public spectacle was the departure of the Emperor for his summer sojourn in Phrygia. From an early hour the streets were thronged with people eagerly waiting for the pageant. At length, from the portals of the palace there issued a gorgeous procession; soldiers in white uniform, with gold-brocaded ensigns; then the body guard, called domestics, with their tribunes and generals arrayed in robes flashing with gold, mounted on horses with golden caparisons; each rider bore a gilded lance in the right hand, and in the left a gilded shield studded with precious stones. In the rear, surrounded by a grand cortége of state officials, came the imperial car, drawn by milk-white mules, clothed in purple housings, which were tricked out with gold and jewels. The sides of the car also were gilded, and flashed out rays of golden light as it moved along towards the harbour, where rode a fleet of barges richly decorated, waiting to convey the royal traveller to the opposite shore of the Bosporus. In strange contrast to all this splendour appeared in the centre of the car the dull and somnolent countenance of the young Arcadius and the wrinkled visage of his old minister. The multitude, ever greedy of show, would eagerly strain forward their necks to catch a glimpse, if it were only of the imperial ear-rings, or the circlet of his diadem, or the strings of pearls upon his robe. With such empty exhibitions of their puppet king did the wily minister seek to amuse the frivolous inhabitants of the capital, while he himself enjoyed the exercise of real power.[394]

CHAPTER 14

DEATH OF NECTARIUS, ARCHBISHOP OF CONSTANTINOPLE—EAGER COMPETITION FOR THE SEE—ELECTION OF CHRYSOSTOM—HIS COMPULSORY REMOVAL FROM ANTIOCH—CONSECRATION—REFORMS—HOMILIES ON VARIOUS SUBJECTS—MISSIONARY PROJECTS.

SUCH WAS THE POLITICAL and social condition of the Empire in the year A.D. 397. In September of that year died Nectarius, Archbishop of Constantinople, a man of an easy, amiable disposition, who, not taking a very elevated or severe view of the duties of his position, had administered the see for sixteen years, without annoyance, but without distinction.[395] A conscientious discharge, indeed, of episcopal duties was at this epoch beset by no small difficulties in the great cities of the Empire. Bishops of important sees now occupied a high social rank.[396] This had to be assumed (in Constantinople at least) in the midst of an intriguing, factious court, a corrupt, frivolous people, and a demoralised, or at least secularised, clergy. "Nothing," said St. Augustine, "can in this life, and especially at this time, be easier or more agreeable than the office of bishop, presbyter, or deacon, if discharged in a perfunctory and adulatory manner; nothing can in this life, and especially at this time, be more laborious and perilous than such an office, if discharged as our heavenly Commander bids us."[397] And the testimony of Chrysostom's friend, Isidore, Abbot of Pelusium, is to the same effect: "True freedom and independence are not to be found in these distinguished positions: it is so difficult to rule some, and to submit to others; to direct some, and to be directed by others; to be complaisant to some and severe to others." Into this difficult and delicate position the pious, single-minded, unworldly, but courageous preacher of Antioch was to be suddenly transplanted, and that in a city where the difficulties incident to such a position existed in peculiar force.

At the time of the decease of Nectarius, several bishops happened to be sojourning in Constantinople on business, and as tidings of the vacancy of the see got abroad, the number of episcopal visitors largely increased; some coming as candidates, others by the invitation of the Emperor, who wished to make the ceremony of consecration as dignified and august as possible.[398] Constantinople became convulsed by all those factious disputes and dissensions which usually attended the election of a bishop to an important see, and which Chrysostom has so vividly described in his treatise on the priesthood.[399] From dawn of day the places of public resort were occupied by the candidates and their partisans paying court, or paying bribes to the common people; canvassing the nobles and the wealthy not without the potent aid of rich and costly gifts, some statue from Greece or silk from India, or perfumes from Arabia.[400] One of the most conspicuous candidates was Isidore, a presbyter of Alexandria. His claims were eagerly pushed by Theophilus, Archbishop of Alexandria, who had a strong personal interest in securing his success. For Isidore was in possession of a rather awkward secret in the past history of Theophilus himself. When the war between Theodosius and the usurper Maximus was impending, Isidore had been despatched by the Archbishop to Italy with letters of congratulation to be presented to him who should prove the conqueror. Isidore waited till victory had declared itself in favour of Theodosius; presented the humble felicitations of the patriarch, and returned to Alexandria. But he was unable on his return to produce the other letter, designed for Maximus had he proved the victor. According to his own account, it had been abstracted by the reader who had accompanied him on the journey. Theophilus, however, suspected the fidelity of Isidore himself, and that some ugly stories which began to circulate respecting the affair had emanated from him. The See of Constantinople, if secured through his interest, would be an effectual means, he thought, of stopping the mouth of Isidore.[401] But he was doomed to disappointment. While the several candidates and their patrons were exhausting all their arts on the spot to obtain the favour of the electors, the clergy and people, distracted by conflicting bribes and arguments, unanimously decided to summon a man from a distance who had not come forward at all. They submitted the name of Chrysostom to the Emperor, who immediately approved their choice.[402] In fact, the election of Chrysostom was in all probability the suggestion of Eutropius. During a recent visit on public business to Antioch, he had heard and recognised the eloquence of the great preacher. Even if the heart of the man was not touched by the pungent warnings, or warmed by the kindling exhortations of Chrysostom, he had plenty of astuteness to perceive, if only such an eloquence could be employed in the service of the Government, what a powerful engine it would be.[403] The appointment, at any rate, was certain to be welcomed by the people, and of popularity Eutropius stood greatly in need. By the people of Antioch indeed Chrysostom was so deeply and ardently beloved, that the question was how to remove him without causing a disturbance of the public peace. The excitable feelings of the populace at Antioch were at all times a train of powder which needed but the application of a spark to cause a serious explosion of tumult. The difficulty was solved by a mixture of force and fraud highly characteristic of the chief designer and executor of the project. Eutropius addressed a letter to Asterius, the Count of the East, who resided in Antioch, and who promptly acted on his instructions. He proposed to the unsuspecting Chrysostom that they should pay a visit together to one of the martyries outside the city walls. Well pleased to make this pious pilgrimage, the saintly preacher accompanied his captor through the Roman gate, and turned his back on his beloved native city, which he was destined never to revisit. At the martyry he was seized by some Government officials, and carried on to Pagræ, the first station on the high road for Constantinople. Here a chariot and horses awaited them, together with one of the imperial chamberlains, a "magister militum," and an escort of soldiers. The bewildered Chrysostom was hurried into the chariot, without any attention being paid to his remonstrances or inquiries; the horses were put into a smart gallop, and the pace well kept up to the next stage, where a similar equipage was in waiting. Such was the rapid, but, considering all the circumstances, undignified approach of the future archbishop to take possession of his see.[404]

Great was the joy of the people on his arrival, great the mortification and consternation of the rival candidates. Theophilus loudly declared that he would take no part in the ordination. "You will ordain him," said Eutropius, "or take your trial on the charges contained in these documents;" producing certain papers of accusations brought against him from various quarters, at the sight of which Theophilus turned pale. His opposition was effectually silenced, though he nourished his revenge for a future day.[405] And we may presume that he took the lead, by virtue of his rank, in the ceremony of consecration—that is, that he pronounced the consecration prayer and blessing, while two other bishops held the gospels over the head, and the other prelates who were present laid their hands on the head of the recipient of consecration.[406] The ceremony took place on February 26, A.D. 398, in the presence of a vast concourse of people, who came, no doubt, not only to witness the spectacle, but to hear from the lips of one so famed for eloquence the "Sermo enthronisticus," or homily on the lesson for the day, which was delivered by the new Patriarch[407] after he had been conducted to his throne, and which was regarded as a test of his powers. This discourse has not been preserved, but Chrysostom alludes to it in the homily numbered xi. against the Anomœans, which was the second discourse he delivered as archbishop. He there reminds his hearers how in his first discourse he had promised, in his warfare with heretics, to trust, not in the carnal weapons of human dialectic, but in the spiritual armour of Holy Scripture, even as David had confronted and prevailed over the Philistine with weapons which the warrior despised, but which were crowned with success because blessed by God.[408] In the review already taken of his discourses against Arians and other heretics, it has been seen how faithfully he adhered to this principle.

The disadvantages of a monastic, secluded training, in one who was called upon to occupy a large and important see, have been pointed out by no one better than by Chrysostom himself,[409] and he now experienced the truth of his own observations. His genius was not of that practical order which displays itself in great discernment of character and tact in the management of men; and his virtues were of that austere kind, the virtues of the monk rather than of the Christian citizen, joined to a certain irritability of temper and inflexibility of will, which were ill calculated to first conciliate and then delicately lead on to a purer way of life the undisciplined flock committed to his care.[410] If Nectarius had been too much the man of the world, his successor was, for the position in which he was placed, too much the saint of the cloister. The new wine burst the old bottles. He began immediately to reform with an unsparing hand—first of all within the limits of his own palace. The costly store of silken and gold-embroidered robes, the rich marbles, ornaments, and vessels of various kinds which his courtly predecessor had accumulated, were sold in exchange for homelier articles, and the surplus was applied to the aid of hospitals and the relief of the destitute.[411] The bishop, and many of the clergy of Constantinople, had been accustomed to entertain and be entertained by the wealthy and the great. Ammianus Marcellinus contrasts the luxurious style of living affected by the bishops of great cities, who "rode about in their carriages, elaborately dressed, and gave princely banquets," with the frugal fare, the cheap clothing, the modest deportment of the provincial bishops.[412] The admonition of Jerome also to an episcopal friend demonstrates the tendency at this period to an immoderate and worldly hospitality on the part of the clergy. "Avoid," he says, "giving great entertainments to the laity, and especially to those who occupy high stations; for it is not very reputable to see the lictors and guards of a consul waiting outside the doors of a priest of Jesus Christ, nor that the judge of a province should dine more sumptuously with you than in the palace. If it be pretended that you do this only to be able to intercede with him for poor criminals, there is no judge who will not pay greater respect to a frugal priest than to a rich one, and show more deference to your piety than to your wealth."[413] Chrysostom, like Jerome, was an uncompromising ascetic in his views on clerical life. He ate in solitude the spare and simple diet of a monk, and declared that he would never set foot at Court except on pressing affairs concerning the welfare of the Church. When one considers what the character of that Court was, it must be confessed that the resolution highly became a Christian bishop.[414] His own seclusion might have been easily tolerated if he had not exacted the same severe simplicity of life in his clergy. He denounced their parasitical flatteries, and their propensity to seek entertainments at the tables of the wealthy, and insisted that their stipends must be quite sufficient to supply them with the necessaries of life. He suspended many from their cures on account of worldly or immoral conduct, and repelled others from the Eucharist. Several of these became the most active organisers of hostile cabals.

But there was another cause of the archbishop's unpopularity with his clergy, which arose from his vigorous assaults upon a deep and apparently most prevalent evil.

Celibacy appears never to have been made obligatory on the clergy of the Eastern Church. The Synod of Elvira, which enjoins celibacy, was a purely Spanish synod;[415] and the decree of Pope Siricius to the same effect, in A.D. 385, could not affect any countries beyond Italy, Spain, and perhaps Southern Gaul. That decree is a remarkable instance of the law-giving spirit of the Western Church, which hardened tendencies into binding statutes. But sentiment and opinion were quite as strong in favour of clerical celibacy in the East as in the West. It was proposed at the Council of Nice that a canon should be passed enforcing it upon every order of the clergy; a proposal which was defeated only by the influence of the aged Egyptian monk Paphnutius, who, though he had never been married, and had always lived an ascetic life, earnestly deprecated the imposition of a burden upon all men which some men only were able to bear. The result was that the clergy were permitted to retain their wives whom they had married before ordination, but were forbidden to marry after ordination. And this is called "the ancient tradition of the Church."[416] There can be no doubt, however, that a profound conviction possessed the minds of all the most earnest Christians in Eastern Christendom that the unmarried life was inherently better than the married; and, consequently, clerical celibacy was honoured and encouraged, though marriage was allowable. On the other hand, there grew up, side by side with the practice of celibacy, a custom which broke it in the spirit while it was preserved in the letter. The same Council of Nice which by one canon freely granted to the clergy the society of their lawful wives, by another prohibits unmarried clergy of every rank to have any woman dwelling under the same roof who was not their mother, sister, or aunt.[417] It was the transgression of this canon which was indignantly complained of by several writers[418] and at councils[419] in or near the time of Chrysostom, as well as by Chrysostom himself. Under the name of spiritual sisters, young women, often consecrated virgins of the Church, lived, as they maintained, in all innocent and sisterly affection with unmarried priests. But the risk to the morals of both was imminent, and the scandal which it brought upon the clergy in the eyes of the world was certain. Chrysostom denounces the custom on both these grounds. Whether two treatises, one addressed to the men, the other to the women, were composed at Constantinople, or, as Socrates says, during his diaconate, they embody his views on the whole subject, and afford a curious insight into clerical life in the great cities at this epoch.[420]

He places the offenders on the horns of a dilemma. "If you are weak, the temptation to evil is so great, that for your own sake you ought to avoid it; if you are strong, you ought to abandon the practice for the sake of those who are weak." They brought a great scandal on the Church and opened the mouths of adversaries. An isolated sin would be less severely visited than one which, though comparatively small in itself, caused others also to offend. They should imitate the wisdom of St. Paul, who would not do a thing in itself desirable or harmless, if the evil resulting to some exceeded any possible advantage to others.[421] A pretext for the reception of these unmarried women was made on the ground that they were orphans who had no protectors. But this became a great snare both to the women and the clergy: they were occupied with the management of property instead of devoting themselves to spiritual concerns. It would be far better that a maiden should marry, than, by abstaining from marriage, involve herself and others in worldly business who ought to be free from it. If poor, it was better she should remain poor and friendless, than be received into a home where the danger incurred by the soul would far exceed the advantages procured for the body. There were many aged women who were poor, friendless, maimed, or diseased; the city was full of them. These were the most deserving objects of clerical charity, and on them it could be exercised without fear of reproach.[422] These "spiritual sisters" appear from Chrysostom's account to have often lived very much like fine ladies of fashion. "How incongruous and ludicrous," he says, "when you enter the house of one who calls himself a single man, to see articles of female dress and instruments of female occupation lying about—girdles, head-gear, wool-baskets, spindles, distaffs!" In the elaboration of their dress these companions often surpassed actresses; they were gossips and match-makers. The man who ought to have renounced all worldly calls might be seen inquiring at the silversmith's if his lady's mirror was ready, her casket finished, her flask returned; from the silversmith's he hurried to the perfumer's to see about her scents; from the perfumer to the linen-draper, and so on upon a round of shopping. All this business and worldly worry made them harsh to the servants, who retaliated by secretly abusing their master and mistress.[423] This was bad enough, but the clergy were not ashamed to display their servile attachment to these women even in the churches. They received them at the doors, forced others to make way for them, and walked in front of them with a proud air, when they ought not to have been able to lift up their heads for shame.[424]

CHAPTER 15

THE FALL OF EUTROPIUS— HIS RETREAT TO THE
SANCTUARY OF THE CHURCH— RIGHT OF SANCTUARY
MAINTAINED BY CHRYSOSTOM— DEATH OF EUTROPIUS—
REVOLT OF GOTHIC COMMANDERS TRIBIGILD AND
GAÏNAS— DEMAND OF GAÏNAS FOR AN ARIAN CHURCH
REFUSED BY CHRYSOSTOM— DEFEAT AND DEATH
OF GAÏNAS. A.D. 399-401.

THE EMPRESS EUDOXIA HAD rejoiced to discover that the new Archbishop, although he mainly owed his promotion to the supreme minister of the Court, was by no means disposed to be ruled by him. If, indeed, Eutropius had expected to be rewarded for the elevation of Chrysostom by finding in him a complaisant servant, he sustained a severe disappointment. Some little pretences which the minister made of assisting the Church, by patronising Chrysostom's missionary projects, could not disguise the iniquitous venality of his administration, or protect him from the solemn warnings and severe censure of one who was no respecter of persons. In fact, when the Archbishop declaimed against the cupidity, injustice, and extortions of the rich, it was obvious to all that Eutropius was the most signal example of those vices. Eudoxia was anxiously aiming to compass the fall of the detested minister; detested by her more especially, not only because he thwarted her influence with Arcadius generally, but had also persuaded him to withhold from her the title of Augusta until she should present a male heir to the throne. She spared no pains therefore to conciliate the

Archbishop, who might prove a valuable ally to her cause. It has been seen with what an appearance at least of humble piety she took part in the nocturnal procession which conducted some sacred reliques to their resting-place outside Constantinople.

Her chamberlain, Amantius (himself distinguished for unaffected Christian piety), was the frequent bearer to the Archbishop of her liberal contributions to the support of churches, or the relief of the poor. With her own hands, it is said, she traced designs for basilicas to be erected at her expense in some of the country districts.[461] Chrysostom was always ready to welcome as genuine any manifestations of religious feeling. Such practical proofs of her attachment to the Church completely captivated him, and for the present his rich vocabulary could hardly furnish language adequate to express his admiration and gratitude.[462]

Meanwhile, the poor doomed minister, not content to remain as he began, enjoying the reality of power without the name, prepared the way for his own destruction by inducing the Emperor to bestow on him the titles of Patrician and Consul. The acquisition of these venerated and venerable names by the eunuch slave caused a profound emotion of indignation and shame throughout the Empire, but especially in the Western capital, where they were bound up with all the most noble and glorious memories in the history of the nation. It is true the consulship was now an empty honour, destitute of all the great duties and responsibilities which formerly were attached to it. But the year was still named after the consul, and the character of the man was by a superstitious feeling projected on to the year which he inaugurated. The name of the odious Eutropius, eunuch and slave, if prefixed to the year, would seem to overshadow it with a kind of ominous and baleful blight, and to be in itself a portent of incalculable disaster. In short, after their indignation had vented itself in much bitter sarcasm, the Romans resolved that the consulship of Eutropius should never be inscribed at the Capitol. A solemn deputation from the people and senate waited on Honorius and Stilicho at Milan, to submit their decision, and to implore the imperial assent. Their spokesman recounted the glorious exploits of Theodosius and (by a flattering courtesy) of his son. The Saxon by the ocean, defeated; Britain delivered from the Picts; Gaul protected from the menaces of Germany! "Through thee Rome beholds the Frank humbled at her feet, the Suevian discomfited, and the Rhine, submissive to thy rule, salutes thee under the name of Germanicus. But the East, alas! envies us our prosperity; abominable conspiracies are fermenting there which tend to break up our unity" ... the revolt of Gildo, the destruction of African towns, the famine of Rome, all these calamities were the work of Eutropius, and for these he was rewarded with the consulship! The East, accustomed to stoop under the sceptre of women, might accept the rule of a eunuch slave; but that to which the Orontes and the Halys submitted as ordinary custom would be a foul stain on the waters of the Tiber. The image of Eutropius should never be placed in the same rank with those of Æmilius, of Decius, of Camillus, the saviours and supporters of their country, the champions of Roman freedom!... "Rise from your tombs, ancient Romans, pride of Latium; behold an unknown colleague on your curule chairs; rise and avenge the majesty of the Roman name!"[463]

Honorius, prompted no doubt by Stilicho, accorded a favourable reply to the supplication of the Roman people. Mallius Theodorus, prætorian prefect of Italy, a man eminent in virtue and ability as lawyer, soldier, and writer, and not less popular than distinguished, was nominated Consul by Honorius amidst general approbation, and his name appears in the Fasti of the West without a colleague.[464]

No doubt some of the virtuous indignation of the Romans is to be attributed to the jealousy which now ran high between East and West, but we may also not fancifully discern genuine sparks of the independent spirit of their forefathers. Amidst the general decadence and degeneracy of the whole Empire, the West did not descend, could not have descended, to such depths of servile adulation as did the Byzantines on the occasion of the inauguration of Eutropius as Consul. When, arrayed in an ample Roman robe, he assumed his seat in the palace of the Cæsars, the doors were thrown open to an eager crowd of flatterers. The senate, the generals, all the high functionaries of the state, poured in to offer their homage to the great personage; emulated each other in the honour of kissing his hand, and even his wrinkled visage. They saluted him as the bulwark of the laws, and the parent of the Emperor. Statues of bronze or marble were placed in various parts of the city, representing him in the costume of warrior or judge, and the inscriptions on their pedestals styled him third founder of the city after Byzas and Constantine.

No wonder that Claudian declaimed with bitter sarcasm against "a Byzantine nobility and Greek Quirites," and even invokes Neptune by a stroke of his trident to unseat and submerge the degenerate city which had inflicted such a deep disgrace upon the Empire.[465]

And in truth a blow of no mean force, though directed not by the hand of a mythic deity, but of a stout barbarian was about to descend on the Eastern capital. The consequences of it were averted only by the sacrifice of the new consul who had chiefly provoked it; upon him it came with crushing effect: he fell never to rise again. In the final scene of this curious drama the Archbishop plays a conspicuous part, and therefore it must be unfolded from the beginning. But, independently of this, it throws light upon the condition of the Eastern Empire at that period.

Tribigild, a Gothic soldier of distinction, had been, according to a usage now prevalent, promoted to the rank of Tribune, and placed in command of a military colony of Gruthongi (a large branch of the Ostrogoths), established in the region of Phrygia, near the town of Nacolea. The recent elevation of Alaric to the rank of Commander-in-chief of the Roman forces in the East had encouraged the pretensions and raised the expectations of all barbarian commanders. In the February or March next after the appointment of Eutropius to the consulship, Tribigild appeared at court to solicit promotion for himself and a higher rate of pay for his martial colonists, who, too ignorant or too proud to maintain themselves by cultivating the soil, were perishing of hunger in the midst of the most productive regions of Asia Minor. His suit was one among many of similar applications at that time constantly brought before the Court, and it was coldly dismissed by the Emperor's minister. Tribigild was not one to return home and brood in sullen and ineffective silence over his repulse. Gaïnas, the Gothic leader, to whom it will be remembered Stilicho had confided the task of putting Rufinus to death, was still in Constantinople; and he was a relation of Tribigild, who found in him a sympathiser to inflame rather than soothe his sense of wrong. In this irritated frame of mind, like a train of powder only needing the application of a match to produce an explosion, he returned to Phrygia. According to Claudian, that match was applied by his wife. He dramatically describes her welcome of the returning husband: "She flies to meet him, embraces him with her snow-white arms, and eagerly inquires what honours or rewards he brings back from the generous prince." When the chieftain relates his ineffectual errand, and the cold disdain with which he had been treated by Eutropius, the chieftainess tears her face with her nails, and with bitter irony bids her husband sheathe his sword and attend to his plough or his vine. She contrasts her own condition with the happy wives and sisters of other warriors; they enjoyed rich spoils in the shape of adornments or of beautiful Grecian handmaids. "Alaric, who broke treaties, was rewarded for it, but those who observe them remain poor. Alaric invaded and pillaged Epirus, and was made commander of the forces; *you* go humbly to solicit your due and are repulsed. Enrich yourself with booty, and you will be a Roman citizen as soon as you please."[466] No doubt this scene, whether wholly imaginary or not, faithfully represents the feelings which, since the fatal promotion of Alaric, must have encouraged treasonable designs on the part of many barbarian chiefs. At any rate, whether the resentment of Tribigild was inflamed or not by the irony of his wife, he resolved to cast off allegiance to the Empire. He mustered his forces, which gladly abandoned their feeble attempts at husbandry to return to the more congenial pursuit of war and plunder. The rich country of Phrygia was rapidly overrun, and some of the fortified towns, owing partly to the decay of their walls, were captured. All Asia Minor was convulsed with apprehension, and appealed to Constantinople for protection.

Eutropius affected to treat the rebellion as a petty insurrection, the suppression of which belonged rather to the judge armed with instruments of torture than to a military force. He declined the proffered assistance of Gaïnas, but secretly negotiated with Tribigild, in the hope of subduing him by means of promotion or of a bribe in money. The Goth, proud to have turned the tables upon the minister who had recently treated him with scorn, steadfastly declined to accept any satisfaction but one— the head of Eutropius himself. Thus war was inevitable; but who was to conduct it? Eutropius dared not trust Gaïnas to act against his own countryman and kinsman. He retained him therefore at Constantinople in command of the city troops, and committed the management of the legions to one of his favourites, Leo, described by Claudian as a man "abounding in flesh, but scant of brains;"[467] once a wool-carder, but, under the administration of the eunuch, a military commander. His obesity made him an object of derision to the army, and, joined to his natural incapacity and ignorance, rendered him the most unfit man to conduct an expedition against the subtle and active barbarian. Leo crossed the Bosporus with a large, ill-disciplined army, whose approach was welcomed by the devastated provinces, which vainly rejoiced at the prospect of speedy deliverance from the ravager. The enemy, meanwhile, had retreated southwards through Pisidia, and after a narrow escape from destruction in the defiles of Mount Taurus, where the inhabitants made a fierce stand, he emerged into Pamphylia, and awaited Leo in the vast plain of the Eurymedon and Melas, which extends between the chain of Taurus and the sea. The doughty commander of the imperial forces eagerly pursued the Goths, and flattered himself, as the artful chieftain pretended to retreat in alarm, that he had cooped him up by the sea. In the confident anticipation of success, the discipline, such as it was, of Leo's camp became still more relaxed. Little or no watch was kept; festivity, drunkenness, and disorder of all kinds prevailed; while the general had allowed himself to be drawn into a fatal position between a wary enemy in front and an impassable morass in his rear. In the depth of a dark night, the Goth swooped down upon his prey: all were asleep in the camp, the slumbers of many deepened by drunkenness. Those who were not killed on the spot fled in wild confusion, but only to flounder in the marsh, in the oozy bed of which large numbers were absorbed. A few scattered remnants reached the Bosporus by devious routes, to carry tidings of the disaster to Constantinople. Leo himself had plunged on horseback into the morass; the animal soon sank under the weight of his bulky rider, who, after vain struggles to extricate himself, was finally sucked beneath the quag. To such a bathos have the annals of Roman warfare descended! A Roman general suffocated in mud![468]

The news of this disaster struck panic into the population and Court of Constantinople. There was but one who rejoiced; for he saw himself master of the situation. This was Gaïnas; he was the only man at hand capable of confronting Tribigild, and he was despatched across the Bosporus with his barbarian auxiliaries. But he did nothing to check the enemy, who had resumed his career of pillage. He represented that the forces opposed to him were insuperable, but expressed a firm conviction that Tribigild would become as loyal a servant as himself on one condition— the surrender of the minister Eutropius, the principal author of all the evils of the State.[469]

Arcadius was placed in a state of cruel perplexity. We need not suppose that he was attached to Eutropius, but his weak and indolent nature shrank from the responsibility and labour to which, through the industry of his ambitious minister, he had been a stranger. Now, however, from all quarters the truth was forced upon him, that if he would save his throne, he must part with his newly-made consul. Ugly rumours were prevalent that Stilicho was meditating a march to the East, and at the same time a new king, hostile to the Empire, had ascended the throne in Persia.[470] But a nearer and more persuasive enemy of Eutropius was at hand to give the finishing impulse to his fall. The profound jealousy of his power entertained by Eudoxia has been already intimated. Not only had the title of Augusta been withheld from her through his influence, but he had even carried his arrogance so far at this time as to declare that his hand, which had elevated her, could also depose her from her present position altogether. The proud Frankish blood of the Empress could ill brook such words from the lips of an upstart menial, consul though he now was. With a passionate gesture she dismissed him from her presence, hastened to her two young children, Flaccilla and Pulcheria, and with them made her way into the apartment of Arcadius. To his inquiries as to the purpose of her sudden appearance she made at first no reply save by a flood of tears, in which the children, from natural sympathy, joined; but presently, in language broken by sobs, she related a tale of insults received at the hands of Eutropius, and the crowning insult of the whole series. This was the blow which was completely to fell the tottering minister. He was summoned to the imperial presence, and having been informed that he was deprived of his official dignity, and his property confiscated, he was commanded instantly to quit the palace under pain of death.[471]

The poor wretch, who had mounted from the lowest dregs of society to the grandest position a subject could occupy, was thus by a single blow suddenly reduced to the position from which he had started; and even worse, for death stared him in the face. The bows and smiles with which courtiers had greeted him that morning, when he was still the royal favourite, concealed, he well knew, a hatred and a scorn which were not confined to them, but animated the whole population, and only needed opportunity to declare themselves. That opportunity had come. He had no friends; whither should he fly? There was but one place to which he could in his extremity naturally turn— the sanctuary of the Church; but here, by the cruel irony of his fate, a law emanating from himself barred his entrance.

The right of asylum, which was once possessed by many of the Pagan temples, passed over, by a natural transition, about the time of Constantine, to Christian churches. However useful in ages of great rudeness and ferocity this right may be, either to shelter the innocent from lawless violence, or to give offenders protection from vindictive rage till the time of equitable trial, it inevitably becomes, sooner or later, an intolerable interference with the natural course of law and justice. Tiberius had found it expedient to restrict or abolish such rights attached to many of the Greek and Asiatic temples. Their suppression was resisted partly from feelings of pride, partly of mercenary interest, partly of respect for the sanctity of the places, as in the case in our own country of the sanctuary of Westminster.[472] In the reign of Theodosius I. a law was passed which excepted gross criminals and public debtors, and another in the reign of Arcadius, which excepted Jewish debtors who pretended to be Christians, from the privileges of asylum;[473] but by a law of September, A.D. 397, suggested by Eutropius, clergy and monks, in whose churches or convents fugitives might shelter, were obliged to surrender them to the officers of justice, though they might appeal to the Court in their favour.[474] The special object of Eutropius had been to cut off all retreat from the victims of his jealous ambition or avarice; and now he was one of the first to want the protection which he had himself abolished. But he knew, no one better, that the law had excited much resentment and resistance on the part of the Church; and it might well be that the Archbishop would gladly connive at the violation of the obnoxious measure by the very person who had framed it. He resolved to make the attempt. In the humblest guise of a suppliant, tears streaming down his puckered cheeks, his scant grey hairs smeared with dust, he crept into the cathedral, pushed aside the curtain which divided the b or sanctuary from the nave, and, clinging closely to the holy table,[475] awaited the approach of the Archbishop or any of the clergy.[476] The enemy was on his track. As he lay quaking with terror, he could hear on the other side of the thin partition the trampling of feet, mingled with the clattering of arms and voices raised in threatening tones by soldiers on the search. At this crisis he was found by the Archbishop, in a state of pitiable and abject terror; his cheek blanched with a death-like pallor, his teeth chattering, his whole frame quivering, as with faltering lips he craved the asylum of the Church.[477]

He was not repulsed as the destroyer of that shelter which he now sought. Chrysostom rejoiced in the opportunity afforded to the Church of exhibiting at once her clemency and power, by taking a noble revenge upon her former adversary. The clamour of the soldiers on the other side of the veil increased. Chrysostom led the unhappy fugitive to the sacristy; and having concealed him there, he confronted his pursuers, asserted the inviolability of the Church's sanctuary, and refused to surrender the refugee. "None shall penetrate the sanctuary save over my body; the Church is the Bride of Jesus Christ, who has intrusted her honour to me, and I will never betray it." The soldiers threatened to lay violent hands on the Archbishop; but he freely presented himself to them, and only desired to be conducted to the Emperor, that the whole affair might be submitted to his judgment. He was accordingly placed between two rows of spearmen, and marched like a prisoner from the cathedral to the palace.[478]

The populace meanwhile had heard of the wonderful event of the day. The news of the detested minister's degradation had circulated through the Hippodrome, where a grand performance had attracted large multitudes. The spectators rose in a mass, uttered a shout of exultation, and vociferously demanded the head of the culprit.[479]

Chrysostom meanwhile maintained before the Emperor his lofty tone of authority in vindication of the Church's right of asylum. Human laws could not weigh in the balance against divine; the very man who had assailed the Church's divine right was now forced, in his day of distress, to plead in favour of it. The Emperor was moved, as he always was by any one who possessed some of that force of character which he himself lacked. Some feelings of compassion also for his late minister's humiliation may have mingled themselves with superstitious dread of incurring Divine wrath. He promised to respect the retreat of Eutropius. But, on learning his decision, the troops which were in the city became indignant and furious in their demands that the culprit should be surrendered to justice. The Emperor made an address to them, entreating them even with tears to remember that they had received benefits as well as wrongs from the object of their present rage, and, above all things, imploring them to respect the sanctity of the holy table, to which the suppliant was clinging. By such words he restrained them with difficulty from the commission of any immediate violence.[480]

The following day was Sunday; but the places of public amusement and resort were deserted, and such a vast concourse of men and women thronged the cathedral as was rarely seen except on Easter Day.[481] All were in a flutter of expectation to hear what the "golden mouth" would utter, the mouth of him who had dared, in defence of the Church's right, to defy the arm of the law, and to stem the tide of popular feeling. But few perhaps were prepared to witness such a dramatic scene as was actually presented, and which gave additional force and effect to the words of the preacher. It was a common practice with the Archbishop, on account partly of his diminutive stature and some feebleness of voice, to preach from the "ambo," or high reading-desk, which stood a little westward of the chancel, and therefore brought him into closer proximity with the people.[482] On the present occasion, he had just taken his seat on the ambo, and a sea of upturned faces was directed towards his thin pale countenance in expectation of the stream of golden eloquence, when the curtain which separated the nave from the chancel was partially drawn aside, and disclosed to the view of the multitude the cowering form of the unhappy Eutropius, clinging to one of the columns which supported the holy table. Many a time had the Archbishop preached to light minds and unheeding ears on the vain and fleeting character of worldly honour, prosperity, luxury, wealth; now he would enforce attention, and drive his lesson home to the hearts of a vast audience, by pointing to a visible example of fallen grandeur in the poor unhappy creature who lay grovelling behind him. Presently he burst forth: "'ματαιότης ματαιοτήτων!—O vanity of vanities!'" words how seasonable at all times, how pre-eminently seasonable now. "Where now are the pomp and circumstance of yonder man's consulship? where his torch-light festivities? where the applause which once greeted him? where his banquets and garlands? Where is the stir that once attended his appearance in the streets, the flattering compliments addressed to him in the amphitheatre? They are gone, they are all gone; one rude blast has shattered all the leaves, and shows us the tree stripped quite bare, and shaken to its very roots."... "These things were but as visions of the night, which fade at dawn; or vernal flowers, which wither when the spring is past; as shadows which flitted away, as bubbles which burst, as cobwebs which rent."... "Therefore we chant continuously this heavenly strain: ματαιότης ματαιοτήτων καὶ πάντα ματαιότης. For these are words which should be inscribed on our walls and on our garments, in the market-place, by the wayside, on our doors, but above all should they be written in the conscience, and engraved upon the mind of every one." Then, turning towards the pitiable figure by the holy table: "Did I not continually warn thee that wealth was a runaway slave, a thankless servant? but thou wouldst not heed, thou wouldst not be persuaded. Lo! now experience has proved to thee that it is not only fugitive and thankless, but murderous also; for this it is which has caused thee to tremble now with fear. Did not I declare, when you rebuked me for telling you the truth, 'I love thee better than thy flatterers; I who reprove thee care for thee more than thy complaisant friends?' Did I not add that the wounds inflicted by a friend were to be valued more than the kisses given by an enemy? If thou hadst endured my wounds, the kisses of thy enemies would not have wrought thee this destruction."... "We act not like thy false friends, who have fled from thee, and are procuring their own safety through thy distress; the Church, which you treated as an enemy, has opened her bosom to receive thee; the theatre, which you favoured, has betrayed thee, and whetted the sword against thee."[483] He thus depicted, he said, the abject condition of the minister, not from any desire to insult the prostrate, not to drown one who was tossed on the billows of misfortune; but to warn those who were still sailing with a fair wind, lest they should be hurried into the same abyss. Who had been more exalted than this man? Had he not surpassed all in wealth? had he not climbed to the very pinnacle of grandeur? yet now he had become more miserable than a prisoner, more pitiable than a slave.... It was the glory of the Church to have afforded shelter to an enemy; the suppliant was the ornament of the altar. "What!" you say, "is this iniquitous, rapacious creature an ornament to the altar?" Hush! the sinful woman was permitted to touch the feet of Jesus Christ Himself, a permission which excites not our reproach, but our admiration and praise.... The degradation of Eutropius was a wholesome example both to the rich and poor. "Let some rich man enter the church, and he will derive much advantage from what he sees. The spectacle of one, lately at the pinnacle of power, now crouching with fear like a hare or a frog, chained to yonder pillar not by fetters, but by fright, will repress arrogance, and subdue pride, and will teach him the truth of the Scripture precept: 'All flesh is grass, and all the glory of man as the flower of grass.' On the other hand, let a poor man enter, and he will learn not to be discontented, or to deplore his lot; but will be grateful to his poverty, which is to him as a most secure asylum, a most tranquil haven, a most impenetrable fortress."[484] The Archbishop concluded by exhorting the people to mercy and forgiveness, following the example of their Emperor. How else could they with a clear conscience join in the Holy Mysteries about to be celebrated, or join in the prayer: "Forgive us our trespasses, as we forgive them that trespass against us?" He did not deny that the offender had committed great crimes, but the present was a season not for judgment but for mercy. If they would enjoy the favour of God, who had declared, "I will have mercy and not sacrifice," they would intercede with the Emperor for the life of their enemy. So would they obtain the mercy of God for themselves, and remission of their own sins; so would they shed glory on their Church, and win the praise of their humane sovereign, while their own clemency would be extolled to the ends of the earth."

The people probably thought that sufficient mercy had already been exercised by respecting the asylum of the Church as against the law, and no further effort, so far as is known, was made on behalf of the fallen minister. He remained for several days more in the sanctuary, and then secretly and suddenly quitted it. Whether he fled designedly, mistrusting the security of his retreat, perhaps even, with the suspiciousness natural to a deceitful person, mistrusting the fidelity of his protectors, and hoping to make his escape from Constantinople in disguise; or whether he surrendered himself on the condition that exile should be substituted for capital punishment, cannot with perfect certainty be determined. It is implied by one writer[485] that he was seized and forcibly removed from the sanctuary. Chrysostom, on the other hand, declares that he would never have been given up, had he not abandoned the Church.[486] However and wherever he may have been captured, some promise appears to have been made that his life at least should be spared. He was put on board a vessel which conveyed him to Cyprus, that island being designed, it was said, to be the place of his banishment for the remainder of his life.[487] But his enemies had determined that his life should be brief. A suit was instituted against him at Constantinople on a variety of charges under the presidency of Aurelian, Prætorian Prefect. Over and above all his other crimes, he was found guilty of mingling with the ordinary costume of the consul certain ornaments or badges which belonged exclusively to the Emperors, and even of harnessing to his chariot animals of the imperial colour and breed. These were found to be treasonable offences, on the strength of which, in spite of some misgivings and hesitation on the part of Arcadius, which were overruled by Eudoxia and Gaïnas, the miserable culprit was recalled from Cyprus to Chalcedon, and there beheaded. As he entered that city, he might have seen affixed to the walls the imperial sentence, by the terms of which his property was declared confiscated to the State, his acts as consul were cancelled, the title of the year was changed, the world invited to rejoice at the purification of the consulship, and to cease to groan over the sight of the monstrosity which had disgraced and disfigured the divine honour of that sacred office. Finally, it was commanded that all statues or representations whatever of Eutropius in public places should be thrown down and broken in pieces.[488]

Thus the earnest desire of Eudoxia was accomplished: she remained mistress of the field, mistress, as she fondly hoped, of the Empire. The government for the present passed from the hands of a eunuch and slave into the hands of a woman. The possible rivals to her supremacy were the Gothic commander Gaïnas and the Archbishop. In what manner she was brought into hostile collision with these two very different personages remains now to be related. The Goth was determined in the ambitious pursuit of power, the Archbishop equally determined in the conscientious discharge of duty. The collision of the ruling powers with him was yet to come, but the contest with Gaïnas immediately succeeded the fall of Eutropius.

The Empress procured the elevation of Aurelian, Prætorian Prefect, to the consulship, and of her favourite (some said her criminal lover[489]), Count John, to the office of Comptroller of the Royal Treasury, or sacred largesses. The public affairs of the Empire were discussed and settled in a sort of cabinet council by her and her friends, of whom three wealthy but avaricious ladies, Castricia, Eugraphia, and Marcia, were the most influential. The haughty and manly spirit of the Gothic warrior naturally disdained to be directed by a coterie of women. He united his army with that of Tribigild, and the two forces assumed a menacing attitude in the vicinity of Constantinople, on the Asiatic side of the Bosporus. Gaïnas opened negotiations with the Emperor, refusing to communicate with any lesser power, complained that his services had been inadequately requited, and demanded, as a preliminary to any further correspondence, the surrender of three principal favourites at Court— Aurelian the Consul, Saturninus the husband of Castricia, and the Count John. The embarrassment of the Court was extreme; but the three ministers, in a genuine spirit, to all appearance, of Roman courage and self-sacrifice for the good of the State, crossed the Bosporus, and sent word to the camp of Gaïnas that they had come to surrender themselves into his hands. The chieftain subjected them to a grim practical jest. He caused them to be loaded with chains, and received them in his tent in the presence of an executioner. After all manner of insults had been heaped upon them, the executioner approached and swung his sword over them with a furious countenance as if on the point of decapitating, but, checking the impending blow, only made a slight scratch on their necks so as just to draw blood. This savage farce having been performed, the three were simply detained in the camp without suffering further violence.[490]

Chrysostom appears to have laboured diligently to mitigate the demands of Gaïnas. His language, in a homily delivered just after the surrender of the three captives, implies that some degree of success had attended his efforts, but it manifests also a feeling of great depression, caused by the unsettled, indeed anarchical, state of public affairs.

"After a long interval of silence, I return to you, my beloved disciples—a silence occasioned, not by any indifference or indolence, but by my absence spent in earnest endeavours to allay a tempest, and to bring into a haven those who were beginning to drown."... "For this purpose I have withdrawn from you for a time, going backwards and forwards" [across the Bosporus], "exhorting, beseeching, supplicating, so as to avert the calamity which was impending over the higher powers. But now that these dismal matters have been concluded I return to you...." He had gone to rescue those who were falling and tempest-tossed; he came back to confirm those who were still standing and at rest, lest they should become victims of some calamity. "For there is nothing secure, nothing stable in human affairs; they are like a raging sea, every day producing strange and fearful shipwrecks. The world is full of tumult and confusion; everywhere are cliffs and precipices, rocks and reefs, fearfulness and trembling, peril and suspicion. No one trusts any one; each man is afraid of his neighbour. The time is at hand which the prophet depicted in those words: 'Trust not in a friend, put not confidence in a guide' (Micah vii. 5); civil strife prevails everywhere, not honest open warfare, but veiled under ten thousand masks. Many are the fleeces beneath which are concealed innumerable wolves; so that one might live more safely among enemies than among those who appear to be friends."[491]

It is possible that the intercessions of Chrysostom may have saved the lives of the three captives, or averted any immediate assault of the Gothic army; but Gaïnas was in a position to dictate any terms he pleased, and his army was like a great swelling wave, threatening at any moment to break in overwhelming force upon the capital. An interview with the Emperor, protected from any insidious attack by the solemn oath of each party, took place in the church of St. Euphemia, situated on a lofty eminence above the city of Chalcedon. The Gothic leader no longer pretended to disguise his ambitious designs. He demanded to be made Consul and Commander-in-chief of the Imperial army, cavalry and infantry, Roman as well as barbarian troops; in short, he aspired to be in position the Stilicho of the East. The Emperor yielded to these ignominious terms, which in effect placed his capital at the mercy of a foreign invader. The troops were rapidly transported from the Asiatic side of the Bosporus and occupied Constantinople. They waited but the word of their commander to fly upon the booty with which the wealthy and luxurious city teemed, and which they beheld with hungry eyes; but for a time the signal was not given.[492]

Gaïnas, either from sincere attachment to the Arian form of faith, or possibly from ambition to display his power to his countrymen, who were mainly of the Arian persuasion, demanded the abolition of that law of Theodosius by which Arians were prohibited from public worship inside the city walls. He represented that it was specially indecorous for the Commander-in-chief of the Imperial forces to go outside the city to pay his public devotions. Arcadius, intimidated, and as usual on the point of yielding, referred the matter to the Archbishop. Chrysostom earnestly and indignantly deprecated any concession; to give up one of the Catholic churches to the Arians would be to cast things holy to the dogs, and to reward the impious at the expense of the reverent worshippers of Jesus Christ. He begged the Emperor to allow the whole matter to be discussed between himself and Gaïnas in the royal presence, when he trusted that, by the help of God, he should succeed in silencing the Gothic heretic, and in repressing any repetition of his profane demand.[493] Gaïnas was not averse from the interview; he rather prided himself on his skill in theological debate, and boasted of having vanquished the monk Nilus on the question of the identity, or similarity, of substance in the first two Persons of the Holy Trinity.[494] The Emperor was well satisfied to act the part of a quiet, irresponsible auditor. Accordingly, on the following day, Chrysostom appeared at the palace, accompanied by all those bishops who were in Constantinople at the time. Gaïnas put forward his demand. The Archbishop replied that it was impossible for a prince who laid claim to piety to take any step adverse to the interests of the Catholic faith. If Gaïnas wished to worship inside the walls, all the churches in the city were open to him. When the Goth claimed a right to possess one for his own sect, in consideration of his great services to the State, Chrysostom repelled the demand with indignant scorn. "You have already rewards far exceeding your deserts; you are Commander-in-chief and Consul. Consider what once you were, and what now you are; consider your former destitution and your present abundance. Look at the magnificence of your consular robes, and remember the rags in which you crossed the Danube. Speak not then of ingratitude on the part of those who have laden you with honours. Remember the oaths by which you swore fidelity to the great Theodosius and to his children." He then cited the prohibitory law issued by Theodosius in A.D. 381, called upon the Emperor to enforce it, and on the Gothic commander to observe it. The ecclesiastical historians concur in affirming that the Goth was completely vanquished by the authoritative demeanour and eloquence of the Archbishop, and for the time at least desisted from pressing his demand; but it appears that Arcadius was obliged to satisfy his rapacity by melting the plate of the Apostles' Church.[495]

Possibly, indeed, extortion of money had been the object of Gaïnas from the beginning in making his demand for an Arian church. The plunder-loving spirit of his army was aroused, and the gold and silver visible on the counters of money-changers, and in the shops of wealthy jewellers, was a temptation constantly dangling before their eyes, till a rumour of violent intentions, or perhaps common prudence, caused the owners to remove these alluring treasures into secret places of safety. If the enemy had entertained any design upon the shops, it was transferred from them to the palace, upon which they made a nocturnal assault. According to some accounts, it was repulsed by the vigorous courage of the citizens, who fell with arms upon the assailants; according to others, Gaïnas was scared in several attempts by a vision of an angelic host planted in bright array around the walls of the palace.[496] The materials for the history of these occurrences are so meagre that it is impossible to ascertain details, but, from whatever cause, Gaïnas resolved to escape from the city. Fearing that if he attempted to quit it openly with his troops, he might be forcibly stopped or impeded in his departure, he pretended to be under the influence of a demon and that he desired to offer up prayers for relief from his affliction at the martyry of St. John at Hebdomon, seven miles outside Constantinople.

As he was going out, however, by one of the gates on this pretext, the guards stationed at the gate perceived that his followers were taking with them a quantity of arms which they endeavoured to conceal. The guards refused to let them pass; a fray ensued in which the guards were killed. The inhabitants were seized with mingled rage and terror. Gaïnas was declared by royal decree a public enemy. He himself was outside the walls, and the city gates were now all closed to cut him off and such forces as were with him from those who were left inside Constantinople. A large number of these assembled in and around the church of the Goths. Here they were attacked by the infuriated populace, which set fire to the building. The Goths perished wholesale in the flames or by the sword. Gaïnas, with the remainder of his followers, betook himself to a life of plunder in the Thracian Chersonese. But he found the inhabitants generally prepared to offer a stout resistance to his pillaging bands, which were soon reduced to great straits for subsistence. Meanwhile, a countryman of his in Constantinople was organising measures for his destruction. Fravitta was one of those Goths who had become assimilated to the people among whom they lived. He had married a Roman lady, and was eminent alike for refinement of manners, for valour in arms, and for honest fidelity to the government which he served.[497] He offered to lead out such forces as could be placed at his disposal, pledged himself to clear the Chersonese of the rebels, and drive them, if necessary, beyond the Danube. The offer was accepted with joy, and Fravitta defeated the enemy in several engagements. Gaïnas attempted to cross the Hellespont, and throw his troops again into the fertile regions of Asia Minor; but his flimsy fleet of hastily-constructed rafts, being attacked by a well-managed body of galleys in the middle of the passage, was dispersed or broken in pieces, and a large part of his army was drowned. Gaïnas then determined, with the remnant of his followers, to beat a hasty retreat in the direction of the Danube, where he hoped to be joined by some of his own countrymen, and renew the offensive. The accounts of his march are not quite harmonious, and somewhat obscure. According to Zosimus,[498] he was hotly pursued by Fravitta from place to place, across the range of Hæmus up to the shores of the Danube, into the waters of which he plunged on horseback, and with a scanty band of followers gained the opposite bank, intending thence to make his way to the settlements of his forefathers on the banks of the Pruth or Borysthenes. But his design was frustrated by an unexpected enemy. The Huns occupied at that time the region immediately north of the Danube, and their king, Uldes or Uldin, was disposed to enter into friendly relations with the Roman Empire. He took up the pursuit which Fravitta had abandoned at the river frontier, chased the unhappy Goth like a wild beast from one hiding-place to another, till at last the prey was caught and killed. His head was carried on the point of a lance to Constantinople, as a visible pledge of the good-will of the Hunnish chief. Sozomen and Socrates,[499] on the other hand, represent him to have been overtaken, routed, and slain by Roman troops in Thrace.[500]

Theodoret has a vague story of his own, that when Gaïnas was ravaging Thrace, neither warrior nor ambassador could be found courageous enough to encounter him but Chrysostom, who, yielding to the public appeal, set forth to intercede, and was most respectfully received by the barbarian, who placed the right hand of the Archbishop on his own eyes, and brought his children to his knees—it may be presumed, to receive his blessing. Theodoret does not venture to affirm that the mission availed to induce the Goth to lay down his arms, and the whole story has an unreal and romantic character.[501]

Three aspirants to the absolute control of the Eastern Empire, widely different in race, character, and original condition of life—Rufinus, Eutropius, Gaïnas—had alike perished by a violent death. Fravitta was made consul, but he was too loyal or too unambitious to go beyond the line of his legitimate power. Eudoxia now stood without a rival in the management of the Emperor and the kingdom. Her influence over her husband was enhanced by the birth of a prince, who afterwards mounted the throne as Theodosius II.; and thus the final obstacle was removed to her being solemnly proclaimed Empress under the venerable title of Augusta.

CHAPTER 16

CHRYSOSTOM'S VISIT TO ASIA— DEPOSITION OF SIX SIMONIACAL BISHOPS— LEGITIMATE EXTENT OF HIS JURISDICTION— RETURN TO CONSTANTINOPLE— RUPTURE AND RECONCILIATION WITH SEVERIAN, BISHOP OF GABALA— CHRYSOSTOM'S INCREASING UNPOPULARITY WITH THE CLERGY AND WEALTHY LAITY— HIS FRIENDS— OLYMPIAS THE DEACONESS— FORMATION OF HOSTILE FACTIONS, WHICH INVITE THE AID OF THEOPHILUS, PATRIARCH OF ALEXANDRIA. A.D. 400, 401.

UP TO THIS POINT the episcopal career of Chrysostom may be pronounced eminently successful. He had distinguished himself not only as a vigorous reformer of ecclesiastical discipline, an eloquent master of pure Christian doctrine, and preacher of lofty Christian morality, but he had done good service to the State; and even while he upheld with inflexible firmness the full rights of the Church, he had not by overbearing or haughty independence forfeited the goodwill, respect, and admiration of the Emperor and Eudoxia. But now the horizon gradually darkens. We have to begin unravelling a tangled skein of troubles, to trace a series of subtle intrigues, against which the single-minded honesty of Chrysostom was ill matched, ultimately bringing about his degradation, exile, and death. We are fortunate in possessing, to guide us among these complicated proceedings, the narrative of one who was not only an eye-witness, but an actor in many of the scenes which he relates.[502]

In the spring of the year A.D. 400, during the military usurpation of Gaïnas, twenty-two prelates had assembled in Constantinople to confer with the Archbishop on ecclesiastical business.[503] Palladius has mentioned the names of a few, Theotimus from Scythia, Ammon an Egyptian from Thrace, Arabianus from Galatia. One Sunday when the conclave was sitting, Eusebius, bishop of Valentinopolis in Asia, apparently not himself a member of the synod, entered the place of assembly, and presented a document addressed to the Archbishop as President, which contained seven grave charges against Antoninus, bishop of Ephesus: "He had melted down some of the sacred vessels to make plate for his son; he had transferred some of the marble at the entrance of the baptistry to his own bath; he had placed some fallen columns which belonged to the Church in his own dining-room; he had retained in his employment a servant who had committed murder; he had taken possession of some property in land which had been left to the Church by Basilina, the mother of Julian; he had resumed intercourse with his wife, and had children born to him, after his ordination; lastly, the worst offence of all, he had instituted a regular system of selling bishoprics on a scale proportioned to the revenue of the sees." Chrysostom probably perceived, or suspected from the eagerness of the accuser, that he entertained some personal animosity towards the accused. He replied with calmness and caution: "Brother Eusebius, since accusations made under the influence of agitated feelings are often not easy to prove, let me beseech you to withdraw the written accusation, while we endeavour to correct the causes of your annoyance." Eusebius waxed hot, and repeated his tale of charges with much vehemence and acrimony of tone. The hour of service was approaching; Chrysostom committed to Paul, bishop of Heraclea, who appeared friendly to Antoninus, the task of attempting to conciliate Eusebius, and passed with the remainder of the prelates into the cathedral.

The opening salutation, "Peace be with you," was pronounced by the Archbishop as he took his seat in the centre of the other bishops, ranged, according to custom, on either side of him round the wall of the choir or tribune. The service was proceeding, when, to the amazement alike of the clergy and the congregation, Eusebius abruptly entered the choir, hurried up to the Archbishop, and again presented the document of charges, adjuring him by the life of the Emperor and other tremendous oaths to attend to its contents. From the agitation of his manner, the people imagined that he must be a suppliant entreating the Archbishop to intercede with the Emperor for his life. To avoid a disturbance in the face of the congregation, Chrysostom received the paper of charges, but when the lessons for the day had been read, and the Liturgy of the Faithful (Missa Fidelium) was about to begin, he desired Pansophius, bishop of Pissida, to "offer the gifts," and, with the rest of the prelates, quitted the church. His serenity of mind was ruffled by the impetuous behaviour of Eusebius, and he dreaded the possibility of infringing our Lord's command to abstain from bringing a gift to the altar when "thy brother hath aught against thee." After the conclusion of the service, he took his seat with the other bishops in the baptistry, and summoned Eusebius into the presence of the conclave. Once more the accuser was warned not to advance charges which he might not be able to substantiate, and was reminded that when once the indictment had been formally lodged, he could not, being a bishop, retract the prosecution. Eusebius, however, intimated his willingness to accept all the responsibility of persevering with the accusation. The list of charges was then formally read. The bishops concurred in pronouncing each of the alleged offences to be a gross violation of ecclesiastical law, but recommended that Antoninus should be tried upon the cardinal crime of simony, since this transcended, and in a manner comprehended, all the rest. "Love of money was the root of all evil;" and he who would basely sell for money the highest spiritual office, would not scruple to dispose of sacred vessels, marbles, or land belonging to the Church. The Archbishop then turned to the accused: "What say you, brother Antoninus, to these things?" The Bishop of Ephesus replied by a flat denial of the charges. A similar question being addressed to some of the bishops there present, described as purchasers of their sees, was answered by a similar denial. An examination of such witnesses as could be procured lasted till two o'clock in the day, when, owing to the lack of further evidence, the proceedings were adjourned. Considering the gravity of the affair, and the inconvenience of collecting the witnesses from Asia, the Archbishop announced his intention of paying a visit to Asia Minor in person. Antoninus, conscious of guilt, and aware of the rigorous scrutiny to which his conduct would be subjected, was now thoroughly alarmed. He made interest with a nobleman at court, whose estates he managed (contrary to ecclesiastical law) in Asia, and besought him to prevent the visit of the Archbishop, pledging himself to present the necessary witnesses at Constantinople. The Archbishop, accordingly, found his intended departure opposed by the Court. It was represented that the absence of the chief pastor from the capital, undesirable at all times, might be especially inconvenient at a crisis when tumults were apprehended from the movements of Gaïnas; and it was unnecessary, as the appearance of witnesses from Asia in due time was guaranteed.[504] Any delay was an immediate relief to the accused; and there was a further hope that, by bribery or intimidation, the ultimate production of the witnesses might be prevented. But he was disappointed; for though the Archbishop consented to defer his own visit to Asia, he appointed, with the sanction of the synod, three delegates to proceed thither immediately and institute an inquiry into the case of Antoninus.

The delegates were instructed to hold their court at Hypœpœ, a town not far from Ephesus, in conjunction with the bishops of the province; and the Archbishop and his synod further determined, that if either the accuser or accused failed to appear there within two months, he should be excommunicated. One of the delegates, Hesychius, bishop of Parium on the Hellespont, was a friend of Antoninus, and withdrew from the mission under the pretence of illness; the other two, Syncletius, bishop of Trajanopolis in Thrace, and Palladius, bishop of Hellenopolis in Bithynia, proceeded to Smyrna, announced their arrival to the accuser and defendant by letter, and summoned them to appear at Hypœpœ within the appointed time. The summons was obeyed, but the appearance of the two was only for the purpose of playing off a farce before the commissioners. Strange to relate, a reconciliation had taken place between Antoninus and his apparently implacable accuser. Eusebius had yielded to the temptation to commit the very crime which he had so vehemently denounced. A bribe of money had quelled his righteous indignation; plaintiff and defendant were now accomplices, whose one interest was to conceal their joint iniquities. They professed great willingness to produce their witnesses, but pleaded the difficulty of collecting persons who lived in different and distant places, and were engaged in various occupations. The commissioners requested the accuser to name a period within which he could guarantee the appearance of his witnesses. Eusebius required forty days. As this space of time covered the hottest part of the summer, it was hoped that the patience or health of the commissioners would be too much exhausted at the expiration of it to prosecute the inquiry. Eusebius then departed, ostensibly to search for witnesses; but, in fact, he quietly sneaked away to Constantinople, and concealed himself in some obscure corner in that great city. The forty days expired, and, Eusebius not appearing, the two delegates wrote to the bishops of Asia, pronouncing him excommunicated for contumacy. They lingered a whole month longer in Asia, and then returned to Constantinople. Here they chanced to light upon Eusebius, and upbraided him with his faithless conduct. He affected to have been ill, and renewed his promises to produce witnesses. During these prolonged delays Antoninus died; and Chrysostom now received earnest solicitations from the clergy of Ephesus, and from the neighbouring bishops, to apply a healing hand to the wounds and diseases of the Asiatic Church. "We beseech your Dignity[505] to come down and stamp a divine impress on the Church of Ephesus, which has long been distressed, partly by the adherents of Arius, partly by those who, in the midst of their avarice and arrogance, pretend to be on our side; for very many are they who lie in wait like grievous wolves, eager to seize the episcopal throne by money."[506]

The death of Gaïnas in January, A.D. 401, set Chrysostom free to comply with this earnest appeal to his authority and aid. It was the depth of the winter season; his health was infirm and impaired by the strain of the past year's anxiety and toil; but the zeal of the Archbishop disregarded these impediments. He embarked at Constantinople without delay, leaving Severian, Bishop of Gabala, to act as deputy bishop in his absence. Such a violent north wind sprang up soon after starting, that the crew of the vessel, afraid of being driven on Proconnesus, lay at anchor for two days under shelter of the promontory of Trito. On the third day they took advantage of a southerly breeze to land near Apamea in Bithynia, where Chrysostom was joined by three bishops, Paul of Heraclea, Cyrinus of Chalcedon, and Palladius of Hellenopolis. With these companions he proceeded by land to Ephesus. There he was received with hearty welcome by the clergy and by seventy bishops.

The first business to which the Archbishop and this council of prelates addressed themselves was the election of a new bishop to the See of Ephesus. As usual there were many rival candidates, and factions supporting each with equal vehemence. Chrysostom fell back on the expedient of putting forward a candidate regarded with indifference by all parties. The plan succeeded, and Heracleides was elected. He was a deacon of three years' standing, ordained by Chrysostom, and in immediate attendance on him; a native of Cyprus, who had received an ascetic training in the desert of Scetis, a man of ability and learning. He comes before us again as a fellow-sufferer with the Archbishop, to whom he had owed his elevation.

Not long after the arrival of Chrysostom, Eusebius, the original persecutor of Antoninus and of the simoniacal bishops, appeared, and requested to be re-admitted to communion with his brethren. The request was not immediately granted; but it was determined to proceed with the trial of the accused bishops, to prove whose guilt Eusebius affirmed that he could produce abundant evidence. The witnesses were examined, and the crime being considered fully proven in the case of six bishops, the offenders were summoned into the presence of the council. At first they stoutly denied their guilt, but finally gave way before the minute and circumstantial depositions of lay, clerical, and even female witnesses as to the place, time, and quality of the purchases which they had transacted. They pleaded partly the prevalence of the custom in excuse for their crime, and partly their anxiety to be exempted from the burden of discharging curial duties; that is, from serving on the common and municipal council of their city. Every estate-holder to the amount of twenty-five acres of land was bound to serve in the curia of his city. Many of the functions incident to that office, such as the assessment and collection of imposts, were (especially under an ill-administered despotism) invidious and onerous. Constantine had exempted the clergy from curial office, and the consequence was that many men got themselves ordained simply to evade the disagreeable duty; and this becoming detrimental both to the Church and State, the law of Constantine underwent modifications by his successors. The Church passed canons forbidding those who were curiales to be ordained, the effect of which was to diminish the number of wealthy men who entered the ranks of the clergy.[507] The Asiatic bishops, therefore, if curiales when ordained, had acted against the laws of the Church, and could not legally have claimed exemption from curial duties on the ground of their orders. They sued for mercy to the council; they entreated that, if deprived of their sees, the money which they had paid to obtain them might be returned. In many cases it had been procured with much difficulty; some had even parted with the furniture of their wives to raise the requisite amount. The Archbishop undertook to intercede with the Emperor for their exemption from curial duty; the ecclesiastical question he submitted to the council. The decision of the prelates, under the influence of their president, was temperate and wise. The six bishops were to be deprived of their sees, but allowed to receive the Eucharist inside the altar rails with the clergy, and the heirs of Antoninus were required to restore their purchase-money to them. The deposed prelates were superseded by the appointment of six men, unmarried, eminent for learning and purity of life.[508]

On his return through Bithynia the Archbishop was detained by a not less difficult and delicate piece of business. Gerontius, Archbishop of Nicomedia, the metropolitan of Bithynia, was a singular specimen of an ecclesiastical adventurer. He had been a deacon at Milan, but was expelled by Ambrose for misconduct. He made his way to Constantinople, where, by general cleverness, and by some real or pretended skill in medicine, he became a favourite with people of rank, and through the interest of some influential friends obtained the See of

Nicomedia. He was consecrated by Helladius, bishop of Heraclea, for whose son Gerontius had managed to procure a high appointment in the army. The new bishop of Nicomedia gained the attachment of his people, again it is said, through his skill in curing diseases of the body rather than of the soul. Ambrose incessantly demanded of Nectarius, then Patriarch of Constantinople, that he should be deposed; but Nectarius did not venture to incur the displeasure of the Nicomedians. The bolder spirit and more scrupulous conscience of Chrysostom did not hesitate to strike the blow which his more worldly and courtly predecessor had shrunk from striking. Gerontius was deposed, whether by the sole authority of the Archbishop, or by the decree of a council acting under his influence, is not stated. Pansophius, formerly tutor to the Empress, a man of piety, wisdom, and gentleness, was promoted to the see. But the Nicomedians bewailed the loss of their favourite; they went about the streets in procession, singing litanies, as if in the time of some great national calamity.[509]

Before quitting Asia, Chrysostom is also said to have taken active measures for the suppression of the worship of Midas at Ephesus, and of Cybele in Phrygia.[510] All these proceedings are worth recording, not only as of some ecclesiastical interest in themselves, but also because they were all remembered and turned against him by his enemies. It has been much debated whether Chrysostom, by his acts in Asia, overstrained his legal powers, or rather, whether he exceeded the legal boundaries of his jurisdiction as Patriarch of Constantinople. The fact seems to be that the importance of his see was in that growing state which enabled the possessor of it, if a man of energy and ability, to go great lengths without any exception being taken to his authority, unless and until a hostile feeling was provoked against him. By the Council of Constantinople, A.D. 381, the Patriarch of that city was restricted in his jurisdiction to the diocese of Thrace.[511] His authority over the dioceses of Asia Minor and Pontus was not established till the Council of Chalcedon, A.D. 451, when there was a long discussion on the subject, and the papal legates especially resisted any claim to such an extension; but it was affirmed that the Patriarchs had *long enjoyed* the privilege of ordaining metropolitans to the provinces of those dioceses, and so it was finally conveyed to them by that Council; and the additional right was granted them of hearing appeals from these metropolitans.[512] Theodoret (c. 28) simply observes that the jurisdiction of Chrysostom extended not only over the six provinces of Thrace, but also over Asia and Pontus. The Council of Constantinople gave the bishop of that see the first rank after the Bishop of Rome, because Constantinople was "a new Rome." The Council of Chalcedon declared him for the same reason to be invested with *equal* privileges.

Chrysostom was welcomed, on his return to Constantinople, with hearty demonstrations of joy. On the following day he was at his post in the cathedral, and once more addressing his beloved flock. In somewhat rapturous language he expresses his thankfulness at learning that their fidelity to the Church, and their attachment to their spiritual father, had not been impaired by his absence, which had lasted more than a hundred days. They were disappointed that he had not returned in time to celebrate Easter with them. But he consoles them by representing that every participation of the Eucharist was a kind of Easter. "*As often* as ye eat this bread, ye do show forth the Lord's death till He come." "They were not tied to time and place like the Jew. Wherever and whenever the Christian celebrated that holy feast with joy and love, there was the true Paschal Festival."[513] They regretted also that so many had been baptized by other hands than his. "What then? that does not impair the gift of God; *I* was not present when they were baptized, but *Christ* was present." "In a document signed by the Emperor, the only question of importance is the autograph; the quality of the ink and paper matters not. Even so in baptism, the tongue and the hand of the priest are but as the paper and pen: the hand which writes is the Holy Spirit Himself."[514]

The thankfulness and joy of Chrysostom at the affectionate reception with which he was greeted by the people were probably felt and expressed the more warmly, owing to some unpleasant accounts which had been forwarded to him by his deacon Serapion, that Severian, Bishop of Gabala, had been endeavouring to undermine his influence in his absence. It will be remembered that to Severian Chrysostom had intrusted his episcopal duties during his visitation journey in Asia. The circumstance of a bishop of Syria residing for so long a time in Constantinople is worth considering, and affords a curious insight into the character of the times. Antiochus, Bishop of Ptolemais in Phœnicia, had a reputation as a learned and eloquent man; he paid a visit to Constantinople, and excited much admiration by his discourses. Severian, hearing of his success, was animated by a spirit of emulation, if not envy, which could not be satisfied till he had exhibited his powers on the same theatre. He carefully composed a large stock of sermons, and set out to try his fortune in the capital. The unsuspicious and generous Archbishop received him cordially, and frequently invited him to preach. Severian possessed some powers of speaking, though he had a harsh provincial accent, and he exerted all his eloquence in the church, and all his arts of flattery out of it, to win the confidence and admiration, not only of the Archbishop, but also of the chief personages at court, and even the Emperor and Empress. It was with their full approval that he remained as deputy of the Archbishop during his sojourn in Asia. But he found himself narrowly and suspiciously watched by the Archdeacon Serapion, who opposed some of his proceedings as arbitrary, and made no concealment of his dislike. One day after the return of Chrysostom, Severian passed through an apartment of the episcopal palace where Serapion was sitting. Serapion rose not to make the customary salutation of respect. Severian, irritated by his discourtesy, exclaimed in a loud voice: "If Serapion dies a Christian, then Jesus Christ was not incarnate." The last clause only of the sentence was repeated by Serapion to Chrysostom. It was corroborated by witnesses; the indignation of the Archbishop was excited. Severian was peremptorily commanded to quit the city. The Empress resented the expulsion of a favourite preacher, and commanded the Archbishop to recall him. Chrysostom yielded so far, but was inflexible in his refusal to admit the offender to communion, till Eudoxia came in person to the Church of the Apostles, placed her infant son Theodosius on his knees, and conjured him by solemn oaths to listen to her request. The Archbishop then, but with some reluctance, consented.[515] He was, however, thoroughly honest in doing that to which he had once made up his mind. Fearing that his congregation, in their zealous attachment to him, might disapprove of the reconciliation, he delivered a short address on the subject. He was their spiritual father, and he trusted therefore they would extend to him the respect and obedience of affectionate and dutiful children. He came to them with the most appropriate message that could be delivered by the mouth of a bishop—a message of peace and love. There was also a further duty incumbent on all—respectful submission to the civil powers. If the apostle Paul said, "Be subject to principalities and powers" (Tit. iii. 1), how especially was this precept incumbent on the subjects of a religious sovereign who laboured for the good of the Church? He besought them to receive Severian with a full heart and with open arms. The request was received by the congregation with expressions of approbation. He thanked them for their obedience, and concluded with a prayer that God would grant a fixed and lasting peace to His Church.

Severian addressed them the next day in a rhetorical and artificial discourse on the beauty and blessings of peace—a subject painfully incongruous with the subsequent conduct of the speaker; for this misunderstanding with the Bishop of Gabala was the first muttering of the storm which was soon to burst over the head of the doomed Archbishop.[516]

The inevitable fate of one who attempts to reform a deeply corrupt society, and a secularised clergy, on an ascetic model befell Chrysostom. He lashed with almost equal severity the most unpardonable crimes and the more venial foibles and follies of the age. His denunciations of heartless rapacity, sensuality, luxury, addiction to debasing and immoral amusements, might have been borne; but he presumed— an intolerable offence!— to censure the fashionable ladies for setting off their complexions with paint, and surmounting their heads with piles of false hair. The clergy, too, might have tolerated his condemnation of the grosser offences, such as simony or concubinage, but they resented his restraint of their indulgence in the pleasures of society, and of their propensity to frequent the entertainments of the noble and wealthy. He was, as Palladius expresses it, "like a lamp burning before sore eyes," for what he bade others be, that he was pre-eminently himself.[517] None could say that he was one man in the pulpit and another out of it. To set an example to his worldly clergy, and to avoid contamination, he gave up his episcopal income, save what sufficed to supply his simple daily wants. He resolutely abstained from mingling in general society, and ate his frugal meals in the seclusion of his own apartment. Thus, with the exception of a few deeply attached friends, who measured practical Christianity by the same standard as himself, he became deeply unpopular among the upper ranks of society. With the poor it was otherwise; they regarded him as a kind of champion, because he denounced the oppressions and extortions of the rich, and the tyranny of masters over slaves, and because he was ever inculcating the duty of almsgiving. In the eyes of his friends he was the saint, pure in life, severe in discipline, sublime in doctrine; in the eyes of his enemies he was the sacerdotal tyrant, odious to the clergy as an inexorable enforcer of a rule of life intolerably rigid, odious to clergy and laity as an inhospitable, if not haughty recluse; a vigilant and merciless censor who rode roughshod over established customs. Individuals at last, among clergy and laity, who conceived that they themselves, or at any rate the section of society to which they belonged, were the butts at which more especially the Archbishop aimed his shafts, began to discuss their grievances, till their conferences gradually assumed the shape of positive organised hostility against the disturber of their peace. But before entering on the troublous history of his enemies' machinations, it may be well to take a glance at the most conspicuous of Chrysostom's friends.

The list of those who are known to us by more than their mere names is soon exhausted. Among the clergy may be reckoned Heracleides, made Bishop of Ephesus in the place of Antoninus; Proclus, afterwards (in A.D. 434) Patriarch of Constantinople, at present the receiver of those who demanded audiences with the

Patriarch; Cassianus, founder of the Monastery of St. Victor at Marseilles, and his friend and companion Germanus; Helladius, the priest of the palace, probably equivalent to private chaplain; Serapion, the deacon[518] or archdeacon,[519] afterwards made Bishop of Heraclea in Thrace, from which see he was expelled in the persecution which befell Chrysostom's followers. With most of these men he maintained a constant and affectionate intercourse or correspondence during his exile to the close of his life. With such intimate companions and friends the austerity and reserve of manner which he assumed towards those outside this circle vanished. All the natural amiability and playful humour of his disposition shone out when he was in their company; he called some of them by nicknames of his own invention, especially those who practised such ascetic exercises as he specially approved.[520]

Three ladies are distinguished as among his most faithful friends. Salvina was the daughter of the African rebel Gildo, and had been married by Theodosius to Nebridius, nephew of his Empress, in the hope—a vain one as it proved—that this tie would attach Gildo to the Empire. Her husband died young; she vowed perpetual widowhood, and became the patroness and protectress at the court of Arcadius of oriental churches and ecclesiastics.

Pentadia was wife of the consul Timasius; and when her husband was banished by Eutropius to the Oasis of Egypt, she had been persecuted by the merciless tyrant, and fled for refuge to the Church, where she was protected in sanctuary by the Archbishop in spite of the opposition of her persecutor.

But by far the most eminent of Chrysostom's female friends was the deaconess Olympias. She sprang from a noble but Pagan family. Her grandfather, Ablavius, was a prætorian prefect, highly esteemed and trusted by Constantine the Great, and her father, Seleucus, had attained the rank of count. She was early left an orphan, endowed with great personal beauty, and heiress to a vast fortune. Her uncle and guardian, Procopius, was a man of probity and piety, a friend and correspondent of Gregory Nazianzenus. Her instructress also, Theodosia, sister of St. Amphilocius, was a woman of piety; one whom

Gregory recommended Olympias to imitate as a very model of excellence in speech and conduct. Under this happy training, the girl grew up to emulate and surpass her preceptress in goodness. Gregory delighted to call her "his own Olympias," and to be called "father" by her.[521] There could be no difficulty in finding a suitor for a lady possessed of every attraction. The anxiety of Procopius was to secure a worthy one. Nebridius was selected; a young man, but high in official rank; Count or Intendant of the Domain in A.D. 382, Prefect of Constantinople in A.D. 386. They were wedded in A.D. 384. Many bishops assisted at the ceremony, but Gregory was prevented from attending by the state of his health. He wrote a letter to Procopius, saying that in spirit, nevertheless, he would join their hands to one another and to God. Part of the letter is written in a vein of sprightly humour. "It would have been very unbecoming for a gouty old fellow like himself to be seen hobbling about among the dancers and merry-makers at the nuptials."[522] He also addressed a poem to Olympias, in which he gives her advice how she ought to conduct herself as a married woman. She did not long need his counsel. Nebridius died about two years after their marriage. Olympias regarded this early dissolution of the marriage-bond as an intimation of the Divine will that she should henceforth live free from the worldly entanglements and cares incident to married life. The Emperor Theodosius desired to unite her to a Spaniard named Elpidius, a kinsman of his own, but she steadfastly refused. The Emperor acted in that despotic manner which occasionally marred his usually generous character. He ordered the property of Olympias to be confiscated till she should be thirty years of age; she was even denied freedom of intercourse with her episcopal friends, and of access to the Church. But she only thanked the Emperor for those deprivations, which were intended to make her hanker after worldly life. "You have exercised towards your humble handmaiden a virtue becoming a monarch and suitable even to a bishop; you have directed what was to me a heavy burden, and the distribution of it an anxiety, to be kept in safe custody. You could not have conferred a greater blessing upon me, unless you had ordered it to be bestowed upon the churches and the poor." The Emperor was softened; at any rate he perceived the uselessness, if not the injustice, of his treatment. He cancelled the order for the confiscation of her property, and left her in the undisturbed enjoyment of single life and of her possessions. Henceforward her time and wealth were devoted to the interests of the Church. She was the friend, entertainer, adviser of many of the most eminent ecclesiastics of the day; the liberal patroness of their works in Greece, Asia, Syria, not only by donations of money but even of landed property. We may not admire what was regarded in those days as among the most admirable traits of saintliness, a total disregard to personal neatness and cleanliness; but we can admire her frugal living, and entire devotion of her time to ministering to the wants of the sick, the needy, and the ignorant. Her too indiscriminate liberality was restrained by Chrysostom, who represented to her that, as her wealth was a trust committed to her by God, she ought to be prudent in the distribution of it. This salutary advice procured for him the ill-will of many avaricious bishops and clergy, who had profited, or hoped to profit, by her wealth.[523] She, on her side, repaid the Archbishop for his spiritual care by many little feminine attentions to his bodily wants, especially by seeing that he was supplied with wholesome food, and did not overstrain his feeble constitution by a too rigid abstinence.[524]

The leaders of the faction hostile to Chrysostom among the clergy were the two bishops already mentioned— Severian of Gabala and Antiochus of Ptolemais. To these was added a third in the person of Acacius, Bishop of Berœa. He had, in A.D. 401 or A.D. 402, paid a visit to Constantinople, and, in a fit of rage at what he considered the mean lodging and inhospitable entertainment of the Archbishop, had coarsely exclaimed, in the hearing of some of the clergy, "I'll season a dainty dish for him."[525] The ladies who acquired a melancholy pre-eminence among the enemies of the Archbishop were the intimate friends of the Empress, already mentioned— Marsa, widow of Promotus, the consul whom Rufinus murdered; Castricia, wife of the consul Saturninus; and Eugraphia, a wealthy widow,— all rich women "who used *for* evil the wealth which their husbands had *through* evil obtained." Proud, intriguing, licentious, they were all exasperated against the Archbishop for the censure which he had unsparingly pronounced upon their moral conduct, as well as their vain and extravagant display in dress. The house of Eugraphia became the rendezvous of all clergy and monks, as well as laity, who were disaffected to him. Among the clergy was Atticus, who was obtruded on the see as Archbishop after the banishment of Chrysostom. This worthy cabal collected, and disseminated with praiseworthy industry, whatever tales could damage the character and influence of the Archbishop. His real failings were exaggerated, others were invented, and his language misrepresented. He was irascible, inhospitable, uncourteous, parsimonious; he had unmercifully assailed Eutropius with harsh language when he fled for refuge to the Church; he had behaved disrespectfully to Gaïnas when he was "magister militum;" but, worse than all, he had audaciously attacked the Augusta herself, and had insulted her sacred majesty by indicating her under the name of Jezebel. This is scarcely credible in itself, and is distinctly contradicted by the most trustworthy authorities; but it is stated that he had reproved the Empress for appropriating with harshness, if not violence, a piece of land; and of course the blows which he directed against inordinate luxury, unseemly parade of dress and the like, fell heavily upon the most prominent leader in these follies. She was probably mortified also to find that her display of religious zeal, her pious attendance on the services of the Church, her pilgrimages, her really liberal donations to good works, did not protect her from censure in other things. Chrysostom was not one of those who would connive at evil for the benefit, as some might have represented it, of the Church. He would not sacrifice what he believed to be the interests of morality, for the supposed advantage either of himself or of the Church over which he ruled. Wrong was wrong and must be rebuked, though the actor was the Empress herself, though that Empress was inclined to be the benefactress and patroness of the Church, and though she might become, as she *did* become, his implacable foe.

The clergy only needed an equally potent leader on their side, and then the organisation of the hostile forces would be complete. Such a chief was to be found in the Patriarch of Alexandria, Theophilus, who had already displayed a malignant spirit at the ordination of the Archbishop, though intimidated by Eutropius into submission. He was only waiting his opportunity for revenge, which a concurrence of circumstances now put into his hands.

After making the most of such charges as gossip, aided by malice, could manufacture at Constantinople, the enemy employed one of the party, a despicable Syrian monk named Isaac, to make a scrutinising inquiry at Antioch into the previous life of Chrysostom. A youth passed in such a licentious and voluptuous city could not fail, they thought, to betray some stains if submitted to a rigorous inspection. But their malevolent expectations were disappointed, for their miserable spy could bring back nothing but unmixed praise of an immaculate youth and a pious manhood.[526]

At this juncture the intriguers applied to Theophilus, and they could not have secured a more willing and able director of their plans. The character of this prelate, and his prominent position in the final events of Chrysostom's career, demand some notice. Of his family and early life little is known. He had a sister who sympathised with him in his ambitious schemes; and Cyril, who succeeded him in the patriarchate, and too largely inherited his spirit, was his nephew. He spent a portion of his younger manhood as a recluse in the Nitrian desert, where he became familiar with the most eminent anchorites of that period, Elurion, Ammon, Isidore, and Macarius. He was secretary to Athanasius, and a presbyter of Alexandria under Peter, his successor; and, on the death of Timothy in A.D. 385, who succeeded Peter, he was elevated to the see. All historians concur in admitting that he possessed great ability; that he was capable of conceiving great projects, and executing them with courage and address. Jerome has described him as deeply skilled in science, especially mathematics and astrology, and highly praises his eloquence.[527] He had a passion for building, and his episcopate was distinguished equally by the destruction of Pagan temples and the erection of Christian churches. The most splendid of these were the church of St. John the Baptist at Alexandria, and another at Canopus. But to gratify this expensive taste he was grasping of money, too often to the neglect of those indigent people who were dependent on the alms of the Church. He combined his efforts with Chrysostom's, as has been already related, in healing the schism of Antioch in A.D. 399, after which little is known of his history, till he becomes Chrysostom's implacable and too successful foe.[528]

CHAPTER 17

CIRCUMSTANCES WHICH LED TO THE INTERFERENCE OF
THEOPHILUS WITH THE AFFAIRS OF CHRYSOSTOM—
CONTROVERSY ABOUT THE WRITINGS OF ORIGEN—
PERSECUTION BY THEOPHILUS OF THE MONKS CALLED
"THE TALL BRETHREN"— THEIR FLIGHT TO PALESTINE—
TO CONSTANTINOPLE— THEIR RECEPTION BY
CHRYSOSTOM— THEOPHILUS SUMMONED TO
CONSTANTINOPLE. A.D. 395-403.

IN TRACING TO ITS starting-point the interference of Theophilus with the affairs of Chrysostom, we have to unravel a curious and tangled skein of controversy. The doctrines of Origen were as much an occasion of strife a hundred and fifty years after his death, as he himself had been during his life. With one hand holding on to the philosophy of the past, and with the other firmly grasping the Christianity of the present, he was persecuted by Pagans, yet never universally accepted and cordially trusted by the Church.[529] So with his system of doctrine; it became a sort of debatable ground for the possession of which contending parties strove. The prize was worth the struggle; for the genius of Origen could not be questioned, but the quantity of his writings being enormous,[530] and the range of his doctrine wide and many-sided, narrow-minded partisans, grasping only a part of it, condemned or extolled him unfairly on a single issue. The mystical element in his teaching was carried by some of his admirers to extremes of fanciful, allegorical, interpretation of Scripture, such as he himself would never have devised or approved.

To others of a more prosaic, material cast of thought this same mystical vein was repugnant, and was denounced by them with characteristic coarseness. Men of larger minds, who had patience to peruse his voluminous works, and ability to criticise them, admired his genius, recognised his great services to Christianity, heartily embraced much of his teaching, questioned some portions, and rejected others. Such were Gregory Nazianzenus, Basil, Chrysostom, and Jerome, who would never have been so great as writers, or commentators, had they not been students of Origen. As a general statement, it may be true to say that he was less acceptable to the colder, more practical, more realistic mind of the Western Church, than to the lively imagination and speculative spirit of Oriental churchmen. The most controverted points, indeed, in his system were of a kind with which the Western mind did not naturally concern itself. The pre-existence of souls; their entrance into human bodies after the fall as the punishment of sin; their emancipation from the flesh in the resurrection; the ultimate salvation of all spirits, including Satan himself,—these are questions singularly congenial to Oriental, singularly alien from Western, thought. The Origenistic controversy fell into abeyance before the engrossing interest and importance of the Arian contest; but when that wave had spent itself, it revived, and just at this period all the greatest names of the day became engaged on one side or the other. As usual, the real questions at issue were too often forgotten amidst the personal jealousies, intrigues, angry recriminations to which the discussion of them gave birth.

In spite of his doubtful orthodoxy, the Egyptian Church could not fail to be proud of so distinguished a son as Origen, and Theophilus was at first his earnest defender. Some of the more illiterate Egyptian monks had recoiled from Origen's highly spiritual conception of the Deity into an opposite extreme. Interpreting literally those passages of Scripture where God is spoken of as if possessing human emotions and corporeal parts, they altogether humanised His nature; they conceived of Him as a Being *not* "without body, parts, or passions;" they obtained, in consequence, the designation of "Anthropomorphites." Against this humanising, material conception Theophilus, in a paschal letter, directed argument and proof.[531] It was received by many of the monks with dismay, sorrow, and resistance. Serapion, one of the most aged, burst into tears when informed that the mind of the Eastern Church concurred, on the whole, with the doctrine of Theophilus, and exclaimed, "My God is taken away, and I know not what to worship."[532]

Rufinus, a monk of Aquileia, and for a time the ardent friend of Jerome, was, during a visit to Egypt, initiated by Theophilus into the doctrines of Origen, conceived a warm admiration for them, extolled him as the light of the Gospel next to the Apostles, and imparted some of his own enthusiasm to John, bishop of Jerusalem, whom he soon afterwards visited. Jerome fully appreciated the merits of Origen, though his larger mind and more extensive knowledge were not blind to his defects.

Such were the amicable relations between the leading churchmen of the East in A.D. 395, when a visitor from the West threw among them the apple of discord. This was Aterbius, a pilgrim, who had a reputation as a subtle theologian, and appears, immediately on his arrival in Jerusalem, to have applied himself to the business of detecting heresy. He entered into friendly intercourse for a short time with the bishop and Rufinus, and then suddenly included Jerome with them both in a public denunciation as Origenists, and declared the whole diocese of Jerusalem to be infected with that heresy. Jerome immediately and indignantly repudiated the charge; he declared that he was not an Origenist, for that he merely read the works of Origen with reservations, as he might those of a heretic.[533] Rufinus would not condescend to make any defence, oral or written, but shut himself up in his cloister in sullen silence till Aterbius had quitted Jerusalem, fearing, so Jerome affirms, to condemn what he really approved, or to incur the reproach of heresy by an open resistance.[534] John of Jerusalem was equally indignant at the accusation, but displeased with Jerome for publicly exculpating himself independently of his bishop. In fact, the episcopal pride of the Bishop of Jerusalem was severely wounded at this time, both by the pre-eminence of the metropolitan see of Cæsarea,[535] and by the reputation of Jerome's monastic establishment at Bethlehem, which attracted visitors from all parts of Christendom.

When the minds of all were thus ruffled, a second and far more mischievous visitor arrived in the person of Epiphanius, the octogenarian Bishop of Constantia, Metropolitan of Cyprus. He was one of those men who, joining some erudition and a high reputation for rigid orthodoxy to a narrow mind and impulsive temper, figure prominently in theological warfare as the very personifications of discord. Shocked at the intelligence of the heretical tendency in Palestine, and vexed that it should have been detected by a stranger rather than by himself, who was a native of Palestine, and the visitor of a monastery between Jerusalem and Hebron, he lost not a moment in setting out for the Holy City. He accepted the hospitality of the Bishop John, and spent the evening in all amity with him, nor was the obnoxious subject of dispute mentioned between them.[536]

A strange scene took place on the following day.

In the church of the Holy Sepulchre, in the presence of a large congregation, Epiphanius fulminated a discourse against Origen, his doctrines, and all who favoured them. Bishop John and his clergy expressed their contempt by grimaces, sneers, and impatient scratchings of their heads. At last an archdeacon stepped forward, and required Epiphanius, in the name of the bishop, to desist from his discourse. The assembly was dissolved, but met again in the afternoon, largely augmented, in the church of the Holy Cross. This time Bishop John discoursed, and denounced the Anthropomorphites, or Humanisers, under which opprobrious name the partisans of Origen endeavoured to include all their opponents. Pale and trembling, and in a voice quivering with passion, the bishop directed his discourse, and turned his body, towards Epiphanius, who sat motionless in his chair. The invective being concluded, the aged Bishop of Constantia rose and pronounced these words with solemn deliberation: "All that John, my brother in the priesthood, my son in age, has just said against the heresy of the Anthropomorphites I thoroughly approve; and as we both condemn that absurd belief, it is only just that we should both denounce the errors of Origen."[537] A general laugh and acclamation on the part of the assembly proclaimed their sense of this speech as a successful hit. John made one more effort to right himself. He preached again in the church of the Holy Cross, this time on the chief verities of the faith, the Trinity, the Incarnation, the Atonement, the condition of souls before and after this life. It was intended to be a grand and convincing display of his orthodoxy, and at the moment Epiphanius expressed even approbation. On subsequent reflection, however, the aged critic thought he discovered that it teemed with error. He abruptly quitted Jerusalem, repaired to Bethlehem, resisted the solicitation of Jerome and his friends to be reconciled, and addressed a circular letter to all the monasteries of Palestine, requiring them to break off communion with the Bishop of Jerusalem.

Rufinus ranged himself immediately on the side of Bishop John; but Jerome, though with somewhat balanced feelings, sided on the whole with Epiphanius. Then the pent-up jealousy of John towards the monasteries of Bethlehem burst forth; they were placed under interdict, and the church of the Holy Manger closed against them. They were in despair for want of a priest to celebrate the Eucharist; but Epiphanius provided one through a forcible ordination. The young Paulinian had always steadfastly declined holy orders, though considered eminently qualified by his learning and virtue. He was now on a visit to the monastery of Epiphanius, near Eleutheropolis. When Epiphanius was celebrating the Eucharist, the young man was seized by the deacons, dragged to the steps of the altar, and there made to kneel. Epiphanius approached, cut off some of his hair, ordained him deacon, and obliged him to assist in the celebration on the spot. At a fresh sign from the bishop he was a second time seized, gagged to prevent his adjuring the bishop in the name of Jesus Christ, and when he rose from his knees he was declared to be a priest.[538] The joy which filled the monasteries of Bethlehem was only to be equalled by the indignation of their opponents at Jerusalem. John actually applied (not without money, it is said) to Rufinus at Constantinople, then Prætorian Prefect, and even procured a decree of banishment against Jerome;[539] but, the murder of

Rufinus taking place soon afterwards, the governor of Cæsarea evaded the execution of the decree. Jerome retaliated by one of those fierce, nervous philippics which exhibit more command of language than of temper. The governor of Palestine made a praiseworthy but ineffectual effort to bring about a reconciliation. John had determined to invite an arbitrator, from whom he expected a strong partiality for his own cause. He appealed to Theophilus, from whom Rufinus, the monk, had derived his first acquaintance with Origen. Jerome indignantly complained of this invocation of a foreign jurisdiction. Was not Cæsarea the metropolitan see of Palestine? why this contempt of ecclesiastical law?[540] Theophilus, however, had no scruples in accepting the appeal. It was just one of those recognitions of pre-eminence which the Patriarch of Alexandria, like the Bishops of Rome, joyfully welcomed. The gratification of ambition was pleasantly disguised from others, and perhaps from themselves, under the semblance of peacemaking. Theophilus despatched Isidore as his legate to Palestine. His arrival was preceded by two letters, one intended for the Bishop of Jerusalem, the other for Vincentius, the presbyter and friend of Jerome at Bethlehem.

Unfortunately the letter intended for the bishop was delivered to Vincentius, and he and Jerome read with indignation assurances of sympathy and friendship towards John, and expressions of contempt for Jerome and his party, the language, in short, of an accomplice rather than of an arbitrator. It set forth in flowery oriental terms the confidence of the legate in the success of his mission; "as smoke disperses in the air, as wax melts before the fire, so will these enemies, who always resist the faith, and seek to disturb it now, by means of simple ignorant men be dispersed on my arrival."[541] The legate took up his abode at Jerusalem, and spent his time in familiar intercourse with the bishop and Rufinus. To Bethlehem he paid occasional visits, where he conducted himself with dictatorial haughtiness. Jerome and the monks plainly perceived that the so-called arbitrator was committed to one side—which was not theirs.

But on a sudden, in A.D. 398, the Patriarch wheeled round; he discovered that he had been in error. "The writings of Origen were fraught with danger to the unlearned, however profitable to philosophic minds." Such was the reason alleged for this sudden revulsion of opinion. The real reasons appear to have been of a less calm and philosophic character. One of the most distinguished presbyters in Alexandria at this time was Isidore, an octogenarian. His youth had been spent in pious seclusion, among the monks of Scetis and Nitria, and his piety had attracted the notice of Athanasius, whom he accompanied to Rome in A.D. 341, and by whom he was afterwards ordained priest. He became the Hospitaller of the Church in Alexandria, whose duty it was to attend to the reception of Christian visitors. In spite of great personal austerity, he was, as became his position, gentle and amiable to all men, even Pagans, when brought into contact with them. In A.D. 398, at the age of eighty, he had been employed to carry to Rome the recognition by Theophilus of Flavian as bishop of Antioch; and now, in the extremity of age, he was destined to become the first victim of a persecution by Theophilus, which, beginning with him, culminated in the deposition and exile of Chrysostom.[542]

An opulent widow committed to Isidore a large sum of money to be expended on clothing for the poor of Alexandria, and adjured him by a solemn oath to conceal the trust from Theophilus, lest the Patriarch's well-known cupidity should be tempted to appropriate the money to aid his grand operations in building. The precaution, however, was vain: nothing said or done in his diocese could escape the vigilance of informers in the employ of Theophilus. Isidore was questioned by the Patriarch concerning the charitable gift, and required to place the money at his disposal; but the hospitaller refused, and boldly maintained that it would be better bestowed on the bodies of the sick and poor, which were the temples of God, than on the erection of buildings. The Patriarch was astounded at the temerity of his disobedience, but dissembled for the moment the depth of his resentment. Two months later, in a convocation of the clergy, he produced a paper containing the charge of a horrible and unmentionable crime against Isidore, which the Patriarch said he had received eighteen years ago, but had been unable to prove from the absence of the principal witness. The whole charge turned out to be a baseless fabrication; but Isidore was ejected from the priesthood by the contrivance of Theophilus.[543]

The aged hospitaller fled to the peaceful retreat of his earlier days, the desert of Nitria. The most distinguished of the monks in this seclusion were four brothers—Ammon, Dioscorus, Eusebius, and Euthymius—eminent alike for their piety and the height of their stature, whence they were known by the name of the "tall brethren." They were venerated as the fathers of the Nitrian monks. Theophilus had in former times professed the highest admiration and respect for their virtues. He had made the eldest, Dioscorus, bishop of Hermopolis, and had persuaded, if not compelled, Eusebius and Euthymius, much against their will, to be presbyters in Alexandria.[544] Their simple piety was so much shocked by the avarice and other failings of the Patriarch, that they implored him to release them from clerical duties and restore them to the freedom of the desert. When Theophilus discovered their real reason for requesting this permission he was furious, and tried to intimidate them into submission by fierce menaces, but in vain. They withdrew, and for a time the Patriarch was at a loss how to execute vengeance on men who had few possessions of any kind to be deprived of. But now the opportunity arrived. Isidore, the excommunicated hospitaller, had been sheltered in their friendly retreat. Theophilus devised a malignant plan for disturbing their peace. The "tall brethren" belonged to that more mystical order of monks which embraced Origen's doctrine of a purely spiritual Deity, and were determined adversaries of the more sensuous and anthropomorphite school. Theophilus now scrupled not to declare himself in favour of the Anthropomorphites, whom he had formerly denounced. He encouraged the more coarse and ignorant to make violent and tumultuous assaults on the monastic retreat of Nitria, and, directed the bishops of the neighbourhood to eject several of the most distinguished monks, including Ammon. They repaired to Alexandria, sought an interview with Theophilus, requested to hear the cause of their ejection, and remonstrated on the treatment of Isidore. Theophilus burst into a violent rage, changed colour at every moment, glared on them with bloodshot eyes, dealt blows to Ammon on his face, and, while the blood trickled down, shouted, "Heretic, anathematise Origen." One of the number was put in prison to intimidate the rest; but they all entered it voluntarily together, and refused to come out unless their companion also was released. This was at length permitted, but the design of persecution was followed up. The Patriarch's paschal letter of A.D. 401 is chiefly occupied with a condemnation of Origen and his disciples. He confesses, indeed, that he had himself at one time been cast into that fiery furnace of error, but, like the three children, he had come out unscathed; "not even his hair or garments had been singed." He describes himself as having now returned from the land of captivity to the true Jerusalem; Origen and his doctrines are condemned with much heat; and a prominent place is assigned to him and all his disciples in the infernal regions.[545]

But Theophilus was far from being contented to stop at this point. He convoked a synod of neighbouring bishops. The monks were not informed of it, nor invited to appear and make their defence. Three of the most eminent were excommunicated as heretics and magicians. It was in vain that the monks protested against the injustice of condemning Origen or his readers on the strength of a few passages only, and those, as they maintained, in many instances garbled or interpolated. A synodical letter was published, addressed to the Catholic world, reprobating the writings of Origen. It produced a profound sensation in Rome, where the Pope Anastasius anathematised Origen.[546] But the humiliation of the Nitrian brethren was not yet complete. Five most insignificant monks, scarce worthy, according to Palladius, to discharge menial offices as lay brethren, were ordained by Theophilus, one to a bishopric, one to be priest, and the three others to be deacons. A small town was created a see, there being none vacant to receive the new bishop. With these tools the Patriarch could rapidly execute his designs. His creatures prepared, under his direction, a list of complaints and charges against the Nitrian monks, which they publicly presented to him in church. Armed with this, he had an interview with the governor of Egypt, and obtained from him an order for the forcible expulsion of insubordinate monks from the settlement at Nitria. With a troop of soldiers and a rabble of rascals, such as in all large towns are ready for the perpetration of any mischief, whom he had previously primed with drink, the Patriarch fell by night upon the monastic dwellings. Dioscorus was the first victim of his rage. He was one of the "tall brethren," who had been compelled by Theophilus to become bishop of Hermopolis. He was now dragged before the Patriarch by some rude Ethiopian slaves, and told that he was deprived of his see. Diligent search was made for the three other brethren, but they were undiscoverably hidden in a well. The fury of the Patriarch expended itself principally upon inanimate objects; the dwellings of the monks were pillaged and burned, together with their valuable libraries, and, to the horror of the pious, even some of the Eucharistic elements[547] were consumed in the general destruction.

The havoc being completed, Theophilus returned to Alexandria. The terrified monks came out of their hiding-places, and, wrapping themselves in their sheepskins, their only remaining property, set out from their beloved solitudes to seek shelter and a new home elsewhere. Three hundred, following the "tall brethren," took their journey towards Palestine; the rest dispersed in different directions. Not more than eighty arrived with the four brethren at Jerusalem, whence they shortly afterwards withdrew northwards to Scythopolis, a place eminently adapted to their wants by its situation in a well-watered valley rich in palm-trees, of which the leaves furnished materials for mats, baskets, and the other articles usually wrought by monkish labour.[548] But distance did not diminish the malice of their persecutor. They were pursued by letters from Theophilus addressed to all the bishops of Palestine, who were admonished not to grant ecclesiastical communion or shelter to the heretical fugitives. Jerome mentions two commissioners who scoured Palestine, and left no hole or cave unexplored in the diligence of their search for the offenders.[549] Thus hunted and harassed, the poor monks at length resolved to embark for Constantinople, throw themselves on the generosity of the Emperor and Archbishop, and submit their cause to their decision. They reached the capital, fifty in number; their foreign aspect, bare arms and knees, and primitive garb of white sheepskins, excited much curiosity and interest among the people of Constantinople. They repaired first of all to Chrysostom, in the hope that his authority would be sufficient to procure them justice, without an application to the civil powers. The Archbishop received them with great kindness and respect, and shed tears of compassion when he heard the tale of their sufferings and wanderings. But he acted with caution; he consulted some Alexandrian clergy who were at this time in Constantinople engaged in distributing presents to conciliate, or, more properly speaking, to bribe, the favour of persons just appointed to civil offices in Egypt. They admitted the virtues and hard usage of the monks, but recommended him not to incur the displeasure of Theophilus by admitting them to communion. The monks were lodged in the precincts of the church of Anastasia; Olympias and other pious women attended to their wants, which were to some extent supplied by the produce of their own manual labour. They were admitted to prayer in the church, but excluded from the Eucharist until the merits of their cause should have been carefully sifted, and their excommunication revoked. Chrysostom, unsuspicious of others, in his own innocence, was sanguine of his power to obtain their restitution. He despatched a letter to Theophilus, in which he besought him in courteous and friendly terms to be reconciled with the fugitives, and thereby to confer a favour on himself, his spiritual son and brother. But no notice was taken of the request; and meanwhile the agents of Theophilus were busily employed at Constantinople in disseminating injurious tales about the monks— they were heretics, magicians, rebels.

Throughout the rest of Christendom Theophilus pursued a different method. He toiled with diligence worthy of a better cause to obtain a wide condemnation of Origen and his works. Could he once secure such a general condemnation, and then prove Chrysostom and the monks to be at variance with it, he would possess a powerful engine in working the ruin of both. It is difficult to believe that even Theophilus would have pursued the monks with such insatiable animosity had they not fled to the patriarch of that see which was regarded with peculiar jealousy by the bishops of Alexandria, and had not the present occupant of that see been elected in preference to the candidate put forward by himself. Thus he clutched at the opportunity of depressing his rival, and punishing his victims, the monks, at the same time.

He found a faction hostile to the Archbishop already existing in Constantinople, and quite ready to submit the management of their interests to his skilful direction. The persecution of the monks was quickly dropped. Their supposed offence was only the handle by which to compass the destruction of a more formidable foe. Jerome contributed powerful aid to the designs of Theophilus by favourable notices of him in his letters, depreciating the conduct of the monks.[550] But a more active auxiliary appeared in the Bishop of Constantia, whose advanced age seems never to have diminished the alacrity with which he entered the lists of controversy. Theophilus, in his Origenistic days, had attacked Epiphanius with some vehemence as an anthropomorphite; but he now wrote a letter to the bishop expressing regret for his former language, and his increasing conviction of the mischievous tendency of Origen's doctrines.[551] He implored his holy brother to convene a council of the bishops of Cyprus without delay, for the purpose of condemning the heretic, and of drawing up letters, announcing their decision, to be sent round to the principal sees, especially Constantinople, where the heretical and contumacious monks were harboured. Epiphanius flattered himself that he had converted the Patriarch, and was delighted to receive such a powerful accession to his side. The council was summoned, the condemnation carried, and the letters despatched.[552] Theophilus himself, at the commencement of A.D. 402, issued a paschal letter, which contained a subtle exposition and refutation of the Origenistic errors. The letter was translated, and highly commended, both for matter and expression, by Jerome.[553]

To Chrysostom himself Theophilus wrote a sharp complaint of his protecting heretics, and violating the canon of Nice, which prohibited any bishop from exercising jurisdiction in matters relating to another see. The cause of the Nitrian monks, he asserted, could not be decided legally anywhere but in a council of Egyptian bishops. It will be borne in mind, however, that Chrysostom had carefully abstained from pronouncing any decision, through a council or otherwise, on the affair of the monks. They, indeed, became provoked with him that he did not espouse their cause more heartily. The agents of Theophilus were busily engaged in damaging their character; a little money easily persuaded the sailors and others employed in the Alexandrian corn trade to point at the monks in the streets as magicians and heretics. The monks declared to Chrysostom their resolution to appeal to the civil powers to obtain a formal prosecution of their accusers as base calumniators. Chrysostom remonstrated, and declined, if that step were taken, to mediate any more in their affair. Some of his enemies in Constantinople did not fail to represent this as a cruel desertion of those whom he had at first befriended.[554]

Thus hostile forces were on all sides closing round the Archbishop, but he continued apparently unconscious of the snares which were being woven for him. The Origenistic controversy, into the vortex of which his enemies sought to drag him, possessed little interest for him. The more mystical, abstract speculations of Origen's theology were alien from his practical sphere of work and practical habit of mind; and, in common with the other chief representatives of the Antiochene school, Diodorus and Theodore, he neither wholly embraced nor wholly rejected his system of doctrine. At any rate, he paid no attention to the letter from Cyprus, which requested him to join in the condemnation of Origen and his writings. This was precisely what his enemies wanted.

The Nitrian monks, cast off by the Archbishop when they had announced their intention of appealing to secular authority, drew up documents filled with charges of the most flagrant crimes against their accusers and against Theophilus. They demanded that their calumniators in Constantinople should be immediately tried by the prefect, and that Theophilus should be summoned to defend his conduct before a council under the presidency of Chrysostom. One day, as the Empress was riding in her litter to worship in the church of St. John the Baptist at Hebdomon, she was accosted by some of those strange skin-clad beings of whom, and of whose wanderings and wrongs, she had heard much. She caused her litter to stop, bowed graciously to the monks, and implored the favour of their prayers for the Empire, the Emperor, herself, and her children. The monks presented their petition; Eudoxia courteously accepted it, and promised them that the council which they desired should be convened; that Theophilus should be summoned to attend it, and that the accusers now in Constantinople should either substantiate their charges, or suffer the penalties of calumnious defamation. This inquiry was immediately instituted; the poor culprits confessed that they had been paid agents of Theophilus, and that their accusations had been dictated by him. They therefore entreated that their trial might be deferred till his arrival. Meanwhile, however, they were put in prison, where one of them died; and as the arrival of Theophilus continued to be delayed, they were banished to Proconnesus for libel. An officer was despatched to Alexandria to serve Theophilus with a peremptory summons to appear at Constantinople, and empowered to enforce his obedience, if he was reluctant.[555]

Thus the preparations for a judicial investigation of the affair of the monks emanated not from Chrysostom, but from the throne, although he was represented by his enemies as the originator, and by Jerome he is styled a parricide for labouring to condemn Theophilus.[556] Chrysostom seems, in fact, to have dismissed alike the business of the monks and the theological question of Origenism from his mind. Intent on edifying the Church, instead of agitating it by personal or polemical strife, he quietly pursued his daily routine of duties as chief pastor, feeding his flock with the wholesome food of the Word and of the bread of life.

Theophilus was unable to evade obedience to the summons which commanded him to repair to Constantinople. His only hope now was to change his position from that of the accused into that of the accuser. The council which was called together for the purpose of investigating his conduct should, by his contrivance, be transferred into a council for arraigning Chrysostom of heresy and misdemeanour. The letters of Epiphanius and Theophilus having failed to obtain from Chrysostom that condemnation which they demanded of the writings of Origen, the

Bishop of Constantia, at the urgent request of Theophilus, set forth at the beginning of A.D. 403 for Constantinople, bringing the decree of the Council of Cyprus for the signature of the Archbishop. Theophilus slowly proceeded overland from Egypt through Syria, Cilicia, and Asia Minor, in order to bring up as many bishops as possible to the council, who would be prepared to act under his direction. Epiphanius, having landed, halted at the church of St. John, outside Constantinople, held an assembly of clergy, and even, it is said, committed the irregularity of ordaining a deacon.[557] Chrysostom, however, acted with all due courtesy and discretion. He sent out a large body of clergy to welcome the visitor by inviting and conducting him to the hospitable lodging prepared for him in the archiepiscopal palace. Epiphanius, acting on preconceived judgment of the two chief subjects in dispute, declined the offer unless the Archbishop would consent to expel the monks, and to sign the decree against Origen. Chrysostom justly replied that he could not anticipate the decision of a council which was being summoned for the very purpose of considering both these questions. Epiphanius, therefore, found a lodging elsewhere, and diligently strove to induce such bishops as he could collect to sign the decree.[558] His reputation for learning, orthodoxy, and piety secured the consent of many, but on the part of many more there was determined opposition. Eminent among these was Theotimus, a Goth by birth, but educated in Greece, who had been made Bishop of Tomis and Metropolitan of Scythia. He was a man of genuine sanctity, ascetic habits, and courageous spirit. Tomis was a great central market of Gothic and Hunnish tribes, and the bishop used boldly to enter the motley concourse and try to win converts. He would invite savage Huns to partake of some hospitable entertainment in his house, and by gifts and little attentions, and courteous treatment, he sought to soften their ferocity, and effect an opening in their hearts for the reception of Christian teaching. He came to be regarded by them with a kind of superstitious reverence, and was commonly called by them "the god of the Christians." Over his half-episcopal, half-barbarian costume flowed the long hair which betokened his Gothic origin. He lifted up his voice with boldness to denounce the present ill-considered condemnation of the works of Origen. It was unseemly and unjust, he maintained, to pass a coarse and sweeping sentence on the entire works of one whose genius had been acknowledged by the whole Church. He produced a volume of Origen, and from it read some beautiful, powerful passages of irreproachable orthodoxy. Then, turning to Epiphanius, he asked him how he could attack a man to whom the Church owed a thousand similar, and even more beautiful, passages. "How call him a son of Satan? Place what is good in him on one side, and what is bad on the other, and then choose."[559]

This courageous protest, however, did not divert Epiphanius and his partisans from their course of action. In fact, they proceeded a step further. It was arranged that when a large congregation was collected in the Church of the Apostles, Epiphanius should enter and harangue the assembly, denouncing both the writings of Origen and his admirers, especially the "tall brethren," and even Chrysostom himself as their protector. Chrysostom, however, received intimation of their design, and by his direction Serapion confronted Epiphanius at the entrance of the church, and told him that "he had already violated ecclesiastical law by ordaining a deacon in the diocese and church of another bishop, but to minister and preach without permission was a still grosser outrage; a popular tumult would probably ensue, and Epiphanius would be held responsible for any violence which might be committed." Epiphanius, though not without angry remonstrances, desisted.[560]

Eudoxia seems to have placed special faith in the intercessions of ecclesiastical visitors of distinction. As she had formerly asked the prayers of the "tall brethren," so now, the young prince her son (afterwards Theodosius II.), being attacked by an alarming illness, she implored the prayers of Epiphanius on his behalf. The bishop replied that her child's recovery depended on her repudiation of the heretical refugees. The Empress, however, declared that she should prefer simply to resign her son's life to the will of God who gave it without complying with the requisition of Epiphanius.[561]

It may be that these incidents were beginning to tell upon the reason of the aged zealot, and open his eyes to the irregularity of his proceedings; at any rate, shortly after this, he granted an interview to Ammon and his brothers. The record of the conversation is instructive. "Allow me to ask, holy father," said Ammon, "whether you have ever read any of our works or those of our disciples?" Epiphanius was obliged to confess that he had not even seen them, and that he had formed his judgment simply from general report. "How then," replied Ammon, "can you venture to condemn us when you have no proof of our opinions? We have pursued a widely different course. We conversed with your disciples, we read your works, among others one entitled the 'Anchor of Faith;' and when we met with persons who ridiculed your opinions, and asserted that your writings were replete with heresy, we have defended you as our father. Is it just, on such slender ground as common report, to condemn those who have so zealously befriended you?" These bold and pungent remarks are said to have wrought compunction in the heart of the aged bishop. He began to perceive that he had been made the agent of a plot, and he lost no time in extricating himself from it by departing from Constantinople. His farewell words to some of the bishops who accompanied him to the ship were: "I leave to you the city, the palace, and this piece of acting."[562]

CHAPTER 18

THEOPHILUS ARRIVES IN CONSTANTINOPLE— ORGANISES A CABAL AGAINST CHRYSOSTOM— THE SYNOD OF THE OAK— CHRYSOSTOM PRONOUNCED CONTUMACIOUS FOR NON-APPEARANCE AND EXPELLED FROM THE CITY— EARTHQUAKE— RECALL OF CHRYSOSTOM— OVATIONS ON HIS RETURN— FLIGHT OF THEOPHILUS. A.D. 403.

REGARDLESS OF THE FORCES which had been set in motion against him, Chrysostom pursued his usual course of work without any variation. The reins of discipline were held tightly as ever; the Word was preached, in season and out of season, with unabated diligence; the people were exhorted, admonished, rebuked with the same irrepressible earnestness. His enemies took advantage of a sermon, specially directed against the follies and vices of fashionable ladies, to represent it as an attack upon the Empress herself.[563] Eudoxia, credulous and impulsive by nature, and probably irritated because the Archbishop did not pay her servile homage, complained to the Emperor of the insult which had been cast upon her, and was induced by the hostile party to expect the arrival of Theophilus as an opportunity for redressing her wrongs. That prelate was now rapidly approaching, with a large number of bishops collected from Egypt, Syria, and Asia Minor. Twenty-eight, on whose partisanship he could reckon, travelled by sea to Chalcedon. Many bishops had become disaffected to Chrysostom in Asia Minor, owing to the rigorous investigation recently made by him into the state of the Church in that region, and they readily joined the camp of Theophilus. Prominent among them was Gerontius of Nicomedia, whom, as will be remembered, he had deposed. The whole force was at length (June 403) assembled at Chalcedon, and a council of war was held, to determine the plan of operations. None was more virulent in his denunciation of Chrysostom, as tyrannical, proud, and heretical, than Cyrinus, bishop of Chalcedon. He was an Egyptian by birth, and Theophilus reckoned on him as a valuable ally, but was deprived of his services by a curious incident. Maruthas, bishop of Mesopotamia, accidentally trod on the foot of Cyrinus: a wound ensued, the wound gangrened, the foot had to be amputated, but the mortification spread, and, after two years of lingering pain, put an end to his life.[564]

Theophilus made his entrance into Constantinople about the middle of June. He had been summoned as a defendant, but, according to his design already indicated, he appeared surrounded by all the pomp and dignity of a judge. None of the bishops, indeed, or clergy of Constantinople came to greet him on landing, but the crews of the Alexandrian corn-fleet gave him a hearty welcome, and he was accompanied by a large retinue, not only of bishops and clergy, but of Alexandrian sailors, laden with some of the costliest produce of Egypt and the East, a very potent auxiliary in obtaining partisans. As on the arrival of Epiphanius, so now, Chrysostom did not fail to offer the customary hospitality due to a brother bishop; but Theophilus disdainfully declined it, passed by the palace and the metropolitan church, which episcopal visitors usually entered on their arrival, and proceeded to the suburb of Pera, where a lodging had been prepared for him in a house of the Emperor's, called the Palace of Placidia.

During the three weeks that he resided here, he refused to hold any communication with Chrysostom, or to enter his church; nor did he vouchsafe any reply to the frequent entreaties of the Archbishop that he would state his reasons for such conduct. His house became the resort of all the disaffected clergy or affronted ladies and gentlemen in the city, who were drawn thither, not only by a common hatred to Chrysostom, but also by the handsome gifts, the elegant and dainty repasts, and the winning flattery with which they were treated by Theophilus.[565] These arts were the more necessary because Theophilus had a double part to play: to arrest the course of the accusation instituted against himself, as well as to organise a powerful cabal against Chrysostom. In the former he was helped by the scruples or peacefulness of Chrysostom himself. The Archbishop was directed by the Court to repair to Pera, and preside over an inquiry into the crimes of which Theophilus was accused. But he declined, on the plea that the ecclesiastical affairs of one province could not, according to the Canons of Nice, be judged in another; partly also, as he affirmed, out of respect for his brother Patriarch. The truth probably was, that he foresaw the vindictive and turbulent spirit of Theophilus would never submit to the decisions of a council under the presidency of his rival in that see of which Alexandria was especially jealous. Otherwise there is no doubt that a General Council at Constantinople would have been competent to judge the Patriarch of Alexandria; whereas a Provincial Council in Egypt could not have judged him, he being supreme there by virtue of his position as Patriarch.[566] Chrysostom himself also might legally have been arraigned before a General Council; but, as will be seen, the synod composed by Theophilus was far from being entitled to that appellation.

The obstacle of his own trial being thus disposed of, it only remained for Theophilus to prosecute his design against his rival with mingled subtlety and boldness. The first step was to secure a sufficient number of witnesses, and a list of accusations, which, being presented to the Emperor, would furnish a plausible reason for summoning a council. The next step would be to pack that council with bishops hostile to Chrysostom. Two despicable deacons, who had been expelled from their office by the Archbishop for homicide and adultery, were well content to draw up a list of charges on a promise from Theophilus that they should be restored to their former position. The accusations seem to have been of a puerile character; and if the source of them was known, it would seem inconceivable that the Court should have entertained them, did we not remember that the influence of the Empress, as well as of many of the most powerful courtiers, was now turned or rapidly turning against the Archbishop, and that the bribes of Theophilus were permeating the whole city.

The attachment of the people, however, to Chrysostom was known to be so strong, that it was deemed prudent by the enemy to hold the synod at a safe distance from the city. A suburb of Chalcedon, called "The Oak," where Rufinus, the late prefect, had built a palace, church, and monastery, was selected as a convenient place for the assembly.[567] The bishops, after all the exertions of Theophilus, did not amount to more than thirty-six, of whom twenty-nine were Egyptians.[568] Among the latter was Cyril, the successor of Theophilus. Chrysostom was summoned to appear before the synod. The scene in the archiepiscopal palace immediately preceding the summons has been described by Palladius, with the vivid and minute exactness of an eye-witness.

"We were sitting, to the number of forty bishops, in the dining-hall of the palace, marvelling at the audacity with which one, who had been commanded to appear as a culprit at Constantinople, had arrived with a train of bishops, had altered the sentiments of nobles and magistrates, and perverted the majority even of the clergy. Whilst we were wondering, John, inspired by the Spirit of God, addressed to us all the following words: 'Pray for me, my brethren, and, if ye love Christ, let no one for my sake desert his see, for I am now ready to be offered, and the time of my departure is at hand. Like him who spoke these words, I perceive that I am about to relinquish life, for I know the intrigues of Satan, that he will not endure any longer the burden of my words which are delivered against him. May ye obtain mercy, and in your prayers remember me.' Seized with inexpressible sorrow, some of us began to weep, and others to leave the assembly, after kissing, amid tears and sobs, the sacred head and eyes, and eloquent mouth, of the Archbishop. He, however, exhorted them to return, and, as they hovered near, like bees humming round their hive, 'Sit down, my brethren,' he said, 'and do not weep, unnerving me by your tears, for to me to live is Christ, to die is gain. Recall the words which I have so frequently spoken to you. Present life is a journey; both its good and painful things pass away. Present time is like a fair: we buy, we sell, and the assembly is dissolved. Are we better than the Patriarchs, the Prophets, the Apostles, that this life should remain to us for ever?' Here one of the company uttering a cry exclaimed: 'Nay, but what we lament is our own bereavement and the widowhood of the Church, the derangement of sacred laws, the ambition of those who fear not the Lord, and violently seize the highest positions; the destitution of the poor, and the loss of sound teaching.' But John replied, striking, as was his custom when cogitating, the palm of his left hand with the forefinger of his right: 'Enough, my brother—no more; only, as I was saying, do not abandon your churches, for neither did the office of teaching begin with me, nor in me has it ended. Did not Moses die, and was not Joshua found to succeed him? Did not Samuel die, but was not David anointed? Jeremy departed this life, but Baruch was left; Elijah was taken up, but Elisha prophesied in his place; Paul was beheaded, but did he not leave Timothy, Titus, Apollos, and a host of others to work after him?' To these words Eulysius, bishop of Apamea, in Bithynia, observed: 'If we retain our sees, it will become necessary for us to hold communion with the authors of your deposition, and to subscribe to your condemnation.'[569] To which the holy John replied: 'Communicate by all means, so as to avoid rending the unity of the Church; but abstain from subscribing, for I am not conscious of having done anything to deserve deposition.'"

At this point in the conference it was announced that certain emissaries from the "Synod of the Oak" had arrived. Chrysostom gave orders that they should be admitted, inquired, when they entered, to what rank in the hierarchy they belonged, and, on being informed that they were bishops, requested them to be seated, and to declare the purpose of their coming. The two bishops, young men recently raised to the episcopate in Libya, replied, "We are merely the bearers of a document which we request that you will command to be read." Chrysostom gave the order, and a servant of Theophilus read the missive. "The holy Synod assembled at the Oak to John" (thus did his enemies deprive him of all his titles). "We have received a list containing an infinite number of charges against you. Present yourself, therefore, before us, bringing with you the priests Serapion and Tigrius, for their presence is necessary." The bishops who were with Chrysostom were very indignant at the insolent tenor of the message. A reply to the following effect was drawn up, addressed to Theophilus, and despatched by the hand of three bishops and two priests: "Subvert not nor rend the Church for which God became incarnate; but if, in contempt of the canons framed by 318 bishops at Nice, you choose to judge a cause beyond the boundaries of your jurisdiction, cross the straits into our city, which is at least strictly governed by law, and do not, after the example of Cain, call Abel out into the open field. For we have charges of palpable crimes against you, drawn up under more than sixty heads; our synod, also, is more numerous than yours, and is assembled, by the grace of God, after a peaceful manner, not for the disruption of the Church. For you are but thirty-six in number, collected out of a single province;[570] but we are forty, from several provinces, and seven are metropolitans. It is only reasonable that the less should be judged, according to the canons, by the greater."

Chrysostom approved of this answer of the bishops, but sent a separate letter on his own behalf: "Hitherto I am wholly ignorant whether any one has anything to say against me; but if any one has assailed me, and you wish me to appear before you, eject from your assembly my declared enemies. I raise no question respecting the place where I ought to be tried, although the most proper place is the city." He proceeds to say that he objected to his declared and implacable enemies, Theophilus, Acacius, Severian, and Antiochus, being allowed to sit on the council at all. "He could convict Theophilus of having said in Alexandria and Lycia, 'I am setting out for the capital to depose John;' which, indeed, is true, for, since he set foot in Constantinople, he has refused to meet or communicate with me. What, then, will one do, after the trial, who has acted as my enemy before it?" When these men should have been eliminated from the synod, or legally constituted as his accusers, he would appear before a council, even if composed of members from all Christendom; but till this condition was complied with, he would refuse to present himself though summoned ten thousand times over.[571]

He demanded, in short, to be tried by an œcumenical synod, as the only tribunal which could legally exact obedience from him. The Synod of the Oak, composed as it was mainly of Egyptians and of declared enemies, could not possibly pretend to that character. If the Imperial Court had been upright and courageous, not susceptible of flattery and bribes, not induced by personal animosity against the Archbishop to favour or connive at the proceedings of his enemies, such a synod could not have been held. That it was held, and succeeded in the purpose for which it met, will ever be a stain upon the Church and the Empire of the East.

But although viciously constituted and, indeed, all the more on that very account, the synod made much display of complying in formalities with the established order of an ecclesiastical court of judicature. The prosecution was to be carried on in the name of a plaintiff who was to be present, and to submit his charge in writing. The defendant was to be cited to appear and defend himself; and if he failed to appear after three or four citations, he would be pronounced contumacious, and as such be punishable by the synod with excommunication and deposition. The further penalties of imprisonment, exile, or death could not be inflicted by any but the secular power.

Theophilus was president of the synod, and the prosecution was conducted in the name of John, Archdeacon of Constantinople, who cherished malice against Chrysostom because he had once been suspended by him for ill-treating a slave, though afterwards restored. The charges were drawn up under twenty-nine heads. The evidence of most worthless witnesses was accepted, or, more properly speaking, invited. A strange medley of monstrous and incredible offences was included in the list of charges prepared by the Archdeacon John— acts of personal violence, as well as violations of ecclesiastical discipline. "He had struck people on the face, had calumniated many of his clergy, had called one Epiphanius fool and demoniac, had imprisoned others, had accused his archdeacons of robbing his pallium for an unlawful purpose; he had despotically and illegally deposed bishops in Asia, and had ordained others without sufficient inquiry into their qualifications, mental or moral; he had alienated the property and sold the ornaments of the Church; he held private interviews with women, he dined on

Cyclopian fare, he ate a small cake after holy communion, he had administered both sacraments, after he himself or the recipients had eaten."[572] The crowning charge was that of treasonable language against the Empress— "he had called her Jezebel." This was the trump card of the cabal. If the Emperor's Court could be persuaded to believe him guilty on this point, exile at least, and probably death, would be the inevitable consequence.

Such were the principal charges in the list presented by the Archdeacon John. A second list, presented by Isaac the monk, accused him of extending sympathy and hospitality to Origenists, of instigating the people to sedition, of using unseemly expressions in his sermons, such as "I exult, I am beside myself with joy," or language which gave a dangerous encouragement to sinners; for example, "as often as you sin come to me and I will heal you."

By artfully making slight alterations in expressions actually used, and tearing them from their context, it was easy to represent them as mischievous or blasphemous. It is not surprising then that Chrysostom steadfastly refused to answer in person such a list of partly monstrous, partly puerile, accusations before such a synod. He pursued the only dignified course possible under the circumstances. When a notary from the Emperor came to him with a rescript, and showed him the petition inserted in it from the synod, that the Emperor would compel the attendance of the Archbishop; and when, presently, a second deputation from the synod, consisting of a renegade priest of his own clergy, and Isaac the monk, brought a peremptory summons from the synod, he inflexibly maintained the same attitude. "I will not attend a synod which is composed of my enemies, and to which I am summoned by my own clergy. I appeal to a lawfully constituted General Council." The citations were rapidly repeated three or four times, and always met by the same response. The cabal expended their fury on the messengers of the Archbishop; they beat one bishop, tore the clothes of another, and placed on the neck of a third the chains which they had designed for the person of Chrysostom himself, their intention having been to put him secretly on board ship, and send him off to some remote part of the

Empire. Some of the clergy were so much intimidated by these violent proceedings that they dared not return to Constantinople. Demetrius, however, Bishop of Pessina, denounced the conduct of the synod, quitted it, and returned to the Archbishop. After several more ineffectual citations, the synod, at its twelfth session, declared that it would proceed to judgment against Chrysostom as contumacious. Either by a happy coincidence, or by the contrivance of Theophilus, a message arrived from the Court on the same day, urging the bishops to decide the cause as speedily as possible. With much alacrity the request was obeyed. They drew up a despatch to the Emperor— a formal statement: "Whereas John, being accused of crimes, has declined to appear before us, and that in such cases ecclesiastical law pronounces deposition, we have hereby deposed him; but as the indictment against him contains charges of treason as well as ecclesiastical offences, we leave these to be dealt with by you, since it belongs not to us to take cognisance of them." The synod waited for the Imperial ratification of their verdict, and meanwhile issued a circular to the clergy of Constantinople, informing them of the deposition of their spiritual father.[573]

Having attained, as he believed, the object of his intrigue, Theophilus went through the form of reconciliation with the "tall brethren" in the presence of the synod. The facility with which they were restored to favour on a simple request for pardon is in strange contrast to the relentless animosity with which they had been hitherto pursued, and indicates that their persecution had been maintained simply as the means to securing a more important victim.

Both Dioscorus and Ammon had recently died, the latter predicting with his dying lips that the Church was about to be distressed by a furious persecution, and torn by a deplorable schism. He was buried in that church of the Apostles, in the suburb of The Oak, where, nine years before, he had baptized the founder, the Prefect Rufinus. The monks of the foundation celebrated his obsequies with great pomp; and Theophilus, his bitter persecutor, condescended to weep over his death, and publicly declare that he had never known a monk of more exalted saintliness.[574]

The triumph of the synod seemed to be completed by the receipt of an Imperial rescript, ratifying the sentence of deposition, and announcing that the Archbishop would be banished. Many members of the synod were probably disappointed at the mildness of the penalty; but the people of Constantinople were enraged, and impeded the execution of the sentence. It was evening when the impending degradation of their Archbishop became known. During the whole of the night, crowds of people watched outside the Archbishop's palace and the cathedral to guard against his forcible abduction. Early in the morning they thronged the church, loudly protested against the injustice of the sentence, and demanded with shouts the submission of his cause to a General Council. For three days and nights the flock incessantly guarded their beloved pastor. Under their protection he passed to and from the palace and the church. On the second day he delivered a discourse to them in the cathedral. The first portion of it is in all respects worthy of Chrysostom; the conclusion, involved and rugged, seems to have been added by another hand, and extracts will not be made from it here.[575]

"Many are the billows, and terrible the storms, which threaten us; but we fear not to be overwhelmed, for we stand upon the rock. Let the sea rage, it cannot dissolve the rock; let the billows rise, they cannot sink the vessel of Jesus Christ. Tell me, what is it we fear? death?— 'To me to live is Christ, and to die is gain.' Or exile?— 'The earth is the Lord's and the fulness thereof.' Or confiscation of goods?— 'We brought nothing into this world, and it is certain we can carry nothing out.'"... "I fear not poverty, I desire not wealth; I dread not death, I do not pray for life, save for the sake of your advancement. I beseech you be of good courage; no man will be able to separate us, for 'that which God hath joined together no man can put asunder.' If man cannot dissolve marriage, how much less the Church of God! Thou, oh my enemy! only renderest me more illustrious, and wastest thine own strength, 'for it is hard to kick against the pricks.' Waves do not break the rock, but are themselves dispersed into foam against it. Nothing, oh man! is stronger than the Church, ... it is stronger even than Heaven, 'for Heaven and earth shall pass away, but my words shall not pass away.' What words?

'Thou art Peter, and on this rock I will build my Church, and the gates of hell shall not prevail against it.' If thou disbelievest the words, yet believe the facts. How many tyrants have attempted to overcome the Church; how often have wild beasts, and the sword, and the furnace, and the boiling caldron, been employed against it, yet have they not prevailed. Where are those who made war upon it? They have been silenced and consigned to oblivion. Where is the Church? It shines above the brightness of the sun. Let none of the things that have been done disturb you. Grant me one favour only,— unwavering faith. Was not St. Peter on the point of sinking, not because of the uncontrollable onset of the waves, but because of the weakness of his faith? Did man's votes bring me here, that man should put me down? I say not this in a spirit of boastfulness— God forbid— but in the desire to settle your agitated minds."... "Let no one trouble you; give heed to your prayers. This disturbance is the devil's work, that he might destroy your zeal in the sacred Litanies; but he does not succeed. We find you even more earnest than before. To-morrow I shall go out with you in the Litany, for where you are, there I am. Though locally separated, we are in spirit united; we are one body, the body is not separated from its head; even death cannot separate us."... "For your sakes I am ready to be slaughtered ten thousand times over, since death is to me the warrant of immortality. These intrigues are tome but the occasion of security. I say these things to listening ears; so many days have you watched, and nothing has moved you from your purpose. Neither length of time nor threats have enervated you; you have done what I have always been desiring, despised the things of this world, bidden farewell to earth, released yourselves from the fetters of the body: this is my crown, my consolation, my anointing; this the suggestion to me of immortality."

Another discourse[576] contains much to the same effect, and a declaration of his belief that the real cause of his deposition was his sturdy opposition to the corrupt manners and morals of the age. "You know," he says, "why they are going to depose me—because I spread no fine carpets, and wear no silken robes; because I have not pampered their gluttony, or made presents in gold and silver." He would comfort and encourage himself with the prospect of being reckoned among those who had suffered for righteousness' sake. The cruel and capricious woman, who one day called him "a thirteenth apostle," and the next "a Judas," would receive a just retribution for her conduct.

The attachment of the people to the Archbishop, and their sense of the injustice with which he was treated, were so strong that, with his powers of swaying their feelings, he might easily have raised a formidable sedition, and defied, for an indefinite time, the sentence of the synod and the edict of the Emperor. But his sentiments were too loyal, too Christian, too peaceful, for any such desperate and violent measures. He might have continued to demand the reference of his cause to a General Council; but, had this been granted, there was the extreme probability that his enemies would refuse, and persuade many more to refuse, a recognition of its decision. Then would follow one of those melancholy schisms, of which the Church already knew too well the misery. He determined to bow to the storm. On the third day after his deposition by the council, and about noon, when the people were not guarding the approaches to the church quite so vigilantly, he passed out, unperceived, by one of the side entrances, and surrendered himself to some of the Court officials, who conducted him at nightfall to the harbour. In spite of the darkness, he was recognised by some of the people, who followed him with loud cries of distress. He besought them to abstain from the commission of violence, commended them to the care of Jesus Christ, cited the example of Job blessing and thanking God in the midst of trouble, and declared that he patiently waited for the decision of an Œcumenical Council. The vessel in which he embarked conveyed him the same night to Hieron,[577] on the Bithynian coast, at the mouth of the Euxine. Perhaps owing to the dangerous proximity of this place to Chalcedon, the headquarters of his enemies, he removed (being apparently uncontrolled in his movements) to a country-house belonging to a friend, near Prænetum, on the Astacene gulf opposite Nicomedia.

When the departure of the Archbishop became generally known on the succeeding day, the indignation of the people burst into a blaze. The places of public resort were thronged with clamorous crowds denouncing the synod and demanding a General Council. They flocked into the churches to pour forth their lamentations, and to invoke the Divine intervention on behalf of their injured Patriarch. A revulsion of feeling in his favour took place among many of the clergy who had hitherto been opposed to him. The arrival of Theophilus with a large retinue was not calculated to allay the agitation. Force was employed to dislodge the people from the churches; the struggle occasioned bloodshed, and even some loss of life, chiefly among monks. The worthless clergy who had been deposed by Chrysostom, some of them for flagrant crimes, were restored by Theophilus. Severian of Gabala mounted a pulpit in one of the churches, and extolled the act of deposition. "Even were the Patriarch," he said, "guiltless of other offences, the penalty was due to his arrogance, for 'God resisteth the proud,' even if He forgave other sins." The people were furious at this barefaced attempt to justify injustice. They thronged the approaches to the Imperial palace itself, and with loud shouts demanded the restoration of the Patriarch.[578]

A natural phenomenon, not rare in Constantinople, but regarded under the circumstances as a Divine visitation, opportunely concurred with this demand. The city, the palace, but more especially the bedchamber of the Empress, were agitated by a severe shock of earthquake. The friends of Chrysostom rejoiced at this manifestation of the wrath of Heaven; his enemies were alarmed. The terrified Empress eagerly promoted the demand of the people for the restoration of the exile. Messengers were sent across the Bosporus to seek him, for the exact place of his retreat appears to have been unknown. Briso, the Empress's chamberlain, a man of Christian piety and a personal friend of Chrysostom, discovered him at Prænetum. He was the bearer of a humble, we might say abject, letter of self-exculpation from the Empress. "Let not your holiness (ἡ ἁγιωσύνη) imagine that I was cognisant of what has been done. I am guiltless of thy blood. Wicked and corrupt men have contrived this plot. I remember the baptism of my children by thy hands. God whom I serve is witness of my tears."

She informs him how she had fallen at the feet of the Emperor, and had represented to him that there was no hope for the Empire except through the restoration of the Archbishop.[579]

Chrysostom yielded to the solicitation so far as to embark and cross the Bosporus, but he declined at first to advance nearer Constantinople than the suburb of Mariamna, two leagues from the capital by sea. He declared that he would not enter the city until he had been acquitted by a General Council. But the impetuosity of the people would brook no delay. Tidings of his approach had preceded him. The Bosporus was studded with boats crowded with his friends, bearing torches and chanting psalms of welcome. The halt at Mariamna was suspected to be a contrivance of the enemy, who wished to deprive the Patriarch of the honours awaiting him. Their denunciations of the Emperor and Empress grew loud and menacing. An Imperial secretary arrived at Mariamna, urging Chrysostom to enter the city without loss of time. The Archbishop consented, and, attended by about thirty bishops, amidst the acclamations of the populace, was conducted to the Church of the Apostles. Again he remonstrated, and expressed scruples at entering till the sentence of deposition should have been revoked by a legitimate council. But the eagerness of the people was irrepressible. He was borne into the church, and compelled to take his seat on the episcopal throne and pronounce a benediction upon the assembly. When he had complied with their request, they would not be satisfied till he had addressed them in an extempore discourse. The address exists only in a Latin translation. Its brevity, and the abrupt style of the opening sentences, indicate the extemporaneous character of it.[580]

"What shall I say, or how shall I speak? 'Blessed be God.' So spoke I when I departed, and I utter the same again: yea, even in my exile I did not cease to say these words. Ye remember how I quoted Job, and said, 'Blessed be the name of the Lord for ever.' Such was the pledge I left with you when I set forth; such is the thanksgiving I repeat on my return. 'Blessed be the name of the Lord for ever.' Our lot varies, but our manner of giving glory is one. I gave thanks when I was expelled, I give thanks when I return. The conditions of summer and winter are different, but the end is one— the prosperity of the field. Blessed be God who permitted the storm, blessed be God who has dispersed it and wrought a calm. These things I say, that I may prepare you to bless God at all times. Have good things happened to you? Bless God, and the good remains; have evil things occurred? bless God still, and the evil is removed."... "Behold what great results have been wrought by the stratagems of my enemies. They have augmented your zeal, inflamed your affectionate longing for me, and procured me lovers in hundreds. Formerly I was beloved by my own people only; now even the Jews pay me respect. My enemies hoped to sever me from my own friends; and, instead, they have brought even aliens into our ranks."... "To-day the Circensian games take place, but no one is present there; all have poured like a torrent into the church, and your voices are as streams which flow to Heaven and declare your affection towards your father." He congratulates them on putting the enemy to flight. "Many are the sheep, yet nowhere is the wolf seen; the devouring beasts are overwhelmed, the wolves have fled. Who has pursued them? Not I the shepherd, but ye the sheep. O noble flock! in the absence of the shepherd ye have routed the wolves. O beauty and chastity of the wife! how hast thou repulsed the adulterer, because thou lovedst thy husband!"... "Where are our enemies? in ignominy;— where are we? in triumph."[581]

On the following day the Archbishop delivered another address, pitched in the same strain, but amplified and more ornate. It opens with a singular comparison between the meditated seduction of Abraham's wife by Pharaoh, and the plot of Theophilus to corrupt the chastity of the Church of Constantinople. The courage and faith of the flock in resisting the wolf during the absence of their shepherd, their enthusiastic welcome of his return, when the sea, as he expresses it, became a city (alluding to the crowds who had gone out to meet him on the Bosporus), and the market-place was converted into one vast church— these are again the topics on which he dilates with thankful joy. He applies to himself the verse: "They that sow in tears shall reap in joy; he that now goeth on his way weeping, and beareth forth good seed, shall doubtless come again with joy, and bring his sheaves with him." The

Empress is extolled in language which to any but oriental ears must sound painfully fulsome and adulatory. She had sent a message to him on the previous evening, saying, "My prayer is fulfilled, my object accomplished. I have obtained a crown better than the diadem itself. I have received back the priest, I have restored the head to the body, the pilot to the ship, the shepherd to the flock, the husband to the home." In return for this complimentary greeting (complimentary, it must be confessed, to herself as much as to the Archbishop) she is styled by him "most devout Queen, mother of the churches, nurse of monks, protectress of saints, staff of the poor." The people were so much delighted with these laudations of the Empress, that the address was constantly interrupted by their acclamations.[582]

When the object of the Synod at the Oak had eventually failed through the recall of Chrysostom, many of the members lost no time in returning to their several sees. Theophilus and a few of his most resolute partisans appear to have lurked in the city, waiting a possible opportunity for resuming their intrigues. This they attempted, according to two historians,[583] by instigating accusations against Heracleides, who had been consecrated Bishop of Ephesus by Chrysostom. The friends of Heracleides and of the Archbishop protested against the illegality of such proceedings in the absence of the defendant. The question was taken up by the populace. Fierce and sanguinary frays were fought in the streets between the citizens and the Alexandrian followers of Theophilus. At length he and his followers consulted their safety by a precipitate flight. This account is not incompatible with the assertion of Chrysostom himself in his letter to Innocent, that after his recall he incessantly demanded the convocation of a General Council to absolve him from the verdict of the false synod, and to reinstate him in possession of his see; that the Emperor consented, and that, as soon as the imperial summonses were issued in all directions, Theophilus, dreading the scrutiny of his conduct, embarked in the dead of night, and sailed in haste for Alexandria.[584] The citation of the council, and the hostility of the people, may well have concurred to hasten his departure. The General Council seems never to have regularly assembled.

Theophilus was cited to attend it after he had returned to Alexandria, but excused himself on the plea that the Alexandrians were so deeply attached to him, he feared a sedition would take place if he were again to absent himself. No less than sixty bishops, however, who had congregated in Constantinople, though not apparently convened in synodal form, solemnly declared their sense of the illegality and injustice of the late proceedings at the Synod of the Oak, and confirmed Chrysostom in the resumption of his see.

CHAPTER 19

AN IMAGE OF EUDOXIA PLACED IN FRONT OF THE CATHEDRAL— CHRYSOSTOM DENOUNCES IT— ANGER OF THE EMPRESS— THE ENEMY RETURNS TO THE CHARGE— ANOTHER COUNCIL FORMED— CHRYSOSTOM CONFINED TO HIS PALACE— VIOLENT SCENE IN THE CATHEDRAL AND OTHER PLACES— CHRYSOSTOM AGAIN EXPELLED. A.D. 403, 404.

THE STORM HAD PASSED over for the moment, and the atmosphere seemed serene: but in reality it was charged with all the old elements of disturbance. The Archbishop owed his restoration to a mere superstitious impulse on the part of the Empress, seconded by the enthusiastic devotion of the common people to his person and his cause. But as the revulsion of feeling which had led to his recall died away, and he himself resumed with unabated zeal his former work of moral and ecclesiastical reformation, the irritation and animosity of the more corrupt portion of the clergy and laity revived. In two months after his return an occasion arose which brought him into serious collision with the Court. This was the signal for the reappearance of his enemies; they flocked from far and near—Egypt, Syria, Asia, as well as his own more immediate diocese—and swooped down upon their prey with the avidity of vultures.

The pride and ambition of Eudoxia were not satisfied by the enjoyment of a power really greater than her husband's, and of respect outwardly equal; she was determined to receive that half-idolatrous kind of homage which custom, handed down from Pagan times, still paid to the Emperor, but to him alone. The smaller forum of Constantinople was a great square,[585] on one side of which stood the grand curia or senate-house, which Constantine had enriched with the sumptuous spoils of many Pagan temples, and especially with the statues of the Muses brought from the grove of Helicon; opposite to it was the entrance of St. Sophia, and the remaining sides of the forum were bounded by handsome public and a few private buildings all faced with colonnades. In the centre was a stone platform paved with various marbles, from which speeches were delivered on great public occasions. On this platform the Empress determined to gratify her vanity by the erection of a lofty column of porphyry surmounted by a silver image of herself. This design was accomplished in September A.D. 403, and the erection of the statue was celebrated by all the Pagan ceremonies and festivities, including music and dancing, with which the adoration of the Emperor's image was usually attended. These rites had been retained by the Christian Emperors because they were supposed to be useful in maintaining a loyal spirit among the people, but the Pagan elements were afterwards suppressed by Theodosius II.[586]

The position of Eudoxia's column in front of the vestibule of St. Sophia, and the disturbance caused to the sacred services within by the noisy, tumultuous proceedings outside, were regarded by the Patriarch as a disgrace to an Empress calling herself Christian, an outrage and insult flung in the very face of the Church. He denounced the heathenish ceremony with his usual vehemence before the people, and complained of it to the prefect of the city. The prefect was a Manichæan, and no friend to Chrysostom. Instead of endeavouring to conciliate both parties, he reported to the Empress, probably with some exaggeration, the condemnation pronounced by the Patriarch on the indulgence of her pride. The resentment of Eudoxia was fierce. She rallied the enemies of Chrysostom around her to devise means for crushing the audacious prelate. Acacius, Severian, and others of the old troop were soon upon the scene, and conferring with their old confederates, the Marsas and Castriccias, the rich worldly dames, and the dandy young clergy of Constantinople. There was no diminution meanwhile in the tide of invective poured forth from the golden mouth, and the pungency of his sarcasms did not lose force in the reports of them which were carried to the royal ears.[587]

Once more the faction applied to the Patriarch of Alexandria, inviting him to come and conduct their operations. But he was too wary to involve himself personally in another campaign, to terminate perhaps in a second ignominious flight. His influence, however, even at a distance, was potent. The stratagem adopted this time was to counterfeit that General Council which had been constantly demanded by Chrysostom; packing it with hostile bishops who were ostensibly convened to revise, but in reality to confirm, the decision issued by the Synod of the Oak. Theophilus, then, having excused attendance at Constantinople in person, sent three "pitiful bishops" (ἐλεείνους ἐπισκόπους), creatures of his own on whom he could rely, to execute his designs.[588] They were armed with the 12th Canon of the Council of Antioch held in A.D. 341, which declared that any bishop who, after deposition, appealed to the secular power for restoration, should, for that very act, be regarded by the Church as permanently and irrevocably deposed. The Council of Antioch had been swayed by Arian influence, and this same canon had been aimed against Athanasius, who had returned from exile to Alexandria under the Imperial sanction. It had been repudiated by the Western bishops, and some of the Eastern, at the Council of Sardica, and indeed by all who maintained communion with Athanasius. Theophilus, however, proposed to base the present proceedings against Chrysostom on this foundation; to turn, in fact, against the greatest luminary of Constantinople the engine which had been originally constructed against the greatest ornament of the Alexandrian see. The instrument would work well if proper hands could be procured to work it. Syria, Cappadocia, Pontus, Phrygia, were once more ransacked to supply the council with disaffected prelates. To the old names of Acacius of Berœa, Severian of Gabala, Antiochus and Cyrinus, may be added, as leaders of the malignants, Leontius, bishop of Ancyra in Galatia, Brison of Philippopolis in Thrace, Ammon of Laodicea in Pisidia; among those honourably distinguished as friendly to the Patriarch were Theodore of Tyana, Elpidius of Laodicea, Tranquillus (see unknown), and Alexander of Basilinopolis in Bithynia. Theodore, however, perceiving the malevolent intention with which the council was convoked, quitted Constantinople soon after his arrival.

The council met about the close of the year A.D. 403. It was customary for the Emperor to attend Divine service in state on Christmas Day, but he was induced by the enemies of Chrysostom to refuse on this occasion, alleging that it was impossible to be present where the Patriarch officiated till he had been cleared of the serious charges brought against him. It was proposed at first to affect to meet the demand of Chrysostom for an equitable trial, and to hear all the charges which had been preferred at the Synod of the Oak. But, the witnesses were so backward to appear, and the attitude of the defendant betokened such confidence in his cause, that it was deemed more prudent by his enemies to stake the whole issue on the canon of the Council of Antioch. If that was once admitted, there would be an end of the whole matter. The Archbishop, having been deposed already once for all, was not competent to appear and plead his cause before a council. Chrysostom and his friends opposed the adoption of such a course with two powerful arguments. They represented that the Council of Antioch had been managed by an Arian bishop and influenced by an Arian emperor, and the object of it had been to harass the great Athanasius. In the next place, the Synod of the Oak had been illegally constituted; sixty-five bishops had repudiated its decision; Chrysostom, therefore, was not legally deposed, and the canon of Antioch was in consequence not applicable to his case. This last objection was not permitted by his enemies. Leontius boldly declared, what appears to have been a palpable lie, that a larger number of bishops than sixty-five had voted against Chrysostom in the Synod.[589]

Thus the question as to the validity of the Council of Antioch became the knot of the whole affair. It was debated with such vehemence on both sides, that at length the adversaries of the Patriarch proposed that a deputation from the two contending parties should plead the case before the Emperor, and submit the decision to him. It may be presumed from their making the proposal that they felt secure of a verdict favourable to their side, and, at the same time, by this step a semblance of impartiality would be imparted to the proceedings. The deputies met in the royal presence. When the heat which marked the beginning of the discussion had cooled down a little, Elpidius of Laodicea with much gentleness of manner made an astute proposal. He was an old man, eminent for stainlessness of character, as well as for learning in ecclesiastical lore. "Let us not," he said, "weary the clemency of your Majesty any longer; only let our brethren, Acacius and Antiochus, subscribe a declaration that they are of the same faith with those who promulgated these canons, which they maintain to be the production of orthodox men, and the controversy will be at an end." The Emperor perceived the adroitness of the proposal, and observed with a smile to Antiochus, that the plan struck him as the most expedient which could be devised. Antiochus and his colleagues turned livid with perplexity and rage, but, being fairly caught in the dilemma, were forced to dissemble their feelings, and simulated a willing consent to sign the proposed declaration. The promise was made, but never executed. The deputies retired, and the adversaries of the Patriarch laboured with redoubled energy to procure his final condemnation; but we have no record of any formal session or formally declared sentence. Chrysostom continued to preach and discharge his other functions with, if possible, increased diligence, and still acted as president over the floating synod of more than forty bishops who constantly adhered to his cause. His enemies, on the other hand, acted as if the sentence of condemnation had been passed, and continually requested the Emperor to put it into execution.[590]

A.D. 404. As Easter approached, they became more importunate in their demand. They dreaded the demonstrations which might be made in favour of their victim by the large congregations which on Holy Saturday and Easter Day were wont to assemble in the churches. They succeeded in prevailing on the Emperor to prohibit the Patriarch, as having been deposed and excommunicated by two councils, from entering or officiating in the church at Easter-tide. Chrysostom had always expressed an earnest desire to be tried before a lawful council, and to abide by its decision. This request had been systematically evaded even when ostensibly complied with. His whole soul rebelled with honest indignation against these insidious and persistent attempts to misrepresent his conduct, and he determined now to resist them by taking his stand on the lofty ground of his Divine mission. "I received this church from God my Saviour, and am charged with the care of the salvation of this flock, nor am I at liberty to abandon it. Expel me by force if you will, since the city belongs to you, that I may have your authority as an excuse for deserting my post."[591]

The Emperor, though with some shame, sent officials who removed the Archbishop from the church to his palace, with a strict injunction that he should not attempt to leave it. This was a cautious preliminary to final expulsion, suggested by superstitious dread of any earthquake or other manifestation of Divine displeasure. Should any such occur again, the Archbishop could be released in a moment; if not, they might proceed to further measures.

Easter Eve arrived, the greatest day in the year for the baptism of converts. Three thousand were to be "initiated" this year. Chrysostom was again commanded to abstain from entering the church, but answered according to the tenor of his former reply, that he would not desist from officiating unless compelled by actual force. The feeble Arcadius was alarmed, and hesitated how to act. He scrupled to use force on so sacred a day, and dreaded an insurrection of the populace. As usual, he tried to shift responsibility from his own shoulders. He sent for Acacius and Antiochus, and requested their advice in the present emergency. They were too far committed now to draw back, and promptly replied that they would take on their heads the deposition of the Archbishop.

One more effort was made to avert the impending calamity. The forty bishops who maintained a close friendship with Chrysostom accosted the Emperor and Empress as they were visiting, according to their custom at this season, some of the martyr chapels outside the city. They entreated their majesties with tears to spare the Church her chief pastor, especially on account of the season, and for the sake of those who were about to be baptized. But Arcadius and Eudoxia turned a deaf ear to their piteous appeal. The bishops retired, grief-stricken, to mourn over the wrongs of their Church and Patriarch; but not before one of them, Paul, bishop of Crateia, had lifted up his voice in bold and solemn warning:—"Take heed, Eudoxia; fear God; have pity on your children. Do not outrage by bloodshed the sacred and solemn festival of Jesus Christ."[592]

The church of St. Sophia became the scene, on the night of that Easter Eve, of shocking tumult. A vast congregation from the city and surrounding towns, including many of the catechumens, was keeping vigil to greet the dawn of the Resurrection morning. Suddenly a body of soldiers burst in with noise and violence, and took possession of the choir. The confusion may be imagined. Women and children fled shrieking in wild disorder. Many of the female catechumens, only half-dressed, in preparation for the reception of baptism, were hurriedly driven out of the baptistry with the deaconesses who attended them. Some were even wounded, and the sacred fonts stained with blood. Some of the soldiers, unbaptized men, penetrated even to the chamber where the Eucharistic elements were kept, and profaned them with their gaze and touch. The clergy were forcibly ejected in their vestments, and several were wounded. The pitiable spectacle of the mingled troop of men, women, children, and clergy, violently chased along the streets by the brutal soldiery, moved even Jews and Gentiles to compassion. The clergy, however, rallied the scattered flock in the Baths of Constantine, the largest public baths in the city. Here they proceeded with the Easter services in due order; some reading the Scriptures, others baptizing. The churches of Constantinople were deserted, which the adversary wished to force the people to attend in the absence of the Archbishop, in the hope that the Court might thus suppose him to be unpopular.

Such is the description of these violent scenes as drawn by the pen of Chrysostom himself, in a letter[593] written soon after the occurrences, and addressed to Innocent I., bishop of Rome, Venerius, bishop of

Milan, and Chromatius, bishop of Aquileia. "You may imagine the rest," he concludes; "great as these calamities are, there is no prospect of their immediate termination; on the contrary, the evil extends every day. The spirit of insubordination is rapidly spreading from the capital to the provinces, from the head to the members. Clergy rebel against their bishop, and one bishop assails another. People are, or soon will be, split into factions. All places are racked by the throes of coming trouble, and the confusion is universal. Having been informed of all these things, then, my most reverend and prudent lords, display, I pray you, the courage and zeal which becomes you in restraining this lawlessness which has crept into the churches. For if it were to become a prevailing and allowable custom, for any at their pleasure to pass into foreign and distant dioceses, and to expel whomsoever any one may choose, and act as they like on their own private authority, be sure that all discipline will go to pieces, and a kind of implacable warfare will pervade the world, all expelling or being themselves expelled. Wherefore, to prevent the subjection of the world to such confusion, I beseech you to enjoin that these acts so illegally performed in my absence, when I had not declined fair judgment, may be reckoned invalid, as indeed in the nature of things they are, and that those who have been detected taking part in these iniquitous proceedings may be subjected to the penalty of ecclesiastical law; while we who have not been proved guilty may continue to enjoy your correspondence and friendship as aforetime." He closes his letter by affirming that he was still prepared to prove his innocence and the guilt of his accusers before a legally constituted council.

This letter is interesting not only in itself, but because it illustrates remarkably the growing tendency of Christendom to appeal to the arbitration of the Western Church, and especially of the Bishop of Rome, in matters of ecclesiastical discipline. The law-making, law-protecting spirit of the West is invoked to restrain the turbulence and licentiousness of the East. The Patriarch of the Eastern Rome appeals to the great bishops of the West, as the champions of an ecclesiastical discipline which he confesses himself unable to enforce, or to see any prospect of establishing. No jealousy is entertained of the Patriarch of the old Rome by the Patriarch of the new. The interference of Innocent is courted, a certain primacy is accorded him, but at the same time he is not addressed as a supreme arbitrator; assistance and sympathy are solicited from him as from an elder brother, and two other prelates of Italy are joint recipients with him of the appeal. The effect of this letter will shortly be related; for the present, the course of events at Constantinople must be followed.

It did not suit the purpose of Acacius and his party to allow the congregation which had been hunted out of St. Sophia to proceed with their service in the baths unmolested. If the Emperor entered the church in the morning and found it deserted, the vacancy on so great a day would reveal too plainly the intense devotion of the people to their bishop. The aim of the conspirators was to force the people to attend the services, which were to be marked by the absence of Chrysostom alone. They accordingly applied to Anthemius, Master of the Offices, to disperse the congregation, if necessary by force. Anthemius, however, was a moderate, prudent man, and kindly disposed towards the Patriarch. He refused to interfere, pleading the advanced hour of the night, the vastness of the assembly, and the risk of serious tumult. He yielded, however, to their persevering and urgent demands so far as to direct Lucius, a subordinate officer, commander of a Thracian corps called the Scutarii, to present himself with his troops at the entrance of the baths, and exhort the people to return to the church, as the more proper place for conducting the services. He was strictly charged to abstain from violence. He acted on his instructions, and harangued the congregation, but without effect. The chanting of the Psalms and the administration of baptism to crowds of catechumens were proceeded with. Lucius returned and reported his errand ineffectual. Acacius and his colleagues urged him with all their eloquence, and with promises of rich reward, probably more effective than their golden words, to make another effort, and to use force if persuasion were not regarded. They gave him some ecclesiastics to accompany him and, as it were, sanction their proceedings. Whether they began by exhortation is not recorded;

at any rate, if it was given, no attention was paid to it, and it was quickly seconded by barbarian violence. Lucius himself pushed his way to the place of baptism, and laid about him with a truncheon upon candidates, deacons, and priests, some of them aged men, and dispersed them in all directions. The soldiers seized and plundered the women of their ornaments, the clergy of their vestments, and the sacred vessels belonging to the Church; they beat the fugitives and dragged them off to the prisons. The natural solitude and silence of the streets, in the hour immediately preceding dawn, were disturbed by the cries of the captives and the shouts of their brutal captors.

In the morning the street walls were covered with proclamations, menacing with severe punishment any who persisted in maintaining intercourse with the Patriarch.[594]

The baths were effectually emptied of the congregation; but to fill the churches could not so easily be accomplished; in fact, they were entirely deserted. Large numbers of the dispersed congregation who had escaped the hands of the soldiers fled outside the walls of Constantinople, and, with indefatigable zeal, sought to complete the celebration of the Paschal rites as best they could in the secure recesses of woods or valleys. A large number assembled in a field called Pempton, because five miles from the Forum of Constantine, an open space surrounded by wood and intended to be used as a Hippodrome. In the course of the day— Easter Day— the Emperor and his retinue happened to ride, or perhaps were maliciously conducted, near the spot. The eye of Arcadius was attracted by the sight of a large body of people, many of them clothed in white, crowded together outside the Hippodrome. Unhappily, the Emperor was attended by courtiers inimical to the Archbishop. They replied to his inquiries respecting the nature of the concourse, that it was a body of heretics who had met to worship there in order to escape interference. Arcadius was weak enough to allow, without further inquiry, a number of soldiers who formed part of his escort to ride in upon the assembly and seize the most conspicuous leaders. A number of priests were captured, and several rich and noble ladies, whom the soldiers despoiled of their head-dresses and earrings with great barbarity, in one instance even tearing away with the appendage a portion of the ear itself.

One more attempt was made to assemble in a wooden hippodrome, built by Constantine, called the Xulodrome; but once more they were driven out, and hunted from place to place with relentless diligence. These repeated assaults broke up the flock of Chrysostom; the prisons were filled with the Johnites, as they were called after the name of their bishop, and the churches were empty. The prison walls echoed to the sound of the chants and hymns of the martyrs, but the churches to the noise of scourge and fierce threats administered to those who ventured to enter. This was done in the hope that they might be coerced by torture to anathematise the Archbishop.[595]

He himself, however, meanwhile continued to reside two months in his palace, though not without risk. Twice, as it was believed, attempts were made to assassinate him, but frustrated. Suspicion fell first on a man who affected demoniacal possession, and hovered much about the precincts of the palace. A dagger was found upon his person; the people seized him and dragged him before the prefect; but Chrysostom procured his release through the intercession of some bishops, just as he was about to be examined by torture. A second attempt was supposed to be intended by a slave, who ran at full speed towards the entrance of the palace, and plunged a dagger, in some instances with fatal effect, into several passers-by who endeavoured to stop him. He was at last surrounded and captured by the people, when he confessed that he had been bribed by his master, a priest named Elpidius, to try and assassinate the Archbishop. The fury of the people was appeased by the imprisonment of the man; but they now resolved to take the protection of their Archbishop into their own hands. They divided themselves into companies, which kept watch by turns, night and day, over the episcopal palace. The hostile party, dreading any further impediments to the execution of their iniquitous sentence, now hurried matters to their conclusion. Five days after Pentecost, four bishops— Acacius, Antiochus, Severian, and Cyrinus— obtained an interview with the Emperor. They represented that the city never would be tranquil till the removal of the Archbishop had been effected, and that his remaining in the palace after his condemnation was a gross violation of ecclesiastical law. They avowed themselves willing to take the responsibility of his deposition on their own heads, and besought the Emperor not to be more lenient and concessive than were bishops and priests.[596]

June, A.D. 404. The long-hoped-for mandate was at length issued. It was conveyed to the Archbishop by the notary Patricius, and informed him that Acacius and three other bishops having charged themselves with the responsibility of his deposition, he must commend himself to God, and quit the church and the palace without delay. The martyr received the cruel order with meek submission, and prepared to act upon it with prompt obedience. He passed from his palace to his church, saying to the bishops who accompanied him, "Come, let us pray and say farewell to the Angel of the Church. At my own fate I can rejoice, I only grieve for the sorrow of the people." One of his friends, a nobleman, conveyed a warning to him to avoid by a secret departure the risk of exciting popular tumult. He informed him that Lucius was waiting with troops in one of the public baths to compel his removal in the event of any delay or resistance, and that the consequences of any attempt at a rescue by the populace might be serious.

Chrysostom acted on his advice. He entered the choir with his friendly bishops, bestowed on them a farewell kiss and farewell words; then bidding them wait for him there while he went to repose, he entered the baptistry, and sent for the deaconesses, Olympias, Pentadia, Procla, and Salvina. "Come hither, my daughters," he said, "and hearken to me: my career, I perceive, is coming to an end; I have finished my course, and perchance ye will see my face no more. Now I exhort you to this: let not any of you break off her accustomed benevolence towards the Church. If any man is appointed my successor without having canvassed the office, and against his own will, but by the common consent of all, submit to his authority as if he were Chrysostom himself; so may ye obtain mercy. Remember me in your prayers." The women threw themselves at his feet dissolved in tears. The Archbishop made a sign to one of the priests to remove the women, lest, as he said, their wailing should attract the attention of the people outside. He directed that the mule on which he was accustomed to ride should be saddled and taken to the western gate of the cathedral; and while the people's attention was diverted by this feint, he passed out, unobserved, by a small door near the east end, and surrendered himself to some soldiers who were at hand to convey him to the port. So he departed from the church, the scene of his indefatigable labours, whose walls were never again to resound to his eloquence. He went out, and, in the emphatic words of the historian to whose narrative we are indebted for the minute picture of these occurrences, "the Angel of the Church went out with him." Two bishops, Cyriacus of Synnada in Phrygia, and Eulysius of Apamea in Bithynia, accompanied him on board the vessel which conveyed him across the straits to the Bithynian coast.[597]

CHAPTER 20

FURY OF THE PEOPLE AT THE REMOVAL OF
CHRYSOSTOM— DESTRUCTION OF THE CATHEDRAL
CHURCH AND SENATE-HOUSE BY FIRE— PERSECUTION OF
CHRYSOSTOM'S FOLLOWERS— FUGITIVES TO ROME—
LETTERS OF INNOCENT TO THEOPHILUS— TO THE
CLERGY OF CONSTANTINOPLE— TO CHRYSOSTOM—
DEPUTATION OF WESTERN BISHOPS TO CONSTANTINOPLE
REPULSED— SUFFERINGS OF THE EASTERN CHURCH—
TRIUMPH OF THE CABAL. A.D. 404, 405.

THE PEOPLE, MEANWHILE, BOTH within the church and outside, were not long in discovering that the Archbishop had disappeared from the building and its precincts. They became furiously agitated: some rushed to the harbour, but too late to obstruct the embarkation. The doors of the cathedral, which had been locked by some of the cabal, who anticipated a rush of the people as soon as the departure of Chrysostom should have been discovered, were fiercely battered by the crowd on both sides. Jews and Pagans looked on, and jeered derisively at the tumult. The horror of this scene of wild confusion was suddenly increased by the apparition of fire bursting forth from the building. How kindled, by accident or design, it is impossible to determine. Each party fiercely charged the other with the guilt of the catastrophe, and some attributed it to miraculous interference of heavenly powers. The conflagration broke out in or near the throne of the Archbishop, which it consumed, and then spread to the roof. In three hours the edifice, whose erection and embellishment had been the work of many years, was reduced to a heap of cinders. The only portion not destroyed was the treasury which contained the sacred vessels of silver and gold, as if expressly to confute one of the charges made against the Archbishop, that he had sold all the most valuable ornaments belonging to the church. Germanus and Cassian, the custodians of the treasury, when they fled to Rome, carried with them a copy of the inventory of all these articles, which, when they surrendered their office, had been handed over to the prefect and some of the other chief functionaries of the city.

The conflagration, however, did not confine itself to the cathedral. A violent north wind carried the flames across the Forum, and ignited the great curia or senate-house; not, however, that side of it which faced the cathedral, but the further side, which looked into the little forum where the royal palace was situated. The whole senate-house was destroyed. The statues of the Muses which Constantine had brought from Helicon were consumed, and all the other principal adornments. The images of Zeus and Athene alone were found intact, beneath a heap of ruins and of masses of molten lead which had dropped upon them from the burning roof.[598]

The real or affected suspicion that the Archbishop and his flock were the incendiaries was quite a sufficient pretext for treating them with rigour. He himself, with Cyriacus and Eulysius, was detained in chains under a strict guard in Bithynia. These two companions were taken from him and conveyed bound to Chalcedon, but after examination were dismissed as innocent. But at Constantinople the persecution was enforced with merciless severity under the auspices of Optatus, a Pagan, now prefect in the place of Studius. All the followers of the Archbishop, clerical and lay, high and low, were subjected, if caught, to rigorous inquisition, and most of them to severe punishment. Chrysostom wrote a letter from Bithynia to the Emperor, imploring that he might at least be allowed to appear and defend himself and his clergy from the atrocious charge of incendiarism, but the letter received no attention; and as the poor exile continued his journey to Nice, his sufferings were enhanced by pitiable intelligence of the persecution inflicted on bishops, priests, and deacons who refused to anathematise him or recognise the validity of his deposition. But the spirit of the exile was not only brave to support his own troubles, but could spare some of its energy to encourage those, who were suffering in his cause, to patience, fortitude, resignation, and even joy.[599]

In times of religious persecution, the language of the New Testament, about the blessedness of tribulation as a pledge of future happiness and a means of preparation for it, comes home to men's hearts with a reality and force which seem to exceed our present application of it to the troubles and sorrows of ordinary life. Those who were firmly persuaded that their cause was the cause of truth and of Jesus Christ read the words, "Blessed are ye when ye are persecuted for righteousness' sake," or, "Happy are ye when men revile you and persecute you," as if spoken directly to themselves; and they really did "rejoice in that day, and leap for joy." Such are the texts which Chrysostom cites for the consolation of his suffering friends. He speaks of their exposure to intimidation by threats, imprisonment, frequent appearance in judges' courts, torture at the hands of the executioner, shameless false evidence, coarse ribaldry, and scurrilous jests; but "blessed were they, yea, thrice blessed, and more than that, to endure imprisonment and chains, for not only was their fortitude the subject of admiration everywhere, but their present sufferings were the measure of their future happiness, and their names had been inscribed in the Book of Life."[600]

The destruction of the church and senate-house was the first pretext for instituting persecution against the adherents of Chrysostom; the second was, their refusal to recognise his successor. One week after his deposition, Arsacius, brother of Nectarius the predecessor of Chrysostom, was, apparently by the simple exercise of Imperial authority, elevated to the see. He was eighty years old, and is quaintly described by Palladius as "muter than a fish, and more incapable than a frog."[601] The probable aim of the Empress was to secure a man whose servility might be depended on. His brother, Nectarius, had once desired to make him Bishop of Tarsus; and, on his declining to accept the promotion, had taunted him with ambitiously reserving himself for the See of Constantinople; whereupon Arsacius had taken an oath that he never would accept any bishopric. But ambition and Imperial authority overcame his scruples. He is described by the historians as a man of pious disposition and mild conduct; with one exception: that he persecuted with relentless vigour the contumacious adherents of his predecessor. By Chrysostom he is denounced as a wolf, and in a figurative sense as an adulterer, on account of his usurpation of the see during the lifetime of its legitimate occupant.[602] Arsacius applied to the civil powers for assistance to compel the Johnites to attend the churches where he and his clergy officiated. A tribune was directed to attack a body of them who had assembled for worship in some remote part of the city. The soldiers dispersed the assembly, took several of the most eminent persons prisoners, and, as usual, stripped the women of their golden girdles, jewels, and earrings. The only consequence of this was, that the Johnites became more attached to the cause and memory of their late Archbishop. Some of them fled the city, and many more refrained as much as possible from appearing in public places, such as the Forum and the baths. Meetings of some kind for worship were not discontinued, or were soon resumed, for we find Chrysostom, in one of his letters written during his exile, reproving two priests, Theophilus and Salustius, for slackness in attending such assemblies.[603] But worshippers ran great risks. The prefect Optatus, who succeeded Studius, probably because the latter was considered too lenient, appears to have entertained all the animosity of a thorough Pagan against Christians, and to have rejoiced in the present opportunity of inflicting sufferings upon them. He combined the two charges of incendiarism and contumacy in his prosecution of the Johnites, and endeavoured to extort confessions of guilt from his victims with merciless barbarity.

A few instances are recorded, and they are quite enough to sicken us of the tale of such horrors. Eutropius, a reader, was commanded to name the persons who had set fire to the church. He refused. He was young and delicate, and it was thought a confession might be wrung from him under the agony of torture. He was lashed with a scourge, his cheeks were scraped, and his sides lacerated with iron teeth, after which lighted torches were applied to the wounded parts. No information could be extorted from him: he was therefore conveyed to prison, and thrown into a dungeon, where he expired. Some priests, adherents of Arsacius, buried him by night, that his mangled body might not be seen by any eyes but those of his enemies. Celestial music was said to have been heard at the time of his interment.

Tigrius, the priest, whose presence with Scrapion had been demanded at the Synod of the Oak, was another victim. He was stripped, scourged on his back, and then stretched on the rack till his bones were dislocated. He survived the torture, and was banished to Mesopotamia. Serapion himself, now bishop of Heraclea in Thrace, was seized, tried on several calumnious charges, barbarously scourged, and sent into exile.

Those ladies also who were most distinguished for their friendship with the deposed Archbishop, and for the dedication of their time and money to the Church, were marked objects of persecution. They were brought before the prefect, and admonished by him to acknowledge Arsacius, and so save themselves from future annoyance. A few from timidity complied; but Olympias, who was subjected to a severer examination, confronted it with a dauntless spirit. She was bluntly asked why she had set fire to the "Great Church." "My manner of life," replied the accused, "is a sufficient refutation of such a charge; a person who has expended large sums of money to restore and embellish the churches of God is not likely to burn and demolish them." "I know your past course of life well," cried the prefect. "If you know aught against it, then descend from your place there as judge, and come forward as my accuser," replied the undaunted Olympias. Perceiving that she was not to be browbeaten, Optatus proposed the same course to her which had been adopted by some other women as a means of exemption from further persecution, namely, communion with Arsacius; but she scornfully rejected the base compromise. "I have been publicly calumniated by a charge which cannot be proven, and I will not accede to any terms till I have been cleared from this accusation. Even if you resort to force, I will not hold communion with those from whom I ought to secede, nor do anything contrary to the principles of my holy religion." She made a request, which was granted, that she might be allowed a few days to consult with lawyers on the proper means of legally refuting the libellous accusation. The prefect, however (on what pretence is not stated), sent for her again, and exacted a heavy fine, in the hope that she would be induced to yield. The fine was paid without any reluctance, but her refusal to acknowledge the usurper was inflexible; and to avoid, if possible, further pressure and persecution, she retired to Cyzicus, on the other side of the straits.[604]

The tidings of her fortitude and loyalty were conveyed to the exiled Chrysostom, and so cheered his spirit in the midst of depression and sickness that his sufferings seemed to him as nothing. "When many men and women, old and young, highly reputed for their virtue, had turned their backs on the enemy almost before the conflict had begun, she, on the other hand, after many encounters, so far from being enervated, was even invigorated; she spread forth the sails of patience, and floated securely as on a calm sea; so far from being overwhelmed by the storm, she was scarcely sprinkled by the spray. In the seclusion of her little house she was able to inspire courage into the hearts of others, and had been to them a haven of comfort and a tower of strength."[605]

The deaconess Pentadia, widow of the consul Timasius, was another victim. She led the life of a recluse, never going beyond the walls of her house except to church. She was now dragged from her retreat through the Forum to the prefect's tribunal, and thence to prison, charged with being an accomplice in the late fire. Several persons were put to the torture before her eyes, in order to intimidate her into a confession; but in vain. Her firm demeanour, courageous answers, and powerful demonstrations of her innocence, confounded and silenced her adversaries, and elicited the admiration of the public. Beyond imprisonment, no indignities seem to have been inflicted on her; and when desirous to quit the capital, she was persuaded by Chrysostom to remain, who represented the great value of her presence and example in animating others to undergo their present afflictions. She had apparently intended to try and join him in his place of exile, when he had been removed to Cucusus, on the confines of Lesser Armenia, for he dwells on the great risk to her delicate health from a journey in winter, and the danger of being plundered by the Isaurian robbers, who were just then, he says, in a powerful condition. He, therefore, on all grounds, begs her to remain where she is, but to relieve his mind from anxiety about her affairs and health by constantly writing to him.[606]

Meanwhile, the injured Church of Constantinople did not cease through letters and emissaries to solicit the interference of the Western Church. The first intimation of the calamities we have been describing which reached the ears of Rome was through a messenger despatched by Theophilus. The letter which he brought was inscribed "From Pope Theophilus to Pope Innocent," and stated in the barest manner, without assigning his reasons or mentioning any assessors in his judgment, that he had deposed Chrysostom, and that it behoved Innocent to break off communion with him. The Pope was displeased by the cool and curt character of the letter, and somewhat perplexed how to notice or reply to so inexplicit a despatch. Eusebius, a deacon from Constantinople, who was in Rome at the time on some ecclesiastical business, obtained an interview with Innocent, and entreated him not to act till information should be received from Constantinople, which, he added (on what grounds does not appear), he had good reason to expect would arrive in a short time. Three days afterwards four bishops did arrive, bearing the letter from Chrysostom to Innocent which contained that pathetic and perspicuous narrative of the recent occurrences, from which extracts have been made in the preceding chapter. They brought two other letters, one from the forty friendly bishops, another from the clergy of Constantinople.

Innocent no longer hesitated to pronounce an opinion. His letter to Theophilus is brief, decisive, almost peremptory in tone. "The See of Rome," he said, "would maintain communion with Alexandria and Constantinople to avoid rending the unity of the Church; but he annulled (ἀθέτησας) the deposition of John apparently made by Theophilus. It was impossible to recognise the validity of a sentence pronounced by such an irregular synod as that lately convened at Chalcedon. If Theophilus had confidence in the justice of that sentence, he must appear in person to prove it before a General Council called together and regulated according to the Canons of Nice." A few days after the despatch of this letter, Peter, an Alexandrian priest, arrived with a deacon from Constantinople, bearing another letter from Theophilus, and certain minutes, so called, of the acts of the Synod of the Oak. Innocent, having perused the minutes, was indignant at the mingled monstrosity and levity of the charges brought against Chrysostom, and at the condemnation having been pronounced in the absence of the defendant. He ordered special prayers and fasts to be observed by the Church for the restoration of concord, and addressed to Theophilus a sharp letter of reproof.[607]

It is not easy to make out precisely how many communications passed each way between the Churches of Rome and Constantinople, or the exact date of each; but several letters are distinctly mentioned. Theotecnus, a priest from Constantinople, brought a letter from twenty-five of the forty bishops who had constantly adhered to Chrysostom, in which they described the expulsion of the Patriarch and the conflagration of the church. Innocent replied by a letter of condolence, and exhortation to bear their trial with Christian fortitude and patience, for at present he confessed, with deep regret, that he saw small prospect of rendering much effectual aid, "owing to the opposition of certain persons powerful for evil," alluding probably to the jealousies between the Courts of the two brothers, Honorius and Arcadius. The cabal also sent a letter to Innocent, containing their version of the late transactions. Their emissary was Paternus, who called himself a priest of Constantinople; "an ugly little fellow," says Palladius, "and very unintelligible." The letter was written in the names of Arsacius, Paulus, Antiochus, Cyrinus, Severian, and some others; and, among other opprobrious charges, distinctly accused Chrysostom of setting fire to the church. Innocent treated the letter with much disdain, and would not condescend to answer it. Some days afterwards, Cyriacus, bishop of Synnada, arrived in Rome as a fugitive, in consequence of an Imperial edict, which directed the deposition of any bishop who refused to communicate with Arsacius and Theophilus, and the confiscation of his property, if he had any. After Cyriacus arrived Eulysius, bishop of Apamea in Bithynia, bringing a letter from fifteen of the forty friendly bishops, which described all the past and present distress of the Church caused by Chrysostom's enemies, and in all respects confirmed the oral account of Cyriacus. In the course of another month, Palladius, bishop of Hellenopolis, fled to Rome from the intolerable harshness of magisterial decrees, which now subjected to confiscation the house of any one who should be found to have harboured bishop, priest, or even layman, who communicated with Chrysostom. From a letter of Chrysostom[608] it appears that Palladius and many others lived for some time in concealment at Constantinople, in the hope of escaping persecution. They were courteously lodged in Rome by one Pinianus and his wife, by Juliana, Proba, and other Roman ladies, whom Chrysostom warmly thanks for their kindness in letters written by him from Cucusus.[609] Germanus the priest, and Cassian the deacon, custodians of the Church treasury at Constantinople, also came to Rome, bringing a letter from the whole body of the clergy who adhered to Chrysostom, describing the violent deposition and expulsion of the Archbishop, and the tyranny of their adversaries under which they were now suffering.[610]

The reply of Innocent to this letter from the clergy of Constantinople is dignified as well as sympathetic. He exhorts, as usual, to patience, and to the derivation of comfort from the remembrance of the sufferings of all God's saints in past times. But he deeply deplores their wrongs, and again expresses his reprobation in the strongest terms of the illegality of the late proceedings. "The canon which prohibited the ordination of a successor during the lifetime of the reigning bishop had been grossly violated. The Canons of Antioch, on which the synod had relied, were invalid, having been composed by heretics, and they had been rejected by the Council of Sardica. The Canons of Nice alone were entitled to the obedience of the Church; but adversaries and heretics were always attempting to subvert them.'"... "What steps, then, should be taken in the existing crisis? Plainly a General Council must be convoked: that was the only means of appeasing the fury of the tempest. He was watching an opportunity to accomplish this: meanwhile, they must wait in patience, and trust the goodness of God for the restoration of tranquillity and good order."

To Chrysostom Innocent wrote, as friend to friend, as a bishop to a brother bishop, a letter of Christian consolation and encouragement, not entering into the legal questions of the case, and not pledging himself to decisive action of any kind. It was not necessary to remind one, who was himself the teacher and pastor of a great people, that God often tried the best of men, and put their patience to the severest tests, and that they are firmly supported under the greatest calamities by the approving voice of conscience.... A good man may be severely tried, but cannot be overcome, since he is preserved and guarded by the truth of Holy Scripture. Holy Scripture supplied abundant examples of suffering saints who did not receive their crowns until they had undergone the heaviest trials with patience. "Take courage, then, honoured brother, from the testimony of conscience. When you have been purified by affliction, you will enter into the haven of peace in the presence of Christ our Lord."[611]

Innocent, however, not only wrote commonplace letters of condolence, but exerted himself to obtain the council which he had recommended to the Church of Constantinople as the only means of redressing her wrongs. He wrote a letter to Honorius, then at Ravenna, representing the lamentable condition of the Church of Constantinople, which elicited from the Emperor an order for the convention of an Italian synod. This synod, after a due consideration of all the circumstances, was to submit its decision and suggestions to himself. The result of the deliberations of the Italian bishops, swayed no doubt by Innocent, was to request the Emperor to write to his brother Arcadius, urging the convocation of a General Council to be held in Thessalonica, which would be a convenient meeting-point for the prelates of East and West. Honorius complied, and the letter was despatched under the care of a deputation from the Italian Church, consisting of five bishops, two priests, and a deacon. The Emperor calls it the third letter[612] which he had written relative to the affairs of Constantinople. He professes great solicitude for the peace of the

Church, "on which," he observes, "the peace of our Empire depends;" and with a view to this object, he urges the convocation of a council at Thessalonica, and specially entreats that the attendance of Theophilus, who was, he is informed, author of all these disturbances, should be insisted upon. He commends the deputation to the honourable care of Arcadius; and that he may know the sentiments of the Italian Church on the present state of affairs, he sends him two letters as samples of many, one from the Bishop of Rome, the other from the Bishop of Aquileia.

The only bishop on the deputation whose see is mentioned was Æmilius, bishop of Beneventum. The Oriental refugees, Cyriacus, Demetrius, Palladius, and Eulysius, accompanied the Italians. They were the bearers not only of letters from Honorius, Innocent, and the bishops Chromatius of Aquileia and Venerius of Milan, but also of a memorial from the Italian synod, which recommended that Chrysostom should be reinstated in his see before he was required to take his trial before a council. He would then, it was observed, have no reasonable excuse for declining to attend it. The deputation was absent four months. On their return the members had a pitiful tale to tell of failure in their errand, and of personal suffering from maltreatment. They touched at Athens on their voyage out, whence they had intended to proceed to Thessalonica, and lay the letters first of all before Anysius, bishop of that place; but at Athens they were arrested by a military officer, who placed them on board two vessels under charge of a centurion, to be conveyed to Constantinople. A furious southerly gale sprang up soon after their departure, and, after a voyage of some danger, they arrived, late on the third day, at the suburb of Constantinople called Victor. But, instead of being allowed to proceed to the city, they were shut up in a fortress named Athyra, on the coast— the Romans in a single chamber, the Orientals in separate apartments. No servant even was permitted to attend them. They were commanded to deliver up the letters which they had brought, but refused, as being ambassadors, to surrender them to any but to the Emperor himself. Secretaries and messengers were sent in succession, but the ambassadors steadfastly adhered to their refusal. The letters were at length wrested from their possession by sheer violence:

one bishop's thumb was broken in the struggle. On the following day a large bribe was offered them if they would recognise Atticus (the aged Arsacius was now dead) as Patriarch, and say no more about the trial of Chrysostom. This base proposal was firmly resisted; and, seeing the utter hopelessness of their mission, they requested to be released as soon as possible, and suffered to return to their dioceses in safety. The Italians saw no more of their companions from the East. They themselves were thrust into a miserable vessel, with twenty soldiers of various grades, and conveyed to Lampsacus, on the Asiatic coast, where they embarked in another vessel, and, after a tedious voyage of twenty days, arrived at Hydruntum, in Calabria.[613]

Neither the Papacy nor the Empire of the West was sufficiently powerful at this time to insist further upon justice being done to the Patriarch, in the face of the determined animosity of the ruling powers at Constantinople; but the friends of the martyr deemed that they read unequivocal signs of the Divine displeasure in the misfortunes which befell some of Chrysostom's greatest personal enemies. Thrace and Illyria were ravaged by an incursion of Huns, and the Isaurians, a predatory barbarian race, which inhabited the fastnesses of Mount Taurus, committed fearful havoc in Syria and Asia Minor. Cyrinus, bishop of Chalcedon, one of the four who had taken on them the responsibility of Chrysostom's condemnation, died in great agony from the wound in his foot, originally caused when his foot had been trodden upon by Bishop Maruthas, more than a year ago, just before the Synod of the Oak. At the end of September, Constantinople was visited by a destructive fall of hailstones of extraordinary size; and on October 6, A.D. 404, died the Empress Eudoxia. Nilus, one of the most eminent anchorites of the day, once prefect of Constantinople, who had abandoned wealth, family, and position for the solitudes of Mount Sinai, addressed two letters of reproof and warning to Arcadius on the iniquitous banishment of Chrysostom and inhuman persecution of his followers. "How can you expect to see Constantinople delivered from visitations of earthquake and fire from Heaven, after the enormities which have there been perpetrated; after crime has been established there by the authority of laws; after the thrice-blessed John, the pillar of the Church, the lamp of truth, the trumpet of Jesus Christ, has been driven from the city? How can I grant my prayers (Arcadius had apparently begged the intercession of the saint to remove the national troubles) to a city stricken by the wrath of God, whose thunder is every moment ready to fall upon her?"[614]

But human and divine warnings were alike wasted; the enemies of the Patriarch had complete sway over the Court, and suffered it not to swerve from the path of persecution. The Western bishops and presbyters, after the disastrous termination of their embassy to Constantinople, returned home, without honour indeed, but unmolested. Their Eastern colleagues did not escape so easily. They were conveyed to places of exile in the most distant and opposite quarters of the Empire. Cyriacus was confined in a Persian fortress beyond Emessa; Eulysius in Arabia; Palladius on the confines of Ethiopia; Demetrius was to have been confined in one of the Egyptian oases, but died of the harsh treatment to which he was subjected on the journey. The exiles suffered such brutal insults and indignities from the soldiers who conducted them to these places, that the desire of life was extinguished. The little money which they had collected for the expenses of their journey was taken from them by their guards, who divided it among themselves. They were forced to perform in one day the distance of two days' journey. They were not permitted to enter any churches on their route, but forced into Jewish or Samaritan synagogues, and lodged at night in low inns, where their ears were shocked by the filthy conversation of abandoned characters of both sexes. Yet even some of these degraded people were won to a more respectful behaviour, if not actually converted, by the Christian exhortations and instruction of the captives. The "Word of God was not bound." Some of the bishops friendly to Theophilus bribed the soldiers to hurry the exiles out of their dioceses as quickly as possible. Distinguished among these malignants were the bishops of Tarsus, Antioch, Ancyra, and of Cæsarea in Palestine. Most of the bishops of Cappadocia, on the other hand, especially Theodorus of Tyana, and Bosporius of Colonia, accorded them a compassionate and courteous reception.[615]

Arsacius died in November A.D. 404. Out of many ambitious candidates for the vacant throne, Atticus, a presbyter, who had taken an active part in the persecution of Chrysostom, a native of Sebaste in Armenia, was appointed. He was a man of moderate abilities and generally mild disposition, but relentless in his determination to crush out the party of the exiled Patriarch. By his influence an Imperial rescript was obtained, which decreed that "any bishop who did not communicate with Theophilus, Porphyry of Antioch, and Atticus, should be ejected from the Church, and his property confiscated." The wealthy, for the most part, bowed to the storm; the poor sought peace of body and of conscience in flight either to Rome or monasteries. This rescript, aimed at the bishops, was followed up by another directed against the laity. Any layman who refused to recognise the above-mentioned prelates was, if a civilian, to be deprived of any office which he might hold; if a soldier, of his military girdle; if an artisan, to be heavily fined or banished. Bishops and presbyters were dispersed as fugitives into all parts of the Empire. Some sought retirement in some secluded little country property of their own, and obtained a precarious livelihood by manual labour, farming, or fishing.[616]

But, in spite of all the various means of coercion at Constantinople, in spite of trials, torture, imprisonment, banishment, the bulk of the people could not be brought to attend the ministration of Atticus and his clergy. Their churches were comparatively empty, while the persecuted adherents of the exile persistently held their services in some sequestered valley, or on some lonely hillside. In fact, persecution, as has always been the case, only intensified the attachment of many to the person and the cause which it was intended to crush, and so far defeated its own object. Chrysostom himself observes,[617] that many of those who had enjoyed a high reputation for piety were the first to fall away when brought to the test of persecution; whereas others, who had formerly been abandoned to frivolity and vice, now renounced the theatre and circus, hastened into the desert to attend the assembly of the Catholics at worship, and displayed the greatest fortitude before the judge when brought to trial, in the face of torture, and with the prospect of imprisonment or exile.

The party now in power could not convert the hearts of clergy or people to their side, but they could, and did, change the outward aspect of the Church. The men of probity and piety with whom Chrysostom had replaced the six simoniacal bishops deposed in Asia were expelled, and the delinquents restored. The Church in that region was reduced to a disgraceful state. Ordinations were conducted, not amidst prayer and fasting, but feasting, drunkenness, and gross bribery. The See of Heracleides, the good bishop of Ephesus, appointed by Chrysostom, was occupied by a eunuch, a monster of iniquity. The people in disgust deserted the churches.

The death of Flavian, bishop of Antioch, nearly coincided with the banishment of Chrysostom. The people of Antioch were much attached to a priest named Constantius, a man described by Palladius as a faithful and incorruptible servant of the Church from his earliest youth, first as a messenger who carried ecclesiastical despatches, then as reader, deacon, priest. He had won the love and admiration of the people by his gentle, amiable disposition, his intelligence, strict integrity, and exemplary piety. There was a general desire to make him bishop, but an ambitious priest named Porphyry frustrated the design. By bribery, and calumnious stories conveyed to the Court at Constantinople, he procured an Imperial rescript condemning Constantius to be banished to one of the oases as a disturber of the people. With the assistance of his friends Constantius escaped to Cyprus. Porphyry meanwhile imprisoned several of the clergy of Antioch, and seized the opportunity of the Olympian festival (when most of the inhabitants had poured out to the celebrated suburb of Daphne) to enter the church with a few bishops and clergy; and then, with doors fast closed, he was hurriedly ordained, so hurriedly that some portions of the service were omitted. Acacius, Severian, and Antiochus, who had officiated, immediately fled. The people were enraged when they discovered the trick, surrounded Porphyry's house, and threatened to burn it to the ground. He applied for protection to the prefect, who lent him a body of troops, with which he forcibly took possession of the church. He contrived to get an unscrupulous and cruel man sent from Constantinople to be captain of the city guards, terror of whom drove the people to attend the churches, though they did so with disgust, and earnestly prayed for retribution from Heaven on the authors of this wickedness.[618]

Innocent remained inflexibly attached to the cause of Chrysostom. The Church of Rome and the Italian bishops broke off all communion with Theophilus and Atticus, and ceased not to demand the convocation of a General Council, as the only tribunal by which the Patriarch could be lawfully acquitted or condemned.[619] But the Court of Ravenna was not in a position to support these demands by intimidation or actual force. All the skill of Stilicho and all the resources at his command were barely sufficient to repel the persevering efforts of Alaric and Rhadagaisus to take the great prize which they so eagerly coveted, the capital of the Roman Empire. The inevitable fall of Rome was averted only for a little while.

Thus the spirit of lawlessness and selfishness took advantage of the impotence of the secular power both in Rome and Constantinople to work its will upon the Church. It dealt a blow to Christian morality and ecclesiastical discipline from which the Church at Constantinople never recovered, and which caused a throb of pain from one end of Christendom to the other; for, in spite of all differences and divisions, Christendom was one then, so that, if one member suffered, all the members suffered with it; and what was done and said, and thought and felt, in the Church of Alexandria, or Antioch, or Constantinople, was not unknown or unregarded by the Churches of Rome or Milan, and through them made its impress on the Churches even of Gaul and Spain.

CHAPTER 21

CHRYSOSTOM ORDERED TO BE REMOVED TO CUCUSUS— PERILS ENCOUNTERED AT CÆSAREA— HARDSHIPS OF THE JOURNEY— REACHES CUCUSUS— LETTERS WRITTEN THERE TO OLYMPIAS AND OTHER FRIENDS. A.D. 404.

IT NOW ONLY REMAINS to follow the illustrious exile along his painful journey to its melancholy or, if we regard him as the Christian martyr, its glorious termination.

He was removed, as has been already seen, from Constantinople on June 20, and conveyed, in the course of a few days, to Nicæa. Here he remained till July 4, and several of his letters to Olympias were written from this place. The soft yet fresh sea air revived his health, which had suffered from the feverish and harassing scenes that he had gone through at Constantinople, and from the journey begun in the very middle of the summer heat. Nothing could exceed the kindness of the soldiers under whose custody he travelled, who discharged towards him all the duties of servants as well as of guards.[620] His ultimate destination was not known for some time by himself or his friends. Common report sent him to Scythia,[621] but the intention of his enemies appears to have changed from time to time. Sebaste in Armenia had been first proposed, but finally Cucusus, a village in the Tauric range on the edge of Cilicia and the Lesser Armenia, was fixed upon. It was a remote and desolate spot, subject to frequent attacks from the marauding Isaurians; and at first Chrysostom earnestly entreated his friends in Constantinople to try and procure a more agreeable place of exile, a favour frequently granted to criminals. Olympias, Bishop Cyriacus, Briso the chamberlain, and a lady named Theodora, repeatedly interceded on his behalf; but their efforts were ineffectual.[622] The Empress herself, it would appear, selected Cucusus, and was inexorable in her decision.[623]

From beginning to end of his exile Chrysostom's mind was occupied with organising such work as yet remained possible to him. It has been seen with what zeal he had planted a missionary settlement in Phœnicia. This project continued to the close of his life to be an object of his most solicitous interest. On July 3, the eve of his departure from Nicæa, he addressed a letter to a priest named Constantius,[624] apparently the superintendent of the missionary work in Phœnicia and the surrounding countries. He implores him to prosecute his labours for the extirpation of Paganism with zeal undiminished, and undismayed by the present afflicted state of the bishop and the see, to whom the mission owed its origin. "The pilot and the physician, far from relaxing their efforts when the ship and the patient are in peril, redouble their efforts to save them." He begs Constantius to inform him year by year how many temples are destroyed, how many churches built, how many good Christians immigrate into Phœnicia. He had himself persuaded a recluse, whom he found at Nicæa, to go and place himself under the direction of Constantius in the missionary work. He had, he says, happily concluded, just about the time of his deposition, arrangements for the suppression of Marcionism, which was very prevalent at Salamis, in Cyprus. He begs Constantius to write to his friend Bishop Cyriacus, if still in Constantinople, and request him to carry these plans into effect. Finally, he implores the prayers of Constantius and all faithful people for the cessation of the present calamities of the Church, especially of the intolerable evils which had befallen it in Asia; alluding no doubt to the restoration of the simoniacal bishops.

On July 4 or 5 the exile started from Nicæa on his toilsome and perilous journey in the midsummer heat, across the scorching plains of Galatia and Cappadocia. He describes himself[625] as an object of great compassion to travellers whom he met coming from Armenia and the East, who stopped to weep and wail over his distress. His route lay in a diagonal line across the centre of Asia Minor, ascending first of all near the stream of the river Sangarius, which in its upper course winds through vast plains of black bituminous soil, scantily cultivated, but supplying pasture to great herds of cattle. Chrysostom had always been an ascetic liver, but he had not a robust frame, and he had been accustomed to wholesome food and the frequent use of the bath. Continuous travelling by night as well as day, the scorching sun, hot dust, hard bread, brackish water, and deprivation of the bath, threw him into a fever; but either from fear of the Isaurians, or of Leontius, bishop of Ancyra, in Galatia, one of his most virulent enemies, the journey was pursued without intermission till he arrived, more dead than alive, at Cæsarea, in Cappadocia.

He has left us a detailed account of the perils which befell him here, and a melancholy picture indeed it is of the ferocity and cunning of which bishops and monks were capable under the influence of fanatical partisanship.[626] Having escaped, he says, from the Galatian (probably meaning Leontius), he was met, as he approached Cæsarea, by several persons, who informed him that Pharetrius the bishop was eagerly expecting him, and preparing to welcome him with affectionate hospitality. He confesses that he himself mistrusted these specious offers, but he kept his suspicions to himself. On his arrival at Cæsarea, in a state of extreme exhaustion, Pharetrius did not appear, but he was enthusiastically received by the people as well as some monks and nuns. The extreme kindness and skill of physicians (one of whom declared his intention of accompanying him to the end of his journey), wholesome food, and the use of the bath, so much renovated his strength and diminished his fever, that he became anxious in a day or two to resume his journey. But just at this juncture the city was thrown into consternation by tidings that a large body of Isaurians was ravaging the neighbourhood, and had already burned a town with much slaughter. All the available troops in Cæsarea were marched out, and the whole male population, including old men, turned out to man the walls. During this time of suspense, the house in which Chrysostom lodged was besieged by a large body of monks, who with furious cries and gestures demanded his surrender. The prætorians who guarded him were terrified by the fierce behaviour of these fanatics, and declared that they would rather face the Isaurians than fall into the hands of these "wild beasts." The governor of the city succeeded in protecting the person of Chrysostom, but not in quelling the fury of the monks, who renewed their assault still more hotly on the following day. The Bishop Pharetrius was very generally suspected to be the instigator of these attacks, and an appeal was made to him to interpose his authority, that the Archbishop might at least enjoy a few days' repose, which the state of his health greatly needed. But the envy of Pharetrius was embittered by the popularity of Chrysostom, and the great kindness and compassion which his hardships had elicited from clergy and people. He refused to interfere; but Chrysostom's friends took advantage of a brief lull in the hostile visits of the monks to convey him in a litter outside the town, amidst the lamentations of the attendant people, and imprecations on the author of the malevolent assaults. When he was once outside the town several of the clergy joined him, and besought him not to think of trusting himself to Pharetrius; it would be worse, they declared, than falling into the hands of the Isaurians: "only escape from our hands, and wherever you fall you will fall safely."

At this crisis a lady named Seleucia, the wife of Rufinus, a man of rank and a friend of Chrysostom, entreated him to accept a lodging at her country house, about five miles out of the city. He accepted the offer; but, unknown to him, Pharetrius, whose rage was inflamed by the rescue of his prey, visited the house, and threatened to take vengeance on the mistress if her guest was not surrendered. This demand was refused, and the lady gave orders to her steward, in the event of any attack by monks, to collect all the labourers on the estate and repel the assault by force. But her courage at last gave way under the pressure of incessant menaces from Pharetrius, and it was resolved to remove the Archbishop, not less for his own safety than for that of the person whose roof had afforded him shelter. In the dead of night, when Chrysostom was sleeping, unconscious of impending danger, he was roused by a companion, the priest Evethius, who told him that he must instantly prepare for flight. It was midnight, and the sky murky and moonless; but they dared not light torches for fear of attracting the observation of their enemies. The road was rugged and rocky; the mule which carried the Archbishop's litter fell, and he was thrown out. Evethius took him by the hand and led, or rather dragged, him along. In such a pitiable plight, faint with fatigue and fever-stricken, did the bishop of the second see in Christendom stumble and totter in the darkness along the Cappadocian mountain path. "Were not these calamities," he writes to Olympias, "sufficient to blot out many sins, and suggest to me a hope of future glory?"

Of the remainder of his journey to Cucusus we possess no detailed narrative. He only speaks in general terms of his sufferings for thirty days from fever, aggravated by the want of a bath, and by deficient accommodation of every kind in a journey made along a rough road, through a desolate mountainous country, liable to an attack at any moment from Isaurian bandits.[627] Desolate though the region was, however, he speaks of monks and nuns occasionally meeting him in large numbers, and loudly bewailing his calamities, exclaiming that it "had been better the sun should have hidden his rays, than that the mouth of Chrysostom should have been closed."[628] About seventy days[629] after his departure from Constantinople, that is, about the end of August or beginning of September, Cucusus was reached. After the fatigues and dangers of his journey, it was a haven of rest to the exhausted exile, though he describes it as in itself the most desolate place in the world; a mere village high up in the eastern range of Taurus, on the confines of Lesser Armenia, Cilicia, and Cappadocia.[630] But it was protected from the Isaurians by a strong garrison, and it contained many warm-hearted friends of the Archbishop, who emulated one another in showing him attention. Several had sent invitations to him, before he left Cæsarea, to accept a lodging at their houses, but more especially one whom he calls "my Lord Diodorus," who had known him in Constantinople. This generous personage not only placed his whole house at the disposal of Chrysostom, betaking himself to a country villa to make room for his guest, but furnished it with every possible defence against the cold of the approaching winter, in that altitude very severe. The Bishop of Cucusus not only received him with great civility, but was even desirous that his own throne should be occupied by the illustrious exile, that his flock might profit by the eloquence of the greatest teacher and preacher of the day; but Chrysostom thought it prudent to decline the honour.[631]

Many of his friends in Constantinople and other places, who owned property near Cucusus, directed their stewards to provide in various ways for the comfort of the exile, and some of his friends actually came to share his fortunes in person. The aged deaconess, Sabiniana, arrived from Constantinople with the fixed determination of accompanying him to his final place of exile, whatever that might be. Constantius, the presbyter of Antioch, whom the people had wished to make bishop, also took up his abode at Cucusus, as well to escape from the persecution of Porphyry as from his zealous attachment to Chrysostom.[632] Thus the natural disadvantages of the place, the want of good physicians and of a plentiful market, the severity of the heat in summer and cold in winter, were largely compensated by the enjoyment of freedom, rest, and the kind attention of friends. He warns his supporters in Constantinople, who were endeavouring to procure a change of destination for him, to be careful that he was not removed to a place worse than Cucusus, where he possessed all substantial necessaries and comforts of life. If, however, they thought there was a chance of obtaining Cyzicus or Nicomedia, they were not to desist from their efforts; but he was convinced that another long and fatiguing journey to a spot as remote and desolate as Cucusus would kill him.[633]

The leisure of the exile was profitably employed in writing letters to every variety of friends— men of rank, ladies, deaconesses in Constantinople, bishops, clergy, missionary monks, and his kind acquaintances in Cæsarea, especially the physician Hymnetius, who had attended him there with affectionate care. As might be expected, none of his letters describe his condition so minutely or pour forth so unrestrainedly his fears and hopes, his causes of distress or joy, as those written to Olympias. The style in which she is usually addressed is at once respectful, affectionate, and paternal: "To my lady, the most reverend and religious deaconess Olympias, Bishop John sends you greeting in the Lord." They are seventeen in number, written at different stages of his exile; nor is it possible to determine precisely the date of each. The first three seem to have been written from Cucusus, and are mainly devoted to the aim of consoling her under the present calamities of the Church; to dissipating, as he expresses it, that cloud of sorrow which surrounded her.[634] "Come now, let me soften the wound of your sadness, and disperse the sad cogitations which compose this gloomy cloud of care. What is it which upsets your mind, and occasions your grief and despondency? Is it the fierce and lowering storm which has overtaken the Churches and enveloped all with the darkness of a moonless night, which is growing to a head every day, and has already wrought many lamentable shipwrecks? All this I know; it shall not be gainsaid: and, if you like, I can form an image of the things now being done so as to represent the tragedy more distinctly to thee. We behold a sea heaved up from its lowest depths, some sailors floating dead, others struggling in the waves, the planks of the vessel breaking up, the masts sprung, the canvas torn, the oars dashed out of the sailors' hands, the pilots, seated on the deck, clasping their knees with their hands, and crying aloud at the hopelessness of their situation; neither sky nor sea clearly visible, but all one impenetrable gloom, and monsters of the deep attacking the shipwrecked crew on every side. But why attempt further to describe the indescribable? Yet, when I see all this, I do not despair, when I consider who is the Disposer of this whole universe— One who masters the storm, not by the contrivance of art, but can calm it by His nod alone. He does not always destroy what is terrible in its beginning, but waits till it has come to its consummation; and then, when most men are in despair, He works marvels and does things beyond all expectation, displaying a power which belongs to Him alone. Wherefore, faint not, for there is only one thing, Olympias, which is really terrible, there is only one real trial— and that is sin. All things else, whether they be insidious assaults of foes, or hatred, or calumny, or abuse, or confiscation of goods, or exile, or the sharpened sword, and war raging throughout the world, are but as a tale; they endure but for a season, they are perishable, and have their sphere in a mortal body, and do no injury to the vigilant soul."... "Why, then, do you fear temporal things, which flow away like the stream of a river?"... "Let none of these things which happen vex you; cease to entreat the help of this person or that, but continually beseech Jesus Christ, whom you serve, merely to bow the head, and all these troubles will be dissolved; if not in an instant of time, that is because He is waiting till wickedness has grown to a height, and then he will suddenly change the storm into a calm...."

He enters into an eloquent review of the sufferings and persecution to which our blessed Lord was subjected from His birth to His death, in order to prove that apparent failure is a fallacious test of the truth and real value of man's character and work.

"Why are you troubled because one man has been expelled and another introduced into his place? Christ was crucified, and the life of Barabbas, the robber, was asked. How many must have been shocked and repelled by this ignominious termination to a life of miracles! But in every stage of His life there was much to surprise and offend and try the faith. His birth was the cause of death to many innocent children in Bethlehem; poverty, danger, exile, marked His infancy. He was misunderstood and suspected throughout His ministry. 'Thou art a Samaritan, and hast a devil;' 'He deceiveth the people;' 'He casteth out devils through the chief of the devils;' 'He was a gluttonous man and winebibber, a friend of publicans and sinners.' His discernment of purity and goodness was questioned, because He permitted the sinful woman to approach Him; 'neither did His brethren believe on Him.' You speak of many having been frightened out of the straight path by the present calamities. How many of Christ's disciples stumbled at the time of His crucifixion! One betrayed Him, another denied Him, the others fled, and He was led to trial bound and alone. How many, think you, were offended when they beheld Him, who a little while ago was raising the dead, cleansing the lepers, expelling devils, multiplying loaves, now bound, forlorn, surrounded by coarse soldiers, followed by a crowd of tumultuous priests? How many when He was being scourged, and they saw Him torn by the lash, and standing with bleeding body before the governor's tribunal? How many, again, when He was mocked, now with a crown of thorns, now with a purple robe, now with a reed in His hand? How many when He was smitten on the cheek, and they cried, 'Prophesy, who is he that smote Thee?' and dragged Him hither and thither, consuming a whole day in jesting and revilement in the midst of the throng of Jewish spectators? How many when He was led to the cross with the marks of the scourge upon His back? How many when the soldiers divided His raiment among themselves? How many when fastened to the cross and crucified?" And, after our Lord's Ascension, what had been the lot of the early Church? Calamity, persecution, discomfiture, weakness, the offence of many and the defection of many. Yet the truth of Jesus Christ's Gospel had not been obscured; it had shone more and more brightly: God had wrought out the triumph of His Church.

The above is a much-condensed rendering of passages which can hardly be too much admired for the spirit as well as style in which they are written. The union of a Christian philosophy and a Christian faith, a philosophy which traces a principle in God's modes of operation, and a faith which contentedly accepts whatever happens, in the firm belief that, be it pleasant or painful, it is part of some purpose of God; a philosophy which traces in every suffering of Christ's servants for the cause of truth a reflection of the Master's sufferings, and a faith which enables the sufferer not only to be cheerful himself, but to cheer others, form, indeed, a noble object of contemplation. In a letter written to Olympias, just after his hardships and perils at Cæsarea, he begs her to rejoice, as he declares he can himself rejoice, in suffering as a pledge of future glory. He never had desisted, and never would desist, from declaring that the only real calamity to a man's self was sin; all other evils were as dust and smoke. Spoliation of goods was freedom; banishment was but a change of abode; death was but the discharge of nature's debt, which all must eventually pay. So much has been at all times, and is still, uttered by Christian writers and preachers about patience and joy in affliction, that we may be disposed to pass over language of this kind sometimes as a hackneyed commonplace; but it must be remembered that, in Chrysostom's case, the speaker was an actual sufferer. His words were not the sentimental utterances of a rhetorical preacher addressing an admiring audience, but convictions deliberately expressed by a persecuted sufferer, who was really living by the principles which he was accustomed to preach.

The rapturous and lavish praise which in some of his letters he bestows upon the virtues of Olympias would by a lady of piety in modern times be distrusted as flattery, and distasteful as a dangerous encouragement to self-righteousness and conceit; but the language of ornate compliment, which would be offensive to Western taste, seems natural to Orientals: and it may therefore be supposed that its effect in elating the mind of the recipient is faint in proportion. Chrysostom begins his second letter by recommending Olympias to divert her mind from those calamities and sins, for which she was no way responsible, by directing it to the final judgment. The awe with which she must contemplate that scene, in which she, together with all others, is individually concerned and interested, will expel the useless grief which mourns over iniquity wrought by others. But he breaks off suddenly from such a line of argument, as inapplicable to the case of so angelic a being as Olympias. "To me, indeed, and those who, like me, have been plunged beneath a sea of sins, such discourse is necessary, for it excites and alarms; but you, who abound in goodness, and who have already touched the very vault of Heaven, cannot even be pricked by such language; wherefore, in addressing you, I will chant another strain and strike another string." He does indeed; he invites her to count over her own perfections, and to dwell with complacent satisfaction on the heavenly rewards which are surely in store for her.... "It would fill a volume to relate the history of her patience, tried in such a variety of ways from her youth. She had laid such vigorous siege to her body, though naturally delicate and nurtured in the lap of luxury, that it might truly be called dead; and these austerities had raised for her such a swarm of maladies as defied the skill of physicians, and involved her in continual suffering. To speak, indeed, of patience and self-control, in reference to her fasts and vigils, would be inaccurate, because those expressions implied a conquest over oppugnant passions. But she had no desires to conquer: they were not merely subdued but extinguished. It was as easy and natural to her to fast as it was to others to eat, as natural to her to pass the night in vigil as to others to sleep." With an admiring comment on her squalid and neglected attire he closes this singular enumeration of her perfections, lest, as he expresses it, he should lose himself in an illimitable sea if he attempted to wade further; his object being, not to make an exhaustive catalogue of her virtues, but only such as might be sufficient to lift her out of her present state of depression.

It is worth making such extracts as these, because they enable us to see how widely remote Chrysostom was from the mind and taste of our own times in some points, although in others he seems so nearly congenial. There is another vein of thought in this letter which is still more alien. "If," he says, "in addition to the rewards of her chastity, her fasts, her vigils, her prayers, her boundless hospitality, she wishes to enjoy the sight of her adversaries, those iniquitous and blood-stained men undergoing punishment for their crimes, that pleasure also shall be hers. Lazarus saw Dives tormented in flames. This you will experience. For if he, who neglected but one man, suffered such punishment, if it was expedient for the man who should offend one little one to be hanged or cast into the sea, what penalty will be exacted of men who have offended so large a part of the world, upset so many churches, and surpassed the ferocity of barbarians and robbers? You will see them fast bound, tormented in flames, gnashing their teeth, overwhelmed with useless sorrow and vain remorse; and they, in their turn, will behold you wearing a crown in the blessed mansions, exulting with angels, reigning with Christ; and they will cry aloud and groan, repenting of the contumely which they fastened upon thee, supplicating, but in vain, thy pity and compassion."[635]

To our ears of course such language is extraordinarily shocking; but it is valuable as a warning, in estimating the character of Chrysostom, not to judge him or any individual by words or deeds, which are not so much the offspring of the man as of the age and circumstances in which he lived. Chrysostom had exercised as well as taught meekness, forbearance, and charity towards all men, enemies as well as friends; but he lived when the minds of Christians had for generations been inured to scenes of persecution, and to such a rigorous system and barbarous execution of criminal law as are hardly conceivable by us. Fierce opposition of party against party, violence and bloodshed put down, if at all, by the stern hand of force, hardened public feeling, and the individual, however amiable and gentle by nature, inevitably becomes infected by the prevailing mode of thought; he must look at things and judge of things more or less from the same point of view as the generality of men amongst whom he lives. What would seem revoltingly cruel to a humane man now, appeared to a man who lived some hundreds of years ago, though perhaps equally humane by nature, and in private life amiable, a merely natural and just retribution.

The letters of Chrysostom to those bishops[636] who remained loyal to his cause are full of asseverations that his affection for them cannot be diminished by separation or distance. He exhorts them to continue their labours with unabated zeal, and carefully to abstain from all communion with the adverse party. Small though their numbers were, yet their fortitude under persecution would so much encourage others that their conduct might be the salvation of the Church. Several of his letters to laymen in Constantinople are models of wise Christian counsel. He is never less than the pastor, while he is always the friend. He writes to one Gemellus,[637] on his promotion to some high magisterial office, that, "while others congratulated him merely on his new honours, *he* would rather dwell with thankfulness on the abundant opportunities Gemellus would now possess of exercising wisdom and gentleness on a large scale. He doubted not Gemellus would prove to those who were attached to the vain glories of this earth, that the true dignity of the magistrate consisted not in the robe or the girdle of office, or in the voice of the herald, but in reforming what was evil, and repairing what was falling to pieces, in punishing injustice, and preventing the right from being oppressed by might. He knew the boldness of Gemellus, his freedom of speech, his magnanimity, his contempt for the things of this world, his mildness, his benevolence; and he was persuaded that he would be as a haven to the shipwrecked, as a staff to the fallen, a tower of defence to those who were oppressed by tyranny." Gemellus appears to have been on the point of receiving baptism, and perhaps on that account to have been exposed to a rather trying degree of persecution. Chrysostom begs him not to delay baptism in the hope of receiving it from his hands, because the grace of the sacrament would be equally effectual by whatever hands administered, and his own joy would be none the less.[638]

So again, in his letter to Anthemius, who had recently been made prefect and consul:— "Nothing has been really added to you; it is not the prefect or the consul whom I love, but my most dear and gentle Lord Anthemius, full of philosophy and understanding. I do not felicitate thee because thou hast climbed to this throne, but because thou hast gained a grander sphere wherein to exercise thy benevolence and wisdom."[639]

He was less distant from Antioch than Constantinople, and was cheered by visits from not a few of his old friends in his native city, and maintained a correspondence by letter with many more; but intercourse of either kind was much impeded by the dangers and difficulties of the roads, and at times by the severity of the climate.[640] The illegal seizure of the See of Antioch by Porphyry, and the harsh treatment to which the orthodox were subjected under his administration, caused them to turn to Chrysostom, not only with sympathy as a fellow-sufferer, but also for guidance, comfort, and some kind of episcopal superintendence. Their presents to him were so numerous that he felt compelled sometimes to decline them, or to request permission that they might be transferred to the aid of the missionary work in Phœnicia.[641]

Much of his thought and correspondence was concerned in providing for the welfare of the Church in Persia, Phœnicia, and among the Goths. In his fourteenth letter to Olympias he begs her to use her best endeavours to detach Maruthas, bishop of Martyropolis in Persia, from the influence of the hostile party; "to lift him out of the slough" is his expression, for he greatly needed his assistance on account of affairs in Persia; and he was very anxious to know what Maruthas had accomplished there, and whether he had received two letters recently sent by himself. From this it would seem as if Maruthas, who had been present at the Synod of the Oak (when he caused the fatal injury to the foot of Cyrinus), had returned to Persia and again visited Constantinople, and that Chrysostom had hopes of working in connexion with him for the good of the Church in Persia.[642] In the same epistle he expresses his sorrow at having heard, through some Gothic monks with whom Serapion had sought shelter, that the Gothic bishop Unilas, whom he had recently consecrated, was dead, after a short but active career, and that the Gothic king had written to request that a new bishop should be sent out. Chrysostom was fearful lest Atticus and his party should appoint one; and he urges that everything should be done to delay the appointment if possible till winter came, when the season would prevent any one being sent till the following spring. Meanwhile, Moduarius, the deacon who had brought the letter from the Gothic prince, was to repair secretly and quietly to Cucusus, and there confer with Chrysostom on this important matter, to avert if possible the appointment of an improper person to so difficult a charge.

But of course the exile's interest was pre-eminently centred on that city of which he could not but consider himself still the chief pastor, although deprived of his external authority over it. Banishment, imprisonment, and intimidation had thinned the ranks of the orthodox; and among the remaining pastors there were some whose neglect of duty, the result of indolence or faint-heartedness, called forth severe rebukes from their former chief. "He had heard with concern, and was vexed that the information had not come direct from the clergy themselves, that a priest, Salustius, had preached only five times between the end of June and October, and that he and Theophilus, another priest, rarely attended Divine service at all."[643] To Theophilus he writes a letter of mingled sorrow and reproof, expressing a hope that the report may be incorrect, and begging him to refute it, or to amend his conduct. He reminds him of the dreadful punishment which was inflicted on the servant who buried the talent which he ought to have used, and of the fearful responsibility of neglecting that most beautiful flock, which, by the grace of God, was being strengthened in goodness, though now agitated by so terrible a tempest.[644] Several of his clergy and friends are upbraided with more or less of affectionate expostulation for slackness in writing to him; others are praised for their unshakable fortitude, patience, and zeal under affliction. He had learned with much concern from Domitianus, to whom the care of the widows and virgins of the Church was confided, that they were reduced to extreme indigence, and he entreats his friend Valentinus to sustain his well-known character for benevolence by relieving their necessities.[645]

Peanius, a man of rank and position in Constantinople, is thanked and praised for the unremitting zeal, yet tempered with moderation, with which he had resisted the usurping party, had stood inflexible in loyalty when others had fled, and had exerted himself for the welfare of the Church, not only in Constantinople, but also in Phœnicia, Palestine, and Cilicia. Chrysostom observes in the same letter that the members of the Church in those regions had, with very few exceptions, refused to recognise Arsacius.[646]

Those clergy and other persons who had been imprisoned on the charge of incendiarism were released in the beginning of September;[647] and Chrysostom, having heard of their liberation, was eagerly expecting a visit from them when he wrote (about the end of October probably) to Elpidius, bishop of Laodicea,[648] in Syria, a prelate venerable in years and eminent in piety, who had as a priest accompanied Meletius to the Council of Constantinople in A.D. 381, and was his counterpart in the moderation and gentleness of his disposition. Chrysostom wrote to thank him for his zeal in endeavouring to retain the bishops, not only in his own region, but in all parts of the world, in loyal fidelity to the exiled Patriarch. Elpidius proved the sincerity of his own attachment to his friend by suffering deposition from his see, and imprisonment for three years in his own house. Alexander, the successor of the usurper Porphyry in the See of Antioch, restored Elpidius to his see about A.D.

414— a recognition of his merits which received the high approbation of Pope Innocent.[649]

Thus by letters did the exile maintain his influence over all varieties of people in distant and opposite quarters of the Empire. Exhortation and reproof, consolation and encouragement, or the mere expression of affectionate goodwill, are the main chords struck, as circumstances require. But there is one tone which pervades all alike— the unshakable Christian faith of the writer. His deep belief that all suffering was sent for a remedial chastening purpose, and that, if resignedly borne, it enhanced the glory of the reward reserved for those who should suffer for righteousness' sake; that sin is the only real evil, that expatriation and persecution, and even death, since they touch only the external and temporal, are to be regarded as mere shadows, cobwebs, and dreams; that distance and material obstacles cannot impede the wings of affection and prayer, and that the cause of right and truth, although long depressed, will eventually triumph— these are convictions firmly rooted, which he never tires of repeating, and on the strength of which he lived cheerful and contented.

The wide range of his influence, and the nobility of his Christian resignation and fortitude, maintained during his exile, have elicited the admiration of a historian not lavish of his compliments to Christian saints. "Every tongue," says Gibbon, "repeated the praises of his genius and virtue; and the respectful attention of the Christian world was fixed on a desert spot among the mountains of Taurus."[650]

CHAPTER 22

CHRYSOSTOM'S SUFFERINGS FROM THE WINTER COLD— DEPREDATIONS OF THE ISAURIANS— THE MISSION IN PHŒNICIA— LETTERS TO INNOCENT AND THE ITALIAN BISHOPS— CHRYSOSTOM'S ENEMIES OBTAIN AN ORDER FOR HIS REMOVAL TO PITYUS— HE DIES AT COMANA, A.D. 407— RECEPTION OF HIS RELIQUES AT CONSTANTINOPLE, A.D. 438.

THUS THE AUTUMN OF A.D. 404 wore away. The time of the exile was occupied, not unpleasantly, by sending and receiving letters, and his spirits were cheered by occasional visits from friends. The destitute in the neighbourhood of Cucusus were relieved by his alms; the mourners comforted by his affectionate sympathy; some persons taken captive by the Isaurians obtained a release through his intercession or ransom. But the winter, always severe in that elevated region, set in this year with unusual rigour: all communication with the outer world was cut off by the impassable condition of the roads, and the cold told cruelly on the delicate constitution of the poor exile. In a letter to Olympias, written just on the return of spring A.D. 405, he draws a pitiable picture of his winter sufferings. For days together he lay in bed; but, in spite of being wrapped under a very pile of blankets, with a fire constantly burning in his room, he could not keep out the cold. He suffered from constant sleeplessness, headache, sickness and aversion from all food; but, with the return of milder weather in spring, "he was brought up again from the gates of death;" and he compares the softness of the climate at that season to the amenity of the air of Antioch. His spirits also were raised by the arrival of messengers from Constantinople, bringing letters from Olympias and other friends.[651]

But the blessings of restoration to health and warm weather were counterbalanced by the misery of constant disturbance from the Isaurian bandits, who commenced their marauding campaigns as soon as the break-up of winter made the country practicable for their operations. They swarmed over the whole neighbourhood, and the roads which had been impassable from snow were now impassable from robbers, who mingled much merciless bloodshed with their plunder. When the full blaze also of summer heat came, Chrysostom found it almost as injurious to his health as the excessive cold; but he kept up his correspondence with his friends with unabated assiduity.[652]

The mission in Phœnicia occupied a great deal of his attention during this year. He had written, as already related, from Nice to Constantius, the superintendent of the mission, exhorting him not to allow the work to flag, owing to his own deposition and banishment, but rather to carry it on with additional energy. The efforts of the missionaries had begun to provoke a rather fierce opposition on the part of the Pagans, and attempts were made to deprive them of the bare necessaries of life. But Chrysostom's confidence and zeal never failed for a moment. The missionaries were to keep him informed of their wants, for, through the liberality of his friends, he could supply them with all that they required. He was ably seconded by Nicolaus, a priest, who, though living at a distance, supplied the mission not only with money but with men. Gerontius, a presbyter whom Chrysostom had persuaded to abandon a solitary ascetic way of life for missionary work, was anxious to visit Cucusus on his way to Phœnicia; but Chrysostom begs him not to delay, as the work was urgent and winter was approaching. He represents the greater advantages of the active life Gerontius was now embracing. There would be nothing to prevent him observing his fasts, vigils, and other ascetic practices, as before, for the good of his own soul, and at the same time, by his missionary labours, he would reap the reward of those who save the souls of others.[653]

The Pagan resistance assumed more alarming proportions as time went on. A letter written to the missionaries seems to imply, by its tone of mingled warning and exhortation, that their courage was beginning to fail. Chrysostom had recourse to his favourite comparisons of the pilot and the physician, who exert twofold energy as the violence of the storm and the disease increase. Rufinus, a presbyter, seems to have been sent into Phœnicia as a kind of special agent to restore peace, and is stimulated to his work by an animated letter. "I hear that the rage of the Greeks in Phœnicia has burst forth again, that several monks have been wounded, and some even killed. Wherefore I urge you the more earnestly to set out upon your journey with great speed, and take up your position."... "If you saw a house in a blaze you would not retreat, but advance upon it as quickly as possible, so as to anticipate the flames. When all is tranquillity it is within the compass of almost any one to make converts, but when Satan is raging and the devils are in arms, then, to make a gallant stand and rescue those who are falling into the hands of the enemy, is the work of a noble, vigilant spirit, a work which befits an alert and lofty mind like yours, an apostolic achievement worthy of crowns innumerable and rewards which defy description." He entreats Rufinus to write to him from every halting-place on his journey, and to keep him constantly informed of all which might take place after his arrival. He would send, if necessary, ten thousand times to Constantinople, in order to provide Rufinus with all things necessary to facilitate his journey and procure his ultimate success. The letter closes with a passage which remarkably illustrates the importance attached to reliques. "With regard to the reliques of the holy martyrs, feel no anxiety, for I immediately despatched the most religious presbyter, my Lord Terentius, to my Lord Oneius, the most religious Bishop of Arabissus, who possesses many reliques indisputably genuine, which in a few days we will forward to you into Phœnicia."... "Use diligence to get the churches which are yet unroofed completed before the winter."[654]

There is no further record of the future progress or ultimate issue of this mission, in which the heart of the exile was so deeply wrapped up. Theodoret (v. 29) merely says that through the energy of

Chrysostom the extirpation of idolatry in Phœnicia, and the destruction of Pagan temples, were successfully carried on. But there are instances of the existence of Paganism mentioned in the middle of the fifth century;[655] and it is only too certain that, under the feeble and degenerate successors of Chrysostom, the work would not receive any powerful impulse. Partly from the absence of a great central organising force like the Papacy, partly from the irregular and unpractical temperament of the Eastern nature, missionary enterprises have not proceeded in great number from the Eastern Church. The preaching of Ulphilas to the Goths, the missions organised by Chrysostom among the Goths and in Phœnicia, and the missionary labours of the Nestorians in Asia, are but the rare exceptions which prove the rule.

The misery and desolation caused in the neighbourhood of Cucusus by the Isaurians seem to have culminated in the winter of A.D. 405-406 and the ensuing spring. The inhabitants of the villages fled from their homes at the approach of these formidable robbers, and sought a precarious refuge in woods and caves. Many perished from cold in these wild retreats, and many more at the hands of the ruffian robbers, who showed no mercy even to the aged, the women and children. Chrysostom himself was, like others, frequently moving from place to place, now in this village, now in that, sometimes in the woods or secluded places. The only spot in which the poor harassed people seem to have found tolerable security was in the strong fortress of Arabissus, a neighbouring town. Yet even here they ran considerable risks. A body of 300 Isaurians attacked and very nearly captured it in the middle of the night; and the discomfort was extreme at all times, for the castle was crowded like a prison; the difficulty of obtaining food was often very great, and the difficulty of corresponding with friends still greater. Privation, anxiety, and frequent hurried movements in cold weather brought severe illness on Chrysostom again. Physicians attended him with great kindness, but the impossibility of procuring comforts and wholesome food rendered their services almost nugatory. His greatest grief, however, seems to have been the difficulty of maintaining regular correspondence with friends. The bearer of a letter from Olympias actually fell into the hands of the robbers, but was released; in consequence of which Chrysostom entreats her not to send any more special messengers, but only to avail herself of such persons as were obliged by business to pass through his place of exile. He would not add to his present sufferings the distress of knowing that any life had been lost on his account.[656]

To the year A.D. 406 belong those letters of affectionate gratitude, written to the bishops of the West, for their zeal in supporting his cause, especially those who had undertaken a long and perilous voyage to Constantinople to intercede in his behalf. These letters were sent by the hands of Evethius, the presbyter, who had for some time been his companion in exile. One letter may be quoted as an example: "I had already been amazed at your zeal, on behalf of the reformation of the Church, displayed for a long time; but most of all am I now astonished at your great earnestness, in having undertaken so long a journey by sea, full of labour and toil, on behalf of the interests of the Church. I have longed continually to write to you, and offer you the salutation due to your piety; but since that is not possible, living as I now am in a region almost inaccessible, I take advantage of a most honourable and reverend presbyter to send you greeting, and to beseech you to persevere to the end in harmony with such a noble beginning. For ye know how great will be the reward of your patience, how vast the return from a benevolent God to those who labour for the common peace, and undergo so great a conflict."[657]

To Chromatius, bishop of Aquileia, he writes thus: "The loud-voiced trumpet of your warm and genuine affection has sounded forth even as far as to me, a clear and far-reaching blast indeed, extending to the very extremities of the world. Distant as we are, we know, not less than those present with thee, thy exceeding and burning love; wherefore we long extremely to enjoy a meeting with thee face to face. But, since the wilderness in which we are imprisoned precludes this, we fulfil our desire, as well as we can, by writing to you through our most honourable and reverend presbyter, expressing our great gratitude for the zeal which you have for so long a time displayed in our behalf; and we beg you, when he returns, or by the hands of chance messengers who may visit this desolate spot, to send tidings of your health, for you know how much pleasure it will afford us to hear frequently of the welfare of those who are so warmly disposed towards us."[658]

The letter written by Chrysostom in A.D. 406 to Innocent is full of grateful acknowledgments for all the efforts which he had made, and was still making, on his behalf. "Though separated by so vast a length of journey, yet are we near your Holiness, beholding with the eye of the soul your courage, your genuine, inflexible firmness, and we derive constant and abiding consolation from you. For the higher the waves are lifted up, the more numerous the rocks and reefs, the more does your untiring vigilance increase.... This is now the third year of my exile, spent in the midst of famine, pestilence, continual sieges, an indescribable wilderness, and the pillage of the Isaurians. In the midst of these distresses and dangers, your constant and firm affection is no ordinary solace to me."[659]

There is a letter also addressed to Aurelius,[660] bishop of Carthage, thanking him for bold and persevering intercession in his behalf. The Church of Africa appears to have adhered to what was at first the resolution of the Roman Church, to maintain communion with both Chrysostom and Theophilus. St. Augustine has bestowed a high eulogium on Chrysostom,[661] and an African council, in A.D. 407, passed a resolution to address a letter to Innocent, praying that the intercourse between the Churches of Rome and Alexandria might be resumed.

The health of the exile appears to have suffered less than usual, in the winter of A.D. 406-7, from the effects of the cold. By carefully remaining in the house, and for the most part in bed, wrapped up in blankets in an apartment where a fire was kept constantly burning, and by use of a medicine sent him by a lady, his attacks of headache and of sickness were averted or alleviated. He had become inured to the want of exercise, the deprivation of the bath, and the smokiness of the room; and even the natives were astonished at the firmness with which so feeble and "spidery" (ἀραχνώδης) a frame endured the severity of the climate. He began to feel a persuasion that God would not have preserved him so miraculously through such various perils, if it were not His purpose to restore him to his former position, that he might accomplish some work for the Church.[662]

But the chief work which he was destined to accomplish was to exhibit to the close of his life, now rapidly approaching, a noble spectacle of Christian fortitude and patience, of one continuing to the last to hope in God, to put his trust in God, and still to give Him thanks. The malicious envy of his enemies was augmented by the admiration and affection which pursued their victim from all parts of Christendom, and the correspondence which was maintained with him even in the mountain fortress which they had selected for his prison. The only remedy was to remove him yet further, to a more remote and still more inaccessible region. They worked upon the Emperor and the Court, whose jealousy had been already excited by the interference of the West; and, in the middle of June, A.D. 407, an order was obtained by them for the removal of the exile to Pityus, on the eastern coast of the Euxine, near the very frontier of the Empire, in the most desolate country, inhabited by savage, barbarous people. The two prætorian soldiers charged with conveying him thither were instructed to push on the journey with the most inexorable haste, and encouraged to hope for promotion should their prisoner die on the road. One of the two had some sparks of humanity, and furtively showed some little kindness to the sufferer; but the other followed out the cruel directions given him with merciless fidelity. Chrysostom had, some time ago, expressed his conviction that he could not survive the fatigue of another long and laborious journey, yet for three months his fragile frame endured the strain till he reached Comana in Pontus. A former bishop of that place, Basiliscus, had suffered martyrdom in the persecution of Maximinus, together with Lucian of Antioch. Chrysostom was lodged in the precincts of the church erected in honour of Basiliscus, above five miles outside the town. Here, so runs the story, the martyred bishop appeared to him in the night, stood beside him, and said, "Be of good cheer, for by to-morrow we shall be together." A similar vision was vouchsafed to one of the presbyters of the church. He was bidden "to prepare a place for our brother John." In the morning, Chrysostom entreated his guards to allow him to stay where he was till eleven o'clock; but they were inflexible, and the weary march was resumed. When, however, they had proceeded about thirty stadia, he became so ill that they were compelled to return to the martyry. Here he asked for white garments, and having been clothed in them, he distributed his own raiment among the clergy who were present. The Eucharist was administered to him, he spoke a few farewell words to the ecclesiastics who stood around him, and with the words "Glory be to God for all things, Amen," on his lips, the weary exile breathed his last.

> "Rest comes at length; though life be long and dreary,
> The day must dawn, and darksome night be past;
> All journeys end in welcomes to the weary,
> And heaven, the heart's true home, will come at last."

The promise of Basiliscus was literally fulfilled— he was buried in the same grave with the martyr, in the presence of a large concourse of monks and nuns.[663]

The enemies of Chrysostom thus succeeded in wreaking their vengeance to the full upon the person of their victim— "Non missura cutem, nisi plena cruoris hirudo;" but they were powerless to obliterate his memory. A sense of the cruelty and injustice with which he had been treated grew throughout Christendom, and he was more honoured and admired after his death than he had been during his life. His followers in Constantinople, under the appellation of Johnites, persisted in refusing to hold any communion with Atticus; and in the course of ten years, Atticus himself was constrained, by the solicitations of the Court and people, by the example of other prelates, especially Alexander of Antioch, and by a natural desire to maintain communion with the Western Church, to admit the name of Chrysostom into the diptychs of the Church of Constantinople. Cyril, the nephew and successor of Theophilus, who inherited in too many points his uncle's spirit as well as his see, yielded a more tardy and reluctant consent to the recognition of his uncle's foe.[664]

But a still higher honour was yet to be paid to his memory by the Church from which he had been so violently expelled. In A.D. 434, Proclus, formerly a disciple of Chrysostom, was elevated to the See of Constantinople. He conceived that the only effectual means of doing justice to the injured saint, and reconciling the Johnites to the Church, would be to transport his remains to the city. The consent of the Emperor Theodosius II. was obtained. On January 27,[665] A.D. 438, the reliques of the banished Archbishop were brought to the shores of the Bosporus. As once before in his lifetime, to greet him on his return from exile, so now, and in still greater numbers, the people, bearing torches, crowded the waters of the strait with their boats to welcome the return of all which remained of their beloved and much-wronged spiritual father. The young Emperor, stooping down, laid his face on the reliquary, and implored forgiveness of the injuries which his parents had inflicted on the saint whose ashes it contained. That reliquary was then deposited near the altar of the Church of the Apostles.[666] It is the sad story, so often repeated in history, of goodness and greatness, unrecognised, slighted, injured, cut short in a career of usefulness by one generation, abundantly, but too late, acknowledged in the next; when posterity, paying to the memory and the tomb the honours which should have been bestowed on the living man, can only utter the remorseful prayer—

"His saltem accumulem donis, et fungar inaniMunere...."

CHAPTER 23

SURVEY OF CHRYSOSTOM'S THEOLOGICAL TEACHING— PRACTICAL TONE OF HIS WORKS— REASON OF THIS— DOCTRINE OF MAN'S NATURE— ORIGINAL SIN— GRACE— FREE-WILL— HOW FAR CHRYSOSTOM PELAGIAN— LANGUAGE ON THE TRINITY— ATONEMENT— JUSTIFICATION— THE TWO SACRAMENTS— NO TRACE OF CONFESSION, PURGATORY, OR MARIOLATRY— RELATIONS TOWARDS THE POPE— LITURGY OF CHRYSOSTOM— HIS CHARACTER AS A COMMENTATOR— VIEWS ON INSPIRATION— HIS PREACHING— PERSONAL APPEARANCE— REFERENCES TO GREEK CLASSICAL AUTHORS— COMPARISON WITH ST. AUGUSTINE.

THE MAIN CHARACTERISTICS OF Chrysostom as a theologian and interpreter of Scripture, as well as a pastor and preacher, have, it is hoped, been already indicated in the course of the preceding narrative; but it may be desirable to supplement, by a fuller and more methodical survey, notices which were necessarily sometimes brief and incidental in the biographical chapters.[667]

Some evidence, therefore, of his theological teaching and method of interpretation will first of all be collected from his writings, and arranged under different heads. Two difficulties in the way of executing this task faithfully should be borne in mind: first, the voluminous bulk of Chrysostom's works (as Suidas observed, that it belonged to God rather than man to know them all), which renders a successful search for the selection of what are really the most telling passages in illustration of each point far from easy; secondly, that Chrysostom, being a preacher rather than a writer, was of course liable to slip into inexact or exaggerated language, under the influence of excitement, or a desire to make an impression on the feelings of his hearers. An attentive perusal, however, of his writings leads the reader to the conclusion that he was very seldom carried away by the impulse of the moment into merely vague or rhetorical expressions, and that he was especially preserved from this failing by his habit of combining the expository with the practical and hortatory line of preaching. His discourses are careful commentaries as well as practical addresses. Week after week it was his custom to go through some book of Holy Scripture, verse by verse, clause by clause, almost word by word; endeavouring with all diligence and patience to ascertain the exact meaning of the passage before him, to place it clearly before his audience, and to base his practical exhortation upon it.

The remark has been so often repeated, as to have become almost a truism, that the theology of the East is distinguished from the theology of the West by its more speculative, metaphysical character. It deals more especially with the most profound and abstract mysteries— the being and nature of the Godhead, of angels, of the whole spiritual realm. It might, therefore, occasion some surprise to find the homilies of Chrysostom marked by such an eminently practical tone. But the apparent contradiction is easily explained. It is precisely because Greek philosophy and theology were chiefly concerned with the most abstract questions, that the Greek preacher, speaking on matters not abstract, but practical, relating to moral conduct, is especially free in his language from philosophical or technical terms. On the other hand, in the Western Church exactly the reverse occurs. The best intellectual powers of the Roman having been mainly exercised on jurisprudence, the mind of Roman theologians naturally turned most powerfully towards practical questions which had most affinity to that science with which they were chiefly conversant— such as the relation of man to God, the nature of sin, the means of discharging the debt owed by man, the problem of the free-will of man, and providence of God. Western theology is coloured by the language of Roman law, as Eastern theology is coloured by the language of Greek philosophy. "Merit," "satisfaction," "decrees," "forensic justification," "imputed righteousness," are terms which do not occur in the writings of the Greek theologian, because they are the expressions of ideas in which he felt no interest. They are the offspring of the Roman mind, in which legal ideas were dominant. Hence the Western theologian is most technical and scientific in the region of practical questions; the Greek, on the other hand, is more entirely free from the influence of philosophy in that region than in any other.

In accordance with this distinction, we find that Chrysostom, in treating of those practical questions with which, as a preacher and pastor, he was mainly concerned— the nature and the work of Jesus Christ, providence, grace, the nature of man, sin, faith, repentance, good works, and the like— casts his thoughts into the most free, natural, untechnical, and therefore forcible language possible.

To consider first of all his exposition of man's nature. The majority of the Oriental fathers made a triple division, into body, soul, and spirit— the soul (ψυχή) being equivalent to the animal life, the spirit (πνεῦμα or ψυχὴ λογική) to the reason. Chrysostom makes a twofold division only, into body and soul, and reserves the word "spirit" to designate the Holy Spirit.[668] Man, when first created, came like a pure golden statue fresh out of the artist's hands, destined, if he had not fallen, to enjoy a yet higher and nobler dignity than he then possessed.[669] His being made "in the image of God" Chrysostom interprets to signify that dominance over the lower animals which God Himself exercises over the whole creation, and the peculiar superiority of man's nature to theirs consists in his reasoning power, as well as in his endowment with the gift of immortality.[670] Man fell through his own weakness and indolent negligence (ῥαθυμία), and then became deprived of that immortality and divine wisdom with which he had been previously gifted; but his nature was not essentially *changed*, it was only weakened.[671] Evil is not an integral part of man; it is not an inherent substantial force (δύναμις ἐνυπόστατος):[672] it is the moral purpose (προαίρεσις) which is perverted when men sin. If evil was a part of our nature, it would be no more reprehensible than natural appetites and affections. If man's will was not unfettered, there would be no merit in goodness and no blame in evil. There is no constraint either to holiness or to sin; neither does God compel to the one, nor do the fleshly appetites compel to the other.[673] The body was not, as the Manichæans erroneously maintained, the seat of sin; it was the creation of God equally with the soul; the whole burden, therefore, of responsibility in sin must be thrown on the "moral purpose." Here was the root of all evil; the conception of necessity and immutability is bound up with the idea of nature. We do not try to alter that which is by nature (φύσει): sin therefore is not by nature, because by means of education, laws, and punishments we do seek to alter that.[674] Sin is through the moral purpose which is susceptible of change, and till the moral purpose has come into activity sin cannot properly be said to exist: infants, therefore, and very young children, are free from sin.[675] Our first parents fell through moral negligence (ῥᾳθυμία); and this is the principal cause of sin now. They marked out a path which has been trodden ever since; they yielded to appetite, and the force of the will has been weakened thereby in all their posterity, who have become subject to the punishment of death; so that though sin is not a part of man's nature, yet his nature is readily inclined to evil (ὀξυρρεπὴς πρὸς κακίαν): but this tendency will be controlled by the moral purpose if that is in a healthy condition.[676]

Chrysostom would thus readily allow the expressions "hereditary tendency to sin," "hereditary liability to the punishment of death," but he shrinks from the expression "hereditary sin." His anxiety to insist on the complete freedom of the human will was very natural in the earnest Christian preacher of holiness, who lived in an age when men were frequently encountered who, in the midst of wickedness, complained that they were abandoned to the dominion of devils or to the irresistible course of fate. They transferred all guilt from themselves to the powers of evil, all responsibility to the Creator Himself, who had withdrawn from them, as they maintained, the protection of His good providence.

To counteract the disastrous effects of such philosophy, which surrendered the will to the current of the passions, like an unballasted ship cast adrift before the storm, it was indeed necessary to maintain very resolutely and boldly the essential freedom of the will, to insist on man's moral responsibility, and the duty of vigilant, strenuous exertion. Chrysostom frequently exposes the absurdity as well as the moral evil of a doctrine of necessity. If human actions are necessary and preordained results of circumstances, then teaching and government become mere pieces of acting, destitute of any practical influence; they are also unjust, since you have no right to punish a person who has acted under compulsion. Such a theory ought, also, logically to paralyse human industry. If a plentiful harvest is predetermined by the decrees of fate, you may spare yourself the trouble of ploughing, sowing, and other laborious operations; or, if Clotho has turned her distaff in the other direction, all your exertions will fail to produce an abundant crop. Such a doctrine is repugnant to our natural sense, and contradicts our own consciousness and inward experience. We feel that we are free, and all human action proceeds on the principle of supposing man to be free. We teach and we punish. The plea of necessity would be rejected in a court of law as an impudent and futile excuse for crime. Such a theory is utterly at variance also with God's mode of addressing man, which always implies freedom of volition; as, for instance, "If *ye will* hearken unto me, ye shall eat the fat of the land; but if *ye will not* hearken, the sword shall devour you."[677]

Profoundly convinced, therefore, of a universal tendency to sin on the one hand, but of an essential freedom of the will on the other, Chrysostom sounds alternately the note of warning and of encouragement— warning against that weakness, indolence, languor of the moral purpose which occasions a fall; encouragement to the full use of those powers with which all men are gifted, and to avoid that despondency which will prevent a man from rising again when he has fallen. St. Paul repented, and, not despairing, became equal to angels; Judas repenting, but despairing, was hurried into self-inflicted death. Despair was the devil's most powerful instrument for working the destruction of man.[678] Chrysostom therefore earnestly combated any view of Christian life which daunted and discouraged man's efforts, by winding them too high, or placing before them an unattainable standard. Men sometimes said we cannot be like St. Peter and St. Paul, because we are not gifted with their miraculous power. But, he replies, you may emulate their Christian graces: these are within the reach of all, and these are, by our Lord's own declaration, the most important. "*By this* shall all men know that ye are my disciples, if ye have love one to another;" the moral works of the Apostles, works of love, mercy, and faith, were far more instrumental in the conversion of the world than their merely miraculous powers.[679]

Urgently, however, as Chrysostom, in his desire to stimulate exertion and strengthen the moral life, insists on the absolute freedom of the will, he maintains no less clearly the insufficiency of man's nature to accomplish good without the Divine assistance. No one has described in more forcible language the powerful hold of sin upon human nature. Sin is like a terrible pit, containing fierce monsters, and full of darkness.[680] It is more terrible than a demon,[681] it is a great demon;[682] it is like fire; when once it has got a hold on the thoughts of the heart, if it is not quenched it spreads further and further, and becomes increasingly difficult to subdue;[683] it is a heavy burden, more oppressive than lead.[684] Christ saw us lying cast away upon the ground, perishing under the tyranny of sin, and He took compassion on us.[685] In the infant weakness and liability to sin are inherent, though not sin itself. The moral nature of the infant is like a plant, which will grow healthily by a process of natural development, unless exposed to injurious influences; but it requires the protection of grace, "therefore we baptize infants to impart holiness and goodness, as well as to establish a relationship with God." This passage is quoted by St. Augustine in his earnest vindication of Chrysostom from Pelagianism.[686] But the passages on which Augustine mainly depends to prove Chrysostom's adherence to the tenet of original sin are in his exposition of Romans v. 12-14:— "Death reigned from Adam to Moses. How reigned? In likeness of the transgression of Adam, who is a figure of One to come. How a figure? Because, as he became a cause of death to those who were born from him, although they had not eaten of the tree, even so Christ has become to His posterity the procurer of righteousness, though they have not done righteousness, which He has bestowed upon us all through His cross." Augustine quotes also his observation on Christ's tears over the grave of Lazarus:— "He wept to think that men, who were capable of immortality, had been made mortal by the devil;" and his remarks on Genesis i. 28, about the subjection of the lower animals to man: "that man's present dread of wild beasts was entirely owing to the Fall, and had not existed previous to that: it was inherited by all Adam's posterity, because they inherited his degradation through the Fall." All these passages, however, do not amount to more than the doctrine of a universally inherited tendency to sin, and therefore liability to its punishment, death. In his interpretation of the passage, "the free gift is of many offences unto justification," this last word is plainly taken by him in the sense of making man righteous, not accounting him as such.[687]

His conception of the relation between the will and power of God on the one hand, and man's freedom on the other, appears to be this:— All men, without exception, are through Christ called to salvation; predestination means no more than God's original design, conceived prior to the Fall, of bringing all men to salvation. So, after the Fall, His redemptive plan or purpose embraces all men; but, on the other hand, it constrains no one. According to His absolute will all men are to be saved; but the accomplishment of His purpose is limited by the freedom of choice which He has Himself bestowed on man, whereby man may either accept the proffered favour and be eternally blessed, or reject it and be eternally condemned. God's election of those who are called is not compulsory, but persuasive;[688] hence, many of those who have been called perish through their rejection of grace: they, and not God, are the authors of their own condemnation. God knows beforehand what each man will be, good or bad; but He does not constrain him to be one or the other.[689] The illustration of the potter in Romans ix. 20 must not be pressed too closely; St. Paul's object simply is to enforce the duty of unconditional obedience. A vessel of wrath is one who obdurately resists God's grace; he was never *intended* by God to be a vessel of wrath. "The vessels of mercy are said to have been prepared afore by God unto glory," but the vessels of wrath to be fitted (not by God— He is not mentioned— but by sin) unto destruction.[690] So again, he acutely observes that, in the account of the final judgment (St. Matt. xxv.), the destiny of the *good* only is referred to God. "Come, ye blessed *of my Father*, inherit the kingdom prepared *for you*;" but, "Depart, ye cursed" (not "of my Father"), "into everlasting fire, prepared" (not for you, but) "for the devil and his angels."

On St. John vi. 44, he remarks, it is perfectly true that only they who are drawn and taught by the Father can come to Christ; but away with the paltry pretence that those who are not thus drawn and taught are emancipated from blame; for this very thing, the being led and instructed, depends on their own moral choice. Two factors, therefore, Divine grace which presents, and human will which appropriates, are co-efficients in the work of man's salvation; God's love and man's faith must work hand in hand. God provides opportunities, encourages by promises, arouses by calls; and the moment these are responded to, the moment man begins to will and to do what is right, he is abundantly assisted by grace. But Chrysostom recognises nothing approaching the doctrine of final perseverance. St. Paul might have relapsed, Judas might have been saved (De Laud. Ap. Pauli, Hom. ii. 4). In his commentary on Phil. ii. 12-13, "It is God which worketh in us both to will and to do of his good pleasure," the spontaneity of man's will is carefully maintained. It may be said, if God works the will in us, why does the apostle exhort us to work? for if God wrought the wish, it is vain to speak of obedience; the whole work is God's from the beginning. No! Chrysostom says, what St. Paul means is, that if your will works, God will augment your will, and quicken it into activity and zeal. Hast thou given alms? you are the more prompted to give; hast thou abstained from giving? negligence will increase upon you. The histories of Abraham, Job, Elijah, St. Paul, and other saints, are frequently cited to prove his central principle, that God in the moral and spiritual sense helps those only who help themselves. "When He, who knows the secrets of our hearts, sees us eagerly prepare for the contest of virtue, He instantly supplies us with His assistance, lightening our labours, and strengthening the weakness of our nature. In the Olympian contests the trainer stands by as a spectator merely, awaiting the issue, and unable to contribute anything to the efforts of the contender; whereas our Master accompanies us, extends His hand to us, all but subdues our antagonist, arranges everything to enable us to prevail, that He may place the amaranthine wreath upon our brows."[691] God does not anticipate (φθάνει) man's own volitions (βουλήσεις), but when these are once bent in the right direction, God's grace powerfully promotes them; and without this divine co-operation holiness is unattainable.[692] But as, according to Chrysostom's conceptions, the first movement towards good moral practice comes from the man himself, he often speaks of a man's salvation depending on his own moral choice. He is not, therefore, in harmony with the mind of our Church as expressed in the Article, that "we have no power to do good works, pleasant and acceptable to God, without the grace of God *preventing* us, that we may have a good will;" but his language thoroughly concurs with the subsequent clause, "and working with us when we have that good will." In the technical language of theology, he recognises assisting, but not prevenient, grace.

It has been well remarked by Mr. Alexander Knox ("Remains," vol. iii. 79), that "the advocates for efficient grace have been too generally antiperfectionists, and the perfectionists, on the other hand, too little aware that we are not sufficient so much as to think anything as of ourselves, but that it is God which worketh in us both to will and to do of His good pleasure." The perfect conception of the true Christian standard of character could only be found, he thought, in a union of the systems of St. Chrysostom and St. Augustine. It must not be imagined, however, that Chrysostom regarded Divine grace as merely accessory or subsidiary to man's own will and purpose. He fails not to represent it as indispensable to every human soul, however powerfully inclined of itself to good. The human will, weakened and depraved by evil, is not for a moment to rank as co-ordinate in its action with the work of the Holy Spirit: the real efficient force in the work of sanctification is the Holy Spirit. The beginnings, indeed (ἀρχαί), are our own, and we must contribute what we can, small and cheap though it be, because, unless we do our part, we shall not obtain the Divine assistance; but though the initiatory step is ours, the accomplishment of the work is altogether God's, and, since the major part is His, we commonly say that the whole is His.[693]

He invariably speaks of the Old Dispensation as a period when Divine grace was given in less measure than under the Gospel, because then sin had not been blotted out, nor death vanquished. The achievements of holy men like Abraham and Job in this period were therefore deserving of peculiar praise, and their faults, on the other hand, were entitled to more indulgent judgment, because they laboured under disadvantages. When the Lamb which taketh away the sins of the world had been slain, and the reconciliation between man and God had been effected, then spiritual gifts of a higher order were imparted as a sign and a pledge that the old hostility had ceased.[694]

Turning now to theology, strictly so called, to the being and nature of the Godhead, we find comparatively little said by Chrysostom, except incidentally, on a subject more congenial to the theologian and student than to the earnest, practical preacher. In opposition to the rationalistic doctrine of the Arians, who affected to comprehend the Divine Nature, he strenuously maintained, as we have seen,[695] its inscrutability, and denounced any curious investigation of it as at once foolish and profane. God has condescended to appear to us in a form which is intelligible, and it is presumption to attempt to penetrate beyond the limits which He has placed to a knowledge of Himself. Chrysostom takes the dogma of the one substance (ὁμοουσία), established at Nice, as the basis of his position against the Arians, and seeks to prove it, not by speculative argument, after the manner of the Alexandrian school, but by reference to Holy Scripture. He uses the word "substance" (οὐσία) to designate the essential nature and "person" (ὑπόστασις), the personality of the Godhead, and points out that words which relate to the οὐσία, as Lord and God, are applied to all the Persons; whereas the other terms— Father, Son, Holy Spirit— indicating distinction of personality, are each applied to one Person only in the Godhead. Yet the Persons are not related to the substance as parts to the whole: God the Son is to God the Father as a beam of the sun, inseparable from Him, identical with Him in substance, yet retaining His own personality.[696] He is equally careful to guard the divinity of Christ against the rationalising school of Paul of Samosata, and the distinctness of His personality as against the Sabellians. St. Paul, he observes, does not dwell too much upon the abasement of Christ, lest Paul of Samosata should take advantage; neither does he dwell exclusively upon the exaltation, lest Sabellius should spring upon him.[697]

The equal divinity and distinct personality of the Holy Ghost are no less clearly and forcibly demonstrated by a collection and comparison of passages. St. Paul, for instance, in 1 Cor. xii. 6, speaks of God as "working all in all;" in verse 11 of the same chapter, he uses the same language of the Holy Spirit. Into any metaphysical, abstract discussion of the nature of the Godhead Chrysostom does not enter. He simply endeavours to guard the faith of the Church by a careful exposition of Holy Scripture, on which that faith was based, and by an exposure of the one-sided, or perverted, interpretations on which the current forms of heresy depended.

The union of the two natures in the person of our blessed Lord was, as is well known, a subject of constant speculation and of prolific error in the first five centuries. Here, again, the good sense of Chrysostom, united to his careful study of Holy Scripture, enabled him to hold the balance between two divergent methods— one which attended too exclusively to the humanitarian point of view, the other which brought out the divinity, but at the expense of the manhood. He earnestly maintains the veritable assumption of humanity by the Word. Our nature could not have been elevated to the divine if the Saviour had not *really* partaken of it; neither could He have brought help to our race if He had appeared in the unveiled glory of His Godhead, for sun and moon, earth and sea, and even man himself, would have perished at the brightness of His presence. Therefore He veiled his Godhead in flesh, and came not as the Lord in outward semblance, but in lowliness and abasement.[698] And this very condescension enhanced His dignity and extended His dominion: before the Incarnation He was adored by angels only, but afterwards by the whole race of redeemed man.[699] He assumed our nature, even in its liability to death, but not as contaminated by sin.[700] There were in Him three elements— body and soul making up the human nature, and the Logos or Word making up the divine. These two natures were *united* but not *fused*. "We, indeed, are body and soul, but He is God and soul and body; remaining what He was, He took that which He was not, and having become flesh, He remained God, being the Word. The one He became He assumed; the other He was. Let us not then confound, neither let us divide; one God, one Christ the Son of God; and when I say one, I speak of union, not fusion" (ἕνωσιν λέγω οὐ σύγχυσιν).[701] Jesus Christ was subject to death, susceptible of pain and all those emotions and sensations which belong to the human body, otherwise His would not have been a real body, but the weakness pertaining to human nature was entirely overruled by the constant operation of the Logos. If He is said to have been lowered or exalted, this was only as man, since the Godhead was incapable of either, being absolutely perfect. When the Holy Ghost is said to have descended upon Him at His baptism, this must be considered to refer to His human nature only; the manhood, not the Godhead, is anointed. Or when we read that He walked not in Judæa, because the Jews sought to kill Him, and then, just afterwards, that He passed through the midst of His enemies unscathed, we have a direct manifestation, in close correspondence, of the Godhead and the manhood.[702]

In speaking of the redemptive work of our blessed Lord, Chrysostom's language is too rapturously eloquent to be very precise. There are in him several traces of the idea which began with Irenæus, and was developed by Origen, that the devil through the Fall acquired an actual right over man, and that a kind of pious fraud was practised upon him to deprive him of this right through the Incarnation and death of Jesus. By the noiseless, unostentatious manner in which our Saviour assumed humanity, veiling His Godhead under it, He, as it were, stole unawares upon the devil, who was not fully conscious of the majesty and might of his adversary. The devil assaulted Christ as if Christ had been merely man, and he was disappointed in his expectation. He was vanquished by his own weapons, his tyranny was destroyed by means of those very things which were his strength; the curse of sin and of death were his most trusted pieces: Christ submitted Himself to be bruised by them, and yet crushed them by His submission.[703]

On the other hand, we find also in Chrysostom the customary conception of a debt discharged, a ransom paid, a sacrifice offered once for all. "Adam sinned and died; Christ sinned not and yet died. Wherefore? that he who sinned and died might be able, through Him who died but sinned not, to throw off the grasp of death. This is what takes place also in money transactions. Often some one who is a debtor, not being able to pay, is detained in bonds; another, who owes nothing but is able to lay down the sum, pays it and releases the responsible person. Thus has it been in the case of man. Man was the debtor, was detained by the devil, and could not pay; Christ owed nothing, nor was He holden by the devil, but He was able to pay the debt. He came and He paid down death on behalf of him who was detained in bondage.[704]

From this point of view the person to whom the debt is due and is discharged is the devil; from another, the satisfaction is regarded as due to God, owing to the violation of man's obedience, and is paid to Him through the sacrifice of a sinless life. "It was right that all men should fulfil the righteousness of God; but, since no one did this, Christ came and completely fulfilled it."[705] He was Himself both the sacrificer and the victim; the cross being the altar. He suffered outside the city that the prophecy, "He was numbered with the transgressors," might be fulfilled, and also that the *universality* of the sacrifice might be proclaimed.[706] Chrysostom is not careful to distinguish between the alienation of man from God, and of God from man through the Fall. He represents the hostility as in some sort existing on both sides. Christ did the work of a mediator by interposing Himself between the two parties, and reconciling each to the other. The references to such a fundamental verity are of course numerous, often full of beauty of expression and tenderness of feeling, and glowing earnestness. What he specially delights to dwell upon, as might be expected from his warm, affectionate disposition, is the exceeding love of Christ to man, and the hearty return which gratitude for such a benefit ought to draw forth from us. Like St. Paul, he often will break forth, in the midst of some argument or practical address, into a burst of rapturous and adoring praise. "What reward shall I give unto the Lord for all the benefits which He hath done unto me? Who shall express the noble acts of the Lord, or show forth all His praise? He abased Himself that He might exalt thee; He died to make thee immortal; He became a curse that thou mightest obtain a blessing.... When the world lay in darkness, the light of the Cross was held up like a torch shining in a dark place, and the light at the top of it was the Sun of Righteousness Himself."[707]

Chrysostom's doctrine of justification is naturally coloured by his ethics. Maintaining, as he did, that the corruption of man's nature consisted in a weakness of the moral purpose, a crooked tendency of the will, rather than in any inherent indelible stain in that nature itself, his exhortations are directed rather to inculcate energetic action, a gradual process of improvement of the will with the Divine help, than that entire dependence through faith on the mercy of God which springs out of a deep conviction of the sinner's own insufficiency. The logical tendency of the Augustinian view of the intense and radical depravity of man's nature is to induce a total repudiation of the efficacy of personal effort, a total disavowal of all personal merit. Hence justification comes to be regarded as purely an act of acquittal on God's part, a boon which the despairing sinner by an act of faith thankfully accepts. Such is not the position of Chrysostom, or of those who, like the Cambridge Divines of the seventeenth century, have trodden in his footsteps. With him the condition of a pardoned sinner consists rather in that renovation of the spiritual and moral life which is the result of long and laborious effort, aided of course by Divine grace, a succession of moral acts eventually producing "a new creature." Faith is not so much regarded merely as the instrument or hand held out, by which God's gift is appropriated, as the first in a row of good works, a fruitful source of all good action. "Abraham," he says, "believed God, and it was counted to him for righteousness. Why? To prove that belief itself, in the first instance, and obedience to the call of God, come from our own good judgment (εὐγνωμοσύνη); but as soon as the foundation of faith is laid, we require the alliance of the Holy Spirit, that it may remain constantly unshakable and inflexible."[708] "Faith is the mother of all good, the sure staff of man's tottering footsteps, the anchor of his tempest-tossed soul, without which he would be like a ship cast adrift on the sea to the mercy of winds and waves."[709] "It is more stable and secure than reason, for it carries its own proof with it; the conclusions of reason may be diverted by counter-arguments, but faith stands above argument, and is not distracted by it."[710]

He does not, indeed, shrink from a bold declaration of the value of good works, but he is far from teaching men to depend on them as efficient causes of salvation. They are to be stored up as a kind of viaticum for our journey to the other world. "As those who are in a foreign country, when they wish to return to their own land, take pains, a long time beforehand, to collect means sufficient for their journey, so surely ought we, who are but strangers and settlers on this earth, to lay up a store of provisions through spiritual virtue, that when our Master shall command our return into our native country, we may be prepared and may carry part of our store with us, having sent the other in advance."[711] On the other hand, he constantly insists that it is the favour and mercy of God alone which, in the end, bestows salvation on us. Faith and good works are necessary conditions, but not efficient causes of salvation. God has graciously willed that they who have faith and good works shall be saved: let no man therefore boast. We could not do good works without God's assisting grace, nor could they in the end and at the best save us if it were not His merciful and gracious will.[712] Therefore, let no one pride himself on his good works; above all things, let him cultivate a spirit of humility and modesty: St. Paul, after all his labours, confessed that he was not meet to be called an apostle, but was what he was by the grace of God.[713] "What is impossible with men is possible with God." "Tell me not I have sinned much, and how can I be saved? *Thou* art not able, but thy Master is able so to blot out thy sins that no trace even of them shall remain. In the natural body, indeed, though the wound may be healed, yet the scar remains; but God does not suffer the scar even to remain, but, together with release from punishment, grants righteousness also, and makes the sinner to be equal to him who has not sinned. He makes the sin neither to be nor to have been.... Sin is drowned in the ocean of God's mercy, just as a spark is extinguished in a flood of water."[714]

It was, no doubt, the trustful dependence of Chrysostom on Divine grace, coupled with his firm conviction of the free capacity of man to turn to what is good, which enabled him to pitch all his exhortations to Christian holiness in such a singularly cheerful, hopeful tone. To his sanguine temperament it seemed as if man's natural capacities for good, aided by grace obtained through prayer, could accomplish anything. "The effect of prayer on the heart is like that of the rising sun upon the natural world; as the wild beasts come forth by night to prowl and prey, but the sun ariseth, and they get them away together and lay them down in their dens, so, when the soul is illuminated by prayer, the irrational and brutal passions are put to flight, anger is calmed, lust is extinguished, envy is expelled; prayer is the treasure of the poor, the security of the rich; the poorest of all men is rich if he can pray, and the rich man who cannot pray is miserably poor. Ahab without prayer was impotent amidst his splendour; Elijah with prayer was mighty in his coarse garment of sheepskin."[715] "It is impossible, impossible that a man who calls constantly on God with proper zeal should ever sin; his spirit is proof against temptation so long as the effect of his praying lasts, and when it begins to fail, then he must pray again. And this may be done anywhere, in the market or in the shop, since prayer demands the outstretched soul rather than the extended hands."[716] Long prayers were to be avoided; they gave great opportunities to Satan to distract the attention, which could not easily bear a lengthened strain. Prayers should be frequent and short; thus we should best comply with the direction of St. Paul to pray without ceasing.[717]

It remains to collect some notices of Chrysostom's teaching with reference to the two Sacraments.

The number of those who, as Christian children of decidedly Christian parents, were baptized in infancy appears to have been small at this period, compared with those who, like Chrysostom himself, joined the ranks of the Church at a later epoch of life. There were many whose parents, or who themselves, hovered not so much between Christianity and any definite form of paganism, as between Christianity and worldliness. The sermons addressed by Chrysostom and his contemporaries to catechumens, and the frequent allusions to them, the minute directions respecting their instruction, their division into classes, the custom of calling the first part of the service to which they were admitted the Missa Catechumenorum, prove that numerous they must have been. I have failed to find any passages in which Chrysostom urgently inculcates infant baptism, and, considering his views respecting original sin, this is not surprising; but he earnestly denounces a custom of deferring baptism, prevalent among those who were already believers, or professing to be such. Often it was delayed till men believed themselves to be at the point of death— a practice which he especially deprecates, because at such a time "the recipient was often in a restless, suffering state of mind and body, most unfit to receive that holy sacrament; the entrance of the priest was regarded by the sorrowful attendants as a certain evidence of the approaching end; and when the sick man could not recognise those who were present, or hear a voice, or answer in those words by which he was to enter into a blessed covenant with our Lord, but lay like a log or a stone, what possible advantage could there be in the reception of the sacrament?"[718] Again, it was often delayed till a man conceived that he had received a distinct call and intimation that it was the will of God. This Chrysostom regarded as being too often a mere cloak for moral indolence, a reluctance of men to bind themselves under the high responsibilities of the Christian vocation.[719]

He certainly considered baptism as being not merely a solemn initiation into the Christian covenant, and instrument of remission of sin, but also of moral renovation. This, however, is represented as a blessing naturally derivable from the entrance into the new and holy federal relation with God. In his comment on the passage, "and such were some of you; but ye are washed, but ye are sanctified, but ye are justified in the name of our Lord Jesus Christ," he observes that such words signify that they were not only purified from past uncleanness, but had become holy and righteous. "For such is the benevolence of the Divine gift; if an imperial letter consisting of a few lines discharges men from liability to punishment for any number of offences, and advances others to great honour, much more will the Holy Spirit of God, which can do all things, release us from all wickedness, bestow on us abundant righteousness, and fill us with much confidence." The nature of the baptized was, therefore, like a vessel which had not only been cleansed from past defilements, but recast in the furnace so as to come out in a new shape.[720] He is far, however, from regarding such a change as final. The virtue of baptism is effectual at the time, but the grace then given is as a trust to be carefully guarded; a talent to be traded with, a seed of righteousness to be diligently cultivated, the dawning of a light to shine more and more unto the perfect day. As Christ becomes at that time the clothing, the food, the habitation of the Christian, the recipient of these favours has to take care that he does not wrong this intimate relationship. Therefore he is ordered to say at baptism, "I renounce thee, Satan;" that is the declaration of a covenant with his Master. A firm determination to abandon past sin and eradicate evil habits— in a word, repentance— should take place previous to baptism. "Just as the painter freely alters the lineaments of his picture, when it is sketched in outline, by rubbing out or putting in, but when once he has added the colour, he is no longer at liberty to make alterations; in like manner erase evil habits before baptism, before the true colouring of the Holy Spirit has been thrown over the soul: take care when this has been received, and the royal image shines forth clearly, that you do not blot it out any more, and inflict wounds and scars on the beauty given thee by God."[721]

In another place he contrasts the baptism of the Jews, of John the Baptist, and of Jesus Christ. "The first was only a cleansing of the body from ceremonial defilements, the second was a means of enforcing an exhortation to repentance, the third was accompanied by remission of sins: it releases and purges the soul from sin, and gives a supply of the Holy Spirit."[722] "When the merciful God saw the extremity of our weakness, and the incurable nature of our sickness, requiring a great work of healing, He conferred upon us that renovation which comes through the laver of regeneration, in order that, being divested of the old man, that is, of evil works, and having put on the new, we might go forward in the path of virtue."[723]

In considering those passages which relate to the Holy Eucharist, it must be carefully borne in mind that Chrysostom lived in an age when that Sacrament had not become a battle-field of controversy. He was under no constraint in his language, because he did not feel that every word he used was liable to be criticised, or misunderstood, or torn to pieces in the strife of contending parties. He enjoyed because he disputed not. Filled with thankfulness and joy to overflowing for the unspeakable benefits derived from that Sacrament, he is not cautious or scrupulously precise in his expressions, but gives the freest rein to the enthusiasm of his feelings; his object being not to support any rigidly defined theory or system, but to infuse a certain spirit, to encourage a proper moral tone and temper in reference to the whole subject.

Three ideas, however, are apparent as dominant in his mind— a sacrifice, a presence of Christ, a reception of Christ. In several of the passages about to be presented, all the three points will appear in similar and simultaneous force. In one homily,[724] where he severely censures the too prevalent custom of attending the Eucharist on great festivals only, and then behaving in a disorderly manner, the worshippers hustling and trampling on one another in their tumultuous haste to approach the holy table, and then hurrying out of church immediately after the reception, without waiting for the conclusion of the service— "What," he exclaims, "O man, art thou doing? When Christ is present, and the angels are standing by, and the awe-inspiring table is spread before thee, dost thou withdraw?... If you are invited to a feast and are filled before the other guests, you do not dare to withdraw while the rest of your friends are still reclining at the table; and here, when the mysteries of Christ are being celebrated, and the holy feast is still going on, dost thou retreat in the middle?" Again: "Since, then, we are about to see this evening, as a lamb slain and sacrificed, Him who was crucified, let us approach, I pray you, with trembling awe. The angels, who surpass our nature, stood beside His empty tomb with great reverence; and shall we, who are about to stand beside, not an empty sepulchre, but the very table which bears the Lamb, shall we approach with noise and confusion?"[725] Again: "It is now time to draw near the awe-inspiring table.... Christ is present, and He who arranged that first table, even He arranges this present one. For it is not man who makes the things which are set before us become the body and blood of Christ, but it is Christ Himself, who was crucified for us. The priest stands fulfilling his part (σχῆμα) by uttering the appointed words, but the power and the grace are of God. 'This is my body,' He says. This expression changes the character (μεταρρυθμίζει) of the elements, and as that sentence, 'increase and multiply,' once spoken, extends through all time, enabling the procreative power of our nature, even so that expression, 'this is my body,' once uttered, does at every table in the churches from that time to the present day, and even till Christ's coming, make the sacrifice perfect."[726] Speaking of the sacrifice of Isaac, he observes that it was perfect so far as Abraham was concerned, because his *intention* did not fail, though the knife was not actually drawn across his son's throat; "for a sacrifice is possible even without blood— the initiated (*i.e.* the baptized) know what I mean: on this account, also, that sacrifice was made without blood, since it was destined to be a figure of this sacrifice of ours."[727]

Perhaps the most significant passage with reference to the sacrificial idea is one where, after contrasting the many and ineffective sacrifices of the Jews with the one perfect, efficacious sacrifice of Christ, he proceeds: "What then? do we not offer every day? We do offer certainly, but making a memorial of His death; and this memorial is one, not many. How one, not many? Because the sacrifice was offered once for all, as that great sacrifice was in the Holy of Holies. This is a figure of that great sacrifice as that was of this; for we do not offer one victim to-day and another to-morrow, but always the same: wherefore the sacrifice is one. Well, on this ground, because He is offered in many places, are there many Christs? Nay, by no means, but one Christ everywhere, complete both in this world and in the other; one body. As then, though offered in many places, He is but one body, so is there but one sacrifice. Our High Priest is He who offers the sacrifice which cleanses us. We offer that now which was offered then; which is indeed inconsumable. This takes place now for a memorial of what took place then: 'Do this,' said He, 'for my memorial.' We do not then offer a different sacrifice as the high priest formerly did, but always the same; *or, rather, we celebrate a memorial of a Sacrifice.*"[728]

There are other passages in which the idea, no less prominently set forth, is that of a holy feast. Elijah bequeathed his mantle and a double portion of his spirit to Elisha, "but the Son of God, when He ascended, left us His own flesh.... He who did not decline to shed His blood for all, and imparts to us again His flesh and blood, what will He refuse to do for our salvation?"[729] Again: "Consider, O man, what kind of sacrifice thou art about to touch, what kind of table to approach; reflect that thou who art but dust and ashes receivest the body and blood of Christ."[730] The sedulous care with which he urges the duty of moral cleansing before venturing to approach the holy table proceeds chiefly from regarding it as a holy feast. "How shall we behold the sacred passover? How shall we receive the sacred feast? How partake of the adorable mysteries with that tongue whereby we trampled on the Law of God and defiled our soul? for if one would not touch a royal robe with defiled hands, how shall we receive the Lord's body with an unclean tongue?"[731]

These passages, which are but a few specimens extracted from a large number on the same subject, are yet sufficient to show how easy it would be for the partisans of contending schools to press the language of Chrysostom into support of their own system. The truth is, that in the case of this, as of other subjects, we find in Chrysostom and his contemporaries the raw material, which has been wrought out by the toil and strife of later times into definite sharply chiselled dogmas. Nothing, therefore, can really be more unfair than to regard, as a direct friend or opponent, one who lived and wrote long before controversy had arisen on the subjects of which he treated. He might innocently employ expressions which we should deem it incautious to use, because we know the interpretation of which they are susceptible, or because we see in them incipient symptoms of an idea which in process of time grew into a mischievous error. It is instructive also to notice how harmless doctrines which afterwards became mischievous were when they were not pushed to an extremity, not made integral parts of a system of belief. It does not occur to us, for instance, for a moment to suppose that such invocation of saints as was manifestly approved by Chrysostom was the least detrimental to that free intercourse which ought to exist between the soul of man and God Himself. As Dr. Pusey has observed: "Through volumes of St. Augustine and St. Chrysostom there is no mention of any reliance except on Christ alone."[732] There is not the least approach to that system of stepping-stones or halting-places between God and man, which the Roman Church established by means of confession, saint-worship, and, above all, Mariolatry.

There is no trace in Chrysostom of priestly confession as an ordinance of the Church. When he speaks of the misery which ensues on the commission of sin, he urges the sinner to relieve his conscience by a free confession with repentance and tears. "And why are you ashamed to do so?" he proceeds, "for to whom do you confess? Is it to a man or a fellow-servant who might reproach or expose you? Nay, it is to the Lord, tender and merciful: it is to the physician that you show your wound."[733] Again, in speaking of prayer, he contrasts the freedom of access to God with the difficulties and impediments which encounter the delivery of a petition to some great man. "This last could be reached only through porters, flatterers, parasites; whereas God is invoked without the intervention of any one, without money, without expense of any kind."[734] This reads like a prophetical sarcasm on a Church which ultimately made a traffic of dispensing what cannot really be dispensed by man, because it is the free gift of God.

Nor is there any symptom in Chrysostom of a tendency to the theory of Purgatory. The condition of man after death is always represented by him as final and irrevocable. His tone, when exhorting to repentance, is always in harmony with the following passage: "For the day will come when the theatre of this world will be dissolved, and then it is not possible to contend any longer: this is the season of repentance, that of judgment; this of contest, that of crowning; this of labour, that of repose."[735]

But of all medieval additions to the purer faith of primitive times, Mariolatry has grown to the most extraordinary dimensions.[736] Of any tendency to this error there is in Chrysostom a remarkable absence. In fact, his notices of the Blessed Virgin, not very frequent, are on the whole, we might almost say, unnecessarily disparaging. In his commentary on the Marriage Feast at Cana, he suggests that the Virgin, in mentioning the failure of wine to our Lord, may have been anxious to draw out His miraculous powers, partly to place the guests under an obligation to Him, partly to enhance her own dignity through the display of her Son's divine powers. He considers that the appeal sprang from the same feeling which prompted His brethren to say, "Show Thyself to the world;" and he proceeds to observe that our Lord, while never failing to manifest dutiful reverence and affectionate care towards His mother, has taught us, by His conduct and language to her, that the tie of mere earthly kindred entitled her not to higher privileges, and placed her in no more intimate spiritual relationship with Himself than any one might through love and obedience enjoy. "Who is my mother, and who are my brethren? and looking round about on His disciples, He said, Behold my mother and my brethren; for whosoever shall do the will of my Father, the same is my brother, and my sister, and mother." "Heavens!" Chrysostom exclaims, "what honour! what reward! to what a pinnacle does He exalt those who follow Him! How many women have blessed the Holy Virgin and her womb, and have longed to be such mothers! What then prevents it? Behold, he opens a broad way for us: not women only, but men also are permitted to be placed in the same rank." "The demand to see Him was made by His mother in an ambitious spirit: she wished to show to the people how much authority she possessed over Him; at any rate, the request was unreasonable and unseasonable. If she and His brethren desired to speak with Him on matters of doctrine, they might have done so in the presence of the others; but if on private matters, it was an ill-timed interruption to His discourse on weightier subjects."[737] Again: "When a woman in the company cried out, 'Blessed is the womb that bare Thee!' He instantly corrected her: 'Yea, *rather* blessed are they that hear the word of God and keep it.'" It is possible that the general sentiment of the age may have regarded the Virgin with more veneration, but Chrysostom could not have ventured to use such language had the cultus been in any but its very earliest stage, if then. She is called holy by him; she intercedes[738] for Eve, who is a type of herself, but of worship paid to her there is not the slightest evidence.[739]

It is almost superfluous to observe that Chrysostom knew and acknowledged nothing of papal supremacy, in the sense which those words conveyed to the minds of later generations. In common with the rest of Christendom, he paid great deference and respect to the metropolitan at Rome, and he was quite free from those feelings of jealousy which were entertained by the patriarchs of Constantinople, as time went on, owing to the increasing pretensions and exactions of the Roman See. If he respects Innocent, as occupying the chair of St. Peter, he equally respects Flavian, bishop of Antioch (who was not in communion with Rome), for the same reason; he calls him "our common father and teacher, who has inherited St. Peter's virtue and his chair." The letter written to Innocent during exile was addressed also to the Bishops of Milan and Aquileia. In his commentary on Galatians ii. he proves the equality of St. Paul with St. Peter. No doubt he assigns an eminent rank to St. Peter, speaking of him as "leader of the band" (κορυφαῖος) of apostles, and as intrusted with the "presidency" (προστασίαν) of the brethren: but these words do not imply absolute authority, and the same appellations are applied to St. Paul also.

Scattered up and down the discourses of Chrysostom there are abundant references to the liturgical forms, and manner of using them, which were in vogue in his time. If we had no other authority, we could learn from him alone that the service consisted of two parts— the first, called Missa Catechumenorum, because the catechumens were permitted to be present at it, which included an opening salutation of "Peace be with you," with the response, "And with thy spirit;" psalms sung antiphonally; appointed lessons according to the season or the day (as Genesis was read during Lent, the Acts of the Apostles in Pentecost, that is, during the fifty days between Easter and Whitsun Day); the sermon, frequently in Chrysostom's case on the lesson for the day, the preacher usually sitting, and the people standing; then prayers, announced by the deacon, for the catechumens, the "possessed," and the penitents; the benediction by the bishop, and dismissal by the deacon, who bade them "depart in peace." The second part of the service then began, called Missa Fidelium, because the baptized only were permitted to be present. Chrysostom strongly denounces an increasing tendency on the part of many to remain during this second and more sacred portion without participating. He plainly declares that all those who were baptized should communicate, and tells them, if they were not worthy to receive the Eucharist, neither could they be worthy to join in the prayers which preceded the reception, and therefore they ought to quit the church, with the catechumens and penitents, when the deacon commanded all unbaptized, ungodly, and unbelieving persons to depart.[740] The usual order of the Missa Fidelium was "the silent prayer" (εὐχὴ διὰ σιωπῆς), on part of the priest and people (which the latter too often abused, Chrysostom feared, to imprecate vengeance on their enemies[741]); then a prayer somewhat equivalent to our bidding prayer in form, and to our prayer for the Church Militant in substance, the deacon bidding or proclaiming the forms, and the people responding; then a prayer of invocation made by the bishop, which was also called "collecta," because in it the prayers of the people were considered to be gathered or summed up; the oblations of the people presented by the deacons; the kiss of peace, the reading of the diptychs, the ablution of the priest's hands, the bringing of the elements to the bishop at the altar, while the priests stood on each side, and deacons held large fans to drive away the flies; a secret prayer offered by the bishop; the benediction, "The grace of our Lord Jesus Christ," etc., to which the people responded "And with thy spirit;" followed by "Lift up your hearts"— "We lift them up unto the Lord;" "Let us give thanks to our Lord God"— "It is meet and right so to do;" a long thanksgiving, terminating with the Ter Sanctus, in which the people joined; the consecration prayer, including the words of our Lord at the time of institution, and an invocation of the Holy Spirit to make the elements become the body and blood of Christ; a prayer for all members of the Church, living and dead; the doxology, the Creed; a prayer of the bishop for sanctification; the words pronounced by him, "Holy things for holy people" (τὰ ἅγια τοῖς ἁγίοις); the reception by the clergy and laity in both kinds, taking the elements into their hands; concluding prayers, and dismissal by the deacon proclaiming, "Go in peace." Nearly all of the forms indicated in this sketch are more or less clearly referred to or quoted in Chrysostom's works, and from these, with the aid of other contemporary writers and documents, we might construct a liturgy which would more nearly resemble that actually used by him than the liturgy called by his name resembles it.[742] For in this, as in the so-called liturgy of Basil, it is impossible now to determine how much was actually composed by the Father who gave his name to it. It cannot be proved that Chrysostom actually corrected or improved at all the liturgy which he found in use at Constantinople. It may only have come to be called after him as being the greatest luminary who ever occupied the see. The statement, however, made in a tract ascribed to Proclus, Patriarch of Constantinople in the fifth century, is not in itself improbable, that Chrysostom found the existing liturgy so long that many of the congregation, being men of business, and pressed for time, left before the service was concluded, or came in after it had begun, and therefore he abridged and otherwise altered it. In any case, many alterations were made by different churches and bishops in the course of time, as in other liturgies, so also in those which bear the name of Basil and Chrysostom; and hence, as Montfaucon, Savile, Cave, and others have remarked, you cannot find any two copies which are exactly alike.

A critical estimate of Chrysostom's value as a commentator hardly falls within the scope of an essay on his life, but a few general observations on this head may not be deemed out of place here. The same fact was the cause in him of much excellence and some defect in this department. He was a preacher whose primary object was to convert souls. This earnest, practical aim, of which he never lost sight, helped to protect him from lapsing into idle, fanciful, mystical interpretations of Scripture; but, on the other hand, it hindered his entering so fully into all the historical, grammatical, or even doctrinal questions which might be raised about a passage as he would have done had he been exclusively a commentator. His dominant aim being to affect the heart and the moral practice of his hearers, he is content when he has elicited from the passage all that will be most useful for that purpose, and the continuity of the commentary is frequently marred by sudden digressions. His ignorance of Hebrew was of course fatal to his being an accurate interpreter of the Old Testament, since he was entirely dependent on the Septuagint translation. And even in Greek, though few would deny him the merit of fine scholarship on the whole, though his command of the language as an orator is masterly, his style luminous, his diction copious and rich without being offensively ornate or redundant, yet his hold upon the language for critical purposes is neither that of a man who spoke it when it was in its purest stage, nor that of a scholar who, living in a later age and speaking a different tongue, has made a careful, laborious study of it as a dead language.

But two invaluable qualifications for an interpreter Chrysostom did possess— a thorough love for the Sacred Book, and a thorough familiarity with every part of it. There is no topic on which he dwells more frequently and earnestly than on the duty of every Christian man and woman to study the Bible; and what he bade others do, that he did pre-eminently himself. He rebukes the silly vanity of rich people who prided themselves on possessing finely written and handsomely bound copies of the Bible, but who knew little about the contents. Study of the Bible was more necessary for the layman than the monk, because he was exposed to more constant and formidable temptations. The Christian without a knowledge of his Bible was like a workman without his tools. Like the tree planted by the water-side, the soul of the diligent reader would be continually nourished and refreshed. There were no difficulties which would not yield to a patient study of it. Neither earthly grandeur, nor friends, nor indeed any human thing, could afford in suffering such comfort as the reading of Holy Scripture, for this was the companionship of God.[743]

The honest, straightforward common sense which marks his practical exhortations was a useful quality to him also as an interpreter. One of his principles is, that sound doctrine could not be extracted from Holy Scripture but by a careful comparison of many passages not isolated from their context.[744] Allegorical interpretations were by no means to be rejected, but to be used with caution; men too often made the mistake of dictating what Scripture should mean instead of submitting to be taught by it: they *introduced* a meaning instead of *eliciting* it.[745] Thus, though he often accepts popular types— as Boaz and Ruth are figures of Christ and His bride the Church; and Noah, Joseph, Joshua, are all in different ways representative of our Lord; though sometimes particular expressions in Messianic prophecies are forced, for instance, in Isaiah's description of Immanuel, the "butter and honey" there spoken of he supposes to be intended to indicate the reality of our Lord's humanity[746]—yet his customary aim is to discover the literal sense and direct historical bearing of the passage. At the same time he fully recognises a general foreshadowing of Jesus Christ, and the complete fulfilment in Him ultimately of prophecies which immediately refer to persons and events nearly, if not quite, contemporaneous with the utterance. He fails not also to point out the moral aspect of prophecy as a system of teaching rather than prediction, as preparatory to the advent of Jesus Christ in the flesh, not only by informing men's minds, but disciplining their hearts to receive Him.[747] Hence the holy men who lived, under the Old Dispensation, in faith on God's promises, knew Christ as it were by anticipation, and were to be reckoned as members of the one body.[748]

He had a clear conception of the essential coherence between the Old and New Testament. He observes that the very words "old" and "new" are relative terms: *new* implies an antecedent *old*, preparatory to it. The condition of the recipients, the circumstances and age in which they lived, being different, necessitated a difference in the treatment. A physician treated the same patient at different times by directly contrary methods; sometimes administering sweet, sometimes bitter medicines, sometimes using the lancet, sometimes cautery, but always with the same ultimate end in view— the health of his patient. So the Old and New Testaments were different, but not, as the Manichæans maintained, antagonistic. The commandment, "Thou shalt not kill," attacked the fruit and consequence of vice; the precept, "Whosoever is angry with his brother without a cause," etc., struck at the root. This was an illustration in a small instance of the general truth that the New Dispensation was only a completion and expansion of the Old. Those, therefore, who rejected the Old Testament dishonoured the New, which was based upon it, and presupposes it.[749]

He is equally rational in his manner of accounting for the variations in the Gospel narratives. That they differ in details, but agree in essential matters, he regards as a powerful evidence of veracity. Exact and verbal coincidence in every particular would have excited in the minds of opponents a suspicion of concerted agreement.[750] Authors might write variously without being at variance; if there had been ten thousand evangelists, yet the Gospel itself would have been but one.[751] Each evangelist tells substantially the same tale, but varied according to the readers for whom he wrote, and the special object which he had in view. So St. Matthew wrote in Hebrew for the Jews, St. Mark for the disciples in Egypt, St. John to set forth the divine aspect of our Lord's life. Thus we have variety in unity, and unity in variety.[752]

In his commentaries on the Epistles he is careful to consider each as a connected whole; and, in order to impress this on his hearers, he frequently recapitulates at the beginning of a homily all the steps by which the part under consideration has been reached. In his introductions to each letter he generally makes useful observations on the author, the time, place, and style of composition, the readers for whom it was intended, the general character and arrangement of its contents. He regarded the Bible as in such a sense written under the inspiration of God, that no passage, no word even, was to be despised;[753] that men wrote as they were moved by the Holy Spirit, but not to the total deprivation of their own human understanding and personal character. The prophet was not like the seer who spoke under constraint, not knowing what he said; he retained his own faculties and style; only all his powers were quickened, energised by the Spirit to the utterance of words which unassisted he could not have uttered.[754]

Chrysostom's influence as a preacher was not aided by any external advantages of person. Like so many men who have possessed great powers of command over the minds of others—like St. Paul, Athanasius, John Wesley—he was little of stature; his frame was attenuated by the austerities of his youth and his habitually ascetic mode of life; his cheeks were pale and hollow; his eyes deeply set, but bright and piercing; his broad and lofty forehead was furrowed by wrinkles; his head was bald. He frequently delivered his discourses sitting in the ambo, or high reading-desk, just inside the nave, in order to be near his hearers and well raised above them. But these physical disadvantages were more than compensated by other more important qualities. A power of exposition which unfolded in lucid order, passage by passage, the meaning of the book in hand; a rapid transition from clear exposition, or keen logical argument, to fervid exhortation, or pathetic appeal, or indignant denunciation; the versatile ease with which he could lay hold of any little incident of the moment, such as the lighting of the lamps in the church, and use it to illustrate his discourse; the mixture of plain common-sense, simple boldness, and tender affection, with which he would strike home to the hearts and consciences of his hearers— all these are not only general characteristics of the man, but are usually to be found manifested more or less in the compass of each discourse. It is this rare union of powers which constitutes his superiority to almost all the other Christian preachers with whom he might be, or has been, compared. Savonarola had all, and more than all, his fire and vehemence, but untempered by his sober, calm good sense, and wanting his rational method of interpretation. Chrysostom was eager and impetuous at times in speech as well as in action, but never fanatical. Jeremy Taylor combines, like Chrysostom, real earnestness of purpose with rhetorical forms of expression and florid imagery; but, on the whole, his style is far more artificial, and is overlaid with a multifarious learning from which Chrysostom's was entirely free. Wesley is almost his match in simple, straightforward, practical exhortation, but does not rise into flights of eloquence like his. The great French preachers, again, resemble him in his more ornate and declamatory vein, but they lack that simpler common-sense style of address which equally distinguished him. Whether the sobriquet of Chrysostomos, "the golden mouth," was given to him in his lifetime is extremely doubtful; at any rate, it seems not to have been commonly used till afterwards. John is the only name by which he is mentioned in the writings of historians who were most nearly contemporaneous, but the other was a well-known appellation before the end of the fifth century.[755]

The preservation of Chrysostom's discourses we owe mainly to the custom, prevalent in the Eastern Church at that time, of having the sermons of famous preachers taken down by shorthand writers as they were spoken; but some of them Chrysostom published himself.[756] To what extent they may have been written before preaching it is impossible to say. The expository parts were evidently the result of previous study and preparation; the actual diction of the practical portions he may have left to the suggestion of the moment, though the main subjects of his address had been always decided upon beforehand. Extempore remarks were frequently called forth by the behaviour of the congregation, or some passing incident. The discourse delivered after his return from exile we also know to have been purely impromptu; and Suidas observes that he "had a tongue which exceeded the cataracts of the Nile in fluency, so that he delivered many of his panegyrics on the martyrs extempore without the least hesitation."[757] His hearers were sometimes rapt in such profound attention that pickpockets took advantage of it:[758] sometimes they were melted to tears, or beat their breasts and faces, and uttered groans and cries to Heaven for mercy; at other times they clapped their hands or shouted— marks of approbation frequently paid at that time to eloquent preachers, but always sternly reproved by Chrysostom.

Although his style is generally exuberantly rich, yet it is seldom offensively redundant, for every word is usually telling; and at times he is epigrammatically terse. A few instances will suffice:— "The fire of sin is large, but it is quenched by a few tears;" "Pain was given on account of sin, yet through pain sin is dissolved;" "Riches are called possessions (κτήματα) that we may possess them, not be possessed by them;" "You are master of much wealth, do not be a slave to that whereof God has made you master;" "Scripture relates the sins of saints, that we may fear; the conversion of sinners, that we may hope." He refers to a visitation of Antioch by an earthquake, as God "shaking the city, but establishing your minds; making the city crumble, but consolidating your judgment."

His familiarity with classical Greek authors is apparent sometimes in direct references. He speaks of "the smoothness of Isocrates, the weight of Demosthenes, the dignity of Thucydides, the sublimity of Plato."[759] He quotes the beginning of the "Apology," to show that if Socrates did not put a high value on mere fine talking, how much less should the Christian.[760] He illustrates the readiness of men to supply the wants of the monk by a passage from Plato, where Crito says that his money, and that of Cebes and many others, is at the disposal of Socrates; and, go where he will, he may rely on finding friends.[761] Sometimes we detect a thought derived, it may have been unconsciously, from classical sources. When he compares the crowd of the congregation before him to the sea, and the play upon the surface of that sea of heads to the effect of a strong west wind stirring and bending the ears of corn,[762] it is impossible not to think that the idea was suggested by the well-known simile in Homer (Il. ii. 147). Again, when, in speaking of David's sin, he compares the body to a chariot and the soul to the charioteer, and says that, when the soul is intoxicated by passion, the chariot is dragged along at random, it can hardly be fanciful to see a reflection of Plato's celebrated image of the charioteer and horses in the "Phædrus."[763]

But whatever admiration Chrysostom may have retained of those authors whom he had studied in his youth, it was confined to their language, for with their ideas and modes of thought he had, so far as we can judge, abandoned all sympathy. Nor was this unnatural. Christianity existed in such close contact with Pagan corruption, and it had suffered so much from Pagan persecution, that the revulsion of earnest Christians from all things Pagan was total and indiscriminating. "The old order changeth, yielding place to new;" and the new, having fought a hard struggle with the old, is for a long time incapable of recognising merit in anything belonging to it. There are several allusions in Chrysostom to the "Republic" of Plato, but they are always depreciative. He fastens on a few points, such as the regulations about marriage and female work, and condemns it on these as absurd and childish, quite failing to consider the idea in its grandeur as a whole.[764] Yet it is instructive to notice that he never hesitates to assign to Plato the first place among the heathen philosophers, dignifying him with the title of Coryphæus.[765] He often compares the failure of Plato's teaching to regenerate men in every rank with the successful labours of St. Paul and the other apostles; but while he rejoices that the writings and doctrine of the philosopher were eclipsed by the tentmaker and fisherman, and well-nigh forgotten, he evidently regarded it as the most signal triumph which Christianity had achieved.[766]

Unquestionable as the intellectual genius of Chrysostom was, yet it is rather in the purity of his moral character, his single-minded boldness of purpose, and the glowing piety which burns through all his writings, that we find the secret of his influence. If it was rather the mission of Augustine to mould the minds of men so as to take a firm grasp of certain great doctrines, it was the mission of Chrysostom to inflame the whole heart with a fervent love of God. Rightly has he been called the great teacher of consummate holiness, as Augustine was the great teacher of efficient grace;[767] rightly has it been remarked that, like Fénélon, he is to be ranked among those who may be termed disciples of St. John, men who seem to have been pious without intermission from their childhood upwards, and of whose piety the leading characteristics are ease, cheerfulness, and elevation; while Augustine belongs to the disciples of St. Paul, those who have been converted from error to truth, or from sin to holiness, and whose characteristics are gravity, earnestness, depth.[768] If Augustine has done more valuable service in building up the Church at large, Chrysostom is the more loveable to the individual, and speaks out of a heart overflowing with love to God and man, unconstrained by the fetters of a severe and rigid system. Yet it is precisely on this account that he has not been so generally appreciated as he deserves. His tone is too catholic for the Romanist, or for the sectarian partisan of any denomination. "It would be easy to produce abundant instances of his oratorical abilities; I wish it were in my power to record as many of his evangelical excellencies." Such is the verdict of a narrow-minded historian,[769] and the comparative estimation in which he held St. Augustine and St. Chrysostom may be inferred from the number of pages in his History given to each: St. Augustine is favoured with 187, Chrysostom with 20. But he whose judgment is not cramped by the shackles of some harsh and stiff theory of Gospel truth will surely allow that Chrysostom not only preached the Gospel but lived it. To the last moment of his life he exhibited that calm, cheerful faith, that patient resignation under affliction, and untiring perseverance for the good of others, which are pre-eminently the marks of a Christian saint. The cause for which he fought and died in a corrupt age was the cause of Christian holiness; and, therefore, by the great medieval poet of Christendom he is rightly placed in Paradise between two men who, widely different indeed in character and circumstances from him and from one another, yet resembled him in this, that they freely and courageously spoke of God's "testimonies even before kings, and were not ashamed"— Nathan the Seer, and Anselm the Primate of all England:—

"Natan profeta, e'l metropolitano
Crisostomo, ed Anselmo...."[770]

APPENDIX

[*Vide ante*, p. 415 note.]

ON THE LETTER TO CÆSARIUS (Chrys. Op. vol. iii. p. 755).

The history of this letter, and the controversy connected with it, are curious and interesting. Peter Martyr transcribed a Latin translation of it, which he found in a manuscript at Florence, carried it with him to England, and deposited it in the library of Archbishop Cranmer. After Cranmer's death, and the dispersion of his library, the letter disappeared. Peter Martyr had not stated the source from which he had derived it, and, therefore, when the assailants of the doctrine of Transubstantiation wished to make use of it, their opponents always maintained that it did not exist. In 1680, however, Emericus Bigotius discovered a copy in the library of St. Mark's Convent, at Florence, probably the same which Peter Martyr, himself a Florentine, had transcribed. Emericus appended it to his edition of Palladius's "Life of Chrysostom," and in his preface endeavoured to vindicate its authenticity; but the Doctors of the Sorbonne suppressed the letter, and such portions of the preface as related to it. Emericus, however, had retained in his own possession some of the entire copies after they were printed, before they came into the licenser's hands. The translation was published by Stephanus Le Moyne in 1685, by Jacob Basnage in 1687, and in 1689 by Harduin, a Jesuit, who strenuously maintained the Roman Catholic interpretation of the passage on the Eucharist. Montfaucon adopted Harduin's version of it, annexing a few fragments in the Greek, picked out of Anastasius and John Damascene.

John Damascene, Anastasius, and Nicephorus refer to the letter as authentic, nor does Harduin venture to dispute it; but there are several points of evidence which seem to mark it as belonging to a later age than that of Chrysostom. It is not quoted before Leontius, in the latter part of the sixth century, although it might usefully have been employed against the Eutychians. There are expressions in it which were not in common use till after Cyril of Alexandria had employed them against Nestorius. The language generally is that of one who had lived in the midst of the Nestorian and Eutychian controversies, and the style of the Greek fragments, as well as the tone of the Latin translation, are extremely unlike Chrysostom's manner: the sentences are abrupt and rugged, and a kind of scholastic, dogmatic tone pervades the whole composition. The general scope of the letter is clear: it is to maintain the doctrine of the two natures under one person in Jesus Christ, against the heresy of the Apollinarians; or, if we accept the theory of Montfaucon, the intention of the author, living in the time of the Eutychian heresy, was to strike a blow at that by forging a letter supposed to be addressed by Chrysostom to a friend, warning him against Apollinarian errors, which had much in common with the Eutychian. The passage in which the writer illustrates his position by a reference to the Holy Eucharist has been construed by Roman Catholics and Protestants in a sense agreeable to their own views on the subject. The writer has been labouring to prove that there were two distinct natures in the one person of God the Son Incarnate, and he proceeds as follows:— "Just as the bread before consecration is called bread, but when the Divine grace sanctifies it through the agency of the priest it is liberated from the appellation of bread, and is regarded as worthy of the appellation of the Lord's body, although the nature of bread remains in it, and we speak not of two bodies, but one body of the Son; so here, the Divine nature being seated in the human body, the two together make up but one Son, one Person."

FOOTNOTES

[1] In the case of Savonarola such a want has now been fairly well supplied by Villari and other writers. For a good portrait of Erasmus, see "Erasmus, his Life and Character," by Robert Blackley Drummond, B.A. 2 vols., 1873.

[2] "That godly clerk and great preacher" is the description of him in the English Homilies, Hom. i.

[3] "Remains," vol. iii. Letters to Dr. Woodward and Mrs. Hannah More.

[4] Wall, on *Infant Baptism*, endeavours to prove that she was a Pagan, in order to account for the delay in Chrysostom's baptism, but his reasons are far from convincing.

[5] De Sacerdot. lib. i. c. 5.

[6] Julian: Misopogon, p. 363.

[7] Epist. 1057.

[8] Epist. ad viduam jun., vol. i.

[9] Ibid. p. 601.

[10] Adv. Oppug. Vit. Monast. lib. iii. c. 11.

[11] Liban. de fortuna sua, pp. 13-137.

[12] See concluding Chapter.

[13] See concluding Chapter.

[14] Quoted by Isidore of Pelusium, lib. ii. ep. 42.

[15] Sozomen, viii. c. 2.

[16] Isidore Pel., lib. ii. ep. 42; De Sacerdot. i. c. 4.

[17] Gibbon, iii. 52, note; Milman's edition.

[18] Gibbon, iii. 53; for an account of the character of lawyers at this period see Amm. Marcellinus, lxxx. c. 4.

[19] As Socrates, book vi. chap. 3, has done.

[20] De Sacerdot. lib. i. c. 1.

[21] De Sacerdot. c. iii.

[22] See references in Bingham, vol. iii. b. xi. Wall, vol. ii.

[23] Basil: Exhort. ad Baptismum; Greg. Nazianz. Orat. 40 de Bapt.; Nyssen, de Bapt.; Chrysost. in Acta Apost. vol. ix. hom. i. *in fine*, and in Illumin. Catechesis, vol. ii. p. 223.

[24] Philostorgius, ii. 7; Socrates, i. 23; Theod. i. 21.

[25] Socr. i. 24; Theod. i. 22.

[26] Athanas. Hist. Arian. 20, 21; Theod. ii. 9, 10.

[27] Socr. ii. 26; he had been deposed from the rank of presbyter because he was a eunuch, in accordance with the provision of the Council of Nice, c. i. Labbe, i. p. 28.

[28] Sozom. iii. 20; Theod. ii. 24.

[29] Sozom. iv. 12-16; Theod. ii. 26. In consequence of an earthquake at Nice, it was removed to Seleucia in Isauria.

[30] Rufin. i. 21; Socr. ii. 36, 37; Sozom. iv. 19; Jerome c. Lucif. 18, 19.

[31] Socr. ii. 42, 43.

[32] Sozom. iv. 28.

[33] Theod. ii. 31; Sozom. iv. 28.

[34] Socr. ii. 45.

[35] The Arian Bishop George having been murdered by the Pagan population, Socr. iii. 5.

[36] Rufin. i. 27; Socr. iii. 6; Sozom. v. 12.

[37] Chrysost. Hom. in Matt. 85, vol. vii. p. 762.

[38] Chrysost. Hom. in Melet.

[39] Tillemont, viii. 374.

[40] Greg. Nazian., Orat. de Bapt. 40; Chrysost. Ep. 132, ad Gemellum.

[41] Tertullian is the first who mentions it; de Prescript. c. 41.

[42] Just. Nov. cxxiii. c. 13.

[43] Quoted in Bingham, vol. i. p. 378.

[44] Conc. Carth. iv. c. 8; Labbe, vol. ii.

[45] *Vide* quotations in Suicer, Thesaur. *sub verb* οφιλοσοφία.

[46] De Sacerdot. i. c. 4.

[47] Ibid. c. 3.

[48] Ibid. c. 5.

[49] For the oppressive manner in which taxes were collected see Gibbon, iii. 78 *et seq.*, Milman's edit.

[50] De Sacerdot. i. c. 6.

[51] Ibid. vi. c. 12.

[52] Socr. vi. c. 3.

[53] Ibid. vi. 3.

[54] In Facund. Hermiana, Pro Def. trium capit., lib. iv. c. 2, in Gall. and bibl. patr. xi. p. 706.

[55] Chrysost. Hom. in Diodor., vol. iii. p. 761.

[56] Socr. vi. 3.

[57] Niceph. σειρά, vol. i. pp. 524 and 436.

[58] Ibid. vol. i. p. 80.

[59] Leont. Byzant. contra Nestor., et Eutych. lib. iii., in Basnage, Thesaur. monum. i. 592.

[60] C. 2-5.

[61] I. c. 8, 9.

[62] C. 9.

[63] C. 10.

[64] Theod. i. c. 11, *in initio*.

[65] C. 11.

[66] C. 13.

[67] C. 14.

[68] C. 17.

[69] C. 16 and 19.

[70] C. 19.

[71] C. 3.

[72] C. 5.

[73] Tillemont maintains that the Theodore to whom the first letter is addressed must have been a different person from the fellow-student of Chrysostom and eventual Bishop of Mopsuestia, but he stands alone in this opinion, and his reasons for it seem inadequate.— Till. xi. note vi. p. 550.

[74] Possid. Vit. August. c. iv.

[75] Sulp. Sever. Vit. St. Martin. lib. i. p. 224. The affectation of reluctance to be consecrated became a fashion in the Coptic Church. The patriarch-designate of Alexandria is at this day brought to Cairo, loaded with chains, as if to prevent his escape.— Stanley, Eastern Church, lect. vii. p. 226.

[76] C. 5. This word may refer to the bishops or the people. Ambrose calls the people his "parentes," because they had elected him bishop.— Comment. in Luc. l. viii. c. 17.

[77] μειράκια; *vide* note at end of Chapter.

[78] I. c. 5.

[79] C. 7.

[80] C. 6.

[81] C. 8.

[82] C. 9.

[83] The words *priest* and *bishop* are employed, in the following translations and paraphrases, to correspond with ἱερεὺς and ἐπίσκοπος, which are used in the original without much apparent distinction. Chrysostom is speaking of the *priesthood generally*, and it is not easy to say which Order he has in his mind at any given moment.

[84] II. c. 2.

[85] III. c. 1, 2, 5.

[86] III. c. 4.

[87] III. 5.

[88] III. 9, 10.

[89] Lamprid. Vita Alex. Sev. c. 45. Paris edit.

[90] Cyprian, Epis. 52.

[91] Ammian. Marcell. lib. xxvii. c. 3. Socrat. lib. iv. c. 29. See a multitude of evidence carefully collected on this subject in Bingham, vol. i. b. iv. ch. 2.

[92] III. 15.

[93] Comp. in Act. Apost. Hom. iii. 5. "Men now aim at a bishopric like any secular office. To win glory and honour among men we peril our salvation.... Consuls and prefects do not enjoy such honour as he who presides over the Church. Go to court, or to the houses of lords and ladies, and whom do you find foremost there? no one is put before the bishop."

[94] III. c. 14.

[95] III. 16.

[96] III. 17.

[97] IV. c. 3-5 and c. 9.

[98] V. c. 1-4.

[99] V. c. 5.

[100] V. c. 6, 7.

[101] V. c. 8.

[102] VI. c. 1.

[103] VI. c. 4.

[104] VI. c. 6-8.

[105] VI. c. 12.

[106] VI. c. 13.

[107] Which is the date assigned by Socrates, vi. 3.

[108] As stated by Palladius, at least in the Latin translation by Ambrose Camaldulensis.

[109] Zosimus, lib. iv. 13-15. Ammian. Marcell. xxix. c. i.

[110] In Act. Apost. Hom. 38, *in fine*.

[111] Cyril. Catech. x. n. 19. Athanas. Synopsis.

[112] Euseb. lib. vi. c. 11. Clemens Alex., Hom., Quis Dives salvetur?

[113] Vide Epiphan. 69. Hæres. n. i., whence it appears that Laura, or Labra, was the name of an ecclesiastical district in Alexandria.

[114] Theod. Lector.II.l. c. col. 102-104.

[115] Jerome, Ep. 77, 5; Ambrose, de Virgin. i. 10, 11.

[116] Baron. 398, 49-52; Giesel.I.251.

[117] Sozom. iii. 14; Sulp. Severus.

[118] At Stridon, on the frontiers of Pannonia and Dalmatia.

[119] Sozom. iii. 14. Palladius, Hist. Lausiaca, 38.

[120] In Matt. Hom. 8, p. 87.

[121] 'The custom of one monk reading the Scriptures aloud during dinner was first adopted, according to Cassian, in the Cappadocian

monasteries.— Cass. lib. iv. c. 17; Sozom. iii. 14; Jerome's translation of the rule.

[122]But sometimes later.

[123]Hom. in Matt. 55, vol. vii. p. 545.

[124]Sozom. iii. 14, 15; Cassian., de Cœnob. Instit. iv. x. 22.

[125]Cod. Theod. ix. 40. 16.

[126]*Vide* Müller de Antiq. Antioch. c. 3.

[127]Chrysost. in Matt. Hom. 69, vol. vii. p. 652.

[128]In Matt. Hom. 68, c. 3. When they received the Eucharist, which they did twice a week, on Sundays and Saturdays, they threw off their coats of skin, and loosened their girdles.— Sozom. iii. 14.

[129]In Matt. Hom. 68, c. 3; 69, c. 3; in 1 Tim. Hom. 14, c. 4, 5.

[130]In Matt. Hom. 72, vol. vii. p. 671.

[131]In 1 Tim. Hom. 14, c. 5.

[132]In Joh. Hom. 44, c. 1.

[133]De Compunct. i. c. 6.

[134]De Compunct. i. c. 1.

[135]C. 2.

[136]C. 3.

[137]C. 4, 5.

[138]C. 7.

[139]C. 8.

[140]C. 9.

[141]De Compunct. ii. 1-3.

[142]C. 5.

[143]ἔχθρα ἀκήρυκτος, lib. i. c. 5.

[144] Lib. i. c. 4.

[145] The word in the decree is "militare," but this term appears to be applied to civil duties as well as military. *Vide* Suicer, *sub v.* στρατεύειν. The Egyptian monks, however, do seem to have been specially forced into the army. De Broglie, v. 303; Gibbon, iv.; Milman, History of Christianity, iii. 47.

[146] Adv. Oppug. Vitæ Mon., lib. i. c. 1-3.

[147] C. 4.

[148] C. 5-7.

[149] C. 8.

[150] Lib. ii. c. 1, 2.

[151] C. 2-5.

[152] C. 6-10.

[153] Lib. iii. c. 6.

[154] Compare similar remarks by Thucydides, book iii., in his account of the Corcyræan sedition, on the misapplication of names to vices.

[155] Lib. iii. c. 6, 7.

[156] C. 8, 9.

[157] Lib. iii. c. 14, 15.

[158] C. 18, 19.

[159] Pallad. Dial. c. v.

[160] Ad Stag. a Dæm. vex., vol. i. lib. i. c. 1.

[161] Ibid. lib. ii. c. 1.

[162] Ad Stag., vol. i. lib. ii. c. 1.

[163] Ibid. c. 5-9.

[164] See *ante*, Chapter II.

[165] See preface to his Orat. xliii.

[166] The bishops of Egypt and the West generally adhered to Paulinus, Sozom. vii. 11, till by the united efforts of Chrysostom and Theophilus the universal acknowledgment of Flavian was obtained in A.D. 398.

[167] So Jerome, Ep. xxvii.

[168] Conc. Nic., can. 18. (Hefele, p. 426.)

[169] Tertull. de Bapt. cxvii. Jerome Dial. contr. Lucif.

[170] Chrysost. Hom. ii. in 2 Cor.

[171] Constit. Apost. lib. viii. c. 10.

[172] Constit. Apost. lib. ii. c. 57. Chrysost. Hom. xxiv. in Act.

[173] Constit. Apost. lib. ii. c. 31, 32. Cyprian, Ep. xlix.

[174] Conc. Nic., can. 18. (Hefele, p. 426.)

[175] Jerome, Epist. lxxxv. ad Evang.

[176] Chrysost. vol. ii. p. 591.

[177] Ibid. vol. vii. p. 762.

[178] Ibid. p. 629.

[179] Euseb. Vita Const. iii. 50. Chrysost. vol. iii. p. 160 and vol. xi. p. 78. *Vide* also Müller de Antiq. Antioch., p. 103.

[180] This description of Antioch is mainly collected from Müller's admirable and exhaustive work on the Antiquities of Antioch, or from the authorities referred to therein.

[181] See Socrates vi. 1, and Montfaucon's preface to "De Sacerdotio."

[182] Ad vid. jun. c. 5.

[183] C. 4.

[184] Ad vid. jun., c. 3.

[185] C. 4. Executed in 371 in the reign of Valentinian, Valens, and Gratian; Ammian. Marcell. xxix. 1, who calls him a Gaul, not, as Chrysostom, a Sicilian.

[186] Constans by Magnentius.

[187] Constantine the younger.

[188] Jovian.

[189] Gallus Cæsar by Constantius. The two who died natural deaths were Constantine the Great and his son Constantius.

[190] The widow of Jovian, whose son Varronian was deprived of an eye. See Gibbon, vol. iv. p. 222.

[191] Doubtful; possibly first wife of Valentinian I., divorced from him and sent into exile.

[192] Constantia, wife of Gratian.

[193] Flacilla, wife of Theodosius. Compare this mournful list of tragic deaths of sovereigns with the splendid passage in Shakespeare's Richard II.:—

"For Heaven's sake let's sit upon the ground,

And tell sad stories of the death of kings," etc.

[194] De Virginitate, c. 15.

[195] C. 14-22.

[196] De Virginitate, c. 57.

[197] τὴν μάλιστα πάντων ἀγαπωμένην, c. 52.

[198] De Virginitate, c. 52.

[199] C. 62, 63.

[200] C. 66, 67.

[201] De Virginitate, c. 83.

[202] Gibbon, iv. p. 111.

[203] Strabo, p. 750.

[204] As Verus, Pescennius Niger, Macrinus, and Severus Alexander.—Herodian, ii. 7, 8, v. 2, vi. 7.

[205] De S. Babyla, c. 14-16.

[206] Hom. in Matt. vol. vii. p. 762.

[207] To the establishment of parochial divisions with separate pastors in Alexandria we have the direct testimony of Epiphanius, Hæres. 69; Arian. c. 1. In Rome, however, and Constantinople, though the churches were numerous, the clergy seem to have been more or less connected with the mother Church.— *Vide* Bingham, chap. viii. 5, book ix.

[208] μειρακίσκος εὐτελὴς καὶ ἀπερῥιμμένος— applied by rather a strong rhetorical licence to a man forty years old.

[209] μηδέπω πρότερον. This seems to prove that he had not preached during his diaconate.

[210] Ecclus. xv. 9.

[211] Hom. xi. in Act. Apost. *in fine*.

[212] Vol. ii. p. 515.

[213] C. 3.

[214] See the Monitum to these Homilies, vol. i. p. 699.

[215] See Newman's Arians, chap. i. sect. i.

[216] Arius, in a letter to Eusebius, addresses him as συλλουκιανιστά, "fellow Lucianist," Theod. i. 5.

[217] I. c. 6, 7.

[218] C. 3.

[219] I. c. 4.

[220] II. c. 3, 4.

[221] II. c. 4, 5; III. 3, 4, 5, 6.

[222] IV. 4.

[223] V. 2, 3.

[224] VII. c. 3, 4.

225 VII. c. 6, 7.

226 III. c. 6.

227 III. c. 6, *in fine*.

228 IV. *in fine*.

229 The colours represented the seasons, and according as one or other was victorious a plentiful harvest or prosperous navigation was indicated.

230 Contra Anom. vii. c. i.

231 De Laz. vii. c. 1.

232 De Anna, iv. 1.

233 De Laz. vii. c. 1.

234 It is a treatise, because too long for a homily, though mutilated of its proper conclusion. It must belong to the first two years of his priesthood, because it promises a more ample discussion of several points, which promise we find redeemed in the homilies against the Jews, and these homilies, again, can be proved, by internal evidence, to have been delivered not later than A.D. 387. See Montfaucon's Monitum, vol. i. pp. 811 and 839.

235 C. 1.

236 See a singular parallel to this thought in the Emperor Napoleon I.'s remarks on Christianity: "Table Talk and Opinions of Napoleon I."

237 C. 9.

238 C. 9.

239 C. 12.

240 C. 13.

241 C. 2.

242 C. 2-5.

243 C. 6.

[244] C. 7.

[245] C. 3.

[246] See Perowne, vol. i. *in loco*; Ps. lxxii. 6; and Delitzsch in Isa. lx. 17.

[247] Milman's History of the Jews, vol. ii. book xix.

[248] Basnage's Hist. des Juifs, vi. 41. Newman's Arians, ch. i. sect. i.

[249] V. *in fine*; robbers may possibly be used in a figurative sense.

[250] I. c. 7. They seem early to have claimed medical skill. When Simon Ben Jochai went to Rome as ambassador, in the reign of Antoninus Pius, to obtain the abrogation of persecuting edicts, he won the favour of the Emperor by curing his sick daughter— Milman, ii. 443.

[251] II. 3; vii. *in initio*; i. c. 3, 4.

[252] I. c. 6.

[253] i. c. 7. So the idle youth of Rome turned for amusement into the Synagogue. Horace, Sat. ix. 69.

[254] ἐπιγινώσκετε ἀλλήλους. i. 4. This admonition "Discern one another" was uttered just at the close of the Missa Catechumenorum, when all but the baptized had to depart.

[255] Newman's Arians, ch. i. p. 16. Hefele, pp. 305, 306.

[256] In Jud. iii. c. 6, iv. c. 4.

[257] According to Theod. iii. 20, the Jews had ceased to offer sacrifices by the reign of Julian, and when he inquired the reason, said, because it was unlawful except on the site of the Temple; and this was one chief reason why Julian commanded the Temple to be restored.

[258] In Jud. v. c. 1.

[259] Ibid. c. 4-7.

[260] He punished the captives by cutting off their ears. It is singular that there is no record of this rebellion in history.

[261] For a full relation of this singular event, see Milman's Jews, book xx.

[262] Hom. viii. 4, and *in fine*.

[263] Hom. de Anathemate, delivered soon after the discourses against the Anomœans. See Monitum, vol. i. 944.

[264] The former chiefly in the Hom. de Philog. vol. i. 752; the latter in the Hom. in Nat. Diem Christi, vol. ii. p. 552.

[265] De Beato Philog. vol. i. p. 753.

[266] In Nat. Christi, vol. ii. p. 560.

[267] De Bapt. Christi, c. 4.

[268] In Kalend. c. 2.

[269] In Ephes. Hom. vi. c. 4.

[270] Perhaps that convulsive twitching which we call "quick blood."

[271] In Ephes. Hom. xii. c. 3. In Hom. viii. and xii. on 1 Cor. he rebukes the heathenish ceremonies performed at the birth of a child. One was, to give it that name which was attached to the candle that burned longest out of a row of candles.

[272] He was executed at Carthage in A.D. 376.

[273] See Gibbon, c. xxvi. xxvii.

[274] Cod. Theod. xvi. 1, 2.

[275] Sozom. vii. c. 12; Gibbon, c. xxvii.; De Broglie, "L'Église et l'Empire," vi. p. 93.

[276] Cod. Theod. xvi. v. 7, lib. 1, 2.

[277] Cod. Theod. xvi. v. 10, lib. 7, 9. Sozomen informs us (vii. 22) that Eugenius, the usurper, after the death of Valentinian II., was persuaded by divinations to take up arms.

[278] Sozomen, vii. 15. Theod. v. 21.

[279] The most distinguished scholar, and orator, and one of the most upright statesmen of his time— quæstor, prætor, and proconsul of Africa.

[280] Fragments of his speeches preserved in Mai's collection, vol. i.

[281] Ambrose, Op. vol. ii. Ep. 18.

[282] Libanius: Pro templis non exscind. The oration was certainly not spoken before the Emperor, and probably not even sent to him.

[283] Cod. Theod. xii. 104-115.

[284] Theodor. v. 19. A funeral oration on her and the infant was pronounced by Gregory Nyssen, Op. vol. iii. pp. 515, 527, 533.

[285] Libanius, Or. 12, pp. 391-395.

[286] Probably the prætorium built in the reign of Constantine for the Count of the East, who from that time resided in Antioch; *vide* Müller, Antiq. Antioch., ii. 16.

[287] Liban. Or. 12, p. 395, and 21, p. 527. Theod. vii. 20. Sozom. vii. 23. Zos. iv. 41.

[288] Chrys. Hom. de Stat. iii. 1; xxi. 1. Zosimus (iv. 41) sends Libanius also to Constantinople, but this is a palpable error. There is no trace of his having gone, either in his own Orations or in any other historian.

[289] Socrat. vi. 5. The most common practice was for the preacher to sit, the people to stand.

[290] Hom. ii. 2.

[291] iii. 6.

[292] iii. 1, 2.

[293] ii. 5.

[294] iii. 3.

[295] iii. 4, 5.

[296] xvi. 6.

[297] iii. 7.

[298] xiv. 1.

[299] v. 7.

[300]xx. 9. A passage in another homily on this subject is curious, as proving that just the same jugglers' feats were performed in Antioch in the fourth century as at the fairs and races of the present day:— "Persons pretended it was next to impossible to conquer an inveterate habit: this was a paltry excuse, perseverance could conquer any difficulty. To unlearn a habit of swearing could not be more impossible than to acquire the art of throwing up swords, and catching them by the handle, or balancing a pole on the forehead with two boys at the top of it, or dancing on a tightrope."— Hom. in Dom. Serv.

[301]iv. 1.

[302]iv. 2.

[303]v. 3. τὸ σῶμα τῇ ψυχῇ περίκειται καθάπερ ἱμάτιον. Comp. Shakespeare: "When we have shuffled off this mortal coil."

[304]v. 3.

[305]ix. 3, 4.

[306]x. 2, 4.

[307]xiii. 2.

[308]xii. 2.

[309]x. 3.

[310]xii. 2-4; xiii. 3. Comp. Aristotle's distinction between natural and conventional law or justice, Eth. v. 7.1: φυσικόν and νομικόν δίκαιον. Compare also his description of προαίρεσις as the ἀρχὴ κινήσεως in b. iii., and of φρόνησις (nearly = Butler's "Conscience") in b. vi.

[311]Comp. again what Aristotle says of the necessity of *training* to improve the *natural* gifts, b. x. 9, and of the formation of *habits* by repeated *acts*. Comp. Chrys. Hom. xiii. 3, with Arist. Eth. ii. 4, 5.

[312]xiii. 4.

[313]xvi. 1.

[314]Liban. Or. 21, in Helleb. and 20, 517.

[315]Theodor. v. 20.

[316] xvii. 1, 2.

[317] Liban. Orat. 20. De Broglie, vi. 150, 151. Chrys. Hom. xvii. 2.

[318] xvii. 2. The colonnades, especially of the great street which ran through the city from east to west; the περιπάτους or promenades were lined by colonnades with seats.— *Vide* Müller, Antiq. Ant. ii. 12.

[319] xvii. 2.

[320] xx. 5, and xviii. *in fine*.

[321] Liban. Or. 21, p. 536.

[322] xxi. 1.

[323] It was the custom to signalise the great festivals by acts of mercy. "The oil of mercy glistens on the Festivals of the Church," says Ambrose, Serm. 14, on Ps. cxviii. 7. Leo the Great also, Serm. 39, alludes to the custom. But, to prevent any abuse of the practice, it was enacted by Theodosius in A.D. 384-385, that it should apply only to those accused of petty offences: the grosser crimes of robbery, adultery, magic, murder, sacrilege, were to be excepted from claims to this indulgence.

[324] xxi. 1-4.

[325] xxi. 4.

[326] Hom. i. de Anna, vol. iv. c. 1, where he recapitulates the arguments which he had used in the Homilies on the Statues.

[327] Hom. de Anna, i. 1.

[328] Called κυριακὴ τῆς ἐπισωζομένης, this last word being the name of Ascension Day among the Cappadocians, possibly because Christ's work on earth for man's redemption was completed by his return into heaven. (*Vide* Leo Allatius, quoted in Suicer, Thesaur., *sub verbo* "Episozomene," and Bingham, Antiq. b. xx. sect. 5.)

[329] Hom. de Stat. xix. 1, vol. ii.

[330] Euseb. de Vita Constant. lib. iv.

[331] Chrys. Hom. xl. in Juvent.

332 Hom. de Cæmet. et Cruce, vol. ii. c. i. in Ascens. Christi, vol. ii., and de Sanct. Martyr. vol. ii. p. 705. The Sunday corresponding to the present Trinity Sunday was kept as a kind of All Saints' Day. See Bingham, b. xx. c. 7, sect. 14.

333 Aug. Hom. xxvi. Gelas. Decret. in Grabe, vol. i. The word "legend" is perhaps derived from these Acts of the Saints, which were to be read—"legenda."

334 Adv. Judæos viii. c. 7.

335 Hom. in Juvent. et Maxim. vol. ii. p. 576.

336 De Bern. et Prosd. vol. ii. p. 640.

337 See the letter in Euseb. lib. iv. c. 15.

338 Aug. de Vera Relig. c. 55.

339 Aug. contra Faustum, lib. xx. c. 21.

340 De Droside, vol. ii. p. 685.

341 Flavian caused the remains of some much-revered saints who were buried beneath the pavement of the church to be taken up, and placed in another separate grave, because the people were distressed that the reliques of such venerated personages should repose in the same vaults with the remains of less saintly, if not heretical, characters.— Hom. in Ascen.

342 De S. Babyla, c. 12. De Stat. i. 2, and viii. 2. Quod Christus sit Deus, c. 7. De Stat. v. 1.

343 In S. Ignat. Mart. c. 4.

344 In Juvent. et Maxim. c. 1.

345 Hom. in Martyres, vol. ii. p. 663.

346 In Sanct. Jul. vol. ii. p. 673.

347 Aug. cont. Faustum, lib. xx. c. 21.

348 Aug. Confess. lib. vi. 2. Epist. 64, ad Aurel. Conc. Carth. iii. c. 30.

349 Basil. Regul. Major., quæst. 40.

[350] See Dr. Hessey's Bampton Lectures, "on Sunday."

[351] Whether it was a regular custom for the rustic population to visit Antioch on this day, or whether it was the first great influx for trade and legal business after the recent suspension of all business, does not appear.

[352] Ambr. Ep. xx.

[353] Ambr. Ep. xx. p. 854.

[354] Sozomen, vii. 13. Ruf. ii. 16.

[355] Ambr. Ep. xxi. Sermo contra Aux. p. 868.

[356] Ignatius is said to have first introduced antiphonal singing at Antioch, Flavian and Diodorus to have established it there; Socr. v. 8; Theod. ii. 19. Basil refers to it as a common practice, but Ambrose is generally allowed to have introduced it to the Western Church, and on this occasion. *Vide* Suicer.

[357] Aug. Conf. ix. 7, and preceding books.

[358] Ambr. Ep. xxi.

[359] Ambr. Ep. xxii. Aug. Conf. ix. 7.

[360] Ambr. Ep. xl. and xli.

[361] Cod. Theod. iv. v. 4, lib. 2. De Broglie, vi. 257.

[362] Sozom. vii. 25. Theod. v. 17. Ambr. Ep. li. De Broglie, vi. 302, etc.

[363] Theod. v. 18. De Broglie, vi. 302 *et seq.*

[364] Sozom. vii. 15. Socr. v. 15. Ambr. Ep. lvi. Theod. v. 23.

[365] Ambr. de ob. Val.

[366] Theod. v. 24. Socr. v. 25. Sozom. vii. 24. De Broglie, vi. 8.

[367] Ambr. Ep. lxi. lxii.

[368] Socr. v. 26. Sozom. vii. 29. Ambros ii Vita a Paul. scripta, de obit. Theod.

[369] Of course I do not forget that the idea and name of Roman Emperor and Roman Empire lived on for centuries more, but the elevation of Charles the Great was a revolt against the old order of things. He can hardly be regarded as a successor of Theodosius so truly as Theodosius was a successor of Augustus.

[370] Claud. de Bello Gild. 293.

[371] Claud. in Ruf. i. v. 137.

[372] Philostorg. xi. 3. For much assistance in his notices of Rufinus and Eutropius, the writer must pay his acknowledgments to the admirable work by Amédée Thierry: "Les trois ministres des fils de Théodose"— Rufin, Eutrope, Stilicon.

[373] Gibbon, iii. 67. Zosim. iv. 51.

[374] Claud. in Ruf. i. v. 220.

[375] See references in Thierry, p. 19.

[376] De Laud. Stil. ii. v. 379.

[377] "Noster Scipiades Stilicho." De Consulat. Stilic. præf. v. 21.

[378] Claud. de Nupt. Honor. et Mariæ.

[379] Zosim. v. 3.

[380] Symmach. Ep. iv. 15 and 16.

[381] Possibly alluded to by Chrysostom in Hom. iv. de Penitentia, c. 2, where he mentions "incursions of enemies" among other recent calamities. These homilies were probably delivered in A.D. 395.

[382] Thierry, pp. 35-78. Claud. in Ruf. lib. ii.

[383] In Eutrop. i. v. 104, 105.

[384] "Contemptu jam liber erat."— Claud. in Eutrop. i. v. 132.

[385] Claud. in Eutrop. i. v. 148, 149.

[386] Sozom. vii. 22.

[387] Philostorg. xi. 5.

[388]Claud. in Eutrop. i. 427, etc.; ii. 97, etc.

[389]Thierry, pp. 97-126. Zosim. v. 5. Claud. in Eutrop. ii.

[390]Zosim. v. 8, 9, 12.

[391]Sozom. viii. 7.

[392]Claud. in Eutrop. i. 235, etc.

[393]Synes. de Regno, p. 16.

[394]Claud. in Eutrop. ii. 95. Thierry, p. 162, etc.

[395]Socr. vi. 2.

[396]See Chrysostom's own remarks in De Sacerdotio, lib. iii., cited above in Ch. iv., and in Act. Apost. Hom. iii. 5.

[397]Epist. xxi. ad Valerium.

[398]Socrat. vi. 2. Sozom. viii. 2.

[399]Lib. iii. c. 15, 17.

[400]Pallad. Dial. c. 5.

[401]Socr. vi. 2. Sozom. viii. 2. Pallad. Dial.

[402]Socr. vi. 2. Sozom. viii. 2.

[403]Pallad. Dial. c. 5.

[404]Sozom. viii. 2. Pallad. Dial. 5.

[405]Socr. vi. 2.

[406]Bingham, b. ii. c. 11, sec. 8.

[407]The title Patriarch is occasionally used in the following pages, although it does not appear to have been a formally recognised title till fifty years later. Socrates (A.D. 440 about) uses it (*vide* c. 8), but the first occurrence of it in any public document is in the acts of the Council of Chalcedon, A.D. 451, where it is applied especially to Leo i. of Rome.— Can. 28. Labbé, vol. iv.

[408]Hom. xi. in Anom. vol. i. p. 795.

[409] De Sacerd. lib. vi. c. 6-8, quoted above, p. 53.

[410] Soc. vi. 3. Sozom. viii. 9.

[411] Pallad. Dial. c. v. p. 20.

[412] Lib. xxvii. c. 3.

[413] Epist. ii. ad Nepotianum.

[414] Pallad. Dial. c. v. and xii.

[415] See Hefele, p. 131, and on the date of this synod.

[416] Stanley, Eastern Church, lecture v. Socr. i. 11. Sozom. i. 23. The truth of the story has been disputed, but apparently on insufficient grounds. *Vide* Hefele, p. 436.

[417] Can. 3. Hefele, p. 379.

[418] Jerome, Ep. xxii. ad Eustoch. Epiphan. Hær. 63.

[419] See references in Bingham, b. vi. c. ii. 13.

[420] Contra eos, etc., vol. i. p. 495.

[421] Ibid. c. 3, 4.

[422] Ibid. c. 7.

[423] Contra eos, etc., c. 9.

[424] Ibid. c. 10.

[425] Ibid. c. 10.

[426] Socr. vi. 4.

[427] Vol. xii. p. 468.

[428] Vol. xii. p. 485.

[429] Contra Lud. et Theat. vol. vi. p. 269, *in fine*.

[430] Ibid. c. 1.

[431] Contra Lud. et Theat. c. 2.

[432] From this and what follows it would appear that communicants went within the rails to receive, and close to the altar. This was the most primitive custom. Sometimes the recipients stood; *vide* passages cited in Bingham, b. viii. ch. 6, sec. 7.

[433] Vol. xii. Hom. ix.

[434] In Coloss. Hom. vii., vol. xi. p. 350.

[435] Hom. xviii. in Genes., vol. iv. p. 150.

[436] The use of silk seems from its first introduction into the Empire to have been regarded as the *ne plus ultra* of luxury. It was condemned by Pliny, vi. 20, xi. 21. Elagabalus was the first *man* as well as the first Emperor who ventured to wear a material hitherto confined to female dress. See Gibbon, vol. vii. c. 40, and his interesting account of the introduction of silk-worms from China to Constantinople by some Persian monks in the reign of Justinian.

[437] In Matt. Hom. xlix., vol. vii. p. 501

[438] In Psalm. xlviii., vol. v. p. 514.

[439] Hom. i. de Lazaro, c. 8.

[440] In Gen. Hom. xli., p. 382.

[441] In Joan. Hom. lxii., p. 340, and Hom. lxix., p. 380.

[442] In Act. Apost. p. 147 *et seq*.

[443] Hom. xx. in Act. Apost. p. 162. This set of fifty-five Homilies on the Acts of the Apostles, of which much use is made in this chapter, was delivered in A.D. 400, between Easter and Whitsuntide, in which interval it was customary to read through the Acts in the Lessons for the day: *vide* Bingham, vol. iv. These homilies are among the least polished of Chrysostom's productions. Erasmus, who translated them into Latin, was thoroughly disappointed and out of humour with them, and even doubts their authenticity. In a letter to Tonstal, Bp. of Durham, he declares that he could have written better matter himself even when "ebrius ac stertens." But most persons familiar with Chrysostom's productions will agree with Montfaucon and Savile that these homilies could have flowed only from that golden vein, though the ore is not so

much refined as usual, and that some passages are in his very best style. None of his homilies, except those on the Statues and St. Matthew, contain more curious revelations of the manners and customs of the age.

[444] In Act. Apost. pp. 74 and 98.

[445] In Act. Apost. p. 256.

[446] See Villari's Life of Savonarola, b. i. c. 3.

[447] In Act. Apost. p. 191.

[448] Hom. in Inscrip. Altaris, i. *in initio*.

[449] In Act. Apost. pp. 189, 190.

[450] Vol. xii. Hom. vi. adv. Cath. pp. 143 and 491.

[451] Vol. xii. Hom. i., "Quod frequenter," etc. Socrates, vi. 22. If we may estimate the man from the account by Socrates, his admirer, who relates a number of his so-called witticisms, the book is no great loss.

[452] Greg. de Vita sua, pp. 585-1097. Orat. xxii., xxvii., xxxii.

[453] *Vide* Gibbon, v. p. 30.

[454] Socrates, vi. 8. *Vide* Dean Stanley, Eastern Church, pp. 131, 132, for specimens of these Thalia; *e.g.* one commences, "Where are those who say that the Three are but one power?"

[455] Sozom. viii. 3. Socrat. v. 15.

[456] Epist. xiv. vol. iii.

[457] Vol. xii. Hom. viii.

[458] Theod. v. 30.

[459] Epist. xiv. and ccvii.

[460] Theod. v. 29. Tillemont, xi. p. 155.

[461] Marc. Diac. ap. Baron, an. 401, 49.

[462] Vol. xii. 471. The titles "mother of churches," "nurse of monks," "staff of the poor," etc., were not bestowed till after his return from his

first exile, vol. iii. p. 446. M. Thierry has erroneously introduced them into this earlier stage of his life.

[463]Claud. in Eutrop. lib. i. The pathetic appeal is by Claudian put into the mouth of an allegorical impersonation of the city. Claudian was the intimate friend and companion of Stilicho, and may not improbably have assisted at this audience. He is a valuable guide to the history of this period, and especially as an indicator of public opinion on the great events of his day.

[464]Gibbon, vol. v. p. 361. Claudian, De Consul. Mall. Theod.

[465]In Eutrop. ii. 39, 136.

[466]Claud. in Eutrop. ii. 187*et seq.*

[467]In Eutrop. ii. 377.

[468]The above account is taken from Zosimus, lib. v.; Claudian in Eutrop. ii. Thierry, "Trois Ministres; Eutrope."

[469]Zosim. v. 17.

[470]Claud. in Eutr. ii. 474 and 534, etc.

[471]Philostorg. xi. 6. Zosim. v. 18.

[472]Stanley, (Appendix,) "Memorials of Westminster."

[473]Cod. Theod. lib. ix. tit. 45.

[474]Ibid.

[475]The altar was sometimes called ἄσυλος τράπεζα (Synesius, Ep. lviii.)

[476]Claud. Prolog. in Eutrop. ii. 25. Chrysost. in Eutrop., c. 3. vol. iii.

[477]Chrysost. in Eutrop. c. 2.

[478]De Capto Eutrop. vol. iii.

[479]In Eutrop. i.

[480]De Capto Eutrop. c. 4.

[481]In Eutrop. c. 3.

[482]Socrat. vi. 5.

[483]In Eutrop. c. 1.

[484]In Eutrop. c. 2-4.

[485]Zosimus, v. 18, ἐξαρπάσαντες.

[486]De Capto Eutrop. c. 1.

[487]Zosim. v. 18.

[488]Zosim. v. 18. Cod. Theod. ix. 40, 17. Philostorg. xi. 6.

[489]Zosim. v. 18.

[490]Zosim. v. 18. Socrat. vi. 6. Sozom. viii. 4.

[491]Hom. cum Saturn. et Aurel. vol. iii.

[492]Socr. vi. 6. Sozom. viii. 4. Theod. v. 31.

[493]Sozom. viii. 4. Theod. v. 32.

[494]Nili Mon. Epist. i. 70, 79, 114, 116, 205, 206, 286.

[495]Sozom. viii. 4. Socr. vi. 6. Theod. v. 32.

[496]Sozom. viii. 4. Socr. vi. 6. Zosim. v. 19.

[497]Eunap. Sard. Fragm. 60. Sozom. viii. 4.

[498]*Vide* c. 21.

[499]Sozom. viii. 4. Socr. vi. 6.

[500]The Alexandrian Chronicle is precise in fixing Dec. 23, A.D. 400, as the date of his defeat on the Hellespont, and Jan. 3, A.D. 401, as the day on which his head was brought into Constantinople. This certainly leaves a very insufficient interval for the events recorded in Zosimus.

[501]*Vide* c. 33.

[502]Palladius, author of the Dialogue prefixed to Migne's edition of Chrysostom's works. On the debated question whether this Palladius was the same Bishop of Hellenopolis who wrote the Lausiaca, *vide* Tillemont, xi. "Vie de Pallade."

[503]There was in fact what might be called a floating synod of this kind always in existence in Constantinople; the Patriarch being *ex officio* President.— Tillemont, xv. 703, 704.

[504]We are in the summer of A.D. 400, and the capture and death of Gaïnas occurred in Jan. A.D. 401.

[505]σοῦ τὴν τιμιότητα; sometimes we have ὁσιότητα, "your Holiness."

[506]Pallad. Dial. c. 14 and 15.

[507]See, on this whole subject, Bingham, viii. 13. 6; and Robertson, i. pp. 187 and 318, and the authorities there cited.

[508]Pallad. Dial. c. 14, 15. Sozomen (viii. 6) says that Chrysostom deposed thirteen bishops of Asia, Lycia, and Phrygia. This is possible, as the synod may have inquired into other simoniacal cases beyond the original six.

[509]Sozom. viii. 6.

[510]Tillemont, xi. p. 170.

[511]Labbé, ii. p. 947. It must always be borne in mind that Diocese was the name of the largest *civil* division of the Roman Empire. Each diocese contained several provinces, *e.g.* Thrace, six; Asia, ten; Pontus, eleven. The whole Empire was divided into thirteen dioceses, and about one hundred and twenty provinces. The Ecclesiastical divisions followed more or less the plan of the civil. An archbishop was bishop of the metropolis of a Province, a Patriarch of one or more *Dioceses*.

[512]Can. xxviii.; and Can. ix. Chalced. in Labbé, iv. pp. 769 and 798.

[513]Comp. Keble, Christian Year, for Easter Day:—

"Sundays by thee more glorious break,

An Easter Day in every week."

[514]Vol. iii. p. 421.

[515]Socrat. vi. 11. Sozom. viii. 10.

[516]Vol. iii. p. 424 *et seq.*

517Pallad. Dial. c. 18, pp. 62 and 67.

518Socrat. vi. 4.

519Sozom. viii. c. 9.

520Pallad. Dial. c. 19.

521Greg. Naz. Epp. lvii. lviii.

522Greg. Naz. Ep. lvii.

523Theophilus is said to have fallen down before her and kissed her knees, an obeisance prompted by avaricious hopes on his part, and repelled by genuine humility on hers.

524Pallad. Dial. c. 16, 17. Sozom. viii. 9.

525Pallad. Dial. c. 6. Tillemont xiv. p. 219 *seq.*: ἐγὼ αὐτῷ ἀρτύ ωχύτραν.

526Pallad. Dial. c. 5, 6, 18, 19.

527Jerome in Ruf. lib. ii. c. 5. Ep. xxxi. p. 203.

528Tillemont, xi.: Vie de Theophile.

529Euseb. Hist. vi. 3, 19.

530Jerome declared that Origen had composed more books than most men would find time to copy.— Epist. xxix.

531The Paschal Letter was a circular addressed to clergy and monks throughout the diocese soon after the Epiphany; the primary object was to announce the date of the first day of Lent and of Easter Day, whence the name; but other matters were, as in the present instance, frequently introduced. See Tillemont, xi. 462.

532Socrat. vi. 7. Sozom. viii. 11, 12.

533Jerome in Ruf. iii.; and Ep. lxi.

534In Ruf. iii. 33.

535The contest for precedence was eventually decided in favour of Jerusalem. The see was made a Patriarchate in the reign of Theodosius

II., and its jurisdiction fixed to the three Palestines by the Council of Chalcedon, A.D. 451.

[536] Jerome, Ep. xxxviii.

[537] Jerome, Ep. xxxviii.

[538] Jerome, Ep. cx.

[539] Ibid. Ep. xxxviii. and xxxix.

[540] Jerome, Ep. xxxviii.

[541] Ibid.

[542] Pallad. Lausiaca, p. 901. Tillemont, vol. xi.

[543] Pallad. Dial. c. 6. Other causes of the enmity of Theophilus are mentioned by Socrates, vi. 9, and Sozomen, viii. 12, but not incompatible with the account of Palladius.

[544] Socrat. vi. 7.

[545] Pasch. Epist. of Theoph. quoted in Tillemont, xi. p. 470. Pallad. Dial. 6. Sozom. viii. 12.

[546] Sulpic. Sever. lib. i. c. 3.

[547] Pallad. Dial. c. 7.

[548] Sozom. viii. 13.

[549] Jer. Ep. lxx.

[550] Jer. Ep. lxxviii. in Ruf. Epp. lxvii. lxxiii.

[551] Socrat. vi. 9. Sozom. viii. 14.

[552] Socrat. (vi. c. 13) says that the writings only of Origen, not the man himself, were condemned.

[553] Ep. lxxviii.

[554] Pallad. Dial. c. 8.

[555] Sozom. viii. 13. Pallad. Dial. c. 8.

[556] Ep. xvi.

557 Socrat. vi. c. 12.

558 Socrat. vi 12. Sozom. viii. 14.

559 Sozom. viii. 14 and 26.

560 Socrat. vi. 14.

561 Sozom. viii. 14.

562 Sozom. c. 15.

563 Socrat. vi. 15. Sozom. viii. 15.

564 Socrat. vi. 15. Sozom. viii. 16.

565 Pallad. Dial. c. 2 (Epist. of Chrys. to Innocent), and c. 8.

566 See Tillemont, vol. xi. ch. 71.

567 *Vide* ante, Ch. XIII.

568 So Palladius, c. 8, on the whole the most trustworthy authority. Photius, Biblioth. (c. 59), says there were forty-five.

569 The language is not very clear in this passage, but such is, I conceive, the drift of it.— c. 8.

570 This must have been a slight exaggeration, but the members do seem to have been mainly Egyptian.

571 Pallad. Dial. c. 8.

572 Phot. c. 59. Chrys. Ep. 125 ad Cyr., where he indignantly repels the charge:— "had he done so, might his name be blotted out from the roll of bishops;" but at the same time he deprecates the treatment of such an offence (had it been committed) with extreme severity: for had not our Lord Himself instituted that holy feast, and had not St. Paul baptized without previously fasting? Chrysostom shrinks in horror from the supposition of such a gross violation of ecclesiastical rule as the act in his case would have been, but refuses to place it on the same footing with the commission of a flagrant moral crime, or direct disobedience to any command of Christ. There are, however, some doubts whether this letter is genuine. See *infra*, p. 317, and note.

[573] Pallad. Dial. 8. Socr. vi. 15. Soz. viii. 17.

[574] Tillemont, vol. xi.

[575] It contains the celebrated passage: "Herodias again dances and demands the head of John;" which recurs as the exordium of another and spurious homily (vol. viii. p. 485), and also an indignant repudiation of the offence of administering baptism after eating.— vol. iii. 427. Socrates, vi. 16. Sozom. viii. 17, 18.

[576] The authenticity of which has been questioned. The style is perhaps not quite worthy of Chrysostom; but in one of his sermons after his return from exile he apparently alludes to some quotations from Job made in this discourse.

[577] More strictly speaking, "the Hieron," "the sacred spot" where the Argonauts were supposed to have offered sacrifice to Zeus on their return from Colchis.

[578] Sozom. viii. 18, 19. Socrat. vi. 16, 17. Zosim. v. 23.

[579] Theod. v. 34. Chrys. vol. iii. p. 446.

[580] Socr. vi. 16. Soz. viii. 18. Chrys. Ep. ad Innoc. in Dial. Pall. p. 10.

[581] It appears from subsequent events that Theophilus had not yet actually quitted Constantinople, but he and his partisans had retired for the time discomfited from the field of active opposition; and this would justify the language of Chrysostom, who is speaking under excitement.

[582] Sermones 1 and 2, post red. ab exsil. vol. iii.

[583] Socrat. vi. 17. Sozom. viii. 19.

[584] Ep. ad Innoc. in Pallad. Dial. p. 10.

[585] As distinguished from the Forum of Constantine, which was elliptical in shape.

[586] Cod. Theod. vi. 102.

[587] The celebrated exordium of a homily supposed to be directed against Eudoxia— "Again Herodias rages, again she demands the head of John"— if actually spoken with reference to John the Baptist, may easily have been represented by the malevolent as aimed at the Empress. But

the whole homily has been pronounced spurious by Savile and Montfaucon, and on perusal of it their verdict seems reasonable. The discourse is the production of a thorough misogynist, describing with much coarseness and acrimony the misery and trouble caused by the wickedness of women. Most will agree with Savile, that it is "scarcely worth reading, and quite unworthy emendation."— Vol. viii. p. 485.

[588]Pallad. Dial. c. 9.

[589]Sozom. viii. 20. Socrat. vi. 18. Pallad. Dial. c. 9.

[590]Pallad. Dial. c. 9.

[591]Pallad. Dial. c. 9.

[592]Pallad. Dial. c. 9. Chrysostom (Ep. ad Innoc. vol. iii.) speaks of more than forty friendly bishops.

[593]Vol. iii. p. 533.

[594]Pallad. Dial. c. 9.

[595]Pallad. Dial. c. 9. Sozom. viii. 21.

[596]Pallad. Dial. 10. Sozom. viii. 21, 22. Socrat. vi. 18.

[597]Pallad. Dial. c. 10.

[598]Pallad. Dial. c. 10. Zosim. v. 24. Sozom. viii. 2.

[599]Pallad. Dial. c. 11.

[600]Ep. ad Episcop. vol. iii. pp. 541 and 673.

[601]C. 11.

[602]Epist. cxxv.

[603]Epist. ccxii.

[604]Sozom. viii. 24. Pallad. Dial. c. 20.

[605]Epist. ad Olymp. vi.

[606]Epp. xciv. and civ.

[607]Pallad. Dial. cc. 1, 2, 3.

[608] Ep. cxiii.

[609] Epp. clxviii. clxix. *et aliæ*.

[610] Pallad. Dial. c. 3.

[611] Sozom. viii. 26.

[612] One previous letter we possess in Chrys. vol. iii. p. 539, in which he expresses his horror at the late outrages in the Church of St. Sophia, and at the gross violation of justice and law in the recent so-called trial of Chrysostom.

[613] Pallad. Dial. c. 4.

[614] Nilus, 2 Epp. cclxv. and cclxxix. Sozom. viii. 25.

[615] Pallad. Dial. 20.

[616] Sozom. viii. 27. Pallad. Dial. 20.

[617] Ep. ad eos qui scandalizati sunt, c. 19.

[618] Pallad. Dial. cc. 15 and 16.

[619] Theod. v. 34.

[620] Epp. x. xi.

[621] Ep. xiii.

[622] Epp. cxx. cxxi.

[623] Ep. cxxv. *in fine*.

[624] Ep. ccxxi.

[625] Ep. viii.

[626] Ep. xiv.

[627] Epp. xiii. lxxxiv.

[628] Ep. cxxv.

[629] Ep. ccxxxiv.

[630] Epp. ccxxxiv. ccxxxvi. It is not mentioned in Pliny or Ptolemy, but appears in the Itinerary of Antonine as Cocusus (pp. 10, 13). It stood at the confluence of several roads, but apparently not high-roads, one of which connected Antioch with Asia Minor.

[631] Ep. cxxv. *in fine*.

[632] Ep. xiii.

[633] Epp. xiii. xiv. ccxxxiv.

[634] Vol. iii. p. 549 *et seq*.

[635] Ep. ii. c. 10.

[636] *e.g.* Epp. lxxxviii. lxxxix. *et aliæ*.

[637] Ep. cxxiv.

[638] Ep. cxxxii.

[639] Ep. cxlvii.

[640] Epp. cxxx. ccxxii.

[641] Epp. l. li. lxi. *et aliæ*.

[642] There seems no doubt that Maruthas was an able and active missionary bishop. Socrates (vii. 8) tells strange stories of his skill in exposing some tricks of the magi, by which they attempted to prejudice the Persian king Isdigerdes against Christianity.

[643] Ep. ccx.

[644] Ep. ccxii.

[645] Ep. ccxvii.

[646] Ep. cciv.

[647] As appears from an edict dated August 29, addressed to Studius, Prefect of Constantinople.— Cod. Theod. vol. ii. p. 16.

[648] Ep. cxiv.

[649] Tillemont, xi. 274.

[650] Vol. v. ch. xxxii.

[651] Ep. vi.

[652] Epp. cxl. cxlvi.

[653] Epp. liii. liv.

[654] Epp. cxxiii. cxxvi.

[655] Photius, p. 1048.

[656] Epp. lxi. lxix. cxxvii. cxxxi.

[657] Ep. clvii.

[658] Ep. clv.

[659] Vol. iii. p. 535.

[660] Ep. cxlix.

[661] Aug. cont. Jul. p. 370.

[662] Ep. v.

[663] Pallad. Dial. pp. 38, 39, who says that they came out of Syria, Cilicia, and Armenia: but how could this be if it took three months to convey Chrysostom from Cucusus to Comana?

[664] Tillemont, xi. 349.

[665] This is his day in the Calendar of the Eastern and Western Church.

[666] The Roman martyrology states that the remains of the saint were afterwards translated to St. Peter's, Rome, but the statement is not supported by any trustworthy historical evidence.— Tillemont, xi. 352.

[667] I must acknowledge my obligations in the composition of this chapter to the very useful and instructive work of Dr. Th. Foerster, Berlin, entitled "Chrysostomus in seinem Verhältniss zur Antiochenischen Schule."— Gotha, 1869.

[668] In Rom. Hom. xiii. 2. 1 Cor. Hom. xiii. 3. In Phil. vii. 5.

[669] Hom. de Stat. xi. 2.

670 In Genes. Hom. xxi. 2.

671 Ibid. xvi. and xvii.

672 In Rom. Hom. xii. 6.

673 In Genes. Hom. xx. 3. In 1 Cor. Hom. ii. 2. In Matt. Hom. lix. 1, 2.

674 Comp. Jeremy Taylor, "On Original Sin," ch. vi.: "A man is not naturally sinful as he is naturally heavy, or upright, naturally apt to weep and laugh; for these he is always and unavoidably." Comp. also Aristot. Eth. ii. c. 1.

675 In Matt. Hom. xxviii. 3, and lviii. 3.

676 In Heb. Hom. xii. 2 and 3.

677 De Fato, Hom. iii.-vi. Comp. Jer. Taylor, Unum Necessar. ch. 6. sec. 5.

678 De Pœnit. Hom. i. 2; et ad Theod. lapsum.

679 In Inscrip. Act. ii. 6.

680 In Psalm. cxlii. 5.

681 In Act. Hom. xli. 4.

682 In Matt. xxxii.

683 De Sanct. Babyla, vol. ii.

684 In Johan. vol. viii. p. 482.

685 In Hebr. Hom. v. i.

686 Contra Julianum, bk. i. ed. Bened. p. 630; but I have failed to find the passage in Chrysostom's works.

687 In Rom. Hom. x. 2.

688 προτρεπτικὴ οὐ βιαστική in Johan. Hom. xlvii. 4; *et* in Matt. H. lxxx. 3.

689 In 1 Cor. Hom. vii. 2. In Ephes. Hom. i. 2. In 1 Cor. Hom. ii. 2.

690 In Rom. Hom. xvi. cc. 8, 9.

691 In Genes. Hom. xlii. c. 1.

[692] In Johan. Hom. xviii. 3.

[693] In Heb. Hom. xii. c. 3.

[694] De Mac. i. 3.

[695] Ch. VIII.

[696] In Johan. Hom. iii. 2.

[697] In Heb. Hom. ii. c. 2.

[698] In Psal. li. Expos.

[699] In Heb. Hom. iv. 2, 3.

[700] In Rom. Hom. xiii. 5.

[701] In Phil. Hom. vii. c. 3.

[702] In Heb. Hom. iii., Hom. iv. c. iii. In Philog. Beat. In Johan. Hom. xlviii. c. i.

[703] In Matt. Hom. iii.; Expos. in Ps. li.; in 1 Cor. Hom. xxiv. 4.

[704] De Resur. J. Chr. c. 3.

[705] De Bapt. Christi, c. 3.

[706] De Cœmet. et Cruce, i.

[707] De Cœmet. et Cruce, 3. See also in Ephes. Hom. xx.; and esp. In Ascens. J. Chr. c. 2.

[708] De Verb. Apost. vol. iii. p. 276.

[709] In Johan. Hom. xxxiii. c. 1.

[710] In Rom. Hom. viii. c. 5.

[711] In Gen. Hom. v. c. 1.

[712] In Ephes. Hom. iv. c. 2.

[713] In Gen. Hom. xxxi. 2.

[714] De Pœnit. Hom. viii. 2.

[715] Cont. Anom. vii. 7.

[716] De Anna, iv. 5.

[717] Ibid. ii. 2.

[718] Ad illum. Catech. i. c. 3.

[719] De Mut. Nom. iv. *in fine*.

[720] Ad ilium. Catech. i. 3.

[721] Ibid. ii. 3.

[722] De Bapt. Chr. c. 3.

[723] In Gen. Hom. xl. c. 4.

[724] De Bapt. J. Chr. c. 7.

[725] De Cœmet. et Cruce, *in fine*, vol. ii.

[726] De Prod. Jud. vol. ii. Hom. i. c. 6.

[727] In Eustath. Ant. vol. ii. p. 601.

[728] In Ep. ad. Hebr. Hom. xvii. c. 3.

[729] Hom. ii. De Stat. c. 9.

[730] De Nat. Christi, c. 7.

[731] De Stat. xi. c. 5. The authenticity of the letter to Cæsarius is so doubtful that I have not ventured to introduce here the celebrated passage which it contains on this subject. It will be found in the Appendix, where the curious history of this letter is related.

[732] Eirenikon, part i. p. 112.

[733] De Laz. Hom. iv. 4.

[734] De Pœnit. Hom. iv. 4.

[735] De Pœnit. Hom. ix.

[736] See Dr. Pusey's history of the cultus and its mischievous effects, in Parts i. and ii. of the "Eirenikon."

737 In Johan. Hom. xxi. 2; and in Matt. Hom. xliv. 1.

738 De Mundi Creat. vi. 10.

739 *Vide* Dr. Pusey, Eiren. i. p. 113: "We could preach whole volumes of the sermons of St. Augustine or St. Chrysostom to our people, to their edification and without offence: were a Roman Catholic preacher to confine himself to their preaching, he would (as it has been said among themselves) be regarded as 'indevout towards Mary.'"

740 In Ephes. Hom. iii. *in fine*.

741 Vol. iii. p. 362.

742 I have not thought it expedient to crowd the margin with references to Chrysostom's works for every one of the liturgical forms above mentioned. They may nearly all be consulted in Bingham, book xv., who has collected them with great care. The fullest passages occur in vol. ii. p. 345; iii. p. 104; x. pp. 200 and 527; xi. p. 323. The so-called prayer of St. Chrysostom in our Prayer-Book is found in the Liturgies of St. Basil and St. Chrysostom, but cannot certainly be traced to either of those fathers. It was inserted at the end of the Litany in 1544, and of the Daily Service in 1661.

743 Vol. ii. pp. 17, 92, 522, *et passim*.

744 Vol vi. 157.

745 In Isai. v. 3, and vi.

746 Ibid. vii. 6.

747 In Is. vii. c. i.

748 In Ephes. Hom. x. 1.

749 De Verb. Apost. vol. iii. p. 282.

750 In Matt. Hom. i. 2.

751 In Galat. i. 6.

752 In Matt. i. *et* in Johan. i.

753 In Rom. Hom. xxxi. 1.

[754] In Psalm xliv.; in 1 Cor. Hom. xxix. 1.

[755] *Vide* Tillemont, xi. p. 37.

[756] Socrat. vi. 4.

[757] Suidas; *vide* verb. Johannes.

[758] Cont. Anom. Hom. iv.

[759] De Sacerdot. iv. 6.

[760] Adv. Oppugn. Vit. Mon. iii. 2.

[761] Adv. Oppugn. Vit. Mon. ii. 4.

[762] De Pœnit. vi. 1.

[763] De Pœnit. ii. 1.

[764] In Johan. Hom. ii. 2, and vol. vii. 30.

[765] Vol. xi. p. 694.

[766] Vol. ix. p. 407. Comp. Jerome: "Quotusquisque nunc Aristotelem legit? quanti Platonis vel libros novere, vel nomen? Vix in angulis otiosi eos senes recolunt; rusticanos vero et piscatores nostros totus orbis loquitur, universus mundus sonat."— In Galat. iii.

[767] Alex. Knox, "Remains," vol. iii. pp. 75-77.

[768] Jebb, "Pastoral Discourses," ii.

[769] Milner, Hist. ii. p. 302.

[770] Dante, Parad. xii. 136.

INDEX

Ablavius, 231
Acacius, 31, 233, 259, 272, 273, 275, 276, 279, 281, 282, 298
Acts of the Saints, 378
Æmilius, 201, 294
Aëtius, 107
Africa, 35, 119, 133, 321, 374
Alaric, 20, 170, 186, 189, 202, 299
Alexander, 21, 25, 55, 274, 314, 323, 333, 370
Alexander of Basilinopolis, 274
Alexander Severus, 55
Alexandria, 24, 32, 41, 63, 70, 71, 102, 122, 133, 135, 138, 140, 176, 180, 192, 235, 242, 243, 244, 246, 248, 250, 256, 259, 269, 273, 290, 299, 321, 360, 364, 366, 371
Alexandrian school,, 40, 334
allegorical interpretations, 40
Amantius, 200
Ambrose, 17, 20, 63, 67, 134, 136, 159, 166, 170, 172, 173, 174, 176, 180, 181, 182, 225, 364, 366, 375, 377, 379
Ammianus Marcellinus, 195
Ammon, 220, 235, 244, 253, 262, 273
Ammonius, 184
Anastasius, 245, 359
Ancyra, 188, 273, 296, 302
Ancyra in Phrygia, 188
Anomœan, 107
Anthemius, 279, 312
Anthropomorphites, 238, 240, 244
Anthusa, 23, 25
Antioch, 18, 19, 23, 24, 26, 27, 28, 29, 32, 33, 39, 50, 64, 67, 68, 69, 71, 84, 85, 88, 90, 91, 99, 102, 103, 105, 107, 115, 116, 121, 122, 123, 124, 127, 131, 140, 141, 143, 148, 152, 154, 155, 156, 158, 159, 160, 169, 176, 180, 182, 185, 186, 192, 193, 235, 236, 243, 273, 274, 292, 296, 297, 298, 299, 305, 312, 314, 316, 322, 323, 348, 356, 367, 369, 375, 376, 379, 394
Antiochus, 92, 121, 125, 228, 233, 259, 273, 275, 276, 281, 291, 298
Antiochus Epiphanes, 92
Antiochus the Great, 121
Antoninus, 220, 221, 222, 224, 230, 373
Antonius, 63
Apamea, 135, 224, 258, 283, 292

401

Apollinarians, 32, 360
Apollo, 64, 92, 99, 135
Aquileia, 173, 239, 278, 294, 320, 348
Arabia, 165, 192, 296
Arabianus, 220
Arabissus, 318, 319
Arbogastes, 180, 181, 186
Arcadius, 70, 140, 159, 183, 184, 185, 187, 188, 189, 199, 205, 207, 212, 215, 231, 276, 277, 280, 291, 293, 295
Archelaus, 80
Arian, 29, 32, 33, 39, 50, 58, 77, 106, 107, 111, 122, 133, 170, 172, 215, 216, 238, 273, 274, 362, 371
Arian controversy, 29, 33
Arian influence, 273
Arianism, 107, 122, 133
Arians, 29, 33, 58, 107, 110, 112, 113, 117, 127, 133, 170, 194, 215, 334, 371, 373
Aristides, 95
Arius, 31, 107, 223, 371
Arsacius, 286, 288, 291, 295, 297, 314
Ascension Day, 162, 167, 377
Asceticism, 66
Asia, 65, 189, 202, 217, 220, 222, 223, 226, 228, 233, 251, 254, 260, 271, 295, 298, 301, 302, 319, 387, 394
Asia Minor, 203, 222, 226, 254
Aterbius, 239

Athanasius, 13, 17, 20, 23, 32, 63, 67, 235, 243, 273, 274, 354
Atticus, 234, 295, 297, 299, 313, 323
Augustine, 13, 20, 24, 63, 164, 166, 171, 330, 357
Aurelian, 212
Aurelius, 166, 321
Auxentius, 172
Babylas, 65, 93, 100
Baptism, 361
Basil, 17, 20, 27, 28, 29, 34, 36, 37, 38, 42, 50, 51, 52, 61, 62, 134, 166, 238, 350, 362, 378, 379, 399
Basiliscus, 322, 323
Baths, 277
Bautho, 185
Benedict, 67, 135
Benedictines, 13, 68
Bethlehem, 240, 241, 242, 307
Biblical, 39
Biblical interpretation, 39
Bishop, 14, 21, 22, 23, 27, 28, 30, 32, 34, 38, 39, 49, 50, 56, 65, 88, 100, 102, 106, 107, 133, 135, 141, 162, 174, 180, 221, 223, 227, 229, 230, 233, 239, 240, 241, 248, 251, 262, 269, 278, 286, 294, 295, 301, 303, 305, 306, 318, 362, 364, 386
Bishops, 135, 180, 191, 242, 297, 348

Bithynia, 222, 224, 225, 258, 274, 283, 285, 292
Bosporus, 190, 204, 205, 213, 214, 266, 267, 268, 324
Botheric, 176
Briso, 266, 301
Brison, 273
Byzantines, 201
Cæsarius, 35, 152, 153, 154, 156, 398
Caligula, 91
Callinicum, 173
Camillus, 184, 201
Capua, 180
Carterius, 39
Carthage, 35, 166, 172, 321, 374
Cassianus, 67, 231
Castricia, 213, 233
Chalcedon, 27, 184, 212, 214, 224, 226, 254, 257, 265, 285, 290, 295, 381, 389
Character, 361
Christendom, 22, 33, 124, 127, 138, 165, 166, 196, 240, 247, 259, 278, 299, 304, 322, 323, 348, 358
Christian holiness, 20, 36, 74, 340, 358
Christian morals, 75
Christian population, 24, 55, 90, 102, 106, 121
Christian wife, 84
Christianity, 17, 18, 19, 23, 24, 31, 36, 39, 55, 66, 72, 76, 77, 79, 84, 96, 103, 106, 117, 119, 120, 121, 125, 129, 138, 158, 160, 163, 165, 172, 173, 230, 237, 341, 357, 368, 372, 394
Christmas, 127, 178, 274
Christmas Day, 127, 274
Chromatius, 278, 294, 320
Chrysostom's homilies, 164
Church, 1, 2, 11, 12, 17, 18, 20, 21, 22, 23, 24, 28, 29, 32, 33, 34, 51, 55, 58, 61, 63, 65, 66, 67, 70, 78, 89, 90, 92, 104, 105, 113, 118, 119, 124, 126, 127, 130, 134, 136, 138, 160, 162, 165, 170, 172, 174, 179, 180, 182, 189, 196, 197, 199, 200, 206, 207, 208, 211, 216, 219, 220, 221, 223, 225, 227, 228, 231, 232, 234, 236, 237, 238, 243, 250, 252, 254, 258, 259, 260, 262, 263, 265, 267, 268, 272, 273, 276, 278, 280, 282, 288, 290, 292, 293, 296, 297, 298, 299, 301, 306, 308, 311, 312, 314, 319, 320, 321, 322, 323, 324, 326, 333, 335, 341, 346, 349, 352, 355, 358, 364, 365, 371, 377, 379, 382, 384, 393, 395
Claudian, 183, 184, 188, 202, 203, 204, 385
Claudius, 91, 184
Clemens Alexandrinus, 66
Clergy, 278
Cœnobia, 67
Comana, 322, 395

Commodus, 93, 100
Conscience, 376
Constantia, 29, 240, 248, 251, 370
Constantine, 29, 92, 121, 125, 138, 158, 162, 202, 206, 225, 231, 272, 277, 280, 281, 285, 370, 375, 391
Constantinople, 2, 18, 19, 20, 24, 26, 27, 30, 33, 41, 56, 67, 71, 88, 90, 102, 106, 112, 115, 118, 133, 138, 139, 143, 154, 156, 176, 179, 182, 183, 186, 188, 191, 192, 195, 197, 200, 203, 204, 205, 211, 213, 214, 215, 216, 217, 219, 222, 223, 225, 226, 227, 228, 230, 232, 233, 235, 241, 246, 248, 249, 250, 253, 255, 256, 257, 259, 260, 262, 263, 266, 267, 268, 270, 271, 272, 273, 277, 279, 280, 285, 286, 290, 291, 292, 293, 294, 295, 296, 297, 298, 299, 300, 301, 304, 305, 311, 312, 313, 314, 317, 318, 320, 323, 324, 348, 350, 371, 375, 383, 386, 387, 391, 394
Constantius, 30, 92, 121, 298, 301, 305, 317, 370
Council, 27, 29, 33, 35, 63, 88, 124, 133, 155, 196, 226, 251, 256, 261, 263, 265, 266, 267, 269, 273, 274, 291, 292, 293, 299, 314, 362, 381, 389

Count, 142, 173, 193, 212, 232, 375
cradle of Arianism, 107
Crateia, 277
Cucusus, 289, 292, 300, 304, 305, 306, 313, 316, 317, 319, 395
Cynegius, 134, 138, 141
Cyprian, 17, 55, 63, 365, 369
Cyprus, 211, 224, 240, 248, 249, 251, 298, 301
Cyriacus, 283, 285, 291, 294, 296, 301
Cyril, 235, 257, 323, 360, 366
Cyrinus, 224, 255, 273, 281, 291, 295, 313
Cyzicus, 289, 305
Damasus, 56, 133
Damophilus, 133
Dante, 400
Danube, 216, 217
Daphne, 93, 99, 155, 166, 298
De Sacerdotio, 50, 369, 381
Dean Stanley, 384
Death, 144, 149, 330
Demetrius, 74, 262, 294, 296
Diocese, 387
Diodorus, 39, 40, 44, 71, 249, 304, 379
Diogenes, 95
Dionysius, 80, 171
Dioscorus, 244, 246, 262
Domitianus, 314
Domninus, 173

Easter, 124, 130, 148, 156, 158, 162, 167, 208, 227, 275, 276, 277, 280, 349, 383, 387, 388
Easter Day, 156, 275
Eastern, 20, 21, 23, 24, 30, 32, 67, 70, 127, 140, 144, 159, 160, 179, 183, 184, 196, 202, 218, 239, 273, 278, 296, 319, 327, 355, 364, 382, 384, 395
Egypt, 66, 67, 68, 70, 77, 82, 188, 231, 239, 245, 247, 251, 254, 255, 256, 271, 353, 369
Egyptian, 66, 67, 70, 81, 184, 196, 220, 238, 249, 255, 296, 368, 390
Elpidius, 232, 273, 275, 281, 314
Elvira, 196
Emperor, 24, 29, 32, 34, 39, 50, 55, 64, 77, 93, 94, 113, 131, 133, 134, 137, 138, 139, 141, 142, 143, 144, 153, 154, 157, 159, 160, 170, 172, 173, 175, 176, 180, 181, 182, 183, 185, 188, 189, 192, 200, 202, 208, 211, 213, 214, 215, 218, 219, 221, 225, 227, 228, 232, 246, 250, 254, 255, 256, 261, 265, 267, 269, 271, 274, 275, 276, 279, 280, 282, 285, 293, 294, 322, 324, 372, 373, 375, 380, 383
Emperors, 26, 64, 94, 118, 212, 272

Empress, 138, 140, 142, 171, 199, 205, 212, 218, 226, 228, 231, 233, 249, 252, 254, 256, 261, 266, 267, 269, 271, 272, 276, 286, 295, 301, 391
Epaminondas, 95
Ephesus, 220, 221, 222, 224, 226, 230, 269, 298
Epiphanius, 240, 241, 248, 250, 252, 253, 255, 260, 371
Essenes, 66
Eucharist, 21, 114, 128, 182, 196, 225, 227, 241, 247, 323, 343, 349, 359, 360, 367
Eucharistic elements, 277
Eudoxia, 171, 185, 199, 205, 212, 218, 219, 228, 250, 252, 254, 271, 272, 277, 295, 391
Eugraphia, 213, 233
Eulysius, 258, 283, 285, 292, 294, 296
Eunomian, 107
Eunomians, 109, 133
Eunomius, 107
Eusebius, 32, 66, 107, 220, 222, 224, 244, 290, 371
Eustathians, 88, 127
Eustathius, 30
Euthymius, 244
Eutropius, 170, 185, 187, 189, 193, 194, 199, 200, 201, 202, 203, 205, 207, 208, 209, 212, 218, 231, 234, 235, 287, 380
Euxine, 265, 322
Euzoius, 31, 32, 33

Evagrius, 39, 180
Evethius, 303, 320
Flacilla, 138, 370
Flavian, 65, 88, 102, 103, 104, 105, 106, 141, 142, 143, 144, 156, 157, 158, 159, 161, 162, 176, 179, 180, 182, 243, 298, 348, 369, 378, 379
Fravitta, 20, 217, 218
Gabala, 223, 227, 229, 233, 266, 273
Gaïnas, 187, 203, 204, 205, 212, 213, 214, 215, 216, 217, 218, 219, 222, 223, 234, 387
Gallus Cæsar, 100, 370
Gelasius, 163
Gemellus, 311
Gerontius, 225, 254, 317
Godhead, 42, 58, 108, 110, 111, 326, 334, 335, 337
Golden Mouth, 26
Gratian, 132, 369, 370
Grecian legend, 99
Gregories, 17, 20, 29, 134
Gregory of Nyssa, 184
Hadrian, 121, 125
Heaven and hell, 44
Helladius, 226, 231
Hellebicus, 152, 153, 154, 156
Hellespont, 217, 222, 386
Heraclea, 220, 224, 226, 231, 288
Heracleides, 224, 230, 269, 298
Hermione, 42, 46, 48, 49
Hermopolis, 244, 246

Hesychius, 222
Hieron, 265, 391
Hilarius, 67
Hilary of Arles, 55
Holy Saturday, 156, 275
Holy Scripture, 22, 27, 28, 41, 42, 47, 73, 87, 91, 110, 113, 172, 194, 293, 326, 334, 335, 352
Homilies, 12, 14, 112, 121, 361, 371, 377, 383
Honorius, 175, 182, 183, 185, 200, 201, 291, 293, 294
Humanisers, 240
Huns, 186, 189, 218, 251, 295
Ignatius, 165, 379
Illyria, 187, 295
Illyrian, 187
influence of the Jews, 124
Innocent, 22, 269, 277, 279, 290, 291, 292, 293, 294, 299, 315, 321, 348, 390
InnocentI., 277
Isaac the monk, 261
Isaurians, 295, 300, 302, 304, 316, 319, 321
Italian, 32, 184, 186, 188, 293, 294, 299
Jerusalem, 52, 121, 125, 155, 239, 240, 241, 242, 245, 246, 388
Jewish, 40, 77, 92, 117, 122, 123, 124, 125, 129, 173, 207, 296, 308

Jews, 44, 52, 58, 99, 107, 112, 117, 120, 121, 122, 125, 126, 158, 163, 268, 277, 284, 336, 342, 344, 353, 372, 373
John, 2, 23, 26, 67, 106, 109, 112, 120, 149, 181, 188, 212, 216, 236, 239, 240, 241, 242, 249, 251, 257, 258, 259, 260, 261, 262, 290, 296, 306, 323, 332, 342, 353, 354, 357, 359, 391
Johnites, 281, 287, 323, 324
Jovinus, 134
Judaising Christians, 121
Julian, 24, 26, 32, 39, 56, 94, 101, 125, 163, 220, 361, 373
Jupiter, 135, 136
Justina, 170, 173
Justinian, 34, 55, 383
Keble, 387
Laodicea, 31, 152, 273, 275, 314
Laura, 67, 366
Law, 58, 96, 99, 123, 345
Lent, 143, 146, 148, 152, 349, 388
Leo, 204, 377, 381
Leontius, 30, 33, 107, 273, 274, 302, 359
Let us pray, 90
Levites, 89
Libanius, 20, 25, 26, 27, 38, 42, 77, 101, 103, 136, 137, 152, 153, 156, 375
Liturgy, 89, 179, 221
Lucian, 107, 322

Lucifer of Cagliari, 32, 88, 180
Lucius, 279, 282
Macedonians, 133
Macedonius, 30, 153
made commander-in-chief, 189
Mallius Theodorus, 201
Manichæans, 58, 95, 133, 328, 353
Marcellina, 67
Marcellus, 135
Marcia, 213
Marcion, 111
Marcionites, 95
Mariamna, 267
Marriage, 96, 347
Martin, 50, 67, 364
martyr, 93, 101, 162, 276, 282, 295, 300, 323
Maruthas, 255, 295, 312, 394
Maximian, 63
Maximin, 66
Maximus, 12, 38, 132, 140, 173, 175, 176, 180, 192
Meletians, 88, 127
Meletius, 28, 29, 31, 32, 33, 34, 39, 50, 65, 88, 103, 104, 106, 314
Mesopotamia, 255, 288
Midas, 226
Milan, 67, 166, 170, 174, 177, 181, 182, 183, 200, 225, 278, 294, 299, 348
Milman, 361, 363, 368, 373
mixed population, 176
Monica, 24, 171

Mopsuestia, 23, 39, 49, 364
Nazianzus, 133
Nectarius, 56, 179, 191, 192, 195, 226, 286
Nestorius, 41, 63, 360
Nice, 29, 63, 124, 133, 196, 248, 256, 259, 285, 291, 292, 317, 334, 362
Nicolaus, 317
Nilus, 215, 295, 393
Nitrian monks, 244, 245, 248, 249
Œcumenical Council, 41, 265
Old and New Testaments, 353
Old Testament, 40, 41, 87, 98, 117, 120, 174, 351, 353
Olympias, 231, 247, 282, 288, 300, 304, 305, 308, 309, 312, 316, 319
Optatus, 285, 287, 288
Origen, 17, 40, 44, 237, 238, 239, 240, 242, 244, 245, 247, 248, 249, 250, 252, 336, 388, 389
Orontes, 30, 39, 65, 91, 99, 201
Ostrogoths, 132, 202
Pachomian monks, 69
Pachomius, 67, 68
Pagan temples, 206, 236, 272, 319
Paganism, 19, 24, 26, 103, 133, 134, 135, 136, 138, 161, 176, 301, 319
Pagans, 25, 60, 117, 135, 138, 160, 172, 237, 243, 284, 317

Palestine, 240, 241, 242, 246, 296, 314
Palladius, 70, 220, 222, 224, 230, 245, 257, 286, 291, 294, 296, 298, 359, 366, 386, 389, 390
Pamphylia, 204
Pansophius, 221, 226
Paradise, 358
parochial divisions, 371
Paternus, 291
Patriarch, 121, 180, 226, 230, 235, 242, 243, 244, 245, 248, 256, 266, 267, 272, 273, 274, 275, 277, 278, 279, 280, 291, 295, 296, 297, 299, 314, 350, 381, 387
Patricius, 282
Paul, 12, 52, 56, 66, 73, 75, 87, 107, 108, 109, 127, 145, 147, 152, 155, 162, 168, 197, 220, 224, 229, 258, 277, 329, 331, 332, 335, 338, 339, 340, 348, 354, 357, 358, 379, 390
Paul of Samosata, 107, 335
Paulinian, 241
Paulinus, 32, 88, 180, 369
Peanius, 314
Pempton, 280
Pentadia, 231, 282, 289
Persecution, 66
Persian fortress, 296
Pessina, 262

Peter, 46, 75, 106, 118, 133, 162, 235, 264, 291, 330, 348, 359, 395
Pharetrius, 302, 303
Philippopolis, 30, 273
Phœnicia, 228, 301, 312, 314, 317, 318, 319
Phrygia, 132, 189, 202, 226, 273, 283, 387
Pityus, 322
Placidia, 182, 255
Plato, 26, 62, 80, 172, 356, 357
Polycarp, 164
Pontus, 186, 226, 273, 322, 387
Porphyry, 297, 298, 305, 312, 314
Prænetum, 265, 266
prefect, 27, 32, 83, 94, 183, 201, 231, 249, 257, 272, 281, 285, 287, 288, 289, 295, 299, 312
Priesthood, 53, 62, 93
Priscillianists, 173
Procla, 282
Proclus, 230, 324, 350
Procopius, 231
Promotus, 185, 233
Protasius, 172
Ptolemais, 228, 233
Ptolemy Philadelphus, 123
Raphanea, 27
religious riots, 71
Rhadagaisus, 299
Rome, 20, 21, 22, 55, 65, 67, 102, 115, 118, 127, 136, 155, 162, 165, 172, 175, 176, 180, 182, 183, 184, 201, 227, 242, 243, 245, 277, 278, 285, 290, 291, 294, 297, 299, 321, 348, 371, 373, 381, 395
Rufinus, 170, 177, 183, 184, 185, 186, 188, 203, 218, 233, 239, 241, 242, 257, 262, 303, 318, 380
Sabellians, 58, 335
Sabiniana, 305
sacrifice of animals, 134
Saturninus, 213, 233
Savonarola, 18, 354, 361, 384
Scythia, 119, 220, 251, 300
Sebaste, 31, 297, 300
sedition, 19, 94, 144, 160, 176, 261, 265, 270, 368
Septuagint, 31, 120, 123, 351
Serapis, 123, 135
Serena, 182
Sermon, 75
Severian, 223, 227, 229, 233, 259, 266, 272, 273, 281, 291, 298
Shakespeare, 370, 376
Sir Henry, 12, 23
Siricius, 196
Sozomen, 69, 218, 361, 374, 379, 387, 389
St. Augustine, 50, 163, 166, 191, 321, 330, 333, 346, 358, 399
St. Jerome, 67
Stelechius, 74, 76
Stephen, 30, 33, 149

Stilicho, 20, 170, 182, 183, 184, 186, 189, 200, 201, 203, 205, 214, 299, 380, 385
Symmachus, 20, 136, 137, 172, 176
Syncletius, 222
Synnada, 283, 291
Synod of the Oak, 258, 260, 270, 273, 274, 288, 291, 295, 313
Syrus, 85
Tarsus, 39, 286, 296
Tertullian, 17, 162, 363
Thalia, 384
Thebaid, 66, 68, 181
Theodore, 23, 39, 41, 42, 43, 44, 48, 62, 249, 273, 364
Theodosius, 26, 93, 131, 133, 134, 135, 138, 139, 140, 142, 154, 156, 157, 158, 159, 170, 173, 174, 175, 176, 177, 180, 182, 183, 184, 186, 188, 192, 200, 207, 215, 218, 228, 231, 232, 252, 272, 324, 370, 377, 380, 389
Theophilus, 180, 192, 194, 235, 237, 238, 239, 242, 243, 244, 245, 246, 247, 248, 249, 250, 254, 255, 256, 257, 258, 259, 260, 262, 266, 268, 269, 273, 287, 290, 291, 294, 296, 297, 299, 313, 321, 323, 369, 388, 389, 391
Theotecnus, 291
Thermopylæ, 189
Thessalonica, 173, 176, 293, 294
Thrace, 127, 132, 139, 186, 218, 220, 222, 226, 231, 273, 288, 295, 387
Tiberias, 121
Tibur, 56
Tigrius, 258, 288
Tillemont, 362, 364, 384, 386, 387, 388, 389, 390, 391, 394, 395, 400
Tomis, 251
Tours, 50, 67
Trajan, 91
Trajanopolis, 222
Tranquillus, 273
Tribigild, 202, 204, 205, 213
Trinity Sunday, 162, 378
tumults, 41, 55, 114, 115, 222
Tyana, 273, 297
Uldes, 218
Ulphilas, 319
Unilas, 313
Ursicinus, 56
Valens, 26, 33, 34, 39, 50, 64, 65, 77, 93, 95, 131, 134, 369
Valentinian, 64, 94, 132, 134, 170, 173, 175, 180, 369, 370, 374
Valentinians, 173
Victor Uticensis, 35
Vincentius, 242
Virginity, 93
Visigoths, 132, 186
Wealth, 145

West, 21, 22, 67, 127, 132, 134, 135, 136, 140, 170, 173, 180, 184, 185, 186, 188, 189, 196, 201, 239, 278, 293, 295, 320, 322, 326, 369

Western, 20, 30, 32, 52, 66, 71, 88, 133, 159, 179, 180, 182, 183, 196, 200, 238, 273, 278, 290, 296, 309, 323, 326, 379, 395

Western theology, 327

Zosimus, 217, 366, 375, 385, 386

QUICK DICTIONARY

abrogate: to abolish formally, to annul

adjuration: a desperate urging, an earnest request

advent: arrival, the coming

alacrity: readiness, willingness

allay: to relieve, to put fears, doubts to rest

anathematise: to denounce, to curse

anchorite: a hermit

animadversion: unfavourable comment, the act of criticizing

anthropomorphize: to give human characteristics to an animal, a god or an object

apocrypha: religious writings of unknown origin

appellation: a calling, a name

archiepiscopal: relating to an archbishop

artifice: cunning, trickery

asseveration: emphatic statement

auguries: predictions, omens

august: noble, awe-inspiring

austerities: stern, severe attitudes

bathos: anticlimax

behove: befits, it is the responsibility of

bequest: wilful giving

billows: cloud, smoke or steam

cabal: a secret political group

calumniate: defame, make false statements about

caparisons: ornamental covering

catechumen: a person who receives teachings in order to be baptized

circlet: a small circular object

cleaveth: to cut

clemency: a pardon

cloister: arrangement of buildings in a monastery

cogent: clear and logical

collation: snack or combination

colonnaded: with columns

commensurate: in proportion to

compunction: disease, anxiety of conscience

concomitants: naturally associated

conflagration: a destroying fire

congregation: a group of people coming together to worship

contumacious: disobedient to authority

conviviality: friendliness

copious: abundant

copyists: someone who copies, often by hand

coterie: a small exclusive group of people

cultus: established religious culture

cumbrous: heavy, bulky

cupidity: greed for money or things

curiales: leading members of the clan

cyclopian: ancient masonry with big blocks

diaconate: a deacon's office or a body of deacons

diadem: a type of crown

diffidence: shyness, lack of self-confidence

diptychs: relief painting, carving, made in two parts

disaffected: dissatisfied with those in power

dissentient: in opposition to official narratives, positions

dissolute: excessively indulging in sensual pleasures

donative: a formal donation

dregs: the leftover part of a liquid leftover in a container

ecclesiastical lore: Christian church traditions

edict: official command, statement, order

effete: weak

ephod: linen apron, vestment of a high priest

extirpation: destruction

factious: inclined to dissent

febrifugal: removing fever

feint: pretended blow

fetters: manacles to restrain a prisoner

folio: a book or booklet

fulminated: protest

gainsaid: denied, contradicted a statement

herald: a sign that something will happen

heresies: believing or practicing something against church teachings

homily: a religious speech

hovel: small dwelling

ignominious: causing public shame

imbibed: drank

imperious: domineering, arrogant

impugn: dispute the truth, value, validity of a statement

inculcate: to instil

indigent: needy

indolence: laziness

inimical: tending to harm

iniquitous: unfair, morally wrong

inopportune: taking place at an inconvenient time

inordinate: huge amount

interpolated: interjected, inserted

intrepid: fearless, adventurous

inured: desensitised to the difficulty, unpleasantness of something

invective: insulting, abusive

inviolability: secure, impenetrable

labarum: symbolic emblems, imagery

laborious: requiring a lot of work

laity: average, everyday people

lance: a weapon of war, similar to a spear

languid: of one who is weak, or does not like to tire or make an effort

languor: inactivity associated with pleasure

league: the distance one can walk in an hour, usually three miles

legates: an official who represents another or others

lenity: kindness and gentleness

levying: to impose (a tax, a fee, etc.)

libation: a drinkable liquid poured in reverence or as an offering to a god

lictor: a Roman servant or bodyguard to a person in power, a magistrate

luminary: a person who is inspired and inspiring, has influence

maceration: the body weakens, fades away due to excessive fasting

magister militum: senior military officer

meed: a portion, a share, usually of praise

mss: manuscripts

nave: central part of a church

nugatory: of no value

obdurate: stubborn, refusing to change

oblations: offering to God.

obsequies: funeral rites

octogenarian: persons in their eighties

œcumenical: representing several Christian churches, implies unity, agreement

offertory: bread and wine offerings at the Eucharist

onerous: involving heavy, tiresome tasks and obligations

opprobrious: describing language of scorn and criticism

oppugnant: antagonistic

opulent: costly, luxurious

ostentatious: pretentious, showy aiming to impress

otiose: idle, without purpose

paganism: the belief in many gods, ecology, witchcraft, unChristian ethnic religions. Judaism is not considered pagan.

pallium: a woollen cloak or a liturgical vestment that goes around the neck

panegyrist: public speaker, orator

parricide: the killing of a parent

patrician: an aristocrat

pecuniary: relating to money

peremptory: requiring immediate obedience

pernicious: having a slow, subtle, seeping harmful effect

philippics: a bitter verbal attack

pontifical: arrogant, as if incapable of error

potentate: an autocratic ruler or monarch

prætorium: tent of a general

precentor: a leader of singing or prayer in a congregation

prefect: person in charge, a magistrate, governor, head officer

prelate: ecclesiastical person of high rank

promulgator: someone who pronounces the law

propitiate: to gain the favour of by doing something pleasing

propitious: favourable

proselyte: a convert

prostrate: face down, stretched on the floor or ground

provost: high-ranking official

puerile: silly, immature

pungent: horrible tasting, smelly

pusillanimity: cowardliness, timidness

quackery: dishonest, fraudulent claims

quag: marshy, boggy place

quirites: a Roman layperson

rapacity: greed

relics: a precious item associated with a saint or martyr

reliques: archaic of relics

remonstrance: passionate and determined protest

repast: meal

reprobate: an immoral person, a sinner

rescript: official written reply or announcement

resplendent: dazzling, rich-looking

retinue: a group of advisors with an important person

ribaldry: coarse, vulgar, disrespectful, amusing talk

rusticity: of rough, natural, unrefined quality

sacerdotal: priestly; supernaturally and spiritually powerful

sacrament: religious practice like baptism, holy communion.

salutary: ultimately beneficial

sanguinary: bloody

sceptre: weapon, a wand

schism: division, a break

scourge: whip

scruples: uneasiness with doing something wrong

scurrilous: spreading scandalous rumours to ruin someone

secede: to formally quit a position

see: area that a religious leader is in charge of

sheaf: bundle bound together, usually stalks or papers

signet: personalized or official seal used in the place of a signature

simony: trying to buy grace, religious powers, the holy spirit and its gifts. Based on Acts 8:18, Simon Magus purchase attempt

sobriquet: nickname

somnolent: drowsy

sophist: deceptive person using untrue arguments

sordid: immoral, corrupt, distasteful

specious: believable but incorrect

spoliation: destruction, the ruining of

stipend: salary of a priest, teacher, public worker

stratagem: a clever plan towards deception

succour: support in difficult times

sunder: sever, divide

suppliant: someone who is pleading, imploring, begging someone in a high position

surfeiting: overindulge

synod: a Christian council

tenet: important principle of a religion

timorous: shy, nervous

toil: work hard

torpid: inactive both physically and mentally

treatise: a formal written work dealing with a significant issue

tumult: uprising with lots of noise

unguent: ointment, lubricator

upbraided: told off, scorned

usurious: of very high rates, a kind of extortion

venal: open of corruption

venerated: highly respected

vicissitude: transformation, change

vociferously: voicing loud opinions forcefully

warden: a supervisor

whet: to sharpen

www.ingramcontent.com/pod-product-compliance
Lightning Source LLC
Chambersburg PA
CBHW030252100526
44590CB00012B/371